BAD NEWS, GOOD NEWS

BAD NEWS, GOOD NEWS

Conversational Order in Everyday Talk and Clinical Settings

DOUGLAS W. MAYNARD

The University of Chicago Press / Chicago & London

Douglas W. Maynard is professor of sociology at the University of Wisconsin, Madison. He is the author of *Inside Plea Bargaining: The Language of Negotiation* and coeditor of *Standardization and Tacit Knowledge: Interaction and Practice in the Survey Interview.*

The University of Chicago Press, Chicago 60637
The University of Chicago Press, Ltd., London
© 2003 by The University of Chicago
All rights reserved. Published 2003
Printed in the United States of America

12 11 10 09 08 07 06 05 04 03   5 4 3 2 1

ISBN (cloth): 0-226-51194-4
ISBN (paper): 0-226-51195-2

Earlier versions of the following chapters were published as follows. Chapter 2 appeared as "On 'Realization' in Everyday Life: The Forecasting of Bad News as a Social Relation," *American Sociological Review* 61, no. 1 (February 1996): 109–31; chapter 4 is a modified version of "The News Delivery Sequence: Bad News and Good News in Conversational Interaction," *Research on Language and Social Interaction* 30 (1997): 93–130; chapter 7 is a modified version of "Praising vs. Blaming the Messenger: Moral Issues in Deliveries of Good And Bad News," *Research on Language and Social Interaction* 31 (1998): 359–95. Any duplication is by agreement with the publishers.

Library of Congress Cataloging-in-Publication Data

Maynard, Douglas W., [date]
    Bad news, good news : conversational order in everyday talk and clinical settings / Douglas W. Maynard.
        p.   cm.
    Includes bibliographical references (p.) and index.
    ISBN 0-226-51194-4 (cloth : alk. paper) — ISBN 0-226-51195-2 (pbk. : alk. paper)
    1. Conversation analysis.   2. Social interaction.   I. Title.

    P95.45 .M36   2003
    302.3'46—dc21

                                                                            2002032047

CONTENTS

ACKNOWLEDGMENTS

This book is the product of a long journey and I have incurred many debts along the way. Most immediately, the writing for individual chapters began in 1996, when I was on a sabbatical supported by Indiana University. Then, in 1998–99 a fellowship from the National Endowment for the Humanities and a complementary Research Leave Support Grant from Indiana University permitted time away from teaching to complete more chapters. Finally, I also received the equivalent of a semester leave in 2000–2001, when I moved back to the University of Wisconsin. Without these sustained times for reading, working with data, and writing, either this book would have been completed much later or not at all. Although traditionally the opportunity to engage in unbridled inquiry has been the scholar's *raison d'etre,* such opportunities seem increasingly rare. I remain extremely grateful for the financial support and other forms of encouragement from my two university homes and the NEH.

As the various chapters were drafted, I asked colleagues and friends for feedback on them. Sometimes this feedback came orally, in more-or-less long conversations, at other times in extensive written form, and various individuals provided commentary in both ways. For their patience and care with my words and thinking, I thank Wayne Beach, Jörg Bergman, Steve Clayman, Bill Corsaro, Mitch Duneier, Derek Edwards, Bob Emerson, Rich Frankel, Jeremy Freese, Harold Garfinkel, Virginia Gill, John Heritage, Jim Holstein, Jason Jimerson, Joan Maynard, Jay Meehan, James Montgomery, Anssi Peräkylä, Anita Pomerantz, Anne Rawls, Emanuel Schegloff, David Silverman, and Don Zimmerman. Gerry Suttles is deserving of special thanks for painstakingly reading and commenting on the entire manuscript, and for directing the way toward the University of Chicago Press. Many others in my home departments at Indiana and Wisconsin have listened, probably more than they wanted, to my worries and elations as this manuscript progressed.

This is to say that I have gained by being in two of the best places on earth to practice the science and craft of sociology. But beyond my home departments at Indiana and Wisconsin, there have been additional presentations, colloquia, symposia, and teaching stints germane to my writing. During the sabbatical in 1996 I was a guest speaker at the Third Symposium on Oral Communication in Organizations at the University of Utrecht, the Netherlands. I also gave a week-long seminar in the Department of Language and Intercultural Studies at the Aalborg University, Denmark. And I presented at an ESRC Symposium on Conversation Analysis at Lancaster University in England. Hanneke Houtkoop-Steenstra, Alan Firth, and Deirdre Boden, respectively, were the parties responsible for helping to organize these occasions and affording me a running start on early chapters.

Taking a longer view, this monograph is the culmination of a project that began in the early 1980s. I have presented preliminary studies of bad and good news at the University of Amsterdam, Universities of California in Los Angeles and Santa Barbara, University of Cincinnati, University of Copenhagen, the Cleveland Clinic, University of Helsinki, Highland Hospital (University of Rochester School of Medicine), Indiana University School of Medicine, University of Kentucky Department of Behavioral Sciences (in the School of Medicine), Linköping University, Maison des Sciences de l'Homme in Paris, Marquette University, Purdue University, San Diego State University, University of Tampere (Finland), Temple University, University of Oregon, University of Surrey, University of Urbino in Italy, Wayne State University, and at other national and international settings and conferences. In some cases, there has been more than one visit. Thanks go to organizers, including Paul ten Have in Amsterdam, Mel Pollner, Steve Clayman, and John Heritage at UCLA, Dede Boden, Gene Lerner, and Don Zimmerman at UCSB, Angela Garcia at Cincinnati, Marianna Hewson in Cleveland, Mie Nielsen and Johannes Waaner in Copenhagen, Anssi Peräkylä and Auli Häkulinen in Helsinki, Rich Frankel in Rochester, Kathy Zoppi at Indiana, Tim Halkowski at Kentucky, Per Linell in Linköping, Michel de Fornel and Louis Quéré in Paris, Gale Miller at Marquette, Jack Spencer at Purdue, Wayne Beach in San Diego, Anita Pomerantz at Temple, Jack and Marilyn Whalen at Oregon, Christian Heath in Surrey, Anssi Peräkylä and Johanna Ruusuvori in Tampere, Aurelia Marcarino in Urbino, Anne Rawls at Wayne State, and numerous others who organized the affairs in which I participated. In something like a dress rehearsal, I could hone my arguments and get crucial reactions and suggestions from diverse audiences, including specialists in anthropology, communications, linguistics, medicine, psychology, and sociology. I am indebted to many individuals in these audiences for their percipient remarks.

Additionally, I have made a regular practice of discussing progressive versions of chapters in my classes and seminars at Indiana University and the University of Wisconsin. My gratitude goes to all the participants in these classes and seminars. With some individuals, there have been long discussions outside of class. I particularly wish to mention Tom Conroy, Brian Costello, Bob Cradock, Jeremy Freese, Virginia Gill, Tim Halkowski, Norm Jensen, Anne Marie Kinnell, Danielle Lavin, Karen Lutfey, John Manzo, Courtney Marlaire, and Bob Moore, for various kinds of direct hands in the progression of this research.

In 1982, Bonnie Svarstad handed me the tapes from a developmental disabilities clinic that prompted my obsession with bad and good news (see chapter 3). At that time I was a fellow in the National Institutes of Mental Health postdoctoral program directed by the late Jim Greenley, who provided strong encouragement to work with the data in whatever way interested me. In subsequent years, with the help of many friends and professional acquaintances and colleagues, I was able to conduct ethnographic investigations and videotape in various clinics where bad and good diagnostic news were prominent, daily experiences. The people and places need to remain anonymous for purposes of confidentiality, but I will not forget the favors I was granted. Funds for collecting data in clinical settings came from Biomedical Research Support Grants (University of Wisconsin and National Institutes of Health), Indiana University College of Arts and Sciences, a New Investigator Research Award from the National Institutes of Health, the Wisconsin Alumni Research Foundation, and the Wisconsin Department of Health and Social Services.

Much, but not all, of my conversational (non-clinical) data is from collections transcribed by Gail Jefferson, used among many conversation analysts, and made available to me by Paul Drew and John Heritage. Students, friends, and colleagues provided additional conversational data through setting up tape recorders on their home telephones. Or they handed me various kinds of recorded and narrative data—newspaper stories, academic references, conversational excerpts, and other materials in which bad or good news turn up. Especially useful pieces of data were contributed by Wayne Beach, Steve Clayman, Nancy and Pete Daly, Patrick Feaster, Alan Firth, Rich Frankel, Virginia Gill, Tim Halkowski, John Heritage, Robert Hopper, Norm Jensen, Manny Schegloff, David Silverman, Constance Steinkuehler, Candace West, Jack Whalen, and Don Zimmerman. Many in my classes and outside of the academy have written heartfelt accounts of bad and good news. I have thanked these individuals directly, and, for purposes of confidentiality, once more refrain from naming them. The willingness of all these parties to share information is an impressive response to the spirit of inquiry. Last but not least, I want to express appreciation to a number of research assistants who have helped in the transcription of audio and video data.

At the University of Chicago Press, my editors have been wonderful. Doug Mitchell is like a "player's coach"—he is an "author's editor," who knows how to inquire, prod, and encourage at just the right time and in just the right measure, with all kinds of interesting anecdotes and humor. Claudia Rex, besides catching little and big typographical and other errors in my manuscript, edited for substance and readability. Robert Devens took exquisite care of the details in between acquisitions and copyediting. I remain extremely grateful to each of these superb professionals.

At various times and in many ways, the members of my family have represented the best bits of good news in my life. With great love and ultimate forms of gratitude because of their forbearance with my obsession, this book is dedicated to my wife Joan, daughter Jessica, and son Theo.

Bad News, Good News, and Everyday Life

The world
was whole because
it shattered. When it shattered,
then we knew what it was.[1]

Monday, May 4, I was interviewing for a company, Clothiers Limited. They were interviewing people on Monday and conducting second and third interviews on the following day. Well, needless to say, I did not receive a call from Clothiers on Monday night, meaning I did not get a second or third interview. I was very upset because I really wanted this position with the company. Well, three more days passed, and I was once again pondering my job search strategies. Friday, May 8 came about and I went home after my classes. I was conversing with my roommates when one of them, Melissa, told me that I had a message on the answering machine from a "Cloth something." I hurried over to the answering machine to hear the message. What I heard was a message from the director of recruitment offering me a position within the company. The message said, *"This message is for Josh. Josh, this is Bill Smith from Clothiers. You'll remember that we conducted an interview with you on Monday, May fourth. As you know, you were not selected for second interviews on Tuesday. But I would like to discuss with you another opening that we think would better suit you. If you could give me a call at 1-800 . . . we can discuss this in more detail. Thanks, bye."* I saved the message on the answering machine and I called my mother and my girlfriend and I played the entire message for them. I was ecstatic, and I wanted to share the news with everyone who was close to me. All of my other roommates were laughing at me for being so giddy and happy.

*

Well I know that we waited seven and a half years to have a baby, after trying all that time. I think she was just a week old when we took her back in to the doctor. And he walked into the office and here I am so proud of this little bitty baby. And he says, "well I have some bad news for you. I've been thinking all night how to tell you this." And as soon as he said that I get this ringing in my head I couldn't even HEAR what he said for the ten seconds. I was so shocked. What's the matter with my baby? And he knew very little about PKU. So he really didn't have any idea how to explain it to me without getting me upset. All he knew was that it can cause mental

retardation. And when I heard that word "retardation," believe it or not it was almost a relief to me. Because I remember thinking to myself, I don't care if she's retarded as long as she's not gonna die. That's how scared I was when he said that.

A graduating college senior, applying for work and seeking a career, experiences rejection and is "upset." Then, from the very company that had seemingly
passed over his application, a message appears on his answering machine saying
that there is another opening. Sharing the message with others, he is "ecstatic,"
and is seen as "giddy and happy." A woman, attempting for years to get pregnant and finally succeeding, proudly gives birth. A week later, she learns that her
child has Phenylketonuria (PKU), a serious metabolic deficiency that, if un-
treated, can result in mental retardation. When the doctor warns her of this impending bad news, she is momentarily dazed, and then shocked. Unfamiliar
with the disease, she is also "scared" until he tells her that it could cause retardation, whereupon she becomes relieved as she gathers the implication that the
baby will not die.

Bad news and good news are pervasive features of everyday life and experience. Waiting for, and then receiving, the news can send a recipient through
cycles of dread, despair, depression, hope, elation, ecstasy, and other emotional
states. Bearers of news are no less susceptible to its disquieting effects. Josh feels
compelled to tell his good news to "everyone" in his immediate environment of
family and friends. The doctor who had to tell his patient about her baby's condition, in contrast, had been "thinking all night" about how to do this and, not
being a specialist, lacked knowledge about the condition and about how to "explain" it without "upsetting" the new mother.

That experiences of bad news and good news profoundly affect participants
is evident from the clarity with which they are remembered. "Flashbulb memory" is how Brown and Kulik (1977) characterize the vivid retention we have of
consequential events in our lives by way of the *circumstances* in which we were
told. Before the 11 September 2001 attacks on the New York World Trade Center, the Pentagon in Washington, D.C., and the crash of Flight 97 in Pennsylvania, the canonical example was the assassination of President John F. Kennedy.
Those old enough to remember can distinctly recall where they were, what they
were doing, how they were informed, what they did next, and how they and
others felt when they heard about his death. More recently, investigators have
probed flashbulb memories involving the attempted assassination of President
Reagan (Pillemer 1984), the Space Shuttle disaster in the United States (Bohannon 1988), the Hillsborough soccer stadium tragedy in the United King-
dom (Wright 1993), and other such events. Now in the United States, at least

until some other cataclysmic event, the "9/11" events may assume the pinnacle of such recollected episodes of bad news.[2]

Beyond such massively public events, we also retain strong memories for having received the news of more private and personal shocks, such as deaths of family members and friends (Brown and Kulik 1977; Rubin and Kozin 1984). Although students of flashbulb memory have concentrated on the recall of tragic events with negative affect (bad news), the phenomenon appears to be present in relation to uplifting events with positive affect (good news) as well (Scott and Ponsoda 1996). However, in various literatures, researchers have showered attention on bad news while mostly leaving good news aside. By exploring both bad and good news, and tracking their differences and intrinsic relations, I hope to fill this lacuna. Whether devastating or uplifting, flashbulb memories of public and private events share properties including surprise or novelty in addition to their emotional consequences for the individual, and the mechanisms for retention may be both physiological and social-psychological.[3] Such events are easily recollected, in part, because they are subject to *rehearsal*—telling and retelling—which may help establish the neural pathways of the memory rather than their being their mere reflection (Brown and Kulik 1977: 85–86).[4] Given the centrality of the informing *process*—involving talk and interaction—its investigation has been neglected compared to its *product,* which is the memory or memory account. The gap in knowledge about real-time conversational news deliveries is another one this book aims to fill.

Maybe not every experience of bad or good news is associated with flashbulb memories. But if my collection of bad and good news stories and events is any indication, participants readily recall not only momentous communications (about births and deaths, for instance), but the more quotidian ones that interrupt the flow of everyday life. These include news about recovery or illness, couples' marriages or breakups, children's accomplishments or transgressions, passed or failed examinations, successful or unsuccessful job and school applications, new cars or expensive repairs, profitable or disadvantageous investments, computer fixes or crashes, on schedule or delayed flights, promotions or demotions, lost or gained weight, found or misplaced possessions, and others. No matter how severe or mild the matter, what is it that makes the telling and hearing about it so compelling? Why is news often remembered so vividly?

To put these questions in a slightly different way, what is so bad about bad news? What is so good about good news? This way of posing the issues suggests that bad and good news are different phenomena and, on purely psychological grounds, the answers are obvious. We deny and fear death, we do not like disease, we abhor failure, we resist and mourn object loss, whereas we enjoy life, celebrate wanted pregnancies and births, are happy when successful at some job, and have a sense of well-being and completeness when we acquire new things. No one likes to speak or hear about a death or disability, a bad grade or failed class, a layoff or firing, a denied application, or, for that matter, a car that has disintegrated. These matters all represent losses of particular kinds. Contrariwise, we love to tell or hear about a new baby, a graduation, a promotion, or even the arrival and attractive appearance of furniture in a remodeled room. These things are experienced as gains.

The compelling and remembered quality of bad and good news, however, can draw these seemingly disparate phenomena — tidings about gains and losses — back together. Do they have a common core? My argument is that they do. When we deliver or receive bad and good tidings, however mild or extreme, it momentarily interrupts our involvement in the social world whose contours we otherwise unthinkingly accept as we carry on with daily activities.[5] Like a roadblock that forces us to stop our car on the highway, with the consequence that we look around and see the hills and valleys we have been traversing in finer relief, interpersonal deliveries of news can force us to attend in novel ways to background features of our everyday lives. It is precisely this interruptive and sometimes utterly disruptive feature of giving or getting news that provides the impetus for this book. From a *social*-psychological perspective, episodes of bad and good news implicate a breakdown, however momentary or prolonged, in the taken-for-granted everyday world. Such interruptions and breakdowns inevitably provoke emotional reactions of one kind or another just as they necessitate a realignment to and realization of a transfigured social world.

My concern, accordingly, is not just with bad and good news per se but with the structure of the mundane social world and its recognition. Sociologies of the everyday world propose that mundane experience depends upon required mutual adherence among society's members to a set of primordial presumptions that the phenomenological sociologist Alfred Schutz (1962) calls the attitude of daily life (ADL). Following Schutz, Harold Garfinkel (1963) developed the field known as ethnomethodology, arguing that the "perceived normality" of events in the everyday world reflects participants' adherence to these presumptions. For example, we take for granted that *objects are as they appear to be*. With regard to the television in my house, I assume it to be just that, a vehicle for watching an infinite variety of mostly innocuous and bland programming aimed at an anonymous audience. I assume you also regard it as such an object, and assume that you assume the same of me. If, however, you tell me seriously that, by way of the TV, the government is monitoring your movements and ordering you to perform certain deeds, the assumptions sustaining the normal perception of that box with sound and pictures may no longer hold. I will stop, wonder what is happening, and reexamine the terrain of the television. I will have to change what phenomenologists call the "accent of reality" accorded to the television and entertain fresh ideas about what kind of object it is. Or, more likely, I will alter my regard for you, your mental status, and your competence. You and I will cease to cohabit a unitary world.

Ordinarily the mutual assumptions the ADL comprises grant the social world a solidity and obduracy — a structure — that is unquestioned, and thereby provide a backdrop to our engagement in an unlimited panorama of everyday projects. As Garfinkel (1967: 173) puts it, our acting *rationally* — by deliberating about a project, planning it, choosing the means appropriate to achieve its completion, and then implementing these means — is like the one-tenth of an iceberg appearing above the water. That is, rational action depends upon the presence of the nine-tenths of the iceberg that lies below the water, a submerged, almost invisible presence of unquestioned matters that are nevertheless indispensable to deliberation, planning, choosing, and implementing. Because of its unquestionable nature, probing this submerged mass, by laying bare the practical interactive work comprising it, is extremely difficult.

Garfinkel's early ethnomethodological program in sociology attempted to examine the iceberg-like stability of everyday social scenes by asking "what can be done to make for trouble" (Garfinkel 1963: 187). How is it possible to upend the iceberg to see the bulk of stuff that is usually below the surface? The answer involved a strategy of now-well-known breaching demonstrations. These demonstrations included such devices as standing very close to a person while maintaining an otherwise regular conversation, saying "hello" to one's interlocutor at the termination of the conversation, or insisting that a conversational partner clarify the sense of commonplace words and phrases ("What do you mean, you had a flat tire?"). More complex manipulations involved playing for a naive subject an audiotape of actors in the roles of a medical school interviewer and an inept applicant, eliciting the subject's usually *negative* assessment, and then providing *positive* information about the "applicant" that therefore was diametrically opposed to the subject's (Garfinkel 1963, 1967). Even as they succeeded in making visible the "seen but unnoticed" or background practices involved in the production of everyday order, these demonstrations were hard on everyone involved. For example, when undergraduates acted like boarders in their own homes, it required an attitude of detachment that made the otherwise familiar household members, their relationships, and activities almost completely strange. The student experimenters became aware of minute behavioral details that were usually ignored, including how they handled silverware, opened a door, greeted one another, or shared the news of the day. Both the student experimenters and others in the environment became anxious, indignant, or bewildered because of the threat to perceived normality.

These affective concomitants of breaching attest to the hold upon us that usual arrangements in the everyday world have, and also imply that purposeful manipulations inducing them are not the ideal or desired method for loosening and making their parameters more available. Garfinkel (1963) himself suggests other strategies, such as observing how neophytes, including young children, become competent members of the adult world, or examining ceremonies of entrance and exit to plays, theater, and religious rites, or probing the experiences of those affected by fatigue, sensory deprivation, psychoactive drugs, and brain injury, or becoming a "stranger" in Schutz's (1964) sense of participating in a culture so alien as to have one's ordinary "recipes" for conduct be inapplicable for even simple tasks. In all, breaches occur naturally in an immense variety of ways, exposing us to the usually unseen structure of everyday life and practices that organize it. Nevertheless, having located them does not tell us exactly how to study these breaches.

The present inquiry, in any case, is roughly in this tradition of exploring "natural" breaches in the routine order or fabric of everyday life. This is not an unfamiliar ploy in sociology, anthropology, and other social sciences. To take one example, John Lofland has argued that suspension of the attitude of daily life may be the beginning point of *collective behavior.* "A situation," says Lofland (1981: 413), "is to some extent defined as unordinary, extra-ordinary, and perhaps, as unreal." For this beginning to transmute into a *social movement,* large numbers of people — crowds or masses — need to be infected by this suspension and the accompanying emotional arousal. Lofland's perspective, drawing on Berger and Luckmann's *The Social Construction of Reality* (1967), is self-consciously *ideal typical,* and the situation it depicts "rarely, if ever occurs" (414). Accordingly, Lofland provides a frame for understanding what incites and sustains collective behavior *generally.* Berger and Luckmann (1967: 30–46) also suggest that everyday interaction is malleable and flexible because it is based on participants' use of typifications to negotiate a social order regarding self, other, and worldly objects. My difficulty with this perspective is that, analytically, typifications remove participants from the here and now of actual conduct. In contrast, if bad and good news events represent ruptures in the fabric of everyday life, it is because the suspension they engender is visible in the concreteness, specificity, and detail of participants' real perceptual and linguistic displays as interactively organized in the here and now. Participants, in telling and receiving bad and good tidings, experience an assault on the ordinary, expected, intended, typical, predictable, moral world of everyday life. As a result, at least momentarily, and however mildly or strongly, they interactively describe and exhibit relative amounts of confusion and anomie.

As through their divulging and grasping of news, participants build a new world, such a world is not the end product of their talk and social interaction. The new world is there, in the co-produced nuances of the disclosure. The closer we approach actual perception and behavior, the more we can appreciate that everyday features of social life are not best captured through hypothetical, typical, or idealized constructions as abstracted from messy negotiations and other loosely characterized behaviors. Instead, news events show how features of everyday life involve an intimate concerting of orderly practical actions to which those worldly features are reflexively tied and in which they actually consist. To put it succinctly, bad and good news as interactively organized episodes of conduct do not represent the social construction of reality.[6] News episodes consist of the substantial employment of embodied social practices that are the constructions or structural features of everyday life existing nowhere else but in the orderliness of those practices. This book, in other words, is not about the social construction of reality out of everyday life but about real social practices *in and as* everyday life.

A Phenomenological Approach To Bad and Good News

Predominating in this study are the practices of talk and social interaction, and I will later describe the conversation analytic mode of inquiry I employ. To fully describe how bad and good news events provide us with access to the structure of everyday life, however, concepts from phenomenological philosophy and sociology are helpful.

Phenomenological philosophy, inspired by Edmund Husserl, aims to clarify and justify theoretical and scientific knowledge by exploring its underpinnings in the "pre-theoretical" and "pre-scientific" realm of understanding in everyday life, from which theoretical and scientific knowledge emanate (Gurwitsch 1964: 148; Husserl 1970b: 209). For Husserl, the pretheoretical realm was that of consciousness, and when he discusses perception, it is acts of consciousness with which he is concerned. According to Gurwitsch (1964), these acts make available

objects of the most different descriptions: objects pertaining to the perceptual world, inanimate things, animals, fellow human beings, as well as the constructs of science, propositions, numbers, geometrical configurations, also artistic objects, social and political institutions.

Phenomenologically, perception of objects is not simple reflection of them, for the mind is not a "mirror of nature," to borrow Rorty's (1979) phrase. Instead, perception of objects involves seeing them in a context, as in the famous figure-ground relation. For example, is the object pictured in figure 1 in a duck or a rabbit? (Wittgenstein 1953: 194). Which one the actor perceives involves initially foregrounding the figure from its background of white paper, and then seeing aspects of the figure in relation to others and to the overall gestalt that assumes the foreground. As Heritage (1984: 86–87) has written, when we see the figure as a duck,

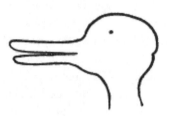

Figure 1.1 The duck/rabbit

the protuberances on the left of the figure are interpreted as a beak and the small indentation on the right of the figure is treated as irrelevant. . . . Once the figure is viewed as a "rabbit," not only does the feature previously identified as a "beak" become the "ears" but also the small indentation, previously ignored as irrelevant to the interpretation of the figure, becomes relevant as the "rabbit's" mouth.

The perceiver, in other words, continuously builds a view of the object by at once cognizing the whole and affording a particular identity to constituents according to this whole. Similarly, the optical illusion presented by the Müller-Lyer figure (Merleau-Ponty 1962: 6–7):

Figure 1.2 Müller-Lyer figure

Although the two horizontal lines are of measurably equal length, with the attachment of auxiliary and differently pointed arrows (angled lines) at each end, they appear unequal. This is because of the way each component refers beyond itself to the "system of perceptions" in which it is embedded (Gurwitsch 1964: 203). Hence the apprehended length of each line is conditioned by its involvement in the configuration it forms with the attached angled lines at either end. Not only does this go against the proposition that perception reflects independent stimuli, it contradicts any easy "transmission" theory about physiology (which would suggest that the body conveys external, particular, simple stimuli piece by piece for registration and reproduction in the mind) and it illustrates that there is an integrative, constitutive, compositional — *active* — element to the way in which we engage the world.

Phenomenologists refer to this active perceptual element as *intentionality.* Directed toward the thing perceived, the consciousness of the subject who is perceiving refers to other acts of perception, and it is these acts that assemble a complete object of perception. As Gurwitsch (173–75) has written, a perceived thing presents itself initially in a one-sided sensuous mode, which Husserl calls the *noema.* While the lines in the Müller-Lyer figure obtain their sense from their relation to co-present angled lines, objects in perception also regularly gain meaningful configurations by their relation to items not seen but *intended,* in part through concepts that can be invoked in conventional ways as part of the perceptual act (Sharrock and Coulter 1998). Accordingly, when we view a building from a given standpoint, we may only see one side, yet we hypothesize its association with other sides not in view. All of these one-sided presentations are *noemata,* and some are anticipated future perceptions that, according to Gurwitsch (1964: 281–82), "extend and complement" our present experience of the one-sided, sensuous presentation. At a party, hearing a sound from another room that we identify as a familiar voice, we move into the room projecting who it is that we will see (285). Weaving anticipations and expectancies into the actual perception, acts of consciousness that assemble noemata into a coherent object are the *noesis,* and the object so assembled is the intended object. Of course, Gurwitsch also points out that we are not guaranteed to have our projections and anticipations always fulfilled, and this means that we are vulnerable to *contingency.* I may find that the sound I heard was a recording, or emanated from someone with a voice similar to my friend.

Phenomenological concepts point to activity on the part of experiencing subjects, but paradoxically we operate most of the time in relation to the social world as if our minds only did mirror its pregiven contents and did not intend or help erect those contents in the first place. Other than when we look at a duck-rabbit or other illustration, we hold to the "constancy hypothesis" (ibid., 163) and the "natural" attitude. Even in viewing the illustration, initially seeing a rabbit and then allowing our perception to oscillate to the duck, we assume that sensory stimuli — for example, the lines that in the former instance are the ears and in the latter instance are the beak — are really there and stay the same as they become rearranged additively in a new pattern. The constancy hypothesis is so called because of a supposition that sensory stimuli are constant across these oscillations in perception as we forget that we may be organizing those stimuli according the particular rabbit-or-duck gestalt that we assemble at a glance. In the

natural attitude, that is, we regard the lines forming the rabbit and duck as having an integrity apart from changing recognitions of pattern. That changing recognition remains as a great mystery, as we assume that somehow the gestalts, or
whole objects we perceive in the world, are outside and preconstituted rather
than inside our acts of perception and actively assembled. This returns us to the
problem we had regarding the attitude of daily life and its component assumptions. How do we penetrate the *as if* quality adhering to the external world?
(the world in perception behaves *as if* it acted unilaterally to imprint itself upon
our conscious thought). How do we gain access to those acts of consciousness
that intend this world when those very acts are inclined to erase their own
biography?

The phenomenological solution lies in its *reduction* of the constancy hypothesis by *bracketing,* which means "suspending" or "putting out of action" our
ordinary stance toward the world (Husserl 1970a: 20). In Schutz's (1962: 122)
terms, if this attitude toward the world—the natural attitude—is one in which
we abandon *doubt* about its existence, the phenomenological reduction (or
epoche) means abdicating *belief.* This involves definitively neither doubting nor
believing in the objective, real nature of the world, however. Instead the strategy
is refusing to take a stance either way so that, *for the philosopher,* the "pure life of
consciousness" in its active mode can be revealed (122–23).

For purposes of my investigation, there are three problems with this latter
statement. These problems indicate wider difficulties with phenomenological
philosophy and the advantages of an ethnomethodological investigation of
language use and social interaction. First, the phenomenological reduction, or
epoche, is something that exists as an experience not just for philosophers but
for ordinary members of society. The analysis of constitutive acts can be connected to actual empirical instances of lay inquiry, when participants in the
everyday world, rather than disciplinary professionals and specialists, suspend
or put out of action belief in that world.[7] Indeed, events of bad and good news
bring members of society to a state of epoche, and my aim is to portray and take
analytic advantage of this situation. The second problem with phenomenology
is its preoccupation with consciousness and subjectivity along with what Heritage (1984b: 71) calls its "abstract" quality. As Dreyfus (1992: 248) points out,
Husserl has an "intellectualist" bias that treats forms of consciousness as separa-
ble from bodily engagement in the social world. And the third problem is that
phenomenologists traditionally have approached perception as a psychological
and cognitive endeavor on the part of perceiving subjects, rather than as a social
and collaborative activity.

The lesson from phenomenology is to transform everyday categories and objects into activities that constitute them. Following Garfinkel's (1996) continuing preoccupation with the "what more" of everyday structures, however, is a concern not for consciousness and its role in assembling the everyday world. Instead, the interest is in *embodied* activity and the *practical* production of worldly accounts in the detail of concrete talk and behavior that participants co-produce.[8] In briefest terms, this translates into a fascination with the in situ *procedures* that participants use in their talk and social interaction for delivering (notifying, forecasting, announcing, reporting, pronouncing, elaborating, explicating) and receiving (obtaining, responding to, affirming, admitting, accepting, evaluating) bad and good news. Such procedures are generic — participants employ them methodically and universally because they are known in common. At the same time, the use of these procedures in concrete situations is singular and particular (Sacks 1984a). Each episode of bad or good news has generic properties *and* a unique, distinctive quality.

Bad and Good News and Suspending Belief: The "Noetic Crisis"

Let us take stock. My thesis is that bad news and good news represent disruptions of quotidian life to the extent of jeopardizing participants' sense of what is real. By creating fissures in the structure of everyday life in the way that contrived and natural breaches do, these events reveal the achieved organizational features of social settings. Episodes of bad and good news are like the "redressive" rituals of social drama that Turner (1969: 94) discusses. Representing a moment in "liminal" time, both apart from and yet intimately involved in daily routines, they are an emotional threshold by which persons exit one social world and enter another. Bad and good news roughly follow the three phases, identified by van Gennep (1909), of *rites de passage* — being separated from the everyday, existing on the margin or *limen,* and reaggregating or reintegrating ordinary experience.

This movement from one to another world is captured in the remarks of a physician who was diagnosed with a cancer in his right leg (synovial sarcoma). Appearing in a Public Broadcasting System program called "When Doctors Get Cancer," he is shown walking on crutches into a hospital and, with a baseball cap covering a bald head, sitting on a bed while undergoing chemotherapy and being examined. The doctor is now a patient, and in a voiceover, he says, "Back in October, a year ago, I was given six months to live. So here I am today, a year later, with a new world, a continuum of my last one but essentially a new world." That bad news can usher one into a "new world" is vividly captured not only in this statement but in the picture of this doctor now in patient garb and in the patient role.

There is, of course, much more to the experience of receiving the bad news of cancer, understanding what it means, accepting the condition, and undergoing treatment, than what happens during the few moments of initial news concerning the disease. However, that informing event is a graphic one in its own right and, as it starts the movement of someone into a new social world, the practices of language and social interaction are its medium. And while the empirical emphasis in subsequent chapters involves relatively bounded conversational episodes, mere moments when bearers bring and give news to recipients who show varying kinds of responsiveness, the episodes nevertheless implicate a disruption in the lived flow of everyday life. From the instant when a potential recipient is first apprised that news may be forthcoming, a short or long interval can transpire in terms of standard time. While waiting for signaled or expected tidings and during the delivery itself, one's inner sense of duration can expand or contract relative to clock time (Flaherty 1999). In terms either of clock time or inner time, it may be agonizingly long or startlingly short as breakdown of the taken-for-granted occurs. Following the phenomenological vocabulary, I will call this breakdown a *noetic crisis,* because participants in a delivery of news are unable to assemble sensuous appearances (noemata) into a coherent object. The noesis, consisting of ordinary acts of gestalt comprehension and involving perception, recollection, retention, and other "modes of consciousness" (Husserl 1970a: 36) as exhibited in embodied action and interaction, is at least momentarily blocked. The crisis has these characteristics: cognitive disorientation and affective arousal when the news is foreshadowed; the beginning of resolution to this disorientation, although not necessarily to the emotional component, when the news is announced; and, after the announcement, retrospective interpretation of previously ambiguous signals along with figuring of what the news means for the future.

Entering the Epoche: Disorientation

In their narratives about giving and receiving news, participants describe discrete features of a lifeworld called into question. Opening the fissure is the indication or prefiguring of an announcement that will reveal some new world:[9]

(1) **Narrative #37**
When I arrived home one morning, there were two messages from my father telling me to call home as soon as possible. One message was from the night before, and the other was from earlier that morning. My roommate said that it sounded urgent. Already my mind began to race with thoughts of death of my grandmother or another relative. I called him back as soon as possible. My cousin

answered the phone, and I asked what the message was. She told me that my uncle had died.

Having the notification to call home, and the roommate's suggestion of urgency, the message recipient's "mind began to race" with various possible scenarios. That would suggest a speeding up of the reflective capacity, but the main matter is a state of disorientation and indeterminacy that the recipient attempts to remedy by conjuring various possible noematic correlates of the inference and prospect that someone close has died. It may be grandmother, it may be another relative, and there is what Mead (1934) called an "imaginative rehearsal" as the individual entertains possible or candidate new worlds marked by the death and therefore absence of a formerly proximate inhabitant.

Thus, when there is a prefiguring of possible news to come, one enters the epoche and may experience disorientation. It may happen inadvertently, not as something a deliverer at all intends. Here is a woman, eighteen months after a successful operation for cancer, returning for what she believed to be a routine checkup and series of tests. At the hospital, she had an ultrasound and a liver scan in the morning, ate lunch, and then received a bone scan:

(2) Macrae 1990: 144

> An hour later I was back in the ward reading my book, feeling pretty smug that I'd finished having all my tests. I suddenly heard a doctor say into the phone, "Could you have another look at Gillian Macrae's lung X-ray? We thought it looked a bit unusual." Time slowed up. I wanted an action replay. It had to be me he was talking about. But this was the sort of thing that happened in bad Hollywood films. Surely this wasn't the way to hear the most serious thing that happened to me in my entire life. I felt mildly hysterical. There were two hours to wait before the consultant's ward round and my husband coming to fetch me home. I couldn't read. I couldn't think. I just wanted to go back to this morning — and not ever have heard that junior doctor's words.

The prefiguring of possible news occurs here as an overhearing. Immediately, "time slowed up" and there are other indications of how unreal the world became: it was like being in a video or movie. Feeling hysterical, the patient is virtually immobilized.[10]

A parent who eventually finds out that a newborn child has some birth defect or disability may be *confused* because of the doing of ambiguity: there may be funny and indecipherable visages of nurses and doctors, consultations between staff in hushed voices, nurses who look at each other and point at something (Darling 1983: 125–27). A mother who learned, twenty minutes after the birth, that her child had a developmental difference, reports this:

(3) Jacobs 1969: 5

> My obstetrician is one of these very sensitive-type people. Most doctors do not display their emotions on their face, but he is one of the few. Now I should have — I should have sensed something in the — in the delivery room — that something was bothering him because he teased me about having another boy. And John was, he wasn't grotesque looking but he was funny looking. He was tiny, but he was real pudgy looking. I noticed how chubby his little hands were and I made a comment about this. And I noticed how puffy his little eyes were, but I didn't say anything about that. But the thing that I thought was strange was that he was thrusting his tongue. Which I thought — well I don't know maybe some babies come out all kinds of ways when they're first born, you know. Cause my oldest was one of these exceptionally pretty babies. Well you can't always have a pretty boy, you know. And he, there was a intern in the room and there were several student nurses and of course they're all saying how cute and I kept saying well he's not as cute as my first one was you know. The doctor still didn't say anything you know. And then when he had gone out and told my husband, my husband came into my room and he already knew that see — and I said to him, gee are you that disappointed because — no well when I went out of the delivery room I told him he was the father of a funny-looking little son, is what I told him. I couldn't help it. He was funny looking. And then after that the doctor told him. And then when he came down to my room I said to him, are you that disappointed because it wasn't a girl — cause he really wanted a girl. No, no, no, he said. I said well what's the matter with you, what is it? And he said, nothing. And I said, well maybe this will be a quiet boy, because the other one was such a loud mouth. And you know he was just acting so strangely and by then you get all these apprehensive feelings which I had during the pregnancy anyhow.

This mother is reading cues from the face of her doctor and his teasing, from what is to her a curious-looking baby, from the incongruous assessments of others ("how cute" the baby is), from the silences of doctor and husband. When her husband withholds responding to her proposal about the son (he is "funny looking") and about his own regard ("disappointed" that it wasn't a girl), she observes that he (the husband) is acting "strangely." Accordingly, the mother is offering interpretive (including normalizing) frameworks in an effort to comprehend these multiple cues, and when no one aligns to her proposals, this intensifies her "apprehensive feelings."

Metaphors for the interval between initial indications and the delivery of news repeatedly invoke images of disorientation, senselessness, imbalance, anomie, and the like. A father whose thirteen-year-old daughter was missing from a California community did not return to work from the time she vanished and describes being stuck in a "Twilight Zone" for weeks (Janofsky 1998). Another family characterizes the nine-year wait to hear about their abducted eleven-year-old son as a time "lived in the half-step, not quite here, not quite there" (Johnson 1998).

It may seem inapposite to equate this kind of agony with that which others experience when in the throes, say, of a competition where the worst that can happen is not winning. Yet the disruption in these circumstances can also be acute. In 1996, Neil Labute won acceptance at the Sundance Film Festival for his movie, *In the Company of Men*. Comparing the experience of anticipating the announcement to the experience of mental patients (he had worked in a psychiatric hospital), Mr. Labute says,

(4) Kennedy 1998

I had so much anxiety that I got to the point where I was hearing the phone ring when it really wasn't ringing. . . . It was really intense. I started to get physically sick. I thought, this is what it must be like to be schizophrenic. They hear voices, I hear phones ringing.

He may be speaking ironically, although hearing phones ringing is not unlike the "ringing in the ear" that the mother of the child with PKU experienced as she received her news, or the "little bell" in her ear that a cancer patient describes after a mammography and prior to obtaining the result (Gordon 1990).

Just as Garfinkel's contrivances demonstrated that disrupting stable meanings evoke affectual experiences and displays, bad and good news do so in a more spontaneous way.[11] Exhibited emotions range from the mild to the overwhelming. Participants describe themselves and others as variously (according to the texture and type of news) feeling upset, sick, struck, stunned, terrorized, falling apart, sad, despairing, helpless, and so on. While most of these adjectives derive from stories about bad news, many of them are present in accounts of good news as well, along with other terms such as happy, elated, giddy, and the like. Consistent with affect control theory (Heise 1999), episodes of bad and good news may mean more or less extreme departures from ordinary definitions of the situation and therefore may provoke relatively drastic negative and positive emotions. In actual talk and social interaction, participants *claim* having such feelings as happiness and sadness and also *display* affect through bodily comportment and by prosodic means or the intonation, pacing, and rhythm of talk.

Resolution of the Noetic Crisis through the Announcement of News

In Mr. Labute's case, a phone call about the Sundance Film Festival eventually came and brought good tidings. When it "finally did come," he said, "it was very freeing. I almost collapsed" (Kennedy 1998). Labute's account and suggestion of being freed when he got the news suggests liberation from the noetic crisis, but the account does not tell us much about the actual episode. If we return to the narrative of the mother who gave birth to the "funny looking" child, it reveals the way in which her quest to assemble a gestalt was an *interactive* one.

(5) Jacobs 1969: 5

> And then the doctor came in and he drew the curtains around my cubicle and I thought, oh no, you know. And he told me the baby was born completely healthy, but he's not completely normal. And I looked at him and I said, he's mongoloid. And I've never seen a mongoloid baby before in my life, but all of a sudden the flat features, the thrusting of the tongue, you know, just kind of hit me in the face. And that poor doctor couldn't bring himself to say the word. He said, it shouldn't have happened to you, not to your age bracket.

The news emancipates this mother from the state of uncertainty in which she was dwelling by enabling her to refashion all the cues according to a fully discerned intentional object or gestalt — her baby's identity as what is now called a Downs syndrome child — that "hits her in the face." Such an idiom, depicting a confrontation with the hard presence of an external force, seems to cancel the intentional acts that are otherwise exhibited in the struggle for comprehension, including the doctor's role in further prompting and confirming the mother's realization. Thereby, such idioms also withdraw from participants' view the interactive resolution of the noetic crisis and socially concerted assembly of the gestalt.[12]

Even when the tidings are bad, recipients recurrently report a feeling of relief concomitant to receiving the news, as the mother did in her story at the front of this chapter concerning how she learned that her baby had PKU. For another example, when the body of her husband could not be found after the 1995 explosion of the Federal Building in Oklahoma City, Gabriella Aleman told a reporter that she could not admit that her husband was gone (Bragg 1995). "We're always hoping," she said. Recognizing that an informing phone call would most likely tell her the body was found and would bring sorrow, Aleman also said, "It would be nice to know." That is, whether the news is good or bad, it ends the suspension of belief and the vacillation between possible noematic anticipations that accrue when the status of objects in the world has become indeterminate. A bad but somewhat intact world capable of being known-in-common may be preferable to this. A woman who complained to her doctor about headaches and was told that it was her "nerves,"

(6) Hackett and Weisman 1962: 122

> asked why was she nervous. [The doctor] returned the question. She replied, "I am nervous because I have lost 60 pounds in a year, the Priest comes to see me

twice a week, which he never did before, and my mother-in-law is nicer to me even though I am meaner to her. Wouldn't this make you nervous?" There was a pause. Then the doctor said, "You mean you think you are dying?" She said, "I do." He said, "You are." Then she smiled and said, "Well, I've finally broken the sound barrier; someone's finally told me the truth."

As one of Charmaz's (1991: 24) subjects, who was diagnosed with a metabolic disorder, put it, "Thank God. At last I *know* it's something real." The delivery of news has this "final," "at last" quality simply because it terminates a state of not knowing, a world of uncertain contents and contingency, and the ambiguity of sensuous presentations. In bringing an end to uncertainty, the delivery and receipt of news help participants reassemble a world with relatively determinate phenomenal features.

Retrospective Interpretations and Prospective Courses of Action

From this vantage point — after the news pronouncement — the obduracy of the new world takes hold, as participants in the event retrospectively interpret or recast the preceding signs and symptoms according to significations now surrounding the discerned object or person. Previous perceptions and indications are seen under fresh auspices, both being formed by and helping to form a new gestalt.

In his ethnographic study of how students become socialized to handle the omnipresence of dying and death during medical school, Hafferty (1991) describes a remarkable hospital scene in which a small group of students observed a psychiatric interview with a nursing home resident, Mr. Kilwauski. Although Mr. Kilwauski began to cough early in the interview and this cough increased in frequency and intensity until he got up, discharged phlegm into a wastebasket, and had to be escorted from the room, the students did not believe that anything was particularly amiss. Nevertheless, outside in the corridor and unbeknownst to the students, Mr. Kilwauski collapsed. No one in the classroom fully understood the seriousness of his condition until, after ten minutes, the group leader returned and said that Mr. Kilwauski had suffered a heart attack. Hafferty (1991: 158–59) writes,

> Following a collective "Oh wow!" the heretofore academically based discussion shifted to a series of anxious questions and opinions about whether Mr. Kilwauski had been pushed too hard during the interview, whether his pulmonary distress was indicative of an impending or full blown heart attack, and whether or not the interview should have been stopped.

Not knowing how serious the situation was and while waiting for further news, the previously witnessed small world of the medical interview collapsed, as the students, with the group leader's provisional disclosure, worked to figure out what had actually transpired. The students Hafferty interviewed report how "unreal" the situation was, how it was a "big shock," and how they "didn't want to believe" their patient was "really sick." The group leader then returned with further bad news: although Mr. Kilwauski's condition had stabilized, he had been deprived of oxygen long enough to raise the likelihood of brain damage. On a final trip, the group leader announced the death of Mr. Kilwauski: "It's all over, they pulled the sheet over his head" (158). Again, following a collective moment of shock, the students raised questions about how it could have happened. Whereas they had initially regarded the interview as "talking to a nice old man," now they saw it as a very sick man having been "peppered" with questions, and sought to assign blame both to Mr. Kilwauski for having denied and obscured the seriousness of his situation, and to themselves for having missed or ignored it (165–69). The new world that succeeded a noetic crisis resolved one set of problems but raised others, as students and faculty engaged in extensive dialogue about what had happened and why.

The medical students' handling of bad news, accordingly, demonstrates not only retrospective interpretation by which, in the staff's and students' discourse, Mr. Kilwauski-as-coughing-but-well newly emerges as Mr. Kilwauski-as-sick and dying (after possibly having been harassed). Additionally, participants in the episode display a functional orientation as they enter the new social world. What lessons can be learned? Rare as the event might be, what are the implications for handling a recurrence of death in the classroom? What is the proper emotional stance toward such an event? The medical students, although plagued with guilt and anxiety about Mr. Kilwauski's unexpected death, resisted their group leader's attempts to talk about the death and favored discussion of the interview context in which the death occurred. Accordingly, from the perspective of participants, a news announcement that ends a noetic crisis does not engender *philosophical* debate, as if the fundamental problem in daily life were to resolve metaphysical questions about the nature of objects, including bodies and selves, that form the social world. Rather, joint adherence is for the sake of engaging that world in a practical way. Put differently, participants uniformly address the nature of the world with a "pragmatic motive" (Schutz, 1962; Zimmerman and Pollner 1970: 85) and work to move ahead in the courses of action that immediately occupy them. Even when a death is closer to home than in the case of Mr. Kilwauski, news conveying the person's demise does not necessarily mean that contemplation of life and death is facilitated. While reflection about death may certainly accompany the experience, under some circumstances tellers strive to avoid such contemplation in both themselves and their recipients.[13] As Charmaz (1975) and Glaser and Strauss (1965: 168) have asserted, this is to avert "scenes"; it is to help relatives in beginning to settle the loved one's affairs and to consider what life will be like now that the former intimate is no longer there.

Episodes of Talk and Social Interaction

In narrative accounts of bad and good news we can see how, in their lay and professional capacities, participants in the everyday world may come to inhabit a rarefied state that phenomenologists thought belonged to the philosopher, one of epoche where the ordinary abandonment of doubt in the objectivity of the external world and the character of certain social objects therein is suspended. Of course, unlike the phenomenologist, who suspends the natural attitude in a strategic fashion, everyday actors often have the epoche thrust upon them in what I previously called "mere moments" of talk and social interaction that are a noetic *crisis*. In episodes consisting of only a few turns of talk, is it also conceivable that speaker and hearer are opening and then closing a deep fissure, and thereby reconfiguring the everyday world? A further question: while the notion of "crisis" may apply to bad news transparently, is it possible that episodes of good news also ensnare participants in crisis? Witness the following telephone call between friends, Andi and Betty. Andi preannounces some "surprising" news (lines 1 and 3). Betty's "go-ahead" signals, which ask for (line 2) and then urge the "telling" (line 4), may, accordingly, display the onset of a noetic crisis. Andi produces the announcement at line 5.[14]

(7) ARL3:18

```
 1   Andi:  Well we have some news for you.
 2   Betty: What?
 3   Andi:  .hhh that may come as a bit of a surprise ehhh!
 4   Betty: I see- what are you telling me?
 5   Andi:  hhhh! Bob and I are going to have a baby.
 6   Betty: Oh my good↑ness hhow- (1.0) did you have a reversal-
 7          he have a reversal?
 8   Andi:  Yea:h.
 9              (1.0)
10   Andi:  .hhh[:::::::::]
11   Betty:     [↑whe::n.]
12   Andi:  tch eyup. Last ↑March.
13              (0.4)
14   Andi:  .mhhh ((sniff))
15   Betty: OH [MY  G:OOD]↑NESS:
16   Andi:     [And  (ituh)]
17   Andi:  It was [very succe̲ssful,] [v̲ery quickly] hh : : h .hhh
18   Betty:        [OH    I'M    SO] [↑HA̲P̲PY.   ]
```

As subsequent questioning by Betty (lines 6–7) reveals, Andi's husband Bob had had a vasectomy. This was something well known by their friends, including Betty. Hence, when she first hears the news, it can be, according to the way the news was preannounced, very surprising indeed, as her upward intoned "Oh my good↑ness" (line 6) displays. As indicated by her subsequent question about whether Bob had a "reversal" (lines 6–7), Betty does not yet know what Andi's announcement means or how to appraise the news. Here, then, is a full-blown suspension — a noetic crisis. We can imagine Betty's puzzle: *How* are they going to have a baby? Is Andi pregnant? Is the forthcoming baby something they want or something forced, as with an accidental pregnancy? Are they adopting? What sort of baby will this be? Is this bad news or good news? The question about reversal, then, elicits further information that can disambiguate the situation. After Andi confirms that Bob did have a reversal (line 8) and responds (line 12) to a further question about its timing, Betty can infer that the pregnancy was a something the couple very actively sought, and relatively recently, which information provides for a more fully intended social object. The projected baby is a wanted, valued addition to Bob and Andi's lives, and the pregnancy represents quick *success* (line 17) after an operation that is known not always to be effective. Having learned this, Betty produces, in crescendo-like fashion, a further receipt of the news with increased volume (line 15) and a claim of being happy, which is also spoken with elevated volume and rising intonation and stress on the focal word (line 18). The noetic crisis is relieved, in other words, in a dramatic celebration or affect-laden show of positive regard for the news.

Other episodes of news delivery and receipt may not be as dramatic as this, and perhaps the fissure in the social world that is opened and closed may be less deep. However, in strong or weak fashion, such moments of talk and social interaction surrounding both bad and good news do involve disruption, suspension, crisis, and resolution as participants move collaboratively from one social world to another. In subsequent chapters, I will further explicate this and similar episodes for what they reveal in terms of the usually submerged, tacit, or taken for granted practices by which these parties made the transition from a social world in which Bob and Andi were a purposefully childless couple to one in which they were now to be a larger family.

Bad and Good News as Phenomena

Bad and good news manifest themselves frequently in the vocabulary and orientations of people living in and through the most ordinary events. "Ordinary" should not imply trivial, however, for these events include births and deaths, health and disease, job losses and promotions, financial ruin and gain, and many other more or less dramatic occurrences. By "ordinary," I mean these events are the stuff of our social existence in daily (and sometimes nightly) encounters. I will explore ways in which the phenomena materialize, and then preview specific features of bad and good news that will be subject to intensive analysis in subsequent chapters.

Bad News and Good News as Everyday Matters

Bad news and good news arise in an astonishing array of environments, regularly attesting to how people, individually and collectively, conduct their lives in terms of this news. For instance, one respondent answered a newspaper's inquiry about when he knew he was in love by saying that his betrothed "was the first person I wanted to share good news with and bad, too." More prosaically, we can hardly read the financial pages of the daily paper without confronting news like this:

(8) **Henriques 1998**
Cendant Corporation, struggling to regain investor confidence amid an accounting scandal that has slashed its share price in half, had a good news, bad news story to tell investors Thursday. The good news was that profits for the first half of 1998 were robust. The bad news? More than $640 million of the profits reported for the last three years were fictional.

Here, a reporter uses a good news/bad news *frame* for portraying corporate performance. More common than the bimodal frame in this story are ones in which corporate performance goes solely in one direction rather than the other. Whether investors obtain such news from the media or other sources, the stories are notorious for having an undue effect on the stock market, with negative reports about earnings driving down the price of the stock to a point of being undervalued, and the effect being opposite when the news is good — stocks can become overvalued. Investors, in part because they emphasize recent information to the neglect of longer-term performance data (De Bondt and Thaler 1985), seem to "overreact" to both bad and good reports of earnings.

The good news/bad news frame appears in other business and organizational settings besides those in which earnings announcements are made. If we go inside such settings, we might find a conversation like this one between a project director at a major research university and one of his collaborators:

(9) **Boden 1994: 135–36 (simplified)**
Vic: Uhm, we have uh- a good opportunity and a problem. Now lemme tell you what the good opportunity is. I've been told by Anderson who's the dean over there of uhm the Research Center, that of course if

> we want to go ahead we can do it? We can ask for a larger amount?
> We can get it as an augmentation to our existing grant in uh
> anticipation of the summer revision.
> Ray: Yes?
> → Vic: Okay that's the good news?
> Ray: Mm hmm?
> → Vic: Now the bad news is- is that we have a very large number of
> competing objectives . . . Okay, the problem is this, that eh John
> Ellis wants a computer . . .

The good news/bad news frame in this excerpt (see arrows) is anticipated, as Boden (137) observes, in Vic's characterization at the beginning of the excerpt of having "a good opportunity and a problem." The contrast being drawn is between having money available to augment what Vic knows to be an existing *teaching* grant and having a colleague speak for a significant piece of that augmentation for a *research* computer. How to arrange priorities, allocate scarce resources, and do so within a system of accounting oversight are all indexed in the framing here (139).

Conversational use of the categories of bad news and good news to raise and manage tasks and agendas is one way that the phenomena make their appearance in organizational settings. More personally consequential in business and government environments are communications about plant or office openings and closings, hirings and firings, and the like. Especially difficult, of course, is a manager's task of presenting the bad tidings of a layoff to a worker. Sometimes, even, the erstwhile bad news messenger becomes victim to the same message:

(10) Uchitelle and Kleinfield 1996

> As an officer in charge of operations of the Standard Chartered Bank, Mr. Allen had to dispose of one of the three currency traders in the Toronto branch. The consensus choice happened to be a woman who was indisputably the top performer, but had the weakest political bonds. "I knew that she was the best in the department," he said. "But she had not networked. And I had to inform her that she was terminated. And she looked at me with tears in her eyes and said, 'But Charlie, you know better.' I will never forget what she said and how she looked that day."
>
> Each afternoon at Mass, he looks to put the past and the present in perspective. "It is a mark on my character," he said. "I feel a lesser person."
>
> There is a sullen irony to Mr. Allen's story. He lost his own job last May and now wanders with the dispossessed.

The good news counterparts to firing involve hiring and promotion, but between hiring and firing or promotion are performance evaluations that can transpire as either bad or good news. According to several surveys, most company appraisal systems are unsuccessful. A *Wall Street Journal* article suggested that this is due to various problems, including managers who do not like to give bad news, employees who do not want to hear it, and a tendency, even when a review is positive, for the recipient "to hear only the negatives" (Schellhardt 1996). There is also the problem of communicating criticism and other kinds of bad news *up* the organizational hierarchy (Roberts and O'Reilly 1974). For either upward or downward communication, business periodicals may publish advisory articles, such as "How to Make the Bad News Less Bad and the Good News Great" (Drennan 1988).

It seems that bad news receives all the attention, and business journals are not the only ones whose advice giving attests to the prominence of this phenomenon as part of the workaday or professional world. Medicine has had a long history of concern about the conveying of adverse diagnostic news, and partly for this reason, I explore the clinical implications of my research in subsequent chapters. The pervasiveness of the role of bad news messenger in some occupations, particularly medicine, can be so well known as to steer people in their career choices. For example, a radiologist, in recounting how he helped diagnose a woman's pancreatic cancer, celebrates only having to do a needle biopsy and making sure that the specimen is adequate (Schragg 1987). In the laboratory, he worked closely with the pathologist who found that the specimen was indeed adequate, and that it unfortunately showed a malignancy. Returning to the patient's room, the radiologist only told the patient about the success of the extraction procedure and not the result. He said to her, "After the pathologist studies the slides, she'll contact your doctor," thereby leaving to that doctor the odious task of presenting the diagnostic tidings. Although he felt "a twinge of guilt" for not revealing the result to the patient, the radiologist also confesses, "Maybe one of the reasons I chose the relatively detached and tranquil field of diagnostic radiology is that we don't have to give patients bad news very often. We let the internists and surgeons be the purveyors of doom." Indeed, the actual ordeal in medical school of having to "purvey doom" to patients and families was the precise reason for a young physician choosing forensic pathology as her career. A crucial experience for this physician was with a fifty-three-year-old woman who had a severe form of leukemia:

(11) **Firstman and Talan 1997: 51–52**

> Then it came time to tell the family. So I went back to find the doctor because it's his patient. And he had left. He had deliberately done that to me, I think to see what I was made of. . . . Well, I went in and started telling this family about this rare, rapidly fatal leukemia and by the time we finished, I was crying harder than

anyone in the family and they were holding me and patting me and telling me, "Please don't cry, it's not your fault." Yes the patient is comforting the doctor. And I thought: This is not going to work. . . . So I decided I needed a layer of doctor between me and the patient. It was either radiology or pathology and to me there's no question pathology is far more interesting.

On the other hand, some clinicians may choose an area of medicine because of the pervading possibility of good news. In an article about the changes that managed care has precipitated in medicine (Kleinfield 1999), one physician was reported to have chosen pediatrics as a specialty because he saw it as a "good-news specialty. Children usually got better."

"Realizing" the News

Because bad *and* good news are such ubiquitous phenomena, it is surprising how little research exists regarding them. To be sure, we are not wanting for journal articles and books about *bad news,* but most of these, full of advice about how to give such news, are remedial and seldom based on systematically gathered and analyzed evidence.[15] And there is simply a dearth of attention to good news or the relations between bad news and good news, even though the contrasting forms are intrinsically connected to one another, and good news is sometimes as problematic to deliver as bad news. Ultimately I aim to redress these various neglects: this is a book based on methodical collection and examination of hundreds of instances, encompassing good news as well as bad news, and, in the effort to capture how participants in everyday life structure their worlds, it investigates how they manage these forms of news in relation to one another such that even in the face of the most dire circumstances participants regularly maintain an optimistic, benign version of things.

The overwhelming remedial concern with bad news, on the part of business, clinical, and other professionals gives us a convenient starting point. Using narrative data: I will probe, in Chapter 2, how best to obtain recipients' *realization* (understanding, acceptance) of bad news. However, close inspection of bad news narratives, and consideration of attitudes toward bad news in different cultures, demonstrates that there are no disembodied techniques for informing that necessarily prevent or assure the realization of bad news. That is, to ensure an effect such as "realization" abstract strategies must be coupled with relevant knowledge of one's recipients and their circumstances; communication is effective according to the contextually embedded particularities of actual social life.

By offering a systematic empirical approach to the interpersonal giving and receiving of news, and by attending to ordinary features of this event glossed or ignored in other investigations, my research seeks to contribute to the applied literature on how best to convey news, including both bad and good kinds. Nevertheless, the starting point is not with professional discourse in such institutional and organizational settings as business and medicine. If these settings are where bad and good news recipients sometimes may first be informed, they still face the task of conveying the news to family members, friends, and others. Patients diagnosed with chronic illness, as Charmaz (1991: 109) observes, must "tell and retell their news to many people."[16] A heart patient who eventually underwent successful transplant surgery had a particularly difficult time with this after his physician first told him of the dire situation:

(12) Lucas 1989

> He tells me that he's been a cardiologist for 10 years and he's never dealt with a case like mine. There's no successful treatment. There's no cure. Nothing. He left the room and that was the longest afternoon of my life because I had to call everybody and tell them.

Eventually, then, it is not the most directly involved parties who are conveying and receiving the news, but others to whom they talk and who may then transmit the news to still others who are some steps removed from the directly involved parties.

My research is occupied with these *conversational* episodes for sound theoretical reasons. As Schegloff (1988b: 455) has argued, the conveying of information, or "telling news," is one action that "ordinary people in ordinary capacities" undertake. When people perform the responsibility by "acting on special occasions or in special capacities—as, for example, with professionals in modern society," they employ canonical or generic devices in an organized manner. In other words, devices for conveying bad and good news, have their home in ordinary conversation, and practitioners shape or adapt them to the particularities and contingencies of professional practice.[17]

In fact—despite the literature on the topic, and efforts by some professional schools and agencies—practitioners in medical settings, welfare bureaucracies, legal environments, and others, very rarely obtain formal instruction about how to deliver news to their clients, to their patients, to family members, or to other involved parties. Consequently, without training about such strategies, the manner in which professionals deliver good, bad, and other kinds of news undoubtedly reflects the tacit or commonsense knowledge (Garfinkel 1967; Polanyi 1958; Schutz 1962) everyone acquires through quotidian linguistic and interactional experience in society. Simply put, by having endured bad and good news in the routines of their more ordinary endeavors, professionals may already know, in taken-for-granted ways, how to design their announcing actions.[18] This is not to say they necessarily know *best* how to do it, but they will have some set of more or less sophisticated skills upon which to rely when facing their work-related tasks of reporting on death, disease, job status, legal involvement, or other matters, to the affected parties. Recipients, as well, will rely on taken-for-granted knowledge for appropriate ways of responding to news. To understand the organization of bad and good news in professional settings, the analytical starting place needs to be with ordinary conversation, for it is here that members of society learn practices for announcing and responding to news as they become proficient at social action and interaction. Each of my analytic chapters, therefore, concentrates initially on conversational instances of bad and good news. Each chapter has a coda that directly examines news deliveries in institutional settings — mostly medical clinics but in one instance the tidings a teacher presents to the mother of one of her students.

Narratives about Bad and Good News versus Recorded Real-Time Interaction

Here and in chapter 2, I rely largely on narrative data — participants' stories in which they observe others giving and receiving news or provide recollections of their own experiences. I obtained this narrative data as a by-product of an "activity focused" inquiry into the interactional giving and receiving of news in a variety of social settings. However helpful these stories are in providing access to inner experience and its relation to behavior and conduct, they are inadequate for any close appreciation of the orderliness in actual exhibits of this behavior and conduct. It is not just that narratives are retrospective accountings and therefore suffer from the distortions that time, memory, and degree of impact can induce in the remembered and told story. These narratives also are glosses or semblances of what participants undergo and produce as part of their *lived* experience.[19] Methodologically, my use of narrative data draws on a mode of inquiry, ethnography, that has a venerable tradition in sociology, anthropology, and other social sciences. Ethnography has an affinity with ethnomethodological conversation analysis (ECA), but ECA, I argue in Chapter 3, illuminates features of bad and good news and hence social organization in the details of real conduct. Subsequent chapters (4 through 8) take up the primarily conversation-analytic inquiry of recorded instances of bad and good news collected from a panorama of everyday settings.

Bad News and Good News as Participants' Own Phenomena

Conveying news in actual interaction is not a matter of some deliverer having a preconstituted newsworthy item with an intrinsic negative or positive character to send, as if down a conduit, to a recipient who grabs the package of bad or good news at the other end. That is, occurrences in the world are not inherently "bad" or "good" or even "news." Instead, participants *work to achieve* a mutual sense of some event-in-the-world as news and as having a good or bad character. Having achieved this sense, participants may have a transformative experience with regard to a noetic crisis in the world of everyday life, but one reason for stressing the achieved character of both bad *and* good news is that it is not easily predictable as to what sort of transformative experience this may be. We have seen that bad news, in resolving the noetic crisis and delivering recipients from uncertainty, can bring *relief.* The "terror" of learning that one has cancer, as Frank (1991: 26) has put it, is counterbalanced by the validation that a diagnosis of serious illness accords: one is not malingering or being difficult. Ratified illness may mean a "reprieve" of sorts, so that a patient can even report being "elated" (Charmaz 1991: 35) because the "sick role" (Parsons 1951) relieves one of responsibility and means that others will work to solve the individual's problems. As well, chronic illness can consolidate, through the discovery of neglected strengths, a more stable sense of self and ultimately can be identity-affirming (Charmaz 1994: 238). A disease like AIDS, Sullivan (1996) has argued, can give victims a life-enhancing sense of purpose and a feeling of integration with others that were missing before the diagnosis.[20]

Such appreciation may not occur when the bad diagnostic news is first delivered, although it can. When one young child learned of the death of his father, the temporary reaction was more positive than negative:

(13) **Wilkinson 1992: 50**

> Christopher was at the playground. The tone of voice of the teacher who sent him to the office made him wonder if he had done something wrong. Then he began to wonder that something had happened to his mother; he thought maybe she had been in a car accident. When he got to the office and she knelt down and told him, he didn't cry. He clenched his fists, and then he said, "Daddy?" Then he said it again. The shock produced in him a kind of exalted state. He said that when he died he was going to tell his father everything that had happened in his life, and what kind of person he had been, and what he had accomplished.

This child's "exalted state" may seem odd, and was no doubt temporary, but it may not be all that unusual: some individuals have an experience of ecstasy because of bad news. For example, Bob Rosenthal, who was poet Allen Ginsberg's secretary for twenty years before Ginsberg's death, recalls how Ginsberg, who was a student of Tibetan Buddhism, dealt with the diagnosis of an inoperable liver cancer through meditative practice:

(14) Van Oss 1998

> In a sense, I think that almost aided his dying in that he — when the terminal di-
> agnosis came, he was in a low form of ecstasy. He was exhilarated by this experi-
> ence. And he put his energy into being aware of the experience.

Just as "bad" news may engender a "good" experience, so may otherwise pleas-
ant tidings be, at least temporarily, a negative experience. In July of 1998, when
thirteen men who had joined in the purchase of a lottery ticket won nearly
$300 million, one of them said, "You go from totally excited to scared to
death. . . . We're really getting nervous and scared what we're going to do with
all this money" (Belluck 1998). After novel drug therapy vastly improved the
treatment of AIDS in the late 1990s and restored the health of some who were on
the brink of death, Sullivan (1996: 52) himself HIV-positive, wrote that it so
dissipated the life-enhancing features of the disease as to "make the good news
almost as unbearable as the bad":

(15) Sullivan 1996: 76

> When you have spent several years girding yourself for the possibility of death, it
> is not so easy to gird yourself instead for the possibility of life. What you expect
> to greet with the euphoria of victory comes like the slow withdrawal of an excuse.
> And you resist it.

That illness comes or goes does not mechanically predict the kind of news one
or the other situation represents. A final example of good news resulting in bad
experience is in the area of genetic testing. In one study of the effects of being informed about their risk for Huntington's disease, approximately 10 percent of
people informed of a *decreased* risk had psychological difficulties coping with this
news, even though (because of family history) they had sought the testing as a
way of relieving uncertainty (Huggins et al. 1992). Again, the adverse reactions
were due in part to the predicament of having to change one's assumptions
about what the future holds. Examining a news delivery sequence in chapter 4,
we can see how participants *work interactionally* with announcements about
events and conditions to establish these events as news, and as bad or good or
neutral, as the case may be.

Bad News, Good News, and Relationship

Events become assembled as news and as a particular kind of news according
to who is telling the news, who is receiving it, and their full set of circumstances,
including their social relationships. To illustrate how presentations of news are
imbued with relational implications, we can consider some extreme cases. Here
is one:

(16) Purdy 1996

> The funeral of a slain police officer is always a tableau of pomp and grief, and 6-year-old Arielle Davis was surrounded by both.
>
> Shifting slightly in her shiny white shoes and wrapped in the embrace of her grieving mother, Arielle watched Friday as the coffins of her slain father, Officer Charles Davis, and of her grandfather [Reginald Skeete], who died after hearing of the slaying, were slid into hearses outside the Cathedral of the Incarnation here.
>
> . . . At the funeral Friday and at the wake for the two men on Thursday in Queens, mourners said they believed that the death of Skeete, a retired postal worker, was hastened by the news of his son-in-law's murder. Friends said the Skeetes had suffered a similar tragedy a few years ago, when Skeete's son was also slain while working as a security guard.

If an announcement about a death in the family can also *cause* death, other kinds of disclosures are perceived to do the same. In a newspaper story about the gay rights movement, one subject suggested that he avoided "coming out" to his parents because he wanted to avoid something a friend experienced: "He came out to his mother, and two weeks later, she died of a stroke. . . . He's convinced that he killed her by telling her" (Johnson 1996). Disclosing a homosexual orientation can also mean rejection from family members, friends, school personnel, co-workers and others (Pilkington and D'Augelli 1995), which, while less severe than death, also means loss of relationship and may be associated with high suicide rates among gay and bisexual youth (Rotheram-Borus and Hunter 1994).[21] And when sexual orientation is not the key, it may be a sexually transmitted disease, such as HIV infection. A young woman who had tested HIV-positive, owing to a history of drug involvement, told me in an interview that when she revealed this news to her live-in boyfriend, he almost immediately began treating her "differently." She told him, "Every time I look at you I feel like I'm in a morgue." Indeed, the boyfriend soon moved out of the apartment.

Sometimes it is not the nature of the news so much as it is the handling of the news that is consequential for relationships. For example, when President Bill Clinton passed over Harold Ickes, his deputy chief of staff, for a promotion after the 1996 election, friends of Ickes "said he was hurt that Clinton had not informed him of his decision to hire Erskine Bowles as White House chief of staff before it was announced Friday" (Purdum 1996). Furthermore, says Purdum, "Clinton's handling of Ickes' departure was in keeping with his well-known distaste for dispensing bad news and with the way he has handled other painful personnel matters in the past." Evidently, Clinton is not the only president to have suffered from this distaste. John Sununu, as chief of staff, was said to have been the bad news bearer for George Bush (Dowd 1991a). In a different public arena, when George Steinbrenner fired Yogi Berra as manager of the New York Yankees in 1985, another member of the Yankee organization, Clyde King, brought the news to Berra, and Berra was so offended by this manner of being told that he vowed not to set foot again in Yankee Stadium so long as Steinbrenner remained as the Yankee owner. Berra stayed away for 14 years until, in 1999, Steinbrenner finally apologized, saying to Berra, "I know I made a mistake by not letting you go personally" (Araton 1999).[22]

Repeatedly, then, the mishandling of bad news demonstrates the severance of relationships. This is no doubt true of good news as well, for withholding one's glad tidings can be a matter for complaint. On the other hand, the sharing of both bad and good news, properly done, enhances relationship, community, and the sense of affinity. Family members and friends generally are under obligation to share major happenings in their lives, and the exchange of news among friends and kin on various topics from births to weddings to deaths and many things in between "defines or redefines the place of the reporter and his audience" in the intimate groups to which they belong (Gans 1962: 77–79).

To obtain analytic access to the embedding of relationship in deliveries of news, we do not need complete ethnographic description of the social context, because participants orient to and exhibit "contextual" matters, including their relationships with one another and to others whom the news concerns in the here-and-now circumstances of delivery and receipt. In their talk and social interaction, for example, parties to the informing episode display their understanding of the consequences of news for those who are most directly affected and for themselves (if they are not the primary figure), and they display their relationship to one another as deliverer and recipient and to other affected individuals. As I show in chapter 5, news may sometimes primarily concern the teller, and at other times may affect the recipient most directly, or even be most significant for neither teller or recipient, but for a third-party friend or acquaintance. Of course, even in the latter situation, teller or recipient or both may demonstrate how they too are touched by the news. One analytic payoff to the investigation of relational matters is to decompose interactional facets of a perplexing problem in the clinic: the frequent occurrence of a "stoic" response to bad diagnostic news.

Asymmetries between Bad and Good News

While employers seek to avoid delivering the bad news of a layoff or firing, for instance, by delegating the task, the opposite may be the case with good news of hiring or promotion. Experimental evidence suggests not only the existence of "discriminatory buckpassing" in organizations—for example, those in the role of manager are more likely to assign the task to a subordinate of conveying bad news about a failed application — but also the tendency to retain the job of delivering good news of successful a application (Rosen, Grandison, and Stewart 1974). As Tesser and Rosen (1975) and other experimental researchers have demonstrated, there is a forceful "mum" effect in many situations: people are much more likely to withhold or delay telling bad news as compared with good news. Accordingly, another phenomenal feature of bad and good news events is their produced *asymmetry,* a matter to be investigated in chapter 6. Illustrations of this feature abound. A first example comes from my clinical data: a psychologist, before presenting two parents the news of their son's mental retardation, says, "Well let me present the bad news and then the good." He proceeds to deliver the news of mental retardation, retrospectively characterizing it with "that's the bad news." Then he goes on, "The *good* news on these kind of developmental things is that as you're seeing he is learning and will continue to learn." For a similar example from a different arena, when the St. Louis Rams lost a preseason game to the Green Bay Packers in 1994, the *Los Angeles Times* quoted Rams coach Chuck Knox as saying, "We didn't win the football game, which is the bad news, but the good news is I think we can profit by some of the mistakes we made" (Simers 1994). There is an ordering here: first the bad news, as if it is something to dispense quickly, and then the good news, which is something to dwell upon. Such was the verdict in a medical encounter when the novelist Morris West learned of his heart disease. The physician began the delivery by saying, "Which do you want first, the good news or the bad news?" West (1994) writes, "I told him I'd prefer to get the bad out of the way."

Another example combines the world of sports with the world of medicine: In 1994, Arizona State baseball coach Jim Brock died of cancer. Before his death, an article in the *New York Times* reported how, even though he was bedridden with his illness, the coach followed what was happening with his team in the College World Series. During the games, he was sometimes sleeping in his hospital room, while his wife Pat Brock was listening to radio reports. She said that during one game, which the team was winning, she would come into the room and wake him every time the team scored. But during a losing effort in the semifinals, she did not wake her husband at all. "I would have if there had been good news," she said (Berkow 1994). The ordering here is that bad news is suppressed at least temporarily and good news is given immediate expression. Hence these orderings are socially organized, and are products of actual conduct in which participants to interaction, in a many ways, produce a vast asymmetry between good news and bad news. Good news obtains a much favored status, not just psychologically among members of society, but in concerted behaviors

that subdue, contain, or "shroud" bad news and "expose" or achieve the ongoing visibility of good news. It is through practices for shrouding bad news and
exposing good news that a benign social world is collaboratively produced.

Bad News, Good News, and Agency

An aspect of the asymmetry between bad and good news concerns the
agency of the bearer, which relates to the *causal texture* of the social world and its
contents — their relation to something that or someone who conditions, effects,
or precipitates what those contents are (Garfinkel 1963). Everyday announcements about occurrences in the lifeworld, in other words, bring to the fore issues of what or who caused the world's objects and events to have the new contents they have. *Blaming the messenger* for bad news goes back at least to the
practice among ancient Persian generals of killing messengers who brought bad
news (Tesser and Rosen 1975: 203). Physicians are well aware of the problem,
and design their death announcements to make a case for the disease process,
rather than their own activities, as having killed a patient (Clark and LaBeff
1982; Sudnow 1967). And figures in political controversy, such as Anita Hill
and Kenneth Starr, may defend themselves against adverse reactions to having
charged a U.S. Supreme Court nominee with sexual harassment (Dowd 1991b)
and a U.S. president with impeachable offenses (Associated Press 1998) by suggesting that they were simply messengers being blamed for unpleasant messages. More sober are stories about a student shooting dead the professor who
told him of a failed doctoral examination (Associated Press 1989) and a bank
customer similarly murdering the branch manager who informed him that his
loan had been denied (Krull 1998). While avoiding blame may be the task a
bearer of bad news faces, we will examine in chapter 7 the asymmetric converse:
those who bring good news often work to take responsibility, and regularly receive credit, for the new state of affairs. Thus, the agency of a bearer of news is
differently configured in interaction according to the type of news it is.

Phenomenal Features of Bad and Good News: Implications

In chapter 8, I explore the implications of my study for the understanding of
public affairs — political and other disasters — in which the interpersonal conveying of bad and good news between major figures may influence the course of
the affair and its public perception. As one illustrative case, I probe the contamination of the U.S. blood supply with HIV virus in the early 1980s, which ad-
versely affected the lives of thousands of hemophiliac individuals and others
who had blood transfusions. The event is a complex one, which has been studied from many different angles. However, no one has looked closely at the in-

teractional dynamics of government, business, foundation, and other actors whose ill-advised decisions in the face of apparent bad news regarding potential contamination jeopardized the lives of so many. I propose that certain features of these actors' decisions are encompassed by an interactional analysis that emphasizes the importance of "everyday rationality" and assumptive orientations to particular social worlds. The possibility is not only that scholars may do better at comprehending communicative processes and actions in public arenas, but that the involved parties, also informed about structures of interaction, may handle crises more effectively than when not aware of their own and others' assumptive worlds and the practices that sustain them.

Once it became clear that blood for transfusions did carry the HIV virus, the evidence is strong that physicians in hemophilia clinics had difficulty imparting this bad news to their patients. They needed to know how to inform them that they might already be infected and that, in any case, they needed to change strategies for treatment. In an epilogue to my research, I make recommendations for better delivery of both bad and good news in professional or occupational settings. Professional bearers of news are messengers *in* the lifeworld because of regular participation in delivering such news. They are messengers *of* the lifeworld because they tell about the status of its desirable and undesirable aspects, and, with their recipients, deal with problems of meaning. I review previous advice in the medical literature about giving bad news. Using my own findings, I consider the efficacy of recommended procedures for conveying news by considering the contingencies that emerge with even the most detailed protocols. If contingencies sometimes render such protocols as inadequate, it does not follow that protocols are invalid. Rather, in Wittgensteinian fashion, we can rearrange what we believe about good professional practice in relation to what we know about language use, and develop protocols that ground deliveries of news in the particularities of participants' circumstances. This will increase the effectiveness of communicative strategies.

TWO

On Realization in Everyday Life

There were two brothers, one of whom owned a beloved cat. Brother A had to go on a trip and needed someone to take care of his cat, so he asked Brother B to do this. Brother B was happy to oblige. Brother A left town and a few days into his trip received a phone call from Brother B, who said, "Hello A, I have to tell you that the cat died." Brother A was taken aback, and said, "Oh how horrible." Then he paused for a few seconds, and added, "This is awful news. And as bad as the news is, what makes it worse is how you told me the news, so bluntly." Brother B replied, "Well I don't know how I could have done any better. The fact is that the cat died." Brother A said, "Well, you could have called me and said something like, 'The cat is up on the roof and we're having trouble getting her down.' Then we would hang up, and you would call a little later, and say, 'The cat is still on the roof and it is looking really bad. I'm not hopeful we're going to get her down.' We would hang up again, and you would call still later, and tell me, 'I'm really sorry to say we couldn't get the cat off of the roof and she died.' That way I could have gotten used to the idea." Brother B answered, "Well, okay, now I know." At this time, Brother A was only at the midpoint of his trip. A few days later, Brother B called again. "Hello A," he said, "Um, mother's up on the roof and we can't get her down."

Recurrent bad news is often *forecasted* as a feature of its telling.[1] The narrative evidence suggests that, compared with the presentational strategies of *stalling* or *being blunt*, forecasting is more effective in procuring a recipient's *realization*, or subjective recognition of the bad news, in part because it implicates a particular social relation between deliverer and recipient. In line with theoretical and empirical challenges to the possibility of differentiating solitary-minded activity from social process, my investigation supports notions that *individual* cognitive apprehension of the world is intimately connected to prior *collective* interpretation, or intersubjectivity, as achieved through the praxis of talk and social interaction (Joas 1985; Levine, Resnick, and Higgens 1993; Rawls 1996, 2001; Schaeffer and Maynard 1996; Schegloff 1991b).

Dictionary definitions of forecasting suggest two meanings: (a) "to serve as an advance indication" of something to come; and (b) to "estimate or calculate in advance." By and large, those who must give bad news forecast in the first sense. That is, they prepare their recipients for the coming news by giving an indication of what it is. Compared with stalling and being blunt, forecasting is a more effective way of procuring recipients' realization of the news because it allows them to forecast the news in the second sense—to estimate and predict what the news will be, such that when it actually arrives it does so in a *prepared social-psychological environment*. Thus, while forecasting is a deliverer's strategy for conveying bad news, it ultimately facilitates realization by involving the recipient in a relational structure of anticipation.[2]

At stake in this chapter is an issue involving ethnographic and conversation analytic methods for inquiry illustrated by the joke recounted in the epigraph. In the joke, Brother B is too blunt in his giving of the bad news about the cat. Consequently Brother A suggests that B's strategy could have been different. He could have forecasted the news so as to better prepare A for the bad news. The joke depicts Brother B as subsequently trying to employ a forecasting strategy, and the punchline has its effect because of B's mechanical style. If we laugh at the joke, it is because B seems to lack commonsense. A competently implemented strategy for giving news cannot be approached in the concrete and literal fashion of Brother B. This is a point not often discussed in the considerable ethnographic literature on giving bad news because of its preoccupation with typology. Forecasting may be a strategy for delivering bad news, but to forecast and prepare a recipient properly involves a bearer's generic knowledge as applied to particular circumstances and relationships, plus competence at signaling and responding in action and in interaction with others. Accordingly, while my proposal is that different devices for conveying bad news—stalling, being blunt, and forecasting—influence a recipient's realization, those strategies and the understanding they demonstrably effect need to be understood as momentary contingent accomplishments in detail. The theme of detail, we saw in chapter 1, is emphasized in ethnomethodology and conversation analysis. It also resonates with something that the sociolinguist Dell Hymes has said about comprehending "the nature and unity" of human discourse. It "must encompass and organize, not abstract from, the diversity of human life" (1974: 33). Hymes could be pointing to the form and structure (unity) of talk and social interaction and to the attempt to capture such form without losing the diversity or detail of what actually happens as part of the interaction. Accordingly, in this chapter I use narrative data both to make an argument about the effect of different presentational strategies on realization and to show the shortcomings of this essentially interview-based approach. This will set the stage for chapter 3 with its more extensive comparison of ethnographic and conversation analytic methods for understanding bad (and good) news in relation to the structure of everyday life.

Forecasting and Realization

Forecasting can involve two major types of interactive practices: nonvocal and vocal. These practices are interrelated, but for purposes of discussion, I will treat them separately.

Nonvocal Forms of Forecasting

Forecasting can be done at some temporal and spatial remove from the actual telling. For instance, when a person has died at the hospital, professionals may call family members at home, tell them that there is a "serious problem" (Clark and LaBeff 1982: 369; see also Sudnow 1967: 118, 127–28), and ask them to come to the scene, thereby enacting what Boden and Molotch (1994) term "the compulsion of proximity."[3] At less of a remove, when loved ones are already on the scene, news givers may isolate recipients (Sudnow 1967: 126), as when nurses take family members to the hospital chapel (Clark and LaBeff 1982: 375), or a physician takes them "somewhere where it is private and discrete" (373). Physicians regard a dying patient's room as taboo for informing, preferring hallways over their own offices, and spaces that are private rather than public. Glaser and Strauss's (1965: 153) term "disclosure space" is an apt one for participants' arranging of their physical environment. Of course, forecasting involves behavior cues—features of a teller's nonvocal comportment—more than spatial management.[4] Sudnow (1967: 120–22) noticed that surgeons entering a waiting room with bad news to deliver provide a show of solemnity. This contrasts with those who have good news to deliver and who therefore walk rapidly and smile at their recipients.

It seems that, in anticipating news, recipients are anxious and intent observers of the setting, and are so regarded by tellers. In fact, clinicians in emergency wards are aware of family members hovering outside the room where they are working on the patient. Families thereby capture glimpses of the patient, and hear how staff regards the situation, and often become suspicious that bad news is forthcoming. A hospital chaplain has said:

(1) **Clark and LaBeff 1982: 374**
They're reading your face, and there's no way you're going to go out with a smile on your face. They can tell by your face . . . They'll read your face and they'll say, "Oh, my God, he's dead" or something like that.

This "reading" of a knowledgeable person's physiognomy can create discomfort for those who indeed are aware of the news but who may not be in a position to tell it. Nurses sometimes wish the attending physician to bring the bad news to a family member, and must stonewall recipients until the physician arrives.[5]

The scrutiny that recipients employ focuses on at least two things: the *demeanor* (Clark and LaBeff 1982: 374) and *identity* (Sudnow 1967) of the teller.

It is clear that a teller's demeanor can be communicative. For instance, in Florida, in 1989, it was discovered that two infants had been mixed up at birth and sent home from their birth hospital with the wrong families. When one of the girls was dying of heart disease, genetic testing showed that she was unrelated to either one of the parents who raised her. These parents began a search that culminated in finding their biological daughter. Robert Mays, who had raised her, then had to inform the girl of her relationship to this other couple. When the girl came home from school on the fateful day, he reported, "She noticed a look of concern on my face and asked what was wrong. I just sat her down on the edge of her bed and told her" (Leisner 1989). A college hockey coach who had a heart transplant recalls that after his original heart became diseased, and some testing was completed, he saw the doctor come in his hospital room with a "serious look on his face" (Lucas 1989). And a physician (Quill 1991: 465) who had to tell a female patient that she tested positive for the HIV antibody, remarks that his patient asked him, when he walked in the room with the results, "Is it AIDS?," and that she "could read the answer" on his face. A related matter about the scrutinizing activities of recipients is that bearers of news, "giving off" impressions (Goffman 1959), may unintentionally provide indications of what is to come. In stonewalling family members, nurses often convey the news through given-off impressions (Clark and LaBeff 1982: 375).

A second aspect of recipients' scrutinizing activities is the tendency to read identity as a feature of comportment. That is, the sheer arrival of a particular type of person in some setting can forecast what they are bringing as news (Sudnow 1967: 119). As a category of persons, police officers are prone to being revelatory in this way, as are military officers and some others (Clark and LaBeff 1982: 370). However, it does not have to be a professional's arrival; meaning can be attached to someone familiar and the place of the person's visit within the local history of a relationship. For instance, after an 18-year-old man accidentally killed himself while examining a gun, his friend had to go to the deceased's family with the news. He reported, "I haven't been around for a while, so when Jon's mom saw me, she knew something was wrong" (Singer 1988). Therefore, *timing* is also a crucial feature of an identifiable someone's appearance on the scene, as with the late night telephone call:

(2) **Narrative #11**
    I got a phone call about 12:15 after midnight and to get a call that late, my friends
    don't call that late and it's either going to be a wrong number or something's

happening. And so I answer the phone and it was my younger sister calling. MY family doesn't call to just chit-chat. And when you get a call that's THAT late then you know something's up.

Indeed, the younger sister was phoning to say that their mother had been hospitalized with pneumonia in a foreign country and that "it didn't look very good."

In a variety of nonvocal ways, then, and whether intentionally or unintentionally, deliverers can forecast the bad news to come. From deliverers' behaviors such as arranging a disclosure space, showing demeanor, and signaling identity, recipients perceive advance indications, project that "something's up," and discern that it may be bad. Additionally, the presenter's nonverbal cues are often coupled with vocalizations of one kind or another.

Vocal Forecasting Strategies

Preannouncements are devices by which an announcer can discover whether a recipient already knows some news-to-be-told. That is, preannouncements act as precursors to some news and yet withhold it; upon a recipient's subsequent request—a "go ahead" signal that completes a preannouncement sequence—the news will be announced (Terasaki 1976: 28). While preannouncements can be minimal and provide few clues as to the nature of the news (e.g., "Have you heard?"), some preannouncements clearly do foreshadow that the news is "awful," "bad," "sad," or "terrible." (In the following extract, square brackets indicate turn types.)

(3) **Narrative #24**
Janey's mother said, "I've got some rather sad news" [preannouncement]. From this statement, Janey knew that something real bad had happened. The first thing she thought was that her grandmother, who had been ill, had died, but she knew that it could not have been her father or brother. Janey asked, "What?" [go-ahead signal]. Janey's mother answered, "Grandpa died this morning" [announcement].

Other preannouncements, even when vague as to the nature of the forthcoming news, still manage to convey it, in part through the serious and concerned tone of the presaging utterance. For instance, here is an account of how a gay man started to disclose his homosexuality to his parents:

(4) **Edgar 1994: 231**
At dinner one night during Christmas break, I said, "There is something that I want to tell you two, and I want you to be an active part of my life, and feel that without telling, you won't be."

Or a teller may speak ironically and jokingly, but still convey the seriousness and difficulty. Carol Neves, a security analyst and vice president of Merrill Lynch, who is in the position of predicting company earnings in the next quarter or year, and rating them accordingly, reports that when she is about to lower or raise her evaluation of a given company, she calls the chief executive officer a few minutes before this information is to become public. "If it's a drop," Neves said, "I usually say something like we're about to find out if we're just fair-weather friends" (Bartlett 1988).

A variation of the preannouncement is *prefacing,* a device that seems to preclude a proposed recipient's "go-ahead" utterance. If one is reasonably sure that the recipient does not know the news, it may be situationally relevant simply to signal what is coming and proceed with the announcement immediately.

(5) **Narrative #2**
> Uh this was two years ago, I was a sophomore, it was reg week in the dorms. And it was on a Friday. I remember on a Wednesday a friend of mine in Milwaukee got in a Moped accident, uh she just hit her head on the curb going about ten miles an hour, no big deal. Or so they thought. And I came into my room on Friday, and my roommate was sitting in there with a few people from the dorm. And I opened the door, he said, "Oh Mark, I've got some bad news, uh Kate's dead."

Apologizing, as a prelude to delivering bad news, works in a forecasting way. Here is an excerpt from a telephone conversation, in which June has called Edward to invite him and his wife, Iris, to come over for drinks. Edward leaves the phone briefly to consult with Iris. When he returns, this ensues:

(6) **Heritage: OI:13:2 (simplified)**
> Edward: June,
>   June: Yes?
> Edward: I must apologize, the answer is negative.

Edward subsequently gives an account for the rejection, saying that Iris is feeling "a little under the weather." However, this account occurs after the "bad news," which in this case is a rejection of the invitation.[6] Before giving the rejection, Edward's apology forecasts the news to come. In general, because of the way that such "dispreferred" actions as rejections are delayed and prefaced (Heritage 1984b: 267), it can be said that these actions are regularly forecast in some manner.

Preceding apologies, however, are often used in conveying more dire bad news than the rejection of an invitation. Here is an instance of a neurologist talking to a patient in New York Hospital:

(7) Maynard 1991a: 163–64

> This combination of cerebellar dysfunction in one arm and corticospinal tract
> dysfunction in the other . . . (shakes head, raises eyebrows, looks at patient). I'm
> sorry you know it's stronger than any other laboratory test we have. It's- there's
> no other disease but multiple sclerosis that will do it.

The apology is accompanied by other gestures that can help forecast the news.
If these gestures and apologizing seem minimal, nevertheless the news itself occupies a later and prognosticated position in the announcing utterance. Despite
the rapidity with which the news arrives after the apology, it does so in what I
earlier called a prepared social-psychological environment.[7]

Some deliverers, Clark and LaBeff note, provide "elaborate" reports, a list-
ing of a *logical sequence* of progressive events and the attempts to deal with them:

(8) Clark and LaBeff 1982: 374

> We (nurses) saw them privately and indicated that there had been some compli-
> cations and that she had started bleeding. We told them what we had done for her
> in terms of starting an IV, giving whole blood, and everything we did in spite of
> all our efforts we were unable to save her. She passed away.

Anspach's (1993: 97–98) research includes an example of a resident who, wanting to encourage parents to withdraw life support from a struggling infant,
employs an elaborated report. In talking to the parents, the resident lists test results (electroencephalogram, CAT scan, liver functioning), the baby's lack of
improvement, consultations with other experts, the medical staff's own efforts
to do "everything" for the child, and other factors that would logically seem
to suggest discontinuing the support mechanisms.

Related to logical elaborations is the use of *syllogism,* as described by Gill
and Maynard (1995). In clinics for developmental disabilities, psychologists
may (a) present testing and other evidence of a child's delays to parents, and
(b) define mental retardation as typically involving those self-same delays, which
are like premises of a syllogism pointing to a diagnosis, and (c) provide for the
parents to conclude that the diagnosis applies to their child. That is, rather than
directly saying, "Your child is mentally retarded," or "your child has mental retardation," the clinician (a) produces the child's test results, (b) suggests,
"*that's* what we call mental retardation," and (c) invites the parents to deduce
that *their child* is retarded.

Realization

The difficulty of realizing bad news is illustrated in the experience of neighbors to a couple living for nine years under the assumed names of Greg Peters

and Jo Elliott in a residential area of Pittsburgh, who turned out to be on the Federal Bureau of Investigation's "Ten Most Wanted List." Claude Marks and Donna Willmott were in hiding because they had been charged in a plot to blow up a federal security prison in Leavenworth, Kansas, to free a Puerto Rican inmate convicted for sedition. The couple took it upon themselves to tell their neighbors.

(9) **Kifner 1994**

> "We were stunned, totally," said Janine Stern . . . an artist who lived across the street . . . , "We were weighed down by the news. It was almost a dream, something you would read or see in a movie. When I looked at him, he was still the Greg that I knew, not this Claude Marks."

This neighbor exhibits her experience of the noetic crisis; it is as if she has retained her footing in a previous world even as the news she has heard proposes a new world for her to enter. The illustration trenchantly raises the problem of recipient realization. Forecasting, I argue, is an effective way of encouraging realization or bringing the recipient of bad news from a relative state of ignorance to a state of knowledge in the situation where the news is to be given. To revert to the definitions of forecasting mentioned earlier, forecasting aids in realization through giving advance indications of bad news in a way that allows recipients an opportunity to estimate or calculate that news in advance. In essence, recipients guess at or venture the news and deliverers are then in a position to *confirm* or *disconfirm* recipients' presentiments.

Confirmations of Guessed or Ventured Bad News

While McClenahen and Lofland (1976: 257) suggest that presaging a piece of bad news can elicit a recipient's own discovery of the news, because "the facts will 'speak for themselves,'" it is possible to be more precise. By preannouncing bad news, by prefacing it, or by presenting a logical sequence, bearers of bad news reveal information from which recipients can make inferences. The recipient may thereby be induced to actually pronounce the news (Schegloff 1988b).

(10) **Terasaki 1976: 28**

1   D: Didju hear the terrible news?
2   R: No. What.
3   D: Y'know your Grandpa Bill's brother Dan?
4   R: He died.
5   D: Yeah.

In this example, D gives a first clue as to the news he bears through a preannouncement at line 1 indicating that it is "terrible." Then D gives a second clue, a naming or identification of the news's primary figure (line 3). Thus, there are clear verbal forecasts in this episode that allow R to guess accurately at the news in line 4, which D confirms (line 5).

Rather than the facts speaking for themselves, then, it is a matter of a deliverer's clues or indicators engaging a recipient's commonsense knowledge of the world, the participants' "recipient-designed" mutual knowledge, and "their orientation to the occasion of the conversation" (Schegloff 1988b: 444). The practices of cluing, guessing, and confirming are also displayed in institutional settings — particularly medical ones — where professionals must convey bad news (Glaser and Strauss 1965; McClenahen and Lofland 1976; Sudnow 1967). Sometimes this occurs almost inadvertently by way of a doctor's nonvocal comportment and verbal allusiveness (Jacobs 1969: 5).[8] However, the cluing-guessing-confirming pattern can be actualized more purposefully and explicitly through use of the "perspective display series," a device that operates in an interactionally organized manner to "coimplicate" the recipient's perspective in the presentation of diagnoses (Maynard 1992). Schematically, the series consists of three turns:

[1] Clinician's opinion query or perspective-display invitation

[2] Recipient's reply or assessment

[3] Clinician's confirming report and assessment

Clinical use of this series derives from a generic conversational strategy for giving one's own report or assessment in a cautious manner by initially soliciting another party's opinion (Maynard 1991b). The parts of this series are numbered and marked with italics in the next excerpt:

(11) **Fallowfield 1991: 44**

I can't speak highly enough of Mr. C. He was very gentle and kind and didn't hurry me even though it was a busy clinic with lots waiting. He let me get dressed, then he sat me down, held my hand and [1] *asked me what I thought was wrong.* When [2] *I said "cancer,"* [3] *he said that I was right but that I shouldn't feel too worried as the lump was very small and there wasn't any lumpiness under my arms, which is a good sign.*

Narrative evidence strongly suggests that inducing recipients to pronounce the news first is related to their realization. For example, coroners' deputies regularly attempt to control death announcements so that it is a relative who initially refers to the deceased as "dead." "Several deputies," reports Charmaz (1975: 313), "remarked that having the survivors themselves say it made the announcement more meaningful to them, and the death more 'real.'"

An additional matter is that the deliverer's own realization may be aided by having the erstwhile recipient pronounce the news. Not only are bringers of the news then in a position to confirm it; they are also placed to *hear* it perhaps yet again. That realization is also a problem for deliverers as well as recipients is apparent in an anecdote the civil rights leader Jesse Jackson's wife, Jackie, tells about how her husband informed her of Martin Luther King Jr.'s assassination:

(12) **Frady 1996: 151**

> On the evening of April 4, 1968, Jackie got a call from Jesse in Memphis. She relates, in a slow, hushed voice, "He said, 'Jackie, I wanted to tell you before you get the news on television. Dr. King has been shot. He is dead.'" A few seconds later, he said again, "Jackie, Dr. King is dead." Jackie says, "He maybe thought he was repeating it to make me understand it, but I think he kept saying it to make himself understand it."

Disconfirmations

Forecasting doesn't always result in an observable or a correct guess. After her mother's preannouncement of having "sad news" above in example (3), Janey initially thought that her grandmother had died. She did not venture this news, and her mother produced the announcement that it was Janey's grandfather. In the next example, Patti Ann McDonald reports finding out that her husband, a police officer, had been the victim of a shooting. She was staying at her sister Julie's house in Yardley, Pennsylvania. Three months pregnant, Patti Ann was taking an afternoon nap when she heard Julie, her husband Kenny, and their children come into the house.

(13) **McDonald, McDonald, and Kahn 1989: 7**

> For a moment, the house was noisy, and I was half-awake, but confused. Why were they home now? They'd said they wouldn't be home for another hour. What happened? Then Julie *shushed* the children and had Kenny send them out again. I came downstairs as the front door was closing. Julie asked me to come into the family room. She had a strange, worried look on her face. What could be so bad? "Patti Ann, I have something to tell you," my sister said. "Sit down. Something's wrong." *My father,* I flashed. *He's had a heart attack!* "Steven's been shot," Julie said quietly.

The next example is from a woman's story of taking care of her neighbor's cat, who died while the neighbor was away.

(14) **Narrative #18**

> She pulled up and I was standing by her door and I, you know, I was like, "Hi." You know I don't even know why I was pleasant. I was like, "Shady is not okay." She's, you know, she says, "Oh is she sick?", you know, and I'm like, "No she died."

These and similar narratives demonstrate that forecasts of various sorts do occasion an inferencing process on the part of a bad-news recipient. Furthermore, if recipients are occasionally wrong, they nevertheless are only partially so. That is, in both (3) and (13), recipients correctly infer that the projected news is bad and that it concerns a family member, and in (14) the neighbor only errs on the severity of the tidings. Therefore, the prepared social-psychological environment in which the news officially arrives provides at least the contours of the news, and the deliverer functions to *correct an aspect* of the recipient's conception. And as Schegloff (1988b) argues, there may be delicate mechanisms for "steering" incorrect guesses about bad news toward more accurate alternatives. The delicacy of such steering lies in how different ways of rejecting a guess can indicate whether the guess needs to be revised upward (because the bad news is better than the guess) or downward (because it is worse). Although prompted by the teller, recipients may be able to perform the corrective themselves, such that a deliverer maintains the position of confirming rather than saying the bad news.

Knowing the News Already

That forecasting induces the recipient to anticipate and preformulate bad-news-to-come is evident when recipients do guess the bad news correctly (whether they are the ones who pronounce it or not): at the very least, they get a "feeling" about what is wrong, and often claim *knowing* the news in advance of its official delivery.[9]

(15) **Narrative #3**

Last October my grandma was in the hospital with brain cancer and she had had brain cancer for awhile. But she'd been in the hospital for a couple days and I was aware of that and I was at class one day and I got home and my roommate had a message that I was supposed to call home. I kinda had a feeling that's what it was, and my mom's the one that told me.

This subject's message to call home triggers an awareness of her grandmother's hospitalization and allows her to anticipate the news. In the next example, the subject receives a forecast of bad news and initially entertains two possibilities, that something had happened to her dad *or* to her grandmother.

(16) **Narrative #12**

I was in a psych class . . . and I got a note in the middle of class that there was a family emergency and that I was supposed to leave. And my mom worked at the medical school so I went over there right away. And this is around Thanksgiving time and I knew my dad was gonna go pick up my grandma . . . and I know my grandma's sick and my dad had been sick, so as I was walking over to the medical school the first thing I thought was that my dad died and then I thought no, no something's wrong with my grandma or something like that. And I went over to the medical school and my mom was there. She said the hospital called and said my dad was in the hospital but they didn't give her any other information. And just by the look on her face and how I was feeling I — we both knew that he was dead but we didn't know — no one told us. So we had to wait at our house until my brother came back because my brother was with him. . . . When he came in, just the look on his face, we knew. And he just said well he died.

When the subject learns that it was her father, her own feelings plus cues from her mother and later from her brother provide for a knowing of what had happened in advance of the brother's actual informing. Sometimes the sense of knowing is so strong that the actual informing seems almost mechanical:

(17) **Narrative #15**
I have a friend who had a brother who was in a lot of trouble all the time over a period of a year. And I got a call from my friend and she said, "Have you talked to Mary?" and she sounded upset. And I said "no," and she sounded so upset, immediately in my brain it turned into *uh oh what's going on*. And she said, "It's Davy." And immediately I said, "Is he dead?" And she said, "Yeah." . . . But like I knew it before she said it. It was really strange because it was almost as if the conversation was just a play, because I knew what was going to happen and I just went through the ritual of the conversation.

In this episode, the recipient has already perceived an altered social world, and from within that perception, is distanced from the conversational ritual that otherwise might have introduced that world.

Stalling, Bluntness, and Misattribution

Alternatives to forecasting bad news are the strategies of stalling and being blunt. While recipients who receive forecasted bad news sometimes still report being shocked by the news, stalling and blunt strategies appear even more disorienting for a recipient. Narrative evidence suggests that this is because forecasting is more effective in aiding realization of the bad news. Stalling or being blunt exacerbate the disruption to perceived normality and raise the probability of *misapprehension* and other impediments to understanding that one's taken-for-granted everyday world has been altered. Episodes of stalling show that one may sense that something is "different" or "not right," and nevertheless be prevented from knowing the news. The result is a prolonging of the noetic crisis, and an experience of indeterminacy. Recipients are more likely to deny the facts and blame themselves for the unpleasantness. Blunt informings require such rapid and unsupported changes of orientation to the lifeworld that they increase the probability taking the informing as a joke, blaming the messenger, or maintaining ordinariness (subsuming present perceptions to past assumptions).

Stalling

Stalling implies that there is bad news to tell, but that those who are "in the know" and are potential deliverers avoid doing so. Nonetheless, there may be inadvertent and/or relatively purposeful cues whereby a potential recipient understands something to be wrong.

(18) **Darling 1979: 129**

> The doctor did not say anything at all when the baby was born. Then he said, "It's a boy," and the way he hesitated, I immediately said, "Is he all right?" And he said, "He has ten fingers and ten toes," so in the back of my mind I knew there was something wrong.

With stalling, there are at least two kinds of misapprehension: normalization and self-blame.

Normalization. Stalling on the part of a deliverer engenders incorrect inferences on the part of recipients in a number of ways. For one, *euphemism* as a way of stalling can lead a recipient to believe something different from the actual state of affairs. Here is a report from a wife whose husband died of cancer of the tongue:

(19) **Seale 1991: 950**

> I knew he was losing weight rapidly so I felt I knew there was something the matter. I was not told anything. *The doctor said it was trapped wind and I believed him.* I wish someone had told me what was wrong. No-one gave me any help. They seemed to skip over things and never tell me anything. (Emphasis added.)

Another form of incorrect inferencing occurs because, in the face of stalling, a potential recipient who senses something amiss is invited to make guesses. We have seen that forecasting also involves guessing on the part of a recipient, but when a deliverer stalls rather than forecasts, the cues are more ambiguous, making it more likely for the ventured "thought" to be erroneous:

(20) **Darling 1979: 133**

> The doctor came in and said "Her cheekbones are high and her eyes . . . it could be her German ancestry." You know he hemmed and hawed. *I thought she was blind or something.* He finally said it was Down's Syndrome. (Emphasis added.)

In this example, the erroneous guess, as compared with the actual news, favors a perhaps less pervasive disorder than the real one. More generally, when recipients guess incorrectly as a result of stalling, it is not in any haphazard way. Depending on other aspects of the interaction, recipients may infer either good news or bad news is on the way.

Optimistic normalizing projections. In the case of disabled children, parents who have been stalled are initially likely to define or explain abnormalities as unimportant, as evidence of idiosyncrasy, as temporary, and so on (Darling 1979: 138–39). Similarly, when a party in an intimate relationship wishes to break it off, stalling seems to be a frequent strategy, partly out of guilt about hurting the other's feelings (Clark and LaBeff 1986: 260). As a result, the other party continues with "business as usual":

(21) **Clark and LaBeff 1986: 259**
. . . because in each letter he would say things like "Oh, I can't wait. I've been looking at apartments. There's a real nice one in Dallas." And I would write him back and say, "Well, don't look too hard now because I'm really not sure on the time and all that," when in my mind I was saying, "no, I don't want to get married to you!"

Stalling, in other words, often leads to optimistic and normalizing inferences, inducing a potential recipient of bad news to interpret cues as a reason to hope for the best when in fact the situation is beyond hope, or when it might be more appropriate to expect the worse.

(22) **Narrative #19**
A man that I had worked for in business had become ill and he wasn't at work for a few days. And his son called the office one day to say that he was in the hospital and was having some difficulty with his heart. And he called back a few times during the morning to say things were getting worse. So a couple of other people from the office that had worked with D for several years went down to the hospital. And we went into a room where his family was—his wife and a son and a daughter and his mother. And a chaplain from the hospital was there. We went in the room and joined them and they were keeping vigil and saying some prayers in hopes that things would improve. And . . . a doctor who was working on him came into the room, and he sat down next to D's wife and began saying this is where we're at right now. This is what we've done up to this point. And he started to explain in great detail what was happening and what kind of treatment. . . . *Myself, I was feeling very hopeful that he was going to explain what the next step was.* But in his fairly elaborate description of what was going on, D's wife stopped him and said, "Doctor is my husband alive?" And my own feeling at that time was shock.

> I thought, how could she even ask that. *Of course he's alive.* And his response to her
> was, "No he's not." And D's wife's reaction, she was fairly calm as if she kind of
> knew, expressed concern for the mother, the children, became very emotional and
> upset. But in that telling it was almost like a misleading, like we were going in an-
> other direction. (Emphasis added.)

The wife of the deceased here had a sense of what was happening despite what
seems to be a stall in delivering the news.[10] On the narrator's part, the doctor's
"elaborate" explanation allows optimistic inferences that are out of keeping with
what has actually happened. Thus, stalling can exacerbate a counterpart to normalization, which is the tendency for *denial*. It is important to observe, as Frank
(1991: 67–68) does, that denial is not a completely psychological mechanism
but can be related to the cues a news bearer imparts or gives off.

Projections of a dreaded world. When stalling occurs because the deliverer of
bad news becomes involved in discussing a "dreaded," worst-case scenario,
the recipient may infer prematurely that bad news is on its way. Silverman
(1997: chap. 5) documents such an outcome in a clinic for HIV-antibody testing. A Counselor (CO), who had test results in hand for a particular Client
(CL) started the session by suggesting "there are a couple of things we need to
go over," and then asking CL where he would "like to begin." The client asks a
question about the predictive validity of one of the tests, which CO answers. After this exchange, in a number of ways CL invites CO to deliver the test results.
At the same time, however, CL's talk formulates other topics, which CO elects
to pursue as part of what Silverman calls "standard counseling activities." One
topic that is occasioned is the time it takes to "seroconvert" or, when infected, to
exhibit the HIV-antibody so that blood tests can find it. At this point, CL offers
a topic closing utterance (arrow 1 below) that, once more, strongly invites disclosure of his results:

(23) **Silverman 1997: 104 (simplified)**
    CL: 1→   I think that pretty well covers what I need to know.
    CO: 2→   Okay.
    CL: I know that there's- I go to AA so I have er support groups if I need
               them and I know where there are HIV positive meetings

After CL's closing offering, CO produces an "okay" token (arrow 2), yet again
delaying the provision of test results. As Silverman observes, the client then exhibits an interpretation of the delay in telling of his test result and the long discussions of risk and seroconversion as indicating that his results were positive for
the HIV-antibody (105). That is, in volunteering that he knows of "support
groups if I need them," CL *projects* his being declared as HIV-positive. Later, just

after being told that, in fact, he was HIV-negative, the client reports his "relief." This expression may reflect the interactional dynamics of having projected a different outcome, Silverman argues (106), as much as a more generalized anxiety about hearing the substance of his results.

Self-blame. Parents of developmentally disabled children are sometimes suspicious that something is wrong and yet can get no news from professionals. In such circumstances, Darling (1983: 106) indicates that parents may develop "pathological reactions, such as blaming the baby's delayed development on their own inadequacies as parents." One mother, after months of sensing that something was wrong with her child, and being told nothing by professionals other than that the baby was not "up to other babies her age," went with the child to a specialist:

(24) Jacobs 1969: 14

> She took one look at her and said "Turner's syndrome. You do have a defective child." I was relieved. Because from that first day in the nursery I knew I had trouble. And all of that time I had accused myself, blamed myself, whipped myself. I was up all night and all day. I knew that a child who got what he needed would be contented, would be peaceful, would be happy. . . . And I thought what am I doing wrong? Where am I failing? I tried harder and harder and harder until I ended up in the hospital.

It is not possible for potential recipients to realize some state of affairs when deliverers withhold telling what they know, and this seems to be why recipients declare that they are relieved, no matter how bad the news, when they are finally told. As we saw in chapter 1, this indicates that it might be worse to live in an ill-defined everyday world, such as that which sufferers of chronic pain experience (Hilbert 1984), than in one where something has changed for the worse but is at least capable of mutual naming and interactional recognition. As the parent of child finally diagnosed with the rare genetic disorder, ectodermal dysplasias (characterized by the deficiency or absence of sweat glands and other bodily elements) said after diagnosis, "I was so relieved when he was finally diagnosed at 13 months. Once we knew what it was we could live with it" (Sheckler 1998). Finally, that is, one no longer need blame oneself for, or deny, bewildering cues, gestures, and other signs of possible collapse in the local field, and can come to know the everyday world anew.

Being Blunt

It might seem that straightforward telling of bad news, as opposed to withholding, would automatically facilitate realization. According to Glaser and Strauss (1965: 124), bluntness may "sharpen" the disclosure and force "direct confrontation of the truth," as when "one doctor walks into the patient's room, faces him, says, 'It's malignant,' and walks out." However, this dropping of bad news upon a recipient with little or no forewarning is also a regular source of complaint:

(25) **Lind et al. 1989: 5**

I was coming out of anesthesia [for a biopsy] and I had had a very, very bad cold. . . . I had a hard time breathing coming out of anesthesia, so they called respiratory therapy, and I was being given all this stuff. And then I had theophylline injects just to get me breathing again. Then the surgeon comes in and said, "Oh, by the way, it's positive." And of course I'm dying again, you know.

(26) **Seale 1991: 949**

It was awful. We'd gone in to see her, my daughters and me and the wife had first gone along the corridor to go to the toilet . . . and a nurse came out of the office and just said "You know your wife is dying don't you, and the doctor wants to see you tomorrow" and she went off. We were completely shattered. We had to hide in the corridor as my wife came back and went into her ward. We couldn't let her see us. We were in tears. Then I went to see the doctor the next morning and told him how the nurse had told us.

(27) **DeBaggio 2000**

Five months after my 57th birthday, my wife, Joyce, and I sat before a neurologist. A nervous limbo had preceded the visit: a brain scan showed evidence of disease.

The doctor started speaking without preface or explanation. "Mr. DeBaggio, you have Alzheimer's," he said with the bluntness of a hammer. He offered no details of the tests or of their results. I gasped, as much at his hurried diagnosis, as at the death sentence his words implied. I held back tears and bit angry words with silence.

After a patient is told of her disease, she may face the prospect of having to inform others. This may also be done bluntly:

(28) **Fallowfield 1991: 45–46**

Interviewer: Did anyone come with you to the hospital to see Mr. B?
    Patient: No, I went on my own. I hadn't told anyone that I was going, as I
              hadn't told them about the lump even. I didn't want them to
              worry and I thought that it was just going to be something simple
              anyway.
Interviewer: So what did you tell them when you got back from the hospital?
    Patient: Well—oh dear, it was awful—I didn't know how to start. They
              were all sitting down watching television after supper and I just

> blurted it out. Everyone was upset, especially my daughter, and my husband went very quiet. He said that he felt hurt that I hadn't told him.

Accordingly, it is not just professionals but patients themselves who, by the succinctness and directness of their own deliveries, can cause recipients to feel "upset" and "hurt."

We will return to the affective consequences of bad-news tellings. Presently, I wish to explore three types of misapprehensions that occur in relation to blunt deliveries: believing the bad news is a joke, blaming the messenger, and maintaining ordinariness. I also seek to demonstrate that forecasting the bad news can help in counteracting these misapprehensions.

Joking responses. If a party delivers bad news bluntly, a recipient may interpret it as the punchline to a joke:

(29) Narrative #8
> This happened when I was a sophomore in high school. I had a really good friend in high school who was just really popular and then on Christmas I got a phone call that he had committed suicide. And then I started laughing, I thought it was a big joke. But it wasn't actually. He hung himself in the basement of his home.

This narrative does not relate an exact manner in which the telling occurred, but suggests the bluntness in delivery that is more apparent in the next excerpt.

(30) Narrative #4
> I was a sophomore in high school and as usual I always came back in the afternoon about 3:30, and it was just like any day. My mom was sitting in the kitchen facing out the window looking at the town we live in, and just as I was walking through the kitchen she just turned around and says to me guess what? And she was smiling, and I says what, and she says grandpa E died. And she was smiling while she was saying this and I thought that was kinda contradictory. I thought she can't be goofin' around can she. So just her actual delivery by the way she was smiling and you know I thought no this can't be true? And I just totally wouldn't believe it until like an hour later somebody else called and she was talking to them and then I first realized you know that he actually did die.

A mother suddenly produces a "guess what" preannouncement just after the daughter has arrived home from school. Although this projects a news delivery, there is no foreshadowing of what type it is, and the actual news is abrupt. Furthermore, the mother's affect (smiling) is reported as being at odds with the message, an incongruence that Tesser and Rosen (1975: 212–13) propose as inhibiting communication. The daughter's conclusion that her mother is "goofin' around," inhibits her realization of her grandfather's death.

Because bad news announcements may be received as jokes, a deliverer of bad news may have to counteract that interpretation, as when the police arrived at a house in England to arrest the son in the household for murder. In reply to the mother's question about whether their visit was important, one policeman told the mother that it was.

(31) Wambaugh 1989: 153

> Another detective said, "We've come to arrest your son for the murder of Dawn Ashworth." "You're joking!" she cried. "Do you think we'd be joking this time of the morning, dear?" the detective asked. The mother later remembered having to catch the side of the settee in the living room to keep from falling down.

Instead of correcting a recipient's joking response *after* the announcement, a deliverer may use a forecasting device to forestall such a response (Sacks 1972). Thus, a caller to a Suicide Prevention Center prefaces his announcement of despair with "it's no joke":

> And believe me, it's no joke because as I say, I just don't feel my life is worth anything at this point. (46)

In contrast to being blunt, forecasting devices like this help recipients realize bad news by anticipating and proposing to contradict possible humorous interpretations.

Blaming the messenger. This phenomenon has been mentioned and will be explored extensively in chapter 7. However, recall the situation of Carol Neves, the security analyst whose tactics were described earlier in this chapter. In performing financial evaluation of companies, and deciding to downgrade a company's rating, she is in some sense responsible for the news she has to deliver. Accordingly, by prefacing the delivery of negative evaluations with a relationship formulation ("we're about to find out if we're just fair-weather friends"), she effectively asks the recipient to put their relationship above the news and any responsibility she has for that news. This is no trivial matter, and Neves' anxiety is well placed. For example, in 1990 one security analyst at Janney Montgomery was dismissed "after he refused to retract a negative report about the financial stability of Donald J. Trump's Taj Mahal casino after Mr. Trump had complained and pushed for Mr. Roffman's dismissal" (Gladstone 1998). Roffman sued Trump for defamation, settling out of court for an undisclosed sum, and then received $750,000 from Janney Montgomery in a New York Stock Exchange arbitration. This case is only one prominent example of how investment firms sometimes lose clients through having to "deliver bad news on a stock" (Gladstone 1998). If they do not lose the company, analysts at the investment firm may be ostracized and barred from access to management sources and information necessary to evaluate growth potential.

Connected with this is that deliverers in fact often *feel* responsible and even guilty for the news they have to present. Physicians, as Clark and LaBeff (1982: 371) remark, can view a patient's death as their own failure. Thus, as mentioned, their procedures for forecasting or giving elaborate explanations picture death as an outcome of a logical sequence of events in which everything was done medically that could be. In this way, Clark and Labeff argue (374, 377), they may "cover" their performances, and attempt to head off any condemnation that recipients might direct their way. Conversely, being blunt leaves the physician more at risk of being faulted, and decreases the probability of realization when a recipient's effort at eradicating the message takes the form of impugning its vehicle.

Maintaining ordinariness. A phenomenon that Sacks (1984b) identifies is how people in the midst of catastrophic events achieve a sense that "nothing happened." If we consider catastrophic events as, in a sense, being their own announcement, they are perhaps the bluntest kind of informing one can experience. When a catastrophe occurs, the sense of nothing unusual happening is reflected in participants' statements of the form, "At first I thought it was X, then I realized it was Y," and the "classically dramatic instance," as Sacks observes (419), is of witnesses to President's Kennedy's assassination who thought they heard backfires rather than gunshots. Here are two other instances, one of a plane hijacking, and the other of a murder:

(32) **Sacks 1984b: 419**
I was walking up towards the front of the airplane and I saw the stewardess standing facing the cabin and a fellow standing with a gun in her back. And *my first thought was* he's showing her the gun, *and then I realized* that couldn't be, and then it turned out he was hijacking the plane. (Emphasis added.)

(33) **Capital Times 1989**
A rural Sauk City man told the Angela Hackl murder trial jury Friday he heard three shots fired in the wooded area near his home and a noisy car leave the area a short time later the night the Lone Rock teen was brutally slain 27 months ago. Robert Wagner, who lives near the Pines, a teenage party area seven miles west of Sauk City, testified *he did not contact police immediately because he thought the sounds were firecrackers* touched off by drinkers in the wooded area. Wagner, a hunter, *didn't realize they were shots from a small-caliber pistol until he heard three days later that Hackl's body had been discovered chained to a tree in the pines.*[11] (Emphasis added.)

Maintaining ordinariness is related to normalization in that both tactics preserve a sense of the social world, or objects within it, as basically intact rather than under alteration. What differentiates the two is a temporal-perceptual element. "Normalization" refers to practices whereby potential recipients, having seen signs of anomaly, face deliverers who are "in the know" about the meaning of such signs and who delay telling for some period of time. During this period, recipients work to define and explain such signs in a way that denies their import. Such work contains as an essential element the phenomenon of *hopefulness*. Recipients may entertain and anticipate alternative possibilities, yet through optimistic definitions and explanations, come to favor normal interpretations. "Maintaining ordinariness" refers to a related set of practices, but condensed to the momentary, whereby recipients instantaneously subsume stimulus items under categories that fit with ongoing and benign or "innocuous" percepts of daily life (Jefferson 1985). The subsumption is so rapid that hope, as a conscious expectation for a desired state of affairs, plays little or no role. Expectations, as they flow from adherence to the attitude of daily life and intentionality, may enter into an initial perception, but only subsequent to this perception do recipients engage alternative possibilities. Either way — through stalling and normalization or bluntness and maintaining ordinariness — realization is inhibited.

Complexities in the Relationship between News Delivery Strategies and Realization

Forecasting, as an alternative to stalling and being blunt, is a way of providing some warning that there is bad news to come without keeping the recipient in a state of indefinite suspense. Instances show that, when one is waiting for news, stalling prolongs the recipient's noetic crisis and prevents realization. Forecasting, on the other hand, is a way of directly conveying the bad news without being so forthright and abrupt as to disconcert and disorient the recipient. Similar to stalls, blunt informings can aggravate a state of anomie, but here the possibility of realization is inhibited by the overwhelming rapidity and boldness of presentation. Blunt informings appear to maximize the chances for panic (Glaser and Strauss 1965: 143), going to pieces (Glaser and Strauss 1965: 149; Lind et al. 1989: 586), and experiencing uncontrollable anxiety or depression (Parkes 1974). Accordingly, stalled and blunt informings exacerbate the senselessness concomitant to lack of typicality, predictability, causality, and morality that bad news portends in the perceived environment. Evidence of an exacerbated noetic crisis is evident not only in recipients' misapprehensions but in their reported emotional experiences as well. Narratives about both stalling and blunt deliveries more regularly contain accounts of recipients' hurt, anger, hostility and indignation than do those narratives that exhibit a forecasted bad-news delivery. The misapprehensions that stalling and bluntness provoke, then, seem to emanate from desperate attempts to resolve anomie, while forecasting, in the way that it aids realization, simultaneously provides for a more settled and accurate apprehension of an altered lifeworld.

The foregoing analysis suggests that forecasting, stalling, and being blunt form the independent variable and that recipient realization is the dependent variable in the interactional handling of bad news. While this is roughly accurate, there are significant complexities that must be taken into account for proper appreciation of this equation. I treat these complexities under the rubrics "historical-cultural variation" and "local interactional contingencies." My argument is that effective strategies of delivery, like forecasting, rather than being context-free or abstract devices that can be manipulated mechanically, are matters of indigenous situational accomplishment. Furthermore, to capture such matters analytically we need to get beyond ethnographically generated narrative data. To inspect more closely the phenomena of bad and good news, to probe more deeply the transitions they represent and the structures of everyday life they show, we want entry to what Garfinkel (1996) calls the "more" and "other" of practical social interaction and experience. To anticipate the argument of chapter 3 in brief form: conversation analysis provides such entry.

Historical-Cultural Variation

The historical and cross-cultural validity of my account of the forecasting–realization equation is open to question. In medicine, reviews (Maynard 1991a; West and Frankel 1991) suggest a change in attitudes held firmly from the time of Hippocrates until at least the mid-twentieth century. Henri de Mondeville, a fourteenth-century French surgeon, Thomas Percivel, the early nineteenth-century English physician who wrote an influential book on medical ethics, and Oliver Wendell Holmes, the Harvard professor of anatomy who was active in the late nineteenth-century, all asserted the propriety of concealing news from patients because it could have adverse effects on their medical condition. The belief was that the physician should be a source of hope and strength. Currently, for a variety of reasons, this stance on concealment has weakened, and pressure for physicians to be frank and to disclose the facts of illness to patients is increasing. In the case of cancer, an often-cited finding is that, in the United States, the medical profession has radically altered its position in regard to telling patients the diagnosis of this dread disease. Whereas in 1961, 90 percent of surveyed physicians said they preferred *not* to reveal the diagnosis to cancer patients (Oken 1961), by 1979 a replication shows 97 percent of respondents *willing* to do so (Novack et al. 1979). This trend has maintained itself over the last twenty years, but it is far from being universal. In a number of countries around the world, physicians continue to avoid telling patients of their cancers (Holland et al. 1987).

Because historical and cross-cultural evidence shows that in some times and places medical informants regularly conceal bad news, it might suggest that healers in some societies are unconcerned with the problem of how recipients come to realize what is happening to them. They may even want to *prevent* such realization. Accordingly it might be that healers in these environments are like Simmel's (1950) "secret societies," seeking to suppress information for internal purposes of sociation, cohesion, and boundary definition in a way that also protects outsiders (patients and their families) from knowledge they otherwise might have. A close look at the cross-cultural evidence, however, presents a more complicated story. The prohibition against revealing cancer is far from absolute even in cultures where there still are official taboos, and these taboos serve different purposes from those that Simmel relates to secrecy. For one thing, if physicians withhold the diagnosis from patients, they regularly do tell family members instead, who may then choose to deliver the news themselves (Beyene 1992; Gordon 1990; Long and Long 1982). When this happens in Ethiopia, it reflects a deeper concern with overcoming the *suddenness* of disclosure rather than with disclosure per se. "The situation is discussed among friends and relatives," says Beyene (1992: 330), "to decide the appropriate time and the least frightening way of breaking the news." For example, Ethiopians regard the evening as a bad time for informing because it might mean a long and sleepless night for the recipient, whereas breaking bad news in the morning, at the person's home, allows friends to keep the person company, to prepare food, and otherwise help the recipient manage.

When potential informants are verbally silent about cancer, they may regard recipients as nevertheless knowledgeable. In Japan, for instance,

(34) **Long and Long 1982: 2105**
    One man told us that he thought his mother knew she had cancer. "She knew, but she did not talk about it *(Shitte imashita kedo, kuchi ni wa dasanakatta)*." The woman [in another interview] whose brother died of cancer said, "he was a surgeon, so he knew. But it seems he did not really want to be told."

Similarly, investigators find that Italians may distinguish between "knowledge felt deeply inside" and that which is more "superficial" or open (Gordon 1990: 282). Both physicians and lay people in Italy believe that even when cancer patients are not officially told of their diseases, they nevertheless come to know the situation. The "real taboo," argues Gordon (289–90), is against public acknowledgment of the condition, for that can entail a kind of "social death" wherein the individual is prematurely separated from the social unit.

In all, cross-cultural accounts suggest that the main purpose in not telling patients is an interest in preventing depression and preserving hope. Thus, the crucial matter in some cultures is not that they prohibit the direct delivery of bad news but that they preserve an orientation to its proper staging, to the quality of social relationships in which the informing occurs, and to modes of knowing other than verbal and cognitively logical ones (Good et al. 1990). Therefore, while there may be times and places wherein healers really do work to prevent recipients from obtaining bad news, the evidence also suggests that cultural taboos are concerned with the proper means whereby recipient realization can occur. In emphasizing affiliation between the recipient and both immediate family and the larger group, these cultures exhibit an understanding that realization can be enhanced by a precise concerting of effort that involves other parties besides the healer or physician. Cultures may urge a particular social psychological form, in this instance *forecasting,* as a social relation for bearing bad news,[12] and eschew bluntness and stalling because the latter strategies *isolate* recipients, leaving them on their own to decipher the meaning of signs and symptoms. It is this extreme anomic situation that cultures sometimes seek to avoid, not a recipient's knowledge or realization of bad news per se.

Forecasting, as a social relation, involves practices whereby those in the know provide advance indications of, but do not yet reveal, bad news. Recipients are enabled, also without necessarily articulating the potential tidings, to estimate what they may be. Thereby, recipients also may come to know the news in a preverbal or preliterate fashion. Rather than secrecy, there is a conspiracy, and it is not against the knowledge of bad news or sharing it, but simply against doing so overtly, officially, verbally, and literally. The conspiracy binds its participants — deliverers and recipients alike — together in silence until the circumstances are more propitious or compelling to break it.

Local Interactional Contingencies

I do not mean to idealize the practices whereby recipients are excluded from the telling of news. Such practices may be subject to complaint, as in this instance of an Italian woman recalling how she learned of her cancer:

(35) Gordon 1990: 284

Several days later I was with my husband when the results arrived. The professor turned to speak only to my husband — and I, I remained there frozen, petrified in

that gesture. He called my husband, but he should have also called me. From that
I understood.

The professor (physician) here is a man, and his conference with the husband
has more the feel of chauvinism and authority[13] than indirect but caring communication with the patient, although her protest in the recollection ("he
should have also called me") is ambiguous as to how strongly she objects to what
happened.

However, another lesson can be derived from this anecdote, which is that announcements of news often occur in a field with many participants for whom
the mode of delivery may operate differently. The professor's speaking to the
husband may have been direct or even blunt, while his manner of avoiding the
patient works as a forecasting indication of, and helps her realize, her condition
("From that I understood"). Also recall excerpt (22), wherein the doctor's detailed way of informing operated like stalling to the narrator and more like forecasting to the wife.

That there are modes of conveyance other than verbal, literal ones, and that
these modes also vary according to the recipient's situation lead to a general consideration of what strategies of forecasting, bluntness, and stalling are as actual
social practices. While the narrative data demonstrate instances of these strategies, exactly how participants perform and respond to them is a topic needing
further investigation for the reason that *one person's or one culture's stall or bluntness might be another's forecast.*

Put differently, stalling, bluntness, and forecasting meld and fuse in many
ways. We have seen how stalling may exacerbate recipients' tendencies to deny
and normalize.[14] Normalization, in turn, produces expectations on the part of
potential recipients:

(36) **Darling 1979: 139**
The child was a twin, whose sister was stillborn. After the birth, the parents were
told, "The other baby's fine," and the mother "didn't realize that anything could still
go wrong." The baby was hard to feed, but the mother "thought it was just because
she was a premie." When the baby was 6 months old, the mother began to realize
that her daughter "was not holding things like other babies" but again attributed
the slowness to her prematurity. When, at the baby's regular 6-month checkup, the
pediatrician suggested the possibility of cerebral palsy, the mother "just broke
down completely in his office." She said that she "just couldn't believe it."

Even though we do not know the pediatrician's exact manner of delivering the
bad news, the indications are that he was gently suggestive in a "forecasting"

manner rather than boldly forthright in presenting the diagnosis (he "suggested the possibility of cerebral palsy"). Nevertheless, in the context of an initial stall ("the other baby's fine") and the mother's resultant normalizing beliefs about her child, the disclosure appears to have been experienced as entirely blunt. In a way, the bluntness of an informing is not an innate property of the deliverer's manner but is relative to the contingently ordered context of delay in which the delivery ultimately occurs and to the set of convictions a potential recipient holds during this time.[15]

Whether any verbal form of delivery exhibits features of forecasting, stalling, or bluntness is dependent upon what participants know, what they expect, and how they hide, provide and discern cues about their worlds of habitation. Consider how even the most terse verbal message can be part of a situational contexture that is utterly communicative to a recipient. A husband who was waiting for his wife to arrive home at a local airport after a brief trip knew that her return involved one change of planes in Denver. While awaiting her arrival, he heard the phone ring, and answered the phone, according to his own account, with a "casual hello."

(37) **Narrative #31**

> The caller sighed heavily and said (without reciprocating my hello), "I'm in Denver." I immediately identified the caller as my wife, and I knew from her sigh, the tone of her voice, her lack of reciprocity, and the violation of the mutually understood expectation that she wouldn't call before I picked her up at the airport that she had bad news. She informed me that her plane had been late and this led to her missing her connecting flight by three minutes.

Here, the utterance "I'm in Denver" merely *reports* the caller's location (Drew 1984). As a report, it does not name the type of news it projects. Nevertheless, the narrator, operating in a context of mutual expectation regarding phone communication between his wife and him, knows immediately "that she had bad news." In another narrative, the recipient of bad news notes how, although she is not a "superstitious person," she sometimes gets the "feeling that something is wrong or that something has happened to someone close to me." Having such a feeling one Saturday, she decided to call her mother:

(38) **Narrative #32**

> Mother: Hello.
> Me: Hi Mom. It's Katie.
> Mother: Hi. I was going to call you tonight. Your grandfather fell and broke his hip. He's in the hospital having surgery right now as we speak.

The narrator, with the prior feeling, and knowing the family situation, was not so surprised by this otherwise bluntly delivered news, and in fact reported being mostly concerned about how her mother was "holding up." So again, the character of the message does not derive from an utterance divorced from the context or particularity of circumstances—and participants' displayed knowledge thereof—in which it is embedded. In chapter 3 I will address this issue of context more fully in relation to the the problem of "indexical expressions" (Garfinkel, 1967).

Coda: In the Clinic

As a practical matter, and recognizing that the adjustment to and acceptance of bad news may take a long time, I recommend that physicians use some kind of forecasting when they have diagnostic news to deliver (Maynard 1997). Both stalling and bluntness isolate a recipient from the deliverer and leave recipients on their own to decipher the meaning of the news, whereas forecasting binds the two parties together in what was earlier called a "structure of anticipation." Effective presentation of a diagnosis is obviously not facilitated by withholding or by forthrightly stating a diagnostic term and figuring it is the patient's own psychological task to adjust. What matters for recipients' apprehension and grasp of news is the social relationship the deliverer works to invoke, which suggests that realization and lack thereof are features of *social* psychology.[16]

For a physician who decides to employ forecasting as a device for delivering news, nevertheless, the joke in the epigraph to this chapter illustrates an important truth. While forecasting, stalling, and being blunt are strategies that influence realization of news in disparate ways, situational contingencies involved in the discernment of these strategies show that they cannot be employed as disembodied techniques. Instead, strategies of forecasting, stalling, and being blunt affect a recipient's realization according to particularized circumstances and relationships. To employ forecasting as a strategy in a mechanical fashion, by using the same device in every situation, can be as alienating and disorienting to a recipient as either bluntness or stalling. Thus, forecasting the bad news of a pet's demise to your brother is different from forecasting the news of your mother's death. For a bearer of news to *competently* forecast, embodied common sense is important. Deliverers must anticipate the nature of the news for recipients—their understandings and expectations—act in terms that enhance relationship, and then presage the news in a relevant way.

Being an effective deliverer of diagnostic news begs another question, however, which is *whether* to tell a patient that she or he has a particular disease. This question has occupied medical ethicists at length, in part because of the earlier-documented historical and cultural differences in attitudes about disclosure. Once more, consider cancer, a disease which is both stigmatized and dreaded, and therefore the most likely candidate for concealment (Freedman 1997: 332). We have seen how, in Japan or Italy or Ethiopia, physicians may withhold news about cancer from the victim, nevertheless informing family members. The grounds for such a practice — preserving the patient's sense of belonging, maintaining hope, and others — seem entirely reasonable to me. On the other hand, and no doubt because of my own cultural upbringing, I would want to know immediately were I found to have the disease. Although I would want to be surrounded by loved ones for support, I would not permit them to mediate the news for me. I think most American physicians and oncologists would respect my wishes, because of the belief that having the capacity for autonomous decision making fosters a sense of control and maximizes the potential for healing or comfort. My position would be consistent with bioethical proposals (Schoene-Seifert and Childress 1986, for example) that, subject to specific "external limits" such as resources, available treatments, and so forth, and presuming the competence of patients, their own wishes and preferences need to be respected. Respecting patients' wishes and preferences, in turn, necessitates full and direct disclosure of diagnostic and prognostic information. But what about situations where there are strongly different cultural orientations, as in an American hospital when a patient from Ethiopia, is diagnosed with stomach cancer, and her husband requests that she not be told this news (Beyene 1992)?

Such ethical issues are compelling in their own right, and, in slightly different form, become even more acute and complex, because DNA sequencing and predictive testing for various diseases make it increasingly possible to tell presently healthy people their odds for developing severe illness (Biesecker 1998; Siebert 1995). Barbara Biesecker, an expert in genetic counseling, highlights a dilemma that arises in connection with tests that can identify a genetic predisposition for diseases whose date of onset cannot be predicted and for which there is no cure:

> There are basically two types of people. There are "want to knowers" and there are "avoiders." There are some people who, even in the absence of being able to alter outcomes, find information of this sort beneficial. . . . The more they know, the more their anxiety level goes down. But there are others who cope by avoiding, who would rather stay hopeful and optimistic and not have the unanswered answered. (quoted in Bloch et al. 1992: 52)

So who should take predictive tests and what should they be told when the results become available?

My research does not address such issues directly, but it may have a role in discussions about ethics along the lines of the "moral topography" of doctor–patient relationships. Too often, Churchill (1997) argues, the bioethicists and the physicians they advise have not adequately mapped this topography before developing standards for communicative conduct. This is because, instead of recognizing how moral quandaries are embedded in local meanings and concrete social exchanges, practitioners may look for consistency across situations, formal principles or codes, and universal, theoretically correct approaches. For example, in the case of the Ethiopian woman with stomach cancer, a physician disregarded the husband's request about nondisclosure, believing that, "regardless of the family's wishes, it is a patient's right to know the diagnosis" (Beyene 1992: 330). We do not know the exact manner of the doctor's presentation, but it appears to have been experienced as blunt. The woman fainted, and then would not talk further to the physician; the family was very upset as well because *they* judged it to be their prerogative and in the patient's best interest for them to manage the information (Beyene 1992: 330). Simply put, the patient and family had principled ideas about communication that contravened those of the doctor. Preempting the family's deeply felt rights and obligations, the doctor *preconceived* the moral topography of the terrain he was entering (Churchill 1997: 312).[17]

To help map the moral topography of the physician–patient relationship, Churchill says that physicians and ethicists need to avoid a "tendency toward universalist assumptions and superordinate theoretical processes" (317) by employing a cross-disciplinary perspective — that is, by implementing the tools and perspectives of a variety of disciplines, including literary criticism, medical sociology, and cultural anthropology. As a kind of sociology, my study introduces a concrete understanding about the moral terrain of conveying diagnostic news in clinical settings.[18] I have argued that such conveyance involves structuring the experienced social worlds of participants, and it can be emphasized that this structuring involves morality in two senses, one plunging deep and the other spreading across a variety of social actions.

The deep sense of morality derives from how participants mutually adhere to presumptions about the perceivedly normal status of objects, including selves and others, within their social worlds. This sense might be termed the morality *of* discourse. Diagnostic news, as it tells about the potential or actual presence or absence of disease and the imminence of life or death in real persons and bodies, often shatters ordinary premises of social actors regarding the manner in which they and others occupy the social world. So diagnostic news, if allowing for joint anticipation and shared realization rather than either confrontation or avoidance, permits patients and family members to explore immersed presumptions about who they are and what their world is. In turn, for clinicians, diagnostic news also potentially reveals what it is they take for granted about themselves, their patients, and the worlds they and these patients occupy separately and together.

The broader sense of morality — morality *in* discourse — refers to how everyday talk exhibits participants' orientations to a variety of matters including what is real, what is bad and good about the worlds they occupy, what their social relationships are and who has rights and obligations for telling and hearing news, what they dread and hope, who is to blame or credit for things that happen, what they are prepared to do for self and others, and other matters already explored or to be probed in subsequent chapters. Particularly relevant is chapter 7 on how participants orient to bearers as having different forms of agency and responsibility for news. Analyzing actual episodes in conversation as well as clinics does not offer prescriptions for ethics, but does alert us to — and increase our awareness of — the profoundly variegated moral topographies bad and good news already display.

THREE

Conversation Analysis and Ethnography:
What Is the Context of an Utterance?

Now the question is, how do you go about doing an observational anthropology or sociology? And what place would narratives of various activities, ceremonies, etc. have?[1]

Forecasting, stalling, and being blunt, if regarded as *types* of news delivery strategies, will present an inevitable problem, which is that, in narrative data, accounts of how bad news is delivered do not cleanly fit one or another of these types. This is the *pigeonhole problem:* while the proposal and findings of chapter 2 are that devices for conveying bad news influence a recipient's realization, fitting the peculiarities of circumstance into one or the other of the types when analyzing news delivery episodes is often not easy to do. Accordingly, instead of regarding these strategies as literal descriptions of complex modes of behavior and relationship, a better approach may be to regard them as contingent accomplishments developed in real time (Garfinkel 1967). Otherwise, strategies for the delivery of news — whether described by the forecasting/stalling/bluntness trichotomy or in other terms — remain as glosses and weak descriptors for the actual, *produced orderliness* of everyday life, and we lose specific features of the phenomena we wish to probe.[2] Such features as the jointly established valence of the news, the specific relationships among involved parties, the imbalance or asymmetries between bad and good news, and the way that a deliverer's agency enters into the interaction, are tackled in subsequent chapters. Here I will explain why my primary approach to everyday social life and experience is ethnomethodological and conversation analytic.

Another way of formulating the pigeonhole problem is to observe that all utterances are *indexical expressions:* how a participant understands an utterance depends upon the relation of that utterance to such things as the person speaking it and the time or place of its production (Garfinkel 1967: 4–5). In other words, for their meaning, utterances depend on their *context;* the character of a message is related to the particularity of circumstances in which it is embedded. The question is, of what does context consist? How is one to analyze context? For me, the short answer is that *an utterance's context is the organized sequence of turns in which it appears,* and because conversation analysis (CA) concentrates on sequential organization, I rely heavily on this perspective for studying recorded instances of

64

bad and good news. This also means using an approach to recorded dialogue that is very disciplined in particular ways. To the extent possible, analytic interpretations of what someone says must be grounded internally on the conversation — in participants' own, turn-by-turn displayed understandings and practice-based orientations — rather than on less technical observations or interview-based narratives about such interaction.

Whereas CA, in this methodologically strong version, eschews ethnographic description because it draws on resources that are external to the participants' ongoing or "real time" situated talk, my research, primarily based on audio and video recordings of interaction, also has been heavily ethnographic. It therefore trenchantly raises the question of how to integrate the ethnographic data with the mechanically recorded data and conversation analysis of news delivery activities. To put the matter succinctly, I regard ethnography as an ineluctable *resource* for analysis, using it in a relationship with CA that is one of *limited affinity*. This is different from other approaches in which the relationship between the analysis of recorded interaction and ethnography is one of *mutual affinity*, and ethnography and CA or discourse analysis are more freely interwoven. The issues involved in this contrast between limited and mutual affinity are complex, and I probe them more fully after discussing what can be called the "activity focus" (Drew and Heritage, 1992; Levinson 1979) of my study.

Collecting Data to Analyze an Activity Rather Than a Setting

I became interested in the phenomena of bad and good news when a colleague who knew of my interest in conversation analysis gave me some discourse data — tape recordings and transcripts — of informing interviews involving clinicians and parents at a clinic for developmental disabilities.[3] As I began to read transcripts and listen to the recordings with as few preconceived ideas as possible,[4] it soon emerged that a dramatic and difficult event was occurring — the tapes exhibited what I call the noetic crisis — in the conveying of diagnostic bad news to families. Clinicians talked quickly, hesitated, used euphemism, backtracked, and engaged other tactics indicating that relaying a diagnosis was no simple naming or labeling matter (Gill and Maynard 1995). Parents responded with questions, silence, stoical statements, emotional outbursts, or in other ways that mirrored and entered into the clinicians' presentational difficulties.

Although I began by listening to someone else's tape recordings, the project soon took on an expansive life of its own and developed into a traditional field study. After working with these audiotapes, I obtained a grant from the National Institutes of Health to expand my investigation by observing, interviewing, and videotaping in a local center for developmental disabilities. In this center full time for one year, and part time for another, I watched the operations of the clinic, participated in meetings, talked to professionals and family members, and took copious notes on the diagnostic process, in addition to recording examinations and diagnostic informing interviews.[5] My idea was that the study of other clinical processes (Marlaire and Maynard 1990; Maynard and Marlaire 1992), complemented by ethnographic inquiry, including observations and interviews, would enhance my analysis of the delivery and reception of diagnostic news during the penultimate meeting when clinicians told parents their official findings. I know that my ethnographic inquiries did augment analysis of these informing interviews, but I also made a decision that studying the delivery of *diagnostic* news in the medical environment would benefit by inquiry into the delivery of news in more casual conversational interaction. In other words, my study should concentrate, not just on the clinic as a setting for the presentation of a diagnosis, but also on the relation of practices involved in clinical presentations to the conversational undergirding on which those practices build. As an *activity,* the delivery of bad news occurs in a many social worlds, and to understand that activity in its fullness and in relation to generic devices for its delivery, data are needed that sample its variety.

Along with expanding my investigation to include ordinary conversation,[6] I made another decision. Following the Sacks, Schegloff, and Jefferson (1974) strategy of collecting data across settings, I wanted to sample diagnostic news deliveries in other kinds of clinics besides the developmental disabilities one. This comparative approach differs from previous ethnographic research on bad news, which tends to be occupationally and substantively confined.[7] Investigators, in studying professionals (clergy, law enforcement personnel, medical practitioners), not only slight participants giving news to one another in more private and ordinary conversational encounters. Substantively, researchers concentrate one particular topic—such as death, cancer, developmental disabilities, or legal entailment. Subsequent to my presence in the developmental disabilities clinic, I gathered data in a department of internal medicine at a midwestern university teaching hospital, at a clinic for HIV-antibody testing in an urban setting, and in the oncology clinic and hospital ward of another university teaching hospital in the eastern United States.

All of my endeavors to assemble comparative clinical data involved observation and interview in addition to the focal aim of tape-recording a multiplicity of diagnostic announcements. My most intensive field study was at the HIV-antibody testing clinic, which was mostly staffed by volunteers. This meant that I could and did become a working member of the setting, and I spent time at the intake desk, being trained as a counselor, and doing HIV-prevention instruction with individual clients.[8] As an ethnographer, in addition to writing field notes, I gathered two kinds of narrative data — about participants' views of bad or good news experienced in the particular setting and about their previous experiences with bad or good news. Placing this information beside stories from students in my classes and from journalistic and research literatures returns us to the original issue. With both tape-recorded "real time" interactions and field research and narrative data in hand, how do we handle the research evidence? Granting primacy to recorded talk and social interaction, as I do, what is the context of utterances occurring within this interaction? What is the relation between conversation analysis and ethnography?

Ethnographers are often much more expansive than conversation analysts in what they consider the context of talk to be, and muster their observations and interviews to describe features of the distant social environment (sometimes referred to as "social structure") thought to be relevant to understanding given utterances. Consequently, ethnographers sometimes criticize CA for its almost exclusive use of recorded interactions, eschewal of field methods, and willed neglect of social structure. However, accepting the ethnographic proposal that I call the "contextual critique" — that CA needs to turn its attention away from local organization and appreciate the provenance of such organization in external structure — would mean distorting the phenomena of everyday life and the social experience of participants. Conversation analysts question whether ethnographers have a systematic enough way of connecting social structure to talk.

What is needed, I believe, is for each perspective — ethnography and CA — to have a deeper appreciation for the other. Conversation analysts have not explicated their use of ethnography, and can benefit from reflective consideration of field methods and the copious ethnographic literature. At the same time, ethnographers need to appreciate the CA rejoinder to their contextual critique, which helps in specifying why using ethnography in a limited way to inform conversation analysis is desirable.

Mutual Affinity

The number of ethnographic investigators who combine traditional methods of participant observation and open-ended interviewing with a more or less heavy use of tape recordings is very large,[9] in part because of the technological advantages.[10] Researchers in the fields of communications (Hopper 1990/91; Nelson 1994), discourse analysis (Potter 1997; van Dijk 1985), linguistically oriented anthropology (Duranti 1997: 98–99; Erickson and Schulz 1982; Goodwin 1990; Gumperz 1982b), pragmatics (Levinson 1983), and sociology

(Corsaro 1982; Grimshaw 1989; Gubrium and Holstein 1997; Jimerson 1998; Miller 1994; Silverman 1993; Spencer 1994) draw on recordings along with ethnographic methods, sometimes as a supplement to participant observation and interview and sometimes without prioritizing either approach. Thus, as opposed to the "primary or exclusive" use of tape recorded material, Emerson, Fretz, and Shaw (1995) propose that such usage is *"one way among others* for closely examining the meaning events and experiences have for those studied" (77, emphasis added).

The penchant for mutual affinity goes beyond technological advantages of incorporating recordings with traditional field research. An extended argument for mutual affinity is to be found in Gubrium and Holstein (1997), who advocate combining ethnographic *naturalism* with ethnomethodological *social constructionism*. In naturalistic inquiry, the stress is on immersion in the social worlds of prison, mental illness, medical settings, street life, schools, and communities. As demonstrated in such classics as Whyte's *Street Corner Society* (1943), Liebow's *Tally's Corner* (1967), or Anderson's *A Place on the Corner* (1976), the attempt is made to secure the *substance* of life in these worlds by capturing members' own words, modes of expression, descriptions of experience, and the like. Social constructionism, which includes the methods of conversation analysis, involves a shift of attention from an ethnographic insider's depiction of substance to the *how* of social life—the methods implicit in talk and interaction whereby social actors sustain the substantive sense that life has. This distinction between grasping substance and studying the methods or practices for the achievement of meaning highlights a shift investigators can make as they probe a given setting. Here, then, is a clear statement of mutual affinity. In my own research using both recordings and ethnography, however, a difficulty is knowing when or how to make the transition between capturing everyday substance through ethnographic naturalism and breaking down that substance into the methodic practices for its achievement. I will specify strategies for making this transition when I discuss limited affinity.

The "Contextual Critique" of Conversation Analysis

Before explicating the notion of limited affinity, other ground needs to be cleared. A point of contention between those who advocate for a mutual affinity between ethnography and conversation analysis and those who, like me, suggest a more limited approach, is whether studying conversation, performing "sequential analysis,"[11] and confining investigation mostly to recordings and transcripts is by itself adequate social science. Indeed, some conversation analysts, particularly those who concentrate on "ordinary" conversation as opposed to that which occurs in institutional settings, eschew ethnography altogether, giving rise to the criticism that close attention to the sequential organization of talk in CA, or what Corsaro (1981: 12–16) calls "autonomous"-seeming structures,[12] without explication of the *larger* context of that talk, misses the forest for the trees.

In Bourdieu's (1977) words, ethnomethodologists and conversation analysts operate with the "occasionalist illusion" that the essence of interaction is entirely contained within it. Other sociologists (Burawoy 1991: 271–76; Cicourel 1987; Grimshaw 1989; Mehan 1991; Miller 1994) have developed this critique, as have discourse analysts (Coulthard 1977; Stubbs 1983) and linguistic anthropologists. The student of Thai language and society Michael Moerman suggests that CA has a preoccupation with the "dry bones" of talk and is "bloodless" and "impersonal" with regard to "richly experienced human reality" (1988: x–xi).[13] Making the case for a "culturally contexted conversation analysis," Moerman writes, "Sequential analysis delineates the structure of social interaction and thus provides the loci of actions. Ethnography can provide the meanings and material conditions of the scenes in which the actions occur" (57). Less trenchantly but similarly, Hanks (1996), in speaking to linguistic traditions, argues that spoken interactions contain elements of both transcendent formal structures of language and more contingent, local, and momentary developments. Conversation analysis, being confined to the proximate realm, disregards the "broader social backdrop" (218) of everyday interactions. While recognizing that "the surrounding discourse in which any expression is embedded is its first tie to context," there are "larger scale discursive formations" in need of analytic appreciation (185, 223).

Judging by the convergence of many fine scholars on the contextual critique of CA, the impulse to grasp the large or wide social backdrop to a particular spoken activity is strongly felt. As strong as it is, however, where the impulse leads is not at all clear. Goodwin and Duranti (1992: 2) argue that "it does not seem possible at the present time to give a single, precise, technical definition of context, and eventually we might have to accept that such a definition may not be possible."[14] Indeed, when advocating for investigations of context, investigators do not often specify what is meant by "broader" or "larger scale" social structures and organizations or precisely how to incorporate features of context residing outside of and purportedly influencing direct interaction and talk. Hanks (1996: 217–22) points to Goffman's (1974, 1979) frame-analytic "participation frameworks," Gumperz's (1982b) "contextualization cues," and Lave and Wenger's (1991) "communities of practice" as notions helpful to the involvement of social environments in the dissection of conversational interaction.[15]

Although these notions are intuitively appealing and are employed pervasively in many studies that fit in the *ethnography of speaking* tradition (Hymes 1974), a close look suggests they nevertheless are like what Blumer (1956) once called "sensitizing concepts," and do not theoretically or methodologically provide a disciplined approach to capturing their referents in the expansive social arenas to which they point.[16] In short, as Schegloff (1987a: 221) argues, investigators have treated "contexts" (frameworks, cues, communities) as utterly transparent, when they may be anything but.

Response to the Contextual Critique

The impulse to grasp wider contexts surrounding an utterance points toward obtaining more ethnographic information and data. Without proper *analytic control* of contextual information, however, investigators paradoxically may *lose* data in which the produced orderliness or important facets of social organization actually reside. I will address the problems of analytic control and data loss in order.

Analytic Control

The burden for investigators is to provide a methodological apparatus — what Kaufmann (1944) describes as inquiry-specific rules of scientific procedure — for decisions about what to include from the wider-than-sequential context or broader social environment surrounding an utterance or other piece of interaction. In many very fine ethnographies, I do not find rules of procedure for incorporating the analysis of social structure. Consequently, like other conversation analysts, I have come to rely on terms that Schegloff (1987a, 1991) raises in his well-known writings on "micro and macro" sociology and "talk and social structure." In examining utterances and interaction, two questions to be posed about larger or broader structures, categories, or organizations are (1) whether such categories are *relevant* to participants and, if so, (2) whether they are *procedurally consequential* in the sense that participants display, in their talk and interaction, an orientation to them. Considerations of relevance point to the many possible ways in which the "same" participant can be identified. Against the "positivist" solution of defining relevance according to sociodemographic categories that may have theoretical provenance or are statistically significant in their correlation with attitudes and beliefs, Schegloff (1987a) proposes a concrete approach. Investigators' characterizations of participants should be grounded in actual displays of participants themselves using such characterizations to perform and understand their actions. Furthermore, if social structure and other abstract aspects of "context" are real to the participants, they will be procedurally consequential, as reflected in participants organizing speech ex-change (turn-taking)[17] and other features of talk, such as *repair* (Schegloff, Jefferson, and Sacks 1977). In CA, repair refers to mechanisms for dealing with troubles or problems in speaking, hearing, or understanding the talk in progress — what someone has just said — and these mechanisms may be encouraged or suppressed in specific environments.[18]

Data Loss

Instead of providing methodological criteria for analyzing context, investigators often rely on those sensitizing concepts that are more-or-less theoretically sophisticated but otherwise ungrounded vernacular depictions of interactions. Consider further the work of Bourdieu (1977: 4–6), who eloquently criticizes "objectivist knowledge" for its ignorance of "practical knowledge of the social world," opposes abstract rule-oriented theories of social action, incorporates real time as a feature to be appreciated about social life, and thereby assimilates an extraordinary amount of complexity and detail in his analysis of everyday social and cultural phenomena. The ground seems well plowed for inquiries alive to all manifestations of ordinary conduct that contingently develop in the course of actual talk and social interaction. Not so, however, for according to Bourdieu actors are situated according to a "habitus" and system of "dispositions" that derive from social structure — the material conditions of class relations — and thereby provide the forms that interaction takes (78–81). While the implications are clear, the mechanism is not; social structure is somehow operating behind the backs of participants. Indeed, when Bourdieu says, "'interpersonal' relations are never, except in appearance, *individual-to-individual* relationships and . . . the truth of the interaction is never entirely contained in the interaction" (81), it could simply imply that, as Grimshaw (1989: 83) puts it, "life is complex." Any strip of interaction, because it is complex, could be accorded "alternative interpretations," and it is difficult to adjudicate among them. But Bourdieu is up to other things. He means that nothing is autonomous in the domain of language use; anything and everything interactionally is related to habitus and its class conditioning.[19] As against the "occasionalist illusion," and despite Bourdieu's (1990, 1991) distancing from objectivism or the mechanical determinism of formal theory, this smacks of a "social-structural illusion," the idea that there is virtually no time out from participants' potential placement according to race, gender, class, and a society's other structural positionings.

Conversation analysts subscribe to a different sensibility — that many social behaviors are ordered according to local principles that are impervious to effects from social structure. Not always or everywhere, for conversation analysts neither dispute the importance of class and other social structural concepts, nor argue with studies documenting, for instance, the distribution of language styles according to people's class or ethnic backgrounds (Schegloff 1997: 413), as in the pioneering work of Labov (1972a, b), Gumperz (1982a), and other sociolinguists, most recently Baugh (1999). In fact, there is a growing number of CA studies in which speech practices are an independent variable predicting bureaucratic decisions (Boyd 1998) or are a dependent variable affected by specific historical, social, or interactional circumstances (Clayman and Heritage in press; Heritage and Stivers 1999; Lavin and Maynard 2001).

Consistent with such studies, and *after* identifying interactional structures involved in news deliveries, it seems not only possible but important to see how the practices they comprise may be distributed among participants according to their sociodemographic and other identities.[20] I am proposing that we not engage in studies of variation until we have grasped the phenomena — bad news and good news — in the full integrity of their locally produced orderly detail. Otherwise, if researchers begin their studies by assuming that vernacular, categorical, or typological references to a setting or its participants are pervasively relevant, and that the social structures and institutions embodied by such references are omnirelevant in their influence on talk and social interaction, it may mean losing analytic grip on the phenomena that participants themselves regard as prominent. This is because a consequence of working with vernacular terms, categories, and types is to discard or subsume particular, discrete circumstances of real-time talk and social interaction. As Schegloff (1991: 60–61) puts it,

> The vernacular characterization "absorbs" the details of the talk as an unnoticed "of course" in such a "formulated-as-institutional" setting, and does not prompt one to note and explicate how the talk enacts "doing being in that setting." . . . If the focus of inquiry is the organization of conduct, the details of action, the practices of talk, then every opportunity should be pressed to enhance our understanding of any available detail about those topics. Invoking social structure at the outset can systematically distract from, even blind us to, details of those domains of event in the world.

Now there are problems with this strong version of CA strategy, which I discuss below in the section on limited affinity. My present point is that ethnographic insistence on the relevance of larger and wider institutional structures can mean a loss of data in and as the interaction, for attention shifts from actual utterances in the fullness of their detail and as embedded within a local interactional context to embrace narrative or other general accounts concerning social surroundings.

If anything has emerged from ethnomethodological and conversation-analytic inquiry in recent decades, it is that participants in real social worlds *do* show orientations to the most immediate, embodied, pragmatic contexts of any given utterance. Analysts in these traditions are concerned to grasp the small-scale practices, impervious to prior theorizing, in which such orientations make their appearance. In CA terms, participants in ongoing conversations work with the concrete sequential context of any given utterance. Not only in complete utterances and turns, but in hesitations, false starts, breathing, silences, speech tokens, prosodic manipulations, and other minutia of interaction, participants accomplish socially big things by virtue of the adjacent positioning of these utterances, turns, and minutia. Among the big things they achieve, independently from possible accretions of social structure, is *intersubjectivity* — mutual understandings and orientations. Such understandings and orientations are what make actual joint activity possible in the real social world.

Limited Affinity

The notion of limited affinity implies precise ways in which ethnography complements conversation analysis. I will discuss three uses to which conversation analysts put ethnography: in descriptions of settings and identities of parties; in explications of terms, phrases, or courses of action unfamiliar to an investigator or reader; and in explanations of "curious" patterns that prior sequential analysis may reveal.

Describing Settings and Identities

A problem with the strong version of CA strategy is its recommendation that especially in analyzing talk in institutional (medical, legal, business, etc.) settings, we need to attend to how participants "do being in that setting" (Schegloff 1991: 60–61). This raises a problem that is highlighted in Garfinkel's (1967: 32) remark that *every* feature of a setting, without exception, is the managed accomplishment of members' practical actions. On what feature, therefore, should the analyst concentrate? One solution is to prioritize whatever activities seem most prominent to the setting's participants. In a courtroom, for instance, although participants' identities as judge and attorney and defendant are an outcome of work that makes those identities visible, an analyst necessarily may need to disattend aspects of identity or "membership category" work (Watson 1997) to concentrate on other, possibly more prominent activities. In studying a rape trial, Drew (1992) might have devoted attention to how participants use a specialized turn-taking system to exhibit their interaction as constituting a judicial setting or court. Likewise, he could have analyzed how they achieved their situated identities as legal actors (judges, attorneys, witnesses, etc.).[21] Instead, Drew pushed turn-taking and other practices to the background, using transparent categorical terms in his references to participants. This enabled analytic attention to attorneys' and witnesses' ways of substantiating, disputing, and defending versions of what happened during a very controversial event (472–78). Witnesses' actions of "avoiding confirming," and providing "alternative descriptions" to those of the attorney come to the fore, as do attorneys' own actions of displaying contrasts with witnesses' claims and summarizing the testimony in ways that discredit these witnesses.

Without choosing which features and activities to concentrate upon analytically in a setting, and which features therefore to describe ethnographically in the background, investigators are faced with an enormously complicated task, a potentially infinite regress, if not an immobilizing paradox, in which all prominent features of a setting—all "doings"—require inquiry before any one of them can be investigated.[22] Using, in a limited way, ethnographically derived descriptions of identity and setting overcomes this complication.

Explicating Unfamiliar Terms, Phrases, or Courses of Action

A second type of limited affinity between conversation analysis and ethnography highlights meanings that participants take for granted but that are not transparent either for an analyst or a reader of a conversational extract. Conversation and discourse analysts' tendency to work in their own language communities, Duranti (1997: 267–77) argues, obscures the extent to which ethnographic knowledge of taken-for-granted expressions is necessary for the detailed analysis of conversational structure. It is a point well taken, for ethnographic knowledge—an insider's understanding of terms, phrases, and courses of action—is something that CA regularly draws upon when displaying and analyzing a particular excerpt.

I can select examples of ethnographic explication by haphazardly grabbing articles from my files. For one, to show how misunderstandings in talk may derive from problems in determining the sequential import of an utterance or turn, Schegloff (1987b: 207) introduces an extract by saying, "Jim and Bonnie are two 15-year-olds talking on the telephone around Christmas time. At one point, Jim's mother can be heard in the background, telling him to thank Bonnie for having sent a Christmas card." This clarification of who the participants are, the time of year, and what is happening "in the background" shows Jim to be part of a wider action context than that between him and Bonnie, and helps the reader see the mismatch between the design of an utterance and its uptake—a serious utterance (Jim's offer of "thanks") is taken nonseriously by its recipient

(Bonnie), because it was heard to be prompted by another person. For another example of ethnographic clarification, Lerner (1996: 308) precedes the display of an extract in which an "anticipatory completion" of a turn of talk occurs by saying, "Marty is explaining to Josh the problems of copying from one tape recorder to another." Such clarification aids a reader in discerning the referent of "machines" in Marty's utterance, "Now most machines don't record that slow," and in understanding the referent of "tape" when he says, "So I'd wanna- when I make a tape," which is the start of a new utterance. The participants are discussing a tape recorder, and Lerner's ethnographic description helps a reader make sense of Josh's anticipatory completion ("be able to speed it up") to Marty's utterance. Ethnography may be necessary not only for comprehending relatively casual references in recorded conversations, but especially for learning the definition of technical nomenclature in such institutional settings as medicine (Cicourel 1987).[23] An analyst of doctor–patient interaction may have to learn about medical procedures or phrases to understand what is being said in a particular sequence and may need to define such procedures or phrases when publishing an analysis.

Explaining "Curious" Sequential Patterns

A third type of limited affinity situates the CA researcher in a setting and involves traditional fieldwork, including observation and interview. Later, when doing analysis and writing reports, participants' vernacular descriptions can help interpret patterns that sequential analysis reveals but does not fully explain. Put differently, ethnography may capture or confirm in abstract terms what the CA inquiry may propose about concrete interactional organization in the setting's talk. In our study of HIV and AIDS counseling, we found that counselors, despite official recommendations about tailoring "safer sex" teachings to the needs of individual clients, often give clients information that appears irrelevant to them personally. Sequential analysis of recorded discourse demonstrated frequent initiations of advice-giving on the part of counselors that, functionally speaking, were unsuccessful in eliciting uptake. Clients give minimal responses, are silent, or openly contest what counselors say (Kinnell and Maynard 1996).[24] A reason for recommendations being ill-fitted to clients, discovered through ethnographic participation in the setting, is that counselors are taught, not only to minister to individual clients (if they can), but also to attempt relaying information to the community — networks of friends and acquaintances — in which the clients are active. Hence, the apparent insensitivity to clients' own needs, evident in the sequencing of counselor-client interaction, is at least partially responsive to a perceived "institutional mandate" (Drew and Heritage 1992: 22–23;

Maynard 1984: 12) to effect social change in communities where HIV is highly prevalent. Counselors work to use clients as conduits of influence for such change.

Another example of the explanatory use of ethnography comes from our research in an oncology clinic. A patient, who had been dealing with gall bladder cancer for a year, had just undergone an unsuccessful operation to remove more of the tumor. Subsequently, the physician needed to tell this patient that the cancer was no longer treatable, and that, although he would be released from the hospital, he was at the end stage of the disease and life process. All that could be medically provided was palliative care. Inspection and analysis of the natural interaction as captured on the videotape revealed no mention of imminent dying and death. Instead, we observed the physician, at a particular juncture in the conversation, broaching the topic of Hospice, the patient and his partner collaboratively shifting the topic from Hospice to a nursing home where the patient could go upon discharge from the hospital, and the conversation thereby developing contingently in ways that avoided discussion of Hospice. Through his references to Hospice, we described the oncologist as somewhat unsuccessfully alluding to the patient's dying. And because allusive talk purposely avoids explicit formulation, it was helpful to consult what the oncologist said to me in an interview about this encounter: "Sometimes I use the discussion of Hospice, not so much because it's important to me that the patient accept a home Hospice program, but . . . to get the conversation really directed where you want it to go, which is on death and dying issues" (Lutfey and Maynard 1998: 325). Only with the ethnographic information was it possible to verify that the physician, when broaching the Hospice topic, was working to inform the patient that the latter was soon going to die. Although use of ethnography in this fashion may be close to what Gubrium and Holstein (1997), Moerman (1988), and others recommend for enriching conversation analytic inquiry, it bears repeating that ethnography is a post-hoc way of explaining the existence of interactional practices, particularly when *prior* sequential analysis reveals curious-seeming patterns.

Interactional Detail as Deep Context

Bad and good news represent naturally occurring breaches in the structure of everyday life. Locating such breaches does not, however, solve the problem of how to study their constituent features and the practices by which participants, faced with having to suspend their ordinary stance of belief, effortfully reassemble a known-in-common world. Participants in episodes of disclosure can provide post hoc accounts that provide initial access to the practices and methods of worldly suspension and reassembly. However, in part because of the pigeonhole problem — fitting the detail of actual modes for conveying news into strategic types — and the associated challenge of dealing with indexical expressions, the bigger sociological prize exists in the contingently formed, real-time particularities of participants' conduct together. An ethnomethodological proposal is that in these particularities — in the *detail* of participants' conduct — resides a produced orderliness. This orderliness — associated with practices, methods, or procedures of minute but socially consequential mundane behavior — is the participants' world as it is or comes to be known-in-common and newly taken for granted.

It can even be said that, because it contains and is the product of concerted actions, *detail itself is a type of context,* and its incorporation analytically involves going "deeper" into the concreteness of a setting, even if it does not "broaden" the investigation abstractly. Wanting to capture this depth, I employ ethnomethodology and conversation analysis because, in theoretical and methodological ways, they enable systematic and rigorous attention to the fullness of participants' spoken sociality and its generic structuring. I use ethnography in a limited affinity with conversation analysis to (1) refer to settings and participants according to institutional or other identities and categories, (2) describe courses of action related to a focal episode and unfamiliar terms within it, and (3) explain curious sequential patterns.

Additional Affinities between Conversation Analysis and Ethnography

While I have so far stressed the limited affinity between CA and ethnography, to differentiate my methodology from that of those who pose mutual affinity, the operative word in both combinations is still *affinity.* An implication is that more linkages can be developed between CA and ethnography.

Ethnographic Use of Conversation Analysis

If ethnography is of use to CA, the reverse also is true: CA can be employed on behalf of ethnographic inquiry. One example is Duneier's (1999) study of the remarks that street vendors direct toward women passersby. In a co-authored methodological discussion about this research, and in a manner similar to Gubrium and Holstein (1997: chap. 7), Duneier and Molotch (1999: 1269–70) suggest that, instead of taking the *unmotivated* CA stance toward interactional detail, such research can in fact be *motivated* by substantive concerns. Recording and analyzing street conversations reveals practices through which male vendors work to open conversations with female passersby and the unreciprocated efforts of the women to close these conversations. Recordings and "applied" conversation analysis of them are used to "enrich the more conventional sociological ethnography" (Duneier and Molotch 1999: 1272). Conversation analysts themselves have used the CA approach in an ethnographic and applied way, as in our probing the use of the concept of "justice" in a jury deliberation (Maynard and Manzo 1993), Heritage and Lindström's (1998) analysis of the phenomenology of shared experiences between a new mother and her British health visitor, and in other studies.

Longitudinal Conversation Analysis

Another bridge to be built between CA and ethnography involves *extended* social activities. My research on singular episodes of bad and good news does not address the ways in which, over long periods of time, participants progressively adjust to some altered social world. When medical personnel first tell them that they have a chronic illness, for instance, patients may not know how to react:

> Ron Rosato recounted, "I said, 'Well, what is this problem?' And they put me in a hospital and took a lot of tests, and they said, 'Everything is fine, Ron, but — so we've come up with multiple sclerosis, a possible multiple sclerosis.' I said, 'What is that?' and they said, 'You'll learn about it.' And I did." (Charmaz 1991: 18)

In learning about a diagnosis, recipients like Ron Rosato progressively alter their response to the initial news delivery, and experience further announcements about the condition. Analysis of the full process as a duration would require something along the lines of what Corsaro (1996) calls "longitudinal ethnography."

A longitudinal approach to bad and good news would allow us to map how the social worlds of participants undergo metamorphosis in and through paced, incremental announcements, as when someone who has suffered disease or accident gets better or worse, or alternates between the two and staying the same, across days, weeks, months, or longer periods. There is also the task that chronically ill persons face, as they inform others about their diagnosis over time (Charmaz 1991).[25] Using CA, longitudinal designs can encompass the activity of news delivery and receipt as an enduring process. Along these lines, Beach (2001, 2002) has collected telephone calls from a family wherein the wife and mother was diagnosed with cancer and ultimately died. Relatives were dispersed and, over the phone for a thirteen-month period, progressively conveyed, learned about, and adjusted to the woman's state of health as the family's world underwent massive changes. In a kind of longitudinal conversation analysis,

Beach documents a serial deployment of the news delivery sequence to manage moments of ambiguity, uncertainty, and impending finality as the disease takes its toll.

Besides applying CA to enhance substantive ethnographic investigations and to develop longitudinal studies of interactional activities, other rigorous linkages between CA and traditional ethnography are being pursued. The affinities between conversation analysis and ethnography may be many.[26]

Coda: In the Clinic

Further exploration of the affinities between CA and ethnography is a topic beyond the scope of my inquiry into bad and good news. For the present, I limit the use of ethnography, or at least that kind of ethnography attempting to grasp the context of an utterance by positing connections to "wider" social structures, because it would embody an abstracting movement away from interactional detail. The ethnographic literature on bad news, along with an example of a diagnostic interview, can illustrate how analytic control and data loss are lively issues for understanding what happens substantively in clinical settings.

One of the first recordings I came across in the developmental disabilities clinic data I was given involves seven-year-old Donald Riccio (pseudonym), whom the clinic diagnosed as "mildly" mentally retarded.[27] The informing interview took place after Donald was referred to the clinic because of speech and other difficulties at school. Two pediatricians were at the interview — Dr. Davidson was the one who evaluated Donald and performed the diagnosis, while Dr. Andrew introduced herself as the physician who would be responsible for seeing Donald at the clinic for subsequent visits. Dr. Andrew does not speak in the excerpt below. Immediately after introductions, Dr. Davidson began the diagnostic news delivery:

```
(1) DD #11
  1    Dr. D:  I think- you know I'm sure you're anxious about (1.0)
  2            toda:y and I know this has been a re:all:y hard year for
  3            you.
  4                    (0.4)
  5    Dr. D:  .hhh and I think you've really done an extraordinary job
  6            (0.4) in (0.8) dealing with something that's very hard
  7            for any human being or any parent.
  8                    (0.8)
  9    Dr. D:  And you know Mrs. Riccio and I can talk as parents as
 10            well as .hhh
 11    Mrs. R: True
 12    Dr. D:  uh my being a professional.
```

```
13                          (0.6)
14    Dr. D:  It's hard when there's something not all right with a
15            child.
16                          (1.0)
17    Dr. D:  .hhhhh very hard.
18                          (1.0)
19    Dr. D:  And I admire both of you really and (0.8) an' (2.2) as
20            hard as it is (0.4) seeing that there is something that
21            is the matter with Donald, he's not like other kids (0.2)
22            he is slow, he is retarded.
23                          (0.2)
24    Mrs. R: HE IS NOT RETAR[DED!]
25    Mr. R:                 [Ellen.]
26    Mrs. R: HE IS NOT RETARDED!=
27    Mr. R:  =Ellen.
28                          (0.3)
29    Mr. R:  Uh plea:s::e
30    Mrs. R: NO: : !
31    Mr. R:  May- look- (0.6) it's their way of:: I'oh'know.
32    Mrs. R: hhhhh HE'S NOT RETAR: (ghh)DED! ((sobbing))
33                          (2.5)
34    Dr. D:  He can learn and he is lear[ning]
35    Mrs. R:                             [hhhh]
36    Mr. R:  Yes [he is learning    ]        [I-   ]
37    Dr. D:      [and he's making    ] good prog[ress.]
38    Mrs. R:     [.hhhhhhhhhhhhhhh]
```

At line 22, Dr. Davidson proposes the diagnosis of retardation, in a straightforward way that Clark and LaBeff (1982) would characterize as "direct." The
mother, Mrs. Riccio, "breaks down" when she hears this suggestion.[28] In contrast, the father's stance toward the diagnosis is not clear; he addresses his wife
and not the clinician. Now, to account for the news delivery and the parents' reactions, potentially we can go in two different directions. One is toward a relatively abstract understanding of the interaction, based on what can be gleaned
ethnographically about the backgrounds of participants. The other direction,
confining ourselves mostly to the recording, but using ethnography in a limited
way, is to pursue detail and to be concrete about the practical organization of the
encounter.

Ethnographic Abstraction

The tendency in the past has been to glean further ethnographic information about the setting and the identities of the parties. Ethnographers of bad
news, in fact, have an admirable record of letting no stone go unturned to
garner facts about a particular research site, the biographies and demographic

identities of participants—ages, ethnicities, genders, socioeconomic classes, occupational categories—and the cultures to which they belong because of these identities. Such effort is particularly evident in McClenahen and Lofland's (1976: 255–57) finding that when bearers of bad news (U.S. marshals) and recipients (ordinary citizens) differ in terms of race, class and education, the less "emotional involvement" there is. Deputies use such "distancing" tactics as employing "more foreboding and formal settings of delivery." Similarly, according to Glaser and Strauss (1965: 146), physicians take into account a family's ethnicity, religion, and educational level in determining whether and how much news to convey about a patient's dying. And Clark and LaBeff (1982), in their study of death-telling, state *conditions* for how professionals convey the news. "The lack of well-defined, normative guidelines for such deliveries," they argue ". . . requires the deliverers to construct various tactics influenced by situation and structural factors, including occupation, setting, characteristics of the deceased, and the type of death" (379). In these accounts, then, authors describe modes of delivery in typological terms and correlate these modes with other abstractions about attributes of the setting and traits of the parties involved.

With this approach, we would be interested in information that Svarstad and Lipton (1977) obtained by interviewing the parents extensively both before and after the informing interview from which excerpt (1) is taken. The Riccio family, by way of the Hollingshead Index of Social Position, was found to be in the lower social class. They were white and of Italian extraction, Catholic in religion, and the parents both had high school educations. The father worked for a utility company, servicing air conditioners, while the mother was a homemaker with three other children besides Donald. This information implies several things, in keeping with previous ethnographic research. The family is a "traditional" one, with a stay-at-home mother and a father who works at a "blue-collar" outside job. Both pediatricians (with M.D.'s) are women, which, in the early 1970s, when the interview was recorded, meant that they had very "nontraditional" occupational roles, and relatively high-paying ones at that. Accordingly, these educational, class, occupational, and gender role differences between family and clinicians imply a great deal of social distance. Furthermore, such social distance may be a basis for the direct delivery of diagnosis, because professionals are less caring about how their recipients will react when they do not share the same social background (Glaser and Strauss 1965: 122–23) and are likely to be more "cold" and "heartless" (Clark and LaBeff 1982: 371–72), possibly to achieve clarity at the expense of shocking recipients (Clark and LaBeff 1986: 257; Glaser and Strauss 1965: 125). Based on our ethnographic background information, then, the pediatrician evoked the mother's strong and emotional reaction because of structural distance from her recipients and to be starkly clear about the diagnosis. As for the father's reaction to the news, the literature has not said much about how or why the partner of one recipient may respond differently.

It needs to be granted that despite the suggestions from ethnographers of bad news about the importance of participants' backgrounds, field researchers often warn against imposing exogenous categories on their data (Emerson, Fretz, and Shaw 1995: 109–12). There is, however, an impetus in some ethnography, especially in studies of bad news, as well in research advocating for a mutual affinity between recordings and ethnography, to attend to such backgrounds and categories when dealing with interactional data. Van Dijk (1999), for instance, describing the position of critical discourse analysis (CDA), remarks, "There is no hesitation in examining text and context separately, and once a feature of context has been observed, postulated or otherwise identified, CDA may be used to explore whether and how such a feature affects, or is affected by, structures of text and talk" (460).[29]

I think it is tenable to state that a "feature of context" is affected by structures of text and talk; the difficulty is in going the other direction. Statements about the influence of external or exogenous factors tend to be based on the observer's often laborious effort to gather demographic or historical information rather than equally rigorous demonstrations *from* the interactional data. In the literature on bad news, most enlightening about the empirical and analytical difficulties are Glaser and Strauss (1965), reflecting on their own previous statements proposing how social factors affect the presentation of bad news:

> The relationship of social factors such as ethnic status, social class, language, religion, education to properties of disclosure to the family (particularly if, when, and how) is an important research problem. The research should also develop the intervening interaction process that links the relationship of a social factor to a kind of disclosure. (146)

Schegloff's notions of relevance and procedural consequentiality seem to be the exacting terms that Glaser and Strauss are calling for, a way of exerting analytic control over what may be said about the processual "links" between social factors and disclosure practices. Beside the issue of analytic control lies that of data loss: our preoccupation with the social distance between clinicians and parents based on knowledge of background factors means that we disattend much of the detail exhibited in the interaction in favor of inferences about interactionally unseen structural influences.

Detail, Concreteness, and the Organization of Practices

The other direction to go when asking questions about how clinicians present and parents handle diagnostic news is to adhere more closely to the interactional stream of data and to use ethnography in a limited way. In introducing the transcript, I characterized the setting as a developmental disabilities clinic and identified the participants as "pediatricians" and "parents" (mother, father). I also provided the level of Donald's mental retardation, assuming the reader's familiarity with this broad term, but also giving the official classification. These limited ethnographic descriptions and clarifications allow for focusing on the central activity of delivering and receiving the diagnosis. Other ethnographic information (concerning the ethnic, class, educational backgrounds) comes into analysis only if the participants themselves display an orientation to it.[30]

With regard to excerpt (1), this means examining the full sequential context of the diagnostic news delivery, which starts with Dr. Davidson moving from introductions (not on transcript) to an assertion recognizing the parents' anxiety and "re:all:y hard year" (lines 1–3).

(2) DD #11 (first part)

```
 1    Dr. D:  I think- you know I'm sure you're anxious about (1.0)
 2            toda:y and I know this has been a re:all:y hard year for
 3            you.
 4                     (0.4)
 5    Dr. D:  .hhh and I think you've really done an extraordinary job
 6            (0.4) in (0.8) dealing with something that's very hard
 7            for any human being or any parent.
 8                     (0.8)
 9    Dr. D:  And you know Mrs. Riccio and I can talk as parents as
10            well as .hhh
11   Mrs. R:  True
12    Dr. D:  uh my being a professional.
13                     (0.6)
14    Dr. D:  It's hard when there's something not all right with a
15            child.
16                     (1.0)
17    Dr. D:  .hhhhh very hard.
18                     (1.0)
19    Dr. D:  And I admire both of you really and (0.8) an' (2.2) as
20            hard as it is (0.4) seeing that there is something that
21            is the matter with Donald, he's not like other kids (0.2)
22            he is slow, he is retarded.
```

Following a silence (line 4), Dr. Davidson also compliments them (lines 2–5) on their "dealing" with a vaguely formulated "something that's very hard. . . ." This

may operate as what Goodwin (1996a) calls a "prospective indexical," anticipating the diagnosis-to-come;[31] the turn also meets with silence (line 8). Then,
Dr. Davidson suggests that she "can talk" with Mrs. Riccio as a "parent" (lines
9–10), a suggestion with which Mrs. Riccio agrees (line 11), as Dr. Davidson
goes on to say "as well as .hhh uh my being a professional" (lines 9–10, 12). Following another silence (line 13), Dr. Davidson again claims to recognize how
"hard" things may be, referring once more to "something" and adding the phrase
"not all right with a child" (lines 14–15). This is a *litotes,* a rhetorical form of nega-
tion that, by its inexplicitness, permits alluding or hinting at a delicate matter that
so far remains unnamed (Bergmann 1992: 148–51). Yet another silence occurs
(line 16), followed by Dr. Davidson emphasizing the difficulty (line 17), pausing
(line 18), and announcing her admiration of the parents (line 19) before producing a stronger version of the "something" phrase. And the stress on "is" in ". . .
something that is the matter with Donald" (lines 20–21) may reinforce how the
phrase in its positive characterization provides a contrast with the previous negative phrase, or litotes. Still, it alludes to rather than names what the "matter" is.

From this point, Dr. Davidson moves into the official diagnosis of retardation, this movement involving another litotes for comparative declaration
(Donald is "not like other kids," line 21) and a vernacular assessment ("he is
slow," line 22) that lead into Dr. Davidson asserting the condition: "he is retarded." Until now, contrary to our ethnographically abstract depiction of this
interaction, Dr. Davidson has been very cautious, alluding several times to
"something" that is "very hard," "not all right," and "the matter," in approaching an announcement of the official diagnosis. Her practices during this approach include claiming recognition of their plight by repeating five times over
how "hard" they have had it, complimenting the parents on the job they have
done, and proposing the relevance of a relationship ("parents")[32] outside of the
professional–client one, in a way that nevertheless recognizes the latter as primary. Consequently, rather than the analyst needing to make inferences about
the relevance of participants' status backgrounds, Dr. Davidson herself formulates such relevance. Putting these practices together, and considering them as
proposals of affiliation, it would be difficult to sustain an argument that this is a
fully "cold" or "heartless" and socially distanced presentation on the part of the
clinician. Nevertheless, the only device that procures any uptake from the parents is Dr. Davidson's invoking of the "parent" identity. Silences meet the actions of complimenting and recognizing the parents' "hard" challenges, and
may exhibit resistance to the Dr. Davidson's affiliative proposals.

Because most of Dr. Davidson's attempts at affiliation appear to fail, the environment for delivery of bad diagnostic news is not a fully auspicious one. Ar-

riving at the term "retarded" (line 22), Dr. Davidson stops talking, and, following a 0.2 second silence, Mrs. Riccio receipts the diagnosis with a series of loudly oppositional turns (lines 24, 26, 30, and 32), and she ends up sobbing (line 32):

(3) DD #11 (continued)

```
22    Dr. D:  . . . he is slow, he is retarded.
23           (0.2)
24  Mrs. R:  HE IS NOT RETAR[DED! ]
25    Mr. R:                [Ellen.]
26  Mrs. R:  HE IS NOT RETARDED!=
27    Mr. R:  =Ellen.
28           (0.3)
29    Mr. R:  Uh plea:s::e
30  Mrs. R:  NO::!
31    Mr. R:  May- look- (0.6) it's their way of:: I'oh'know.
32  Mrs. R:  hhhhh HE'S NOT RETAR:(ghh)DED! ((sobbing))
33           (2.5)
34    Dr. D:  He can learn and he is lear[ning ]
35  Mrs. R:                              [hhhh]
36    Mr. R:  Yes [he is learning    ]          [I-  ]
37    Dr. D:      [and he's making  ] good prog[ress.]
38  Mrs. R:      [.hhhhhhhhhhhhhhh]
```

As Mrs. Riccio vigorously displays her disagreement, Mr. Riccio addresses Mrs. Riccio by her first name (line 25), produces a plea (line 29), and after her strong rejection ("NO::," line 30), appears to refer to the diagnosis as the clinic's "way of . . .," but then abandons the effort with a knowledge disclaimer ("I 'oh 'know," line 31). Mr. Riccio, accordingly, does not himself exhibit a reaction to the diagnosis. Subsequent to Mrs. Riccio's sobbing rejection of the diagnosis (line 32), there is a substantial silence (line 33), whereupon Dr. Davidson engages a *good-news exit* (chapter 6) from the bad news, suggesting that Donald "can learn" and "is learning" (line 34). Mr. Riccio agrees with this (line 36), as Dr. Davidson continues with the assessment of Donald as "making good progress." Mr. Riccio's line 36 utterance is the second instance of his aligning with what the pediatrician has to say. Meanwhile, at lines 35 and 38, Mrs. Riccio is audibly sighing in overlap with her husband's and the pediatrician's talk.

A Puzzle: Contrasting Parental Reactions to a Forceful Presentation of Diagnosis

Detailed analysis of recorded interaction gives a finer appreciation of the pediatrician's work to mitigate the impact of the clinic's bad news, and demonstrates that if social distance is maintained between the Dr. Davidson and the parents it is partly a product of their resistance to her overtures, rather than residing solely in her manner of presentation to them. Of course, she does forge ahead in a relatively blunt way to present the parents with the diagnosis of mental retardation. Is there more that can be said about this strategy? And how do we analyze the quite different ways these parents receive the news?

Social structure, psychology, and natural periodicity. If we were to draw on previous literature, we would be on thin ground, because it does not say much about how recipients reply to bad-news announcements in the environment of and in relation to the announcement itself. In the bad-news literature, discussions of social structural effects are about the strategies *deliverers* choose for presentation and neglect recipients' practices for handling the news.

When ethnographers discuss responsiveness, they concentrate more on psychological phenomena than on practices. From their experiences with surviving spouses and other relatives, coroner's deputies report that a prominent reaction to death tidings is some expression of *grief* (Charmaz 1975: 307–9). Likewise, experts in the area of developmental disabilities see parents experiencing this emotion, or "sorrow," because a diagnosis means loss of the "fantasized normal child" (Olshansky 1962; Wikler, Wasow, and Hatfield 1981). However consistent proposals about grief and sorrow may be with the premise that recipients are losing a taken-for-granted social world in a noetic crisis, these proposals mostly invoke the psychological impact of bad news, and investigators do not discuss where and how *in interaction* these emotions are expressed. Nor do they account for unemotional reactions, such as silence and withholding and attempted assuagement of a partner on the order of Mr. Riccio's actions after the news delivery.

Glaser and Strauss (1965: 121–35) provide the most comprehensive analysis of reactions to bad news, arguing that they occur as a series of *stages*. First is depression, which is followed by acceptance or denial. Denial, in prolonging the adjustment to bad news, may eventuate in acceptance. Each of these stages can be described in behavioral terms, acceptance being characterized by *preparations* for handling the condition that has been announced, while denial can involve *blocking communication*. In these terms, Mrs. Riccio appears to be blocking communication through her denials and Mr. Riccio to be accepting and prepared to deal with his son's retardation. These parents, accordingly, would be seen to be at different stages in the response process, but this process in either case represents a trajectory occasioned by the delivery of an official diagnosis but otherwise psychologically independent of it. That is, the description of stages mostly detaches them from their concrete relations to the diagnostic presentation and posits a natural progression with its own periodicity.

Conversation analysis and ethnography. So a puzzle remains. In this episode, how are the delivery of diagnosis and the parents' differential responsiveness to be understood concretely and interactionally, rather than in abstract relation to social structure or psychology or natural periodicity? What more can we say about the pediatrician's affiliative-but-blunt mode of delivering the diagnosis? About the mother's crying and the father's relatively restrained response? I offer two promissory notes, because instead of fully answering these questions, they project us toward subsequent chapters.

One note is about the delivery and involves my third form of limited affinity—explaining a curious pattern by way of observation and interview. I did not collect the developmental disabilities data from which the present excerpts derive, and do not have my own ethnographic information, but I can draw on another ethnographic inquiry to propose that Dr. Davidson's blunt approach may have been a *purposeful* device to provoke an emotional reaction. As I describe in chapter 6, counselors at an HIV testing clinic deliver bad news that a client is HIV-positive in a straightforward and assertive manner similar to Dr. Davidson's eventual bluntness. This confrontational style was apparent in the recordings I obtained from the clinic, but what was not evident from the tapes was why the counselors employed such a style. My ethnographic inquiry, we will see, reveals what was afoot in the HIV testing clinic and may generalize to the developmental disabilities data here.

The other promissory note on this interactional puzzle concerns the parents' contrasting responsiveness and draws on sequential analysis to portray their responses as a produced orderliness. After analyzing the news delivery sequence in chapter 4, I will explore in chapter 5 how in clinics this sequence is configured to promote the pair of reactions Mr. and Mrs. Riccio exhibit—hers of crying, or flooding out, and his of restraint, or stoicism. In short, the analysis of news delivery sequencing in chapters ahead will show how their reactions, while capable of description in psychological terms, are also deeply socially organized.

The News Delivery Sequence

> Doctor: *I've got good news for you, Mrs. Brown.*
> Patient: *It's Miss Brown, actually.*
> Doctor: *I've got bad news for you, Miss Brown.*

Reported as "the classic waiting room joke" (MacIntyre 1976: 160), the exchange in the epigraph displays two important features related to the purpose of this chapter. One is a formal structure, a *preannouncement,* through which hearers of the joke as well as the fictional Miss Brown can anticipate a delivery of news (although the news does not get explicitly delivered within the joke). The visibility of some spate of talk as "news," then, is something that participants provide through their analyzable practical actions. The joke also illustrates that whether the news is to be regarded as good or bad depends on a variety of things, including who the teller is, who the recipient is, who the main figure is, the presumptions of each party, and other matters. In this instance, the doctor, no doubt assuming cultural standards to the effect that pregnancy is uniformly desirable for married women and undesirable for the not married, alters the projected valence of the news by what is learned in situ about the conjugal status of the recipient, whom the news is "for." Although the joke includes neither the actual delivery nor the recipient's response to the news, both of which are crucial to the determination of its valence, the lesson should be clear. Whether news is good or bad is not inherent in events and instead is something that is, relative to the exhibited concerns, perspectives, and identities of co-participants, their own interactional production. To put it succinctly, for an event-in-the-world to be news of a particular kind is always a conditional matter, dependent on, among other features of embodied activity, the actions and responses of participants in conversational interaction.

The purpose of this chapter is to explore the conditional nature of good and bad news. Three matters are at stake here. First, participants often share information about events-in-the-world, but it emerges as *news* only as these participants work it up that way in their interaction. Second, while members of society often presume that news of some events (death of a loved one, getting cancer, failing an exam) is inherently bad, and that news of other events (getting engaged, having a healthy baby, earning a good grade) is invariably good, they still must *interactively* establish the valence of the news and just how good or bad it is.[1] Third, participants display that the news has direct consequences for some particular party or parties, whom I call the *consequential figures*. In short, when participants approach, tell, and receive bad or good news, they often converge in understanding the conveyed information as news and as of a particular kind, affecting various parties. This convergence, rather than reflecting prior or general agreement about the objective nature of events-in-the-world, depends on participants' in-course practical activity. To paraphrase Garfinkel (1967: 33), good and bad news emerge from the particularities in conduct of co-present parties and, like other features of a setting, are a "contingent accomplishment of socially organized common practices."

I will examine how news qua news and the valence of that news evolve, in ordinary conversation, from the time of participants' introduction and through articulation of a *news delivery sequence* (NDS). How interactants display consequential figures as they deliver and receive good or bad news is a phenomenon to which, when it is relevant, I only point, and treat more fully in chapter 5. As much as possible I illustrate analytical points with instances of each kind of news, but even when using an example of just one kind, the general points in this chapter apply to both bad and good news.[2] Consequently, this chapter represents a movement away from a preoccupation with bad news to consider the news delivery sequence as a generic device for the gestalt-like activity of bearing news — bad, good, or indifferent — in interaction. As a generic device, the NDS represents a way that participants organize the actions of announcing and receiving news as *courses* of action through deploying a regular sequence of turns (Schegloff 1997: 410).

Presenting "Information" as an Account or as News: News Inquiries and Preannouncement Sequences

For some event-in-the-world to become news-for-participants, one has to report it to another. Previous conversation analytic research has identified what might be called *occasioning practices,* sequences by which potential deliverers and recipients provide for such reporting. A potential deliverer's mechanism is the Preannouncement (Terasaki 1976). Referenced in the joke in the epigraph to this chapter, a preannouncement (e.g., "Hey we got good news!") is designed to handle a central contingency in the development of conversational news, which is a recipient's prior knowledge of the occurrence to be reported. After a preannouncement, a potential recipient can either produce a "blocking" move or a "go-ahead" token or phrase that solicits an announcement (Schegloff

1996). Potential recipients of news can occasion its delivery through what Button and Casey (1985) call the *itemized news inquiry* ("How is Dez anyway?") that
nominates a particular item for reporting, or through a *topic initial elicitor*
("What's new with you?") that provides a more open domain for reporting
news. I will refer to such devices as *news inquiries*.

In suggesting that events-in-the-world become news in a conditional matter,
I am also proposing something more fundamental than the necessity of using
occasioning practices, such as preannouncements and news inquiries, to implicate a news announcement. The deeper point is that interactional organization
and structure supersede utterance content in achieving and displaying the talk as
news. Items that participants could treat as announcements of news are sometimes produced and heard in a way that makes them a different kind of object
(Terasaki 1976: 6):

(1) **NB:II:1:R:2**
```
 1   Emma:   So: Elizabeth 'n Willy were spoze tuh come down las'
 2           night but there was a death 'n the fam'ly so they
 3           couldn' come so Guy's asked Dan tuh play with the
 4           comp'ny deal so I guess he c'n play with 'im. So,
 5   Lottie: Oh:: goo::d.
```

The boldfaced utterance, as a kind of informing about death, is here given as a
reason for one party in a couple not being present for a golf game. The focal
news — in the sense of occupying the part of A's turn that is "sequentially implicative"—is A's announcement that, because of the death, another party
("Dan") can play. B's stretched and emphasized "Oh:: goo::d" is directed to that
and not to the "death in the family."[3]

Accordingly, there can be "information" that is packaged within actions
other than announcing, and recipients can ignore it or retrieve it as news for
assessment. Only when participants retrieve such information for independent
announcement and/or assessment does it achieve the official status of bad or
good news in a particular interaction. Whereas information about the death was
ignored in the last excerpt, information about illness occurs in excerpt (2) below
and is retrieved; Steven has called and Leslie has answered the phone. This excerpt also illustrates the four-part news delivery sequence (see arrows) that we
will probe in detail throughout the chapter:

(2) **H17B/Holt:88:2:3:1**
```
 1   Steven:   Oh: Leslie sorry (.) beh to bother you? °h[h
 2   Leslie:                                             [Oh: right.
 3   Steven:   ↑Could you a::sk Ski:p if- °hmhat- when you go: to
 4             this meeting tomorrow °hm could'e give Geoff:
```

```
 5                    Haldan's a↓pologies thro͟u͟gh sickn͟e͟ss?
 6                             (.)
 7    Leslie:         ↑Y͟e͟:s:. Yes. Oh [↑d͟e͟a:r what's the ↑ma͟l͟tt͟e͟r with=
 8    Steven:                    [ U h  I  (  m͟e͟t  ) ]
 9    Leslie:         =G͟e͟eoff.
10                             (.)
11    Steven: 1→  Well'e he's got this wretched um (0.3) he's got
12             →  this wretche[d
13    Leslie:                 [d g͟o͟[u͟t͟.h
14    Steven:                     [gout.
15    Leslie: 2→  O͟h: ↓ye[s. °hhhh
16    Steven: 3→        [An' he-eh he: he's right fl͟a͟t on iz b͟a͟:ck.
17    Leslie: 4→  A͟h͟::::.  [P͟o͟o͟:r Geoff]
18    Steven:              [But ͟i͟f Sk͟i͟p] c͟o͟u͟ld give iz apologies because
19                    th͟a͟t's the reason eez not g'nna be the͟↓͟:re.
20    Leslie:         Y͟e͟:s ↓fi:ne.
```

Initially, Steven offers Geoff Haldan's "sickness" as an account and not as bad news per se. That is, the sickness is a reason for an anticipated absence at an upcoming meeting (lines 4–5), and Steven's action here is to initiate a request-response sequence for Leslie to have her husband (Skip) convey apologies. Leslie accepts the request (line 7, "yes yes") and then, through a "solicitous inquiry" (Button and Casey 1985), retrieves the embedded account for development as news ("Oh dear what's the matter with Geoff?"). In lines 11–14 (arrow 1), Steven, with help from Leslie in a word search, announces the news of Geoff's gout, to which Leslie responds with a token of receipt (arrow 2).[4] Next, Steven elaborates a further aspect of the news (arrow 3), and Leslie produces a sympathetic assessment (arrow 4). This essentially completes a news delivery sequence, consisting of the (1) *announcement*, (2) *announcement response*, (3) *elaboration*, and (4) *assessment*.[5] Now Steven, in overlap with part of Leslie's line 17 assessment, re-requests conveyance of apologies, recasting (via "that's") the sickness not to be news as such but as the "reason" for Geoff's absence at the meeting (lines 18–19). Leslie again grants the request (line 20), which also works to occasion the closing of the conversation (not included in the excerpt). To reiterate: "sickness" of a mutual acquaintance is initially offered as an account, is momentarily retrieved for treatment as (bad) news, and then is reembedded in a request-response sequence to once more account for the request.

Occasioning the News Delivery Sequence

The news delivery sequence can be occasioned by a potential recipient making inquiry or by a potential deliverer issuing a preannouncement. Additionally, rather than following or being part of a presequence, the announcement in an

emerging NDS can itself initiate topic, mark a stepwise move, or institute a
change of topic in conversation, as when an announcement is the reason for a
call and constitutes its first topic. In excerpt (3), Carrie has telephoned Leslie and
almost immediately announces that she has a new granddaughter:

(3) H13G/Holt:1988:2:4:1
```
 1   Leslie:   Hello↑?h
 2   Carrie:   Oh Les↑lie it's Carrie.
 3   Leslie:   °t hOh: ↑Carrie: ↑Yes he↑llo [:.hh °hh hh
 4   Carrie:  →                             [I: thought you'd like to
 5                   know I've got a little gran'daughter
 6   Leslie:   °thlk ↑Oh: how love↓ly.
```

When callers preempt otherwise routine sequences (such as greetings and how-
are-you's) at the opening of telephone conversations, this often portends bad or
good news.

By whatever route the NDS emerges, participants shape each component according to a myriad of contingencies. Any NDS, in other words, emerges in and
as the detailed course of action by which participants in interaction progressively
and precisely configure and achieve some event-in-the-world as good or bad
news. Shortly, we will consider each of the component turns—announcement,
announcement response, elaboration, assessment—to demonstrate this configuring process. First, I wish to observe some features of the presequences that
occasion bad and good news announcements.

Preannouncements and news inquiries help provide for the understanding
of a subsequent turn as announcing good or bad news and can foreshadow the
valence of the news. In excerpt (2), Steven's initial "sickness" account permits
Leslie to ask "what's the matter?," a colloquial query form that foreshadows the
valence of the news-to-come. However, some queries, as in line 1 in the excerpt
below, are neutral in terms of marking expected valence:

(4) NB2B/NB:II:5:R:3
```
  1   Lottie:   Wt's new with you:.
  2   Emma:    .hhhh Oh:: ah wen'tih th'dentis'n [uh:: G]od'e
  3   Lottie:                                    [Ye:ah?]
  4   Emma:    wantuh pull a tooth 'n [make me a] new go:ld uh:=
  5   Lottie:                         [ (t'hhhhh) ]
  6   Emma:    =bridge fer EI:GHT HUNDER'DOLLARS.
  7   Lottie:  °Oh:: sh::i[ :t. °]
  8   Emma:               [ Shi]:t.
  9                          (0.2)
 10   Emma:    Is ri:ght.
```

Responding to Lottie's inquiry, Emma's bad news (lines 2, 4, 6) arrives in a story about visiting the dentist, and it is within this story that Emma originates an exhibit of valence (discussed below).

Like some news inquiries, preannouncements may be neutral in any lexical assessment of the news they augur:

(5) HS ST:2:4 (Terasaki, 1976: appendix III: 3)

```
 1  A:  → Oh you didn't- You didn' hear the news didju. We were out
 2          there before Thanksgiving.
 3  B:    Oh. You were.
 4  A:    Yeah. Were we?
 5  B:    Oh. Out here?
 6  A:    Yeah.
 7  B:    Yeah. Yeah. Right. Right.
 8  A:    Yeah. Angie's gonna have a baby.
 9  B:    Oh really.
10  A:    Yeah
11  B:    Well, congratulations
```

Of course, preannouncements also may indicate a positive evaluation ("Hey we got good news"), a negative one ("Did you hear the terrible news?"), or some other stance toward the news, and thereby locate the kind of assessment a recipient should produce upon completion of the delivery. However, some preevaluations appear to withhold valence ascription in a kind of dramatic build up. In excerpt (6), Andi's preannouncement, which stretches from line 3 to line 5, both signifies upcoming "news" and indicates her news would come "as a bit of a surprise."

(6) ARL3:18

```
1  Andi:  .hhh well: speaking of bot↑toms are you sitting down?
2  Betty: Ye↑ah.
3  Andi:  Well we have some news for you.
4  Betty: What?
5  Andi:  .hhh that may come as a bit of a surprise ehhh!
6  Betty: I see- what are you telling me?
7  Andi:  hhhh! Bob and I are going to have a baby.
8  Betty: Oh my good↑ness!
```

After Andi's line 7 announcement, Betty at line 8 indeed shows surprise with her upward-intoned exclamation (Freese and Maynard 1998; Local 1996). Whether this surprising news is good or bad is something that the participants, in subsequent talk, systematically work to display (see chapter 1 and excerpt (23) below).

Configuring Events as Bad or Good News through the NDS

The four parts of the news delivery sequence are: announcement, announcement response, elaboration, and assessment. In discussing how the emotions of "joy" and "sorrow" get expressed in conversation, Sacks (1992b: 572) mentions this sequence as consisting of

> an announcement of some big *news* and an expression of *surprise* by the recipient. . . . Then there's some more talk about it by the announcer, and *then* the expression of the appropriate emotion.

Each of these components is itself an achievement or site of detail (Garfinkel 1988) that is consonant with its orderly, collaborative production. By this I mean that each part of the sequence, just as the overall sense of bad or good news, comes into being according to actions and responses of co-participants. A gross example is in excerpt (2), where Steven, the news deliverer, starts an utterance ("he's got this wretched um . . .") that his recipient, Leslie, helps to complete ("gout"), and the announcement turn thereby emerges as a co-production. Furthermore, the in-course actions and response of co-participants determine whether, upon the production of an announcement, a news delivery sequence, as opposed to some other activity such as gossip (see (11) below), will be pursued. Responses to announcements also help configure *how far* the news will be pursued: Some deliveries of bad or good news come to occupy only two or three turns rather than the prototypical four-part sequence. Figure 4.1 presents the NDS schematically; I will discuss each turn constituting the sequence.

The Announcement Turn

If presequences to the NDS help provide for the subsequent interpretation of news, this is not the whole story, because design features displaying it as a telling of or report on some event (Schegloff 1996: 13–14) and as having a positive or negative valence can be intrinsic to an announcing utterance. For instance, speakers (with more or less collaborative contributions) regularly format an announcement utterance as an assertion or declaration (e.g., "He's got this wretched gout," "God he wanted to pull a tooth 'n make me a new gold bridge fer eight hunder dollars," "Angie's gonna have a baby," "Bob and I are going to have a baby"). Some announcements of news, however, consist not of an assertion or declaration but of a small narrative, as in excerpt (4) when Emma tells her bad news by way of a story about her trip to the dentist. Because announcements draw from the biography of the speaker (Labov and Fanshel 1977: 62), that party displays "firsthand knowledge" (Button and Casey 1985: 62)—i.e., a

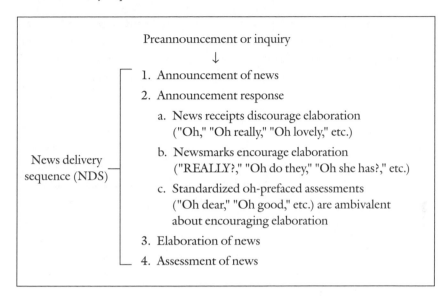

Figure 4.1 The news delivery sequence

particular epistemological stance (Whalen and Zimmerman 1990) — in relation to the event. Connected with this is some formulation, like the ones displayed in excerpts (2) through (5), that provides for the event being recent or current such that the recipient would not have previous knowledge.

As for valence, announcements may be marked lexically in particular ways, as in (2), when Steven characterizes Geoff Haldan's condition as "wretched." Whether or not there is lexical marking, news may be marked in prosodic ways to display a valence (Freese and Maynard 1998). Consider excerpt (4), in which Emma announces the cost of a prospective new bridge. Her intonation on "Oh:: ah wen'tih th'dentis'" wavers in a low key that sets a turn-internal context (Couper-Kuhlen and Selting 1996) for hearing as infelicitous the gold tooth price, which she speaks with elevated volume and emphasis ("EI:GHT HUNDER'DOLLARS").

Contributing to the achieved valence of a news delivery (as well as to the "newsness" of a report) are not only the deliverer's turn 1 announcement and turn 3 elaboration. In turn 2 (the announcement response) and turn 4 (assessment), the recipient becomes involved in exhibiting the valence.[6] Therefore, bad and good news as interactional events have a jointly accomplished character. That participants jointly accomplish the accountable valence of news does not mean, however, that their contributions are equal and symmetrical. Rather, a deliverer, whose epistemological access to an event-in-the-world is displayed as closer than the recipient's, works to set the valence or tone in preannouncing, announcing, and/or elaborating turn(s), and a recipient is usually but not always in the position of aligning to that tone. When the recipient is the primary consequential figure for some news, for example, he or she may determine the valence texture of the news more strongly than the deliverer.

Following Terasaki (1976), I observed that interactional organization and conversational structure supersede content in displaying an event-in-the-world as conversational bad or good news. Reinforcing how structure matters to participants' sense of the nature of news is that very diverse utterance types can convey its substance. For instance, a co-participant, invited by way of a news inquiry to provide an announcement, may respond by admonishing the speaker not to ask, and by refusing or postponing production of discrete information about the situation. A recipient can then appraise that action, infer something negative, and offer responses as if news had been told substantively. Prior to the next excerpt, Edward had asked Donna about school. She indicated it was difficult, and then returned the question:

(7) **ZG:6**
```
1   Donna:   How's yours?
2   Edward:  Htunh. (.) don' a:sk. Ih- It [gets-   ]
3   Donna:                              [Really?]
4   Edward:  .hh [hh I've got-]
5   Donna:      [How bad? ]
6   Edward:  I've got so much homework assignment.
```

Edward's reply ("Don' ask," line 2) resists the question and prefaces a complaint (lines 2, 4, 6) about how much homework he has. However, in overlap with his start of the complaint (line 2), Donna produces a newsmark ("Really?," line 3) and then a querying understanding of his initial resistance as signifying something "bad" (line 5). Hence, Donna's responsiveness displays an understanding of "bad news" *before* its substance is put on the table. Edward's fully formed complaint (line 6), now produced as an answer to Donna's query, confirms her understanding of his circumstances.

In a different conversation, Robbie delicately asks about Leslie's house, and her response, like Edward's in (7), is a *virtual* bad news announcement:

(8) **H14B/Holt:M88:1:5:25**
```
1   Robbie:  Dare I ask how: the house is or sh'l I not.
2                     (0.5)
3   Leslie:  Uh:m::: no eht- neyss not at the moment ehh ↑hheh hheh
4            [heh
5   Robbie:  [Oh::: drat
```

```
  6    Leslie:  H̲m̲:.
  7    Robbie:  It-it's (0.2) it's- as you al:re̲ady ↓know it's a ba:d
  8             time to [↓try 'n [(              )
  9    Leslie:         [°hhhh [I̲ ↓know I̲ know but I'm qu̲ite happy:
 10             so:
```

Leslie (at line 3) rejects the inquiry, her appended laughter perhaps showing "troubles resistance" (Jefferson 1984). Robbie, in producing an oh-prefaced assessment (line 5), thereby exhibits taking this rejection as nonetheless informative, and goes on with a further display of understanding and perhaps sympathy (lines 7–8). Next, Leslie agrees with Robbie's formulation about the "bad time," and contrastingly produces personal-state news indicating happiness (lines 9–10), which appears to counteract the bad news trajectory of Robbie's talk with a further show of troubles resistance. This episode demonstrates that when the giving of information is resisted in a sequential environment that provides for it—when, that is, a participant rejects the request for news—a potential recipient, no doubt drawing on commonsense knowledge of the situation, can take the refusal itself as "bad news." Thus, participants can fill the "slots" (Sacks 1992a: 262) embedded in organized sequences with various kinds of objects. The sequencing itself communicates substantive matters. Produced structures and their mutual articulation help form content, and figure heavily in participants' sense of there being news and of the kind that it is.

Accordingly, participants can convey bad and good news "in so many words." A further example is how news bearers can design their talk in a way that, while informing about one thing, allows a recipient to respond to another. Referring to the device of "burying," Sacks (1992b: 177–78) analyzes a fragment of conversation in which Anne telephones her neighbor Gilda and reports that her (Anne's) husband, Bob, put the newspaper on Gilda's porch.

(9) **NB18G/NB:IV:11:R:1**
```
  1    Anne:   Ah did↑ju̲[ge:tche]r p̲aper this: morning it wz=
  2    Gilda:           [ Ahshh ]
  3    Anne:   =o̲u:t'n [fro̲n'v a̲:r pl↓a:ce.=
  4    Gilda:          [m-
  5    Gilda:   =Ye̲s dear a̲h di↓:d.
  6    Anne:   Bo̲b to̲o̲k't o̲ver on the p̲orch he di̲dn'know whether yih
  7            w'r u↓:p.h
  8    Gilda:   u-Well tha̲nk you ye̲s I di̲d I'm just u̲p a li̲ttle whi:le
  9            en do̲ing the .hh cho̲res . . .
```

In a context where, after an argument, Bob had left Anne for several days, this effectively tells Gilda that he has come back home. However, because Anne here reports a favor, Gilda, rather than being obligated to deal then and there with the mention of Bob's return, can produce a "thank you" (line 8) for the favor, can respond to the other information at her discretion. Later in the conversation, Sacks (1992b: 178) observes, Gilda does pick up on this information and appraise it. Her query at lines 1 and 3 below is a topic change after she had declined Anne's invitation to "come over" (not in excerpt).

(10) NB18G/NB:IV:11:R:3
```
    1  Gilda:  Bu:t uh
    2  Anne:   .hh[hh
    3  Gilda:      [An' Bil-u-an' Bhob ghot dho: [wn.
    4  Anne:                                      [.hhhh YE:S HE wz
    5          HE:RE: uafter I: came ho::me, I: uh went tuh Lottie's
    6          fer a fih- li'l whal'n then he'd gone up tih get some
    7          PAI[:NT. So he ca] :me o:n in en: uh
    8  Gilda:     [°° I  s e e °°]
    9                    (.)
   10  Anne:   .p[.hhh
   11  Gilda:  [Well that's fi:ne.
```

At lines 4–7, Anne confirms Gilda's observation and elaborates the news, whereupon Gilda now receives this *as* news (line 8) and assesses it (line 11) in a measured way. This example returns us to the phenomenon of retrieving "information" for treatment as good or bad news; it may not be happenstance that such information appears as an account for another action and not as a delivery of news. Both an informant who does bury information and a recipient who grasps that doing and later provides for officially recognizing the information as bad or good (or some other kind of) news are artful users of structural knowledge. Their skills at introducing information and then, according to the developing course of conversation, disregarding or regarding its *newsworthiness* or implicativeness as news, displays the possible delicacy of this very information (Sacks 1992a: 47).[7]

The Announcement Response

Deliverers structure their announcements, which can embody a variety of utterance types, to exhibit the information within the turn as news, and lexically and/or prosodically to mark the news as to valence. Recipients, in next turn, display the announcement as "news-for-them" (Terasaki 1976: 7), and also may show an orientation to valence. In displaying the announcement as news-for-them, recipients *accept* that an announcement is news. For example, in regard to "oh" as a change-of-state token, Heritage (1984a: 304) has put it well:

a particle that proposes that its producer has undergone a change of state may be nicely responsive to prior turns at talk that are produced as informings. With the act of informing, tellers propose to be knowledgeable about some matter concerning which, they also propose, recipients are ignorant. Correspondingly, in proposing a change of state with the production of "oh," recipients thus confirm the presupposition, relevance, and upshot of the prior act of informing as an action that has involved the transmission of information from an informed to an uninformed party.

This implies not just that recipients can confirm a previous turn as informing (see the oh-prefaced responses in examples (2), (3), (4), and (5)), but that, after some announcement (arrows 1 below), they can *reject* its newsworthiness (arrow 2):

(11) **Frankel:I:1:4**

```
 1   Sally:      In any eve::nt?hhhhh That's not all thet's ne:w.
 2   Judy:       W't e:lse.
 3   Sally:   1→ .t.hhhhh W'l Vickie'n I hev been rilly having
 4               problems.
 5   Judy:       M-hm,
 6   Sally:   1→ .hh En yesterday I talk'tih her. .hhhh A:n' (0.3)
 7               apparently her mother is terminal.
 8                        (0.5)
 9   Judy:    2→ .tch Yeh but we knew that befo[:re.
10   Sally:                                    [.hhh Ri:ght. Well, (.)
11               now I guess it's official.
12   Judy:       Mm-hm.
13   Sally:      °t°hhh So she's very very upset.
14   Judy:       W'l how long did they give'er.
15   Sally:      Get thi:s. Fifty percent chance of three years.
16                        (0.7)
17   Judy:       W'l that's not bad et a::ll.=
18   Sally:      =I ↑kno:w.
```

How this news progresses and is assessed is a complicated matter, and, in the interests of space, I will gloss matters considerably. As put of her announcement, Sally's lead-in at lines 3–4 can signal upcoming gossip (Bergmann 1993). That is, her indication of "problems" with Vickie may project a moral posture whose contours will be filled in as the talk progresses.[8] The focal part of the announcement at lines 6–7 could be taken as bad news about Vickie's mother, but Judy rejects its newsworthiness by claiming prior knowledge (line 9). Furthermore, if it was Vickie who told Sally of the mother's terminal status, this announcement response, incorporating a "we" reference that can include both Sally and Judy, may be rejecting Vickie's proposed news-to-Sally rather than Sally's proposed news-to-Judy. In other words, Judy can be saying, "This is not news for us," and aligning with Sally against Vickie. Subsequently, Sally adds a component suggesting that the news of something "terminal" is now "official" (lines 10–11). This is another point at which the announcement could be taken as bad news about the mother, but at line 12 Judy simply provides for continuation. Next (line 13), Sally formulates Vickie's state in relation to the news about her mother. Once more, Judy is provided with an opportunity to align as having received bad news, this time concerning Vickie herself. However, Judy subsequently asks about the length of time given the mother (line 14), and Sally answers (line 15) with a temporal formulation of the condition, prefaced with "get this," which, in gossiping context, can indicate a particular moral stance. At line 17, Judy assesses the temporality with a litotes ("not bad"), and immediately Sally agrees (line 18), suggesting that Judy's "get this" preface may have been understood as indicating just this stance: that the proper attitude toward having "fifty percent chance of three years" is that it's not a bad prospect. Accordingly, the conversants here collaborate in aligning critically toward Vickie by displaying skepticism toward how bad her mother is and how upset Vickie herself should be.[9]

In all, Judy forgoes three opportunities for granting the newsworthiness of Sally's announcements — subsequent to the reports of Vickie's mother being terminally ill, of this being officially so, and of this as upsetting to Vickie. If such resistance is in the service of other activities, such as gossiping about an involved figure, the point remains that after a report or announcement is a position in which a recipient may accept or reject it as news. That there is an organized position at which participants can respond positively or negatively to the purported newsworthiness of announcements implies accordingly that potential recipients are not limited to ratifying an announcement as news of a particular kind. Instead, recipients are strongly, collaboratively involved in developing the news implicativeness and valence of a deliverer's announcement.[10]

News receipts and newsmarks: Encouraging or discouraging elaboration of news. When recipients respond to announcements as news, they can use their turns in different ways. With *news receipts,* they show a retrospective orientation, primarily acknowledging an announcement as news while acting to deter development of the news. Accordingly, news receipts are *discouraging* announcement responses. Recipients use *newsmarks,* not only to acknowledge the announcement as news, but to promote its development and elaboration. Newsmarks, then, are *encouraging* announcement responses.

News receipts include freestanding "oh's," "oh really's," and nonsyntactical queries ("she did?"), as Jefferson (1981) and Heritage (1984a: 339–44, n. 13) have shown.

(12) NB:II:2:3
```
1  Emma:      Hey that was the same spot we took off for Honolulu.
2             (0.4) Where they put him on, at that chartered
3             place,
4  Nancy:  → Oh really?
5  Emma:      y::Yea::h.
6  Nancy:     Oh:? For heaven sakes.
```

In other words, news receipts, like the one arrowed above, may elicit a confirmation in next turn but no elaboration, and sometimes may mark the end of an informing sequence altogether, such that the news delivery may consist of only two turns. Freestanding "oh's," for instance, "instruct the informant that a gap in information has now been filled and that the informant may lawfully withhold from further talk" on the news (Heritage 1984a: 333). When news receipts appear in four-part sequences consisting of (1) announcement, (2) newsmark, (3) confirmation, and (4) assessment, as per Jefferson's (1981: 62) analysis, this differs from the prototype news delivery sequence in which turn (3) is an elaboration, and it demonstrates that the response to an announcement, while not determinative, nevertheless highly influences just how much or how far a deliverer's news will be explicated.

Discouraging announcement responses often consist of oh + assessment turns, such as "oh good," "oh lovely," "oh dear," and the like (Heritage 1984a: 302; Local 1996):

(13) R8G/Rahman:A:1:IMJ(2):2
```
1   Ida:     °hhh Well thez eh: few things arrived fer you,
2   Jenny:  → Oh goo:d. [°hhh
3   Ida:             [eeYes.
4   Jenny:   Oh cz the boys w'r ahskin 'ow long they'd been . . .
```

At line 3, Ida follows Jenny's oh-prefaced assessment with a token of confirmation, but no more, and the NDS occupies just three turns (announcement, response, confirmation), followed by the recipient's on-topic talk.

With bad news, when deliverers are the primary consequential figures in the news, they may treat an oh-prefaced assessment as a news receipt by producing an exhibit of troubles resistance. Before the excerpt below, Ann had been telling Jenny about some newly arrived furniture, and here (lines 4–6) announces one of the negative outcomes from this arrival:[11]

(14) R3B/Rah:B:1:JA(11):4
    1   Jenny: So have you g̲ot it all o̲hrganized then [more'r=
    2   Ann: [We̲ll
    3   Jenny: =less?
    4   Ann: Well excep'thet thez m̲u̲:d fr'm the f̲ront do̲:h r̲i:ght
    5   up. tuh the °hh tr̲a̲i:led u̲p̲'n down t'the g̲arage with
    6   screwdriviz 'n [G̲od knows [what   ( ).]
    7   Jenny: [O h̲: : :   [d e a̲ : u h.]
    8   Ann: N̲evuh mind it'll a̲ll come right in the end.
    9   Jenny: Yeh. Okay y̲ou go'n getta clean trousihs on . . .

After Jenny's "oh dear" response (line 7) to the bad news about mud, Ann produces (line 8) an "optimistic projection" (Jefferson 1988) that seems to comment on the entire set of problems the furniture arrival had entailed. As in excerpt (13), the NDS here is three turns (announcement, response, optimistic projection). Subsequently, Jenny moves to close the conversation (line 9).

Newsmarks, by contrast with news receipts and as encouraging responses, include oh-plus partial repeats ("Oh do they"), freestanding but query-intoned objects ("really?"), and syntactical queries ("did she?") that both receive an announcement as news and promote development or elaboration of that news (Heritage 1984a, n. 13; Jefferson 1981).[12] Compared to "Oh really," for example, a freestanding "really" solicits elaboration. In (15), R's newsmark (arrow 2) is freestanding and is spoken with high volume, which may enhance the encouragement:

(15) Terasaki 1976:9
    D: 1→ °hh And I got athl̲etic award.
    R: 2→ REALLY?!?
    D: 3→ Uh huh. From Sports Club.
    R: 4→ Oh that's terr̲ific Ronald.

D both confirms the news and elaborates in line 3. In other words, newsmarks, more strongly than news receipts, have both a retrospective (news acknowledging) and prospective (sequence expanding) character.[13]

A final complication. Whereas "oh" most regularly operates as a curtailing newsmark, Heritage (1984a: 344) notes the possibility that, rarely, intonation may alter the usual status of the "oh" and help it to function as an encouraging announcement response. Such is the case in excerpt (16). The news announcement [1] below is a stepwise move; Leslie and Robbie have been discussing a mutual acquaintance who has allergies to clothing dyes, the sun, and other things, when Leslie produces her announcement at lines 1–2:

(16) **H15B/Holt:M88:1:5:28**
```
 1    Leslie:  1→ Well: th:this ↑is eh why I'm not ↑quite ↓so well at
 2                   th'moment I'd thought I'd got t'the: bottom a'my
 3                   ↑allergies but I came out'n most ↑terr↓ible rash last
 4                   week, °hhhh[hh
 5    Robbie:  2→              [↑Oh:[↓:
 6    Leslie:  3→                   [An' I wz telling th'm all at school
 7                   how m'ch better I wa:s but I: ↑think it might've been:
 8                   um primulas I touched.
 9                            (.)
10    Robbie:  4→ ↑Oh you poor ↑↑thi::ng.
```

Leslie's announcement (arrow 1) reaches back to an earlier sequence, when Robbie had inquired "how're you," and Leslie had replied with what Jefferson (1980: 162–63) calls a "downgraded conventional" response, "Oh fine- well nah yes I am fairly fine." Such responses may *premonitor* a report on a trouble, such as Leslie's announcement here of her rash. After that announcement, Robbie produces a surprise-intoned newsmark (Freese and Maynard 1998; Local 1996); the "oh" at arrow 2 begins in an upper register and slides downward in tone as the marker is stretched. It thereby may help occasion Leslie's elaboration (arrow 3), which overlaps the completion of the oh-token, and describes her having told others about "how m'ch better" she was and provides an account of the source of her rash.

In sum, recipients respond to particular announcements and what they project, and more or less encourage development of the news delivery through lexical and prosodic manipulations that strengthen or weaken the response. Two further points are relevant here, one having to do with oh-prefaced assessments and the other with in-course modifications of announcement responses.

Standardized oh-prefaced assessments as announcement responses. It has been argued that, as announcement responses, oh-prefaced assessments largely operate as news receipts, and appear to curtail elaboration of a news delivery. However, such items as "oh good," in response to good news, and "oh dear," in response to bad news, may be designedly ambivalent in terms of encouraging or discouraging elaboration. That is, they may straddle the news receipt/newsmark distinction in terms of articulating a primarily sequence terminating, discouraging stance toward elaboration of the news, or sequence expanding, encouraging orientation.

Put differently, both "oh good" and "oh dear" are *standardized,* having an abstract and laconic quality that endows them with a utility for responding to very diverse kinds of news. Therefore, recipients can use them to align to announced good or bad news without being either overly committed or unduly distanced in conveying an appreciation of the valence so far displayed. Accordingly, while they often appear in environments where elaboration of news is curtailed, they nevertheless may permit a subsequent proposal of elaboration. In short, while other items such as "oh," "oh really," and the like may be *strong* news receipts (suggesting sequence termination), and other items such as "really?" and "oh do they" are *strong* newsmarks (promoting expansion), "oh good" and "oh dear" as standardized oh-prefaced assessments are *weak* in terms of either treating an announcement as complete enough or requesting elaboration. They neither strongly resist nor encourage development of the news, as in examples (17) and (18):

(17) H20G/Holt:SO88:1:11:2

```
 1    Mum:    1→ Auntie Vi is he↑:re=
 2    Leslie: 2→ =h-↑Oh goo[d,
 3    Mum:    3→            [She's bin here all [the wee↑:k ['n
 4    Leslie: 4→                                 [°hhhh      [Oh: how
 5                 nice.
 6                            (.)
 7    Mum:        M[m:.
 8    Leslie:      [°hhhh Are you having her dinner?hh
```

After her recipient's "oh good" here (and in slight overlap with ending of that turn), Mum elaborates on her news about Auntie Vi. This receives a different oh-prefaced assessment, and the informing has a produced structure that fits the prototypical four-part NDS before a topic shift is produced at lines 7–8. Here is an instance of bad news:

(18) H7B/Holt:X(C)1:1:6:15

```
 1    Leslie: 1→ Well I'm I'm s:- (.) proba'ly going to a funeral on
 2                 Tuesday.
 3                            (0.4)
 4     Mum:   2→ ↑O[h ↓dea: [r.
 5    Leslie: 3→    [°t    [°ukhhh-hu °p°thh D'you 'member- You know
 6                 Philip Cole you ↑know 'e had this u-very: good °hhhh
 7                 very busy little mother that wz al[ways
 8     Mum:                                          [↑Oh:: ↓ye[s.
 9    Leslie:                                                   [busy
10                 doing thin:gs 'nd, (.) She die:d.
11     Mum:   4→ Ah↓::::.
12                            (0.2)
13    Leslie:    eh-in the week ↑very peace↓fully:
14     Mum:      Yes.
```

In this excerpt, Leslie's first turn serves as a kind of "headline" (Button and Casey 1985: 23); after her recipient's "oh dear," the elaboration presents the central news. (She produces a cough at line 5 partially in overlap with the line 4 announcement response.) The elaboration occupies lines 5–7 and 9–10; Mum's "↑Oh:: ↓yes" at line 8 permits continuation. Following the elaboration, Mum issues an assessment (line 11),[14] and there is further topical talk—a "bright side sequence" (Holt 1993) in lines 13–14 and beyond (in talk not included in the excerpt).

Whether a proposed elaboration that follows a standardized oh-prefaced assessment receives a further assessment as bad or good news is far from guaranteed. For instance, when the primary figure of bad news is the deliverer, elaborative talk after an oh-prefaced assessment may involve "exposition" of the deliverer's troubles (Jefferson 1988). In the conversation from which excerpt (19) is taken, Leslie's line 1 utterance is a topic change in which she announces some bad news about her son and his driver's examination. Kevin produces an oh-prefaced assessment at line 2:

(19) H21B/Holt:S088:1:5:2 (modified)
```
 1   Leslie:  ˙hhhh Gordon didn't pass his test I'm afraid, h=
 2   Kevin:   =Oh dear.
 3   Leslie:  ˙k˙tch He's goin- (.) Well ˙hh he was hoping tih get
 4            it (0.2) in: uh the summer but u (.) they're getting
 5            very booked up so I don't know if he'll even: get it
 6            in the:n.h
 7                       (1.1)
 8   Kevin:   Yes I: ah: no doubt he's back e(.)t uh . . .
```

Leslie's turn at lines 3–6 may display her understanding of Kevin's "Oh dear" as aligning him as a troubles recipient, which would make a possible exposition of the trouble now due or relevant. However, subsequent to Leslie's possible elaboration/exposition, Kevin waits (line 7) and then produces a token of receipt (line 8, "Yes") rather than any further assessment, and follows with an inquiry about where Gordon is going to school. Thus, Kevin avoids aligning as a troubles recipient, and the talk (not included in the excerpt) moves to different topics, about Leslie and her husband going to visit Gordon and about the visitors they soon would be hosting in their own home. Kevin's receipt and query provide for a retrospective understanding of his previous "oh dear" as a news receipt that was not asking for elaboration.[15]

In-course modifications of announcement responses. Recipients may produce an announcement response that at first encourages elaboration and then modify this response in the course of its production to de-escalate a display of commitment to hearing more about the news. In excerpt (20), Leslie's announcement emerges not as a reason for the call but after Leslie and her Mum, who talk regularly, had been discussing facial pain and "jaw trouble" among various members of the family (excerpt (21) below). After an extinguishing of the jaw trouble topic through the production of token utterances and a series of brief silences, Leslie (line 1 below) starts a turn of talk, which is like a sighing lead-in to next topic. Mum produces some indecipherable talk in overlap (line 2), and Leslie restarts her turn to produce a topic-shifting, bland announcement of news ("We had a very nice evening," lines 4–5).

```
(20)  H3G/Holt:X(C)1:2:7:8
    1   Leslie:  ↑Ah: .hhhh [Well ud-
    2   Mum:              [ (              )
    3                   (0.3)
    4   Leslie:  We had a ↑very nice evening at the (k) (0.3) Ditchit-
    5            (0.2) Old Time Musi[c Ha:ll.]
    6   Mum:                        [↑O h : ] ↓did ↑you ↓that's
    7            goo↑:[d
    8   Leslie:       [°t °hhh An' Gordon went to watch Big Country
    9            las' week at um the Sharring Pavillion (Chetsham
   10            Mallet)?
```

Leslie's announcement ends with downward intonation. Mum's response at lines 6–7, perhaps dealing with the bland characterization of the news and its routine introduction, has two components. While the "Oh did you" would promote elaboration in the manner of a newsmark, the appended assessment ("that's good") can stand as a news receipt that marks completion of the sequence. Furthermore, across Mum's turn, the intonation starts high, falls, rises, falls, and rises again, in a sing-song manner suggestive of no particularly strong commitment to either curtailment or development of the news. Although like a standardized oh-prefaced assessment, this may not resist elaboration, it can help suggest that a stepwise topic shift is relevant. Leslie makes such a shift in her next turn (lines 8–10). Both excerpts (20) and (19), located deep within conversations occupied with many other matters, are prosaic announcements of the sort that occur through parties' sheer continuing co-presence. Thus, they represent *routine* rather than special news of the sort that prompts a telephone call in the first place, as in example (3) where Carrie calls Leslie with news about her new granddaughter.

In short, depending on how deliverers produce their announcements as special or routine good or bad news, and how recipients respond with different kinds of news receipts, newsmarks, standardized oh-prefaced assessments, and the like, the delivery of news may occupy a minimal two-turn set, three turns, four turns, or more (see figure 4.1). News receipts as announcement responses are discouraging or topic curtailing, while newsmarks are encouraging topically and promote elaboration of the NDS. Standardized oh-prefaced assessments regularly appear as newsmarks, but may only weakly operate to suggest completion of a news delivery. They also allow a deliverer to propose elaboration so that the news and its valence receive more extended recipient treatment. However, proposed elaborations following standardized assessments appear vulnerable to a retrospective casting of such announcement responses as having invited topic discontinuation. Hence, the character of good and bad news — specifically whether the news and its valencing deserve pursuit beyond an initial announcement and response — is something that deliverer and recipient work up in the first moments of its telling and response, as well as in subsequent turns of talk.

Elaboration Turns

Use of the standardized oh-prefaced assessment shows that recipients, beyond allowing for a deliverer to elaborate on some news, may be cautious and circumspect when they first hear the news, evaluating the news relatively abstractly. In the course of further interaction, and depending on the actions of the deliverer, recipients determine whether and how a more precise and particularized response should be produced. If a deliverer chooses to elaborate, it provides for a subsequent, more fitted assessment, as participants complete a four-turn news delivery sequence:

(21) H8B/Holt:X(C)1:2:7:7
```
 1  Leslie:  1→ °hh Well I've ↑written to you in the letter
 2               Katherine's: ↓face is still hurting he:r?
 3                              (.)
 4   Mum:     2→ ↑Oh ↓dea:r.=
 5  Leslie:  3→ So uhm: she's going t'see our doctor when she comes
 6               ho[me.
 7  (Mum):       [ (    )
 8  Leslie:   → °hh An' I'll: get her fixed up with a de:ntist too:,
 9                         (0.7)
10   Mum:     4→ Oh w't a ↓nuisance isn't ↓it. Is it ↓ey:e tee:th?
```

After Mum's turn 2 announcement response, Leslie elaborates on the news in a way that shows the news to involve not just her daughter Katherine but also herself (arrow 3). Mum follows this (arrow 4) with an "affiliation response" (Jefferson 1988: 428). That assessment is fitted to the particularities of the developed news — it formulates the "nuisance" of going to the doctor and fixing Katherine up with a dentist because of her difficulties.

Just as a standardized oh-prefaced assessment may precede elaboration and a more particularized, fitted assessment, newsmarks and assessments may be separated by an elaboration turn. Prototypically, after a newsmark, turn 3 elab-

orations offer the focal piece of the news, or provide details, such that a recipient can assess the news in a precise manner. As Sacks (1992b: 573) has argued
in discussing the expressions of joy and sorrow that accompany deliveries of
news, were assessments to be placed before a deliverer has "a chance to fully develop what it is that happened," it could be taken as cutting off the delivery and
not "really caring" because it might discourage the deliverer from elaborating
the news in a way that allows particularized appreciation.[16] Separating the newsmark from the assessment, accordingly, allows an early display of understanding
that some announcement underway is news and a later, careful, exhibit of the recipient's comprehension of just what sort of news it is. In excerpt (22), Jenny
and Vera had been discussing a missed hair appointment, and why it had been
missed:

(22) R2G/Rahman I:8
```
 1   Vera:      Well ah think it wz the wea↑the:r yih kno:w,
 2              she didn like- feel like goin in the weather
 3              yi[ know °real]ly[:    (y'know)°
 4   Jenny:        [A o h : : :.]  [Oh I-e sh- cuz she said she wouldn'
 5              be going if Milly wz going t'thaht keep fit thing.
 6   Vera:  1→ uRight yeh °hh Oh I met Milly:, eh:::m yestihday en
 7              she'd hahdda foh:rm from the Age Concehrn about thaht
 8              jo:b.h=
 9   Jenny: 2→ =<Oh=she=hahs?>
10   Vera:  3→ So: eh she wz sending the foh:rm bahck
11              [the:n  you]  know]
12   Jenny: 4→ [Oh she di-] aOH w]'l thaht's goo:d ah'm s- ↓pleased
13              she applie:d,
```

Vera's news announcement about Milly's obtaining a job form (arrow 1) is a
change of topic that is touched off by Jenny's mentioning of Milly in the previous discussion. The oh-prefaced newsmark here (arrow 2) is of the [oh +
partial repeat] form that Jefferson (1981: 62–64) suggests is associated with a
pursuit of further talk, which Vera provides in her elaboration (arrow 3). This
is prefaced with a "so" token hearably connecting this part of her announcement with her previous turn. In overlap, Jenny (arrow 4) appears to produce
another newsmark ("Oh she di-"), abandoned as she goes on with an utterance
of the form oh + assessment that attends to the announcement sequence as
complete, and through which she exhibits pleasure not just at Milly having the
form, but at her having sent it back and having "applied" for the job, as Jenny
herself formulates the matter. Notice also that, even as the news is about a third
party, in being "pleased," Jenny exhibits the news to be consequential for herself as well.

Recall from chapter 1 how the development of Andi's news of her pregnancy demonstrates that marking something as news and providing for elaboration before assessing that news can be critical to an appropriate assessment:

(23) (Excerpt 6 continued)
```
 7   Andi:  1→ hhhh! Bob and I are going to have a baby.
 8   Betty: 2→ Oh my goodness↑ hhow- (1.0) did you have a reversal-
 9              he have a reversal?
10   Andi:  3→ Yea:h.
11                          (1.0)
12   Andi:     .hhh[: : : : : : : : : :]
13   Betty:        [whe::↑n.]
14   Andi:   → tch eyup. Last Mar↑ch.
15                          (0.4)
16   Andi:     .mhhh ((sniff))
17   Betty: 4→ OH [MY   G:OOD]↑NESS:
18   Andi:        [And    (ituh)]
19   Andi:   → It was [very successful,] [very quickly] hh::h .hhh
20   Betty:          [OH    I'M   SO] [↑HAPPY.   ]
```

After Andi announces her news about being pregnant (line 7), it is marked (line 8) as "surprising" news but not yet assessed. In response to Betty's questions (lines 8–9, 13), Andi elaborates (lines 10, 14) that the pregnancy came about after Bob's vasectomy had been reversed. I said earlier that this possibly informs Betty that the pregnancy was a sought happenstance, and more clearly allows for positive appraisal than the news of the pregnancy alone, which might have been accidental and unwanted. After the elaboration, Betty produces another "OH MY G:OOD↑NESS:" utterance (line 17), this time with increased pitch and volume, and (overlapping Andi's characterization of the vasectomy, line 19) she follows this with a claim and display of being happy (line 20).

As recipients locate what may be, for them, missing constituents in an announcing turn—e.g., "when" and/or "how" and/or "why" some event happened—they participate in the elaboration of an announcement in the news delivery sequence.[17] For example, Sacks (1992b: 573) refers to the *why* in Nancy's announcement response (arrow 2 in the following excerpt) as an expression of "surprise" about Emma's bad news (arrow 1). That response occasions Emma's elaboration (arrow 3), after which Nancy displays "sorrow" in the assessment turn (arrow 4).

(24) NB:II:4:R:1
```
1   Emma:       HI: HONEY HOW ARE y[uh.
2   Nancy:                          [Fine how'r you.
3   Emma:  1→ .kh.hh.hh.hahh. AOH: AH'M PRETTY GOO::D I HADDA
```

```
4  ·              LIDDLE O:P'ration on my toe this week I had t'have (0.2)
5                 n toenail TAKEN O:FF,hh
6                       (.)
7  Nancy:  2→  Why[:
8  Emma:   3→     [.hhh.hh Oh:: [I have a fungus 'n I: had'n=
9  Nancy:                    [(What wuhhh)
10 Emma:      =inf::↓ECtion,
11                   (.)
12 Emma:      'T's a [hell of a]
13 Nancy:  4→      [O h : : :]::: E:m↓mah
```

More than this, recipients may even collaborate in producing the elaboration
and the news, as when a deliverer engages in a word search that the recipient
helps to complete (excerpt (2), for instance), or when the recipient produces
an upshot for deliverer's confirmation because an announcing turn is vague or
elliptical in presenting the news (see excerpt (29) below). Components of the
four-part news delivery sequence (announcement, response, elaboration, assessment), rather than being deployed statically for telling and receiving good
and bad news, reflect dynamically concerted behavior of participants who offer
and seek perceptibly relevant aspects of the news and concertedly provide for its
suitable understanding and appreciation.

Assessment Turns and Beyond

The assessment turn may mark the completion of a news delivery sequence.
However, following an initial assessment, a deliverer may produce further, em-
bellishing elaborations that also receive evaluation. This is apparent in Carrie's
news about her new granddaughter:

(25) (Excerpt 3 with continuation)
```
1  Leslie:      Hello↑?h
2  Carrie:      Oh Les↑lie it's Carrie.
3  Leslie:      °t hOh: ↑Carrie: ↑Yes he↑llo [:.hh °hh hh
4  Carrie:                                   [I: thought you'd like to
5                know I've got a little gran'daughter
6  Leslie:  A→  °thlk ↑Oh: how love↓ly.
7  Carrie:      ↓Ye:s bo:rn th's <early hours'v this ↓morning.
8  Leslie:  B→  ˙k↑Oh: joll[y goo:d, [h
9  Carrie:                  [↓Ye:s   [↑Christi:ne ↓Ru[th.
10 Leslie:  C→                                     [˙hhhhh ↑hOh::
11               that's ↓ni::ce:.h What a nice name. eh
12 Leslie:      ↑hhah[↑heh hu ˙hhhhh
13 Carrie:           [ (Yeh'v ↑cou:rse.)
14 Leslie:      Ye:s. hheh he he ˙hhhhhhh
```

Leslie's response (arrow A) to the initial announcement (lines 4–5) is an oh-prefaced assessment; she gives high tone and emphasis to the "↑Oh:," and inserts a modifier as part of the assessment, ("how love↓ly"). These features appear to encourage progression of the sequence to Carrie's next turn elaboration (line 7). Carrie, in fact, produces two elaborations (lines 7 and 9), each of which also meets with intensified oh-prefaced assessment (arrows B and C) before the news delivery is brought to completion (lines 12–14).

Similarly, after Jenny's assessment and declaration of being pleased at the Vera's news of Milly's job application (lines 12–13 below), a further elaboration offers information (lines 14–15) about "when" and also meets with a positive assessment (line 16):

(26) (Excerpt 22 continued)
```
 6   Vera:   uRight yeh °hh Oh I met Milly:, eh:::m yestihday en
 7           she'd hahdda foh:rm from the Age Concehrn about thaht
 8           jo:b.h=
 9   Jenny:  =<Oh=she=hahs?>
10   Vera:   So: eh she wz sending the foh:rm bahck
11           [the:n  you]  know]
12   Jenny:  [Oh she di-] aOH w]'l thaht's goo:d ah'm s- ↓pleased
13           she applie:[d,
14   Vera:              [Ye:s, yes she appl- eh she: rahng up on
15           th'Mondee moh:rning.vih[know
16   Jenny:                         [M:mm Oh goo:d, [Mm↑:
17   Vera:                                          [And she's got
18           the application fohrms.=
19   Jenny:  =Ooh:: su when is ehr interview d'd she sa[:y?
20   Vera:                                             [She didn't
21           u Well ushe's gotta send thehr foh:rm ↓bahck.
22           Sh[e d'sn't know w]hen=
23   Jenny:    [O  h  :  :  .]
24   Vera:   =the [interview i : s [yet.]
25   Jenny:       [Oh it's jist th' [foh ]:rm,=
26   Vera:   =N[o.
27   Jenny:    [Yes, M[m,
28   Vera:           [No.
29   Jenny:  Ye:s °h What's happ'ning nex ↑doo:r they moving ↓in or
30           moving out . . .
```

Bad and good news deliveries therefore may involve a number of turns at talk beyond a four-part sequence, although at some point participants segue to producing "informational" topical talk (as at line 17–18 and subsequent utterances above) to which recipients respond with receipts, questions, and so on (lines 19,

23, 25, 27). At some point also, participants move to a different topic (lines 29–30), or work to bring the conversation to a close.

Assessments in relation to foregoing news delivery components. Because they represent the last components of the news delivery sequence, and are almost wholly devoted to displaying valence, assessment turns are especially important to the co-production of bad or good news. Indeed, the fourth turn of the NDS may have a feature that disavows an evaluation of the news altogether, so that it appears as something that is "just" news rather than either of the polar opposites.[18] The following instance of a death announcement was occasioned when Jenny was telling Marian about having gone for coffee next door. This discussion seems to touch off the announcement at lines 1, 3, and 5 below:

(27) **R6B/W:PC:1:MJ(1):35**
```
 1    Jenny:   1→ Oh en the o:l'la:dy. e- (0.2) °the othuh si::de.°
 2    Marian:      Ye:s:,=
 3    Jenny:    → =die:d ehm (0.5) °t (0.3) lahs'Sahtid-eh[week lahs'=
 4    Marian:                                            [↑u
 5    Jenny:    → =Sahti[day.
 6    Marian:  2→     [↑Oh:::: did -she:::::::[ee.↑h
 7    Jenny:   3→                             [Well she'd been een
 8            →  be:d.
 9    Marian:      Ye::::s::,=
10    Jenny:    → =So: uh: (0.3) Miss Carmichael's theahr on'er o:wn
11                no:w,
12    Marian:  4→ Oh:::::::,h
13                    (0.2)
14    Marian:      Mm::[:,
15    Jenny:          [And eh (0.3) yihknow she likes a little, (0.2)
16                ta:lk . . .
```

While Marian responds to the announcement encouragingly, with a newsmark (arrow 2), and Jenny elaborates on the news (arrow 3, lines 7–8, 10), Marian receives the elaboration with a stretched but otherwise bare "oh" token that only denotes her having been informed. She does not evaluate it, as might be expected, as sad or bad. Of course, the identification of the victim is an anonymous one ("the old lady on the other side"), and Marian responds to this with a continuation token ("yes," line 2) rather than a display of recognition, indicating that she may not have been acquainted with her.

When there is a valence ascription by a news recipient, it is not something that is suddenly assigned in the second turn or fourth turn in the NDS. Rather, in announcement and elaboration turns, lexical and prosodic cues often exhibit a valence and more or less induce or solicit an assessment term fitted to it. The fourth turn in particular, far from separately constituting valence, is the site of valence-ascribing work that regularly corresponds to how matters have been so far presented. Since deliverers largely produce announcements and elaborations, they, rather than recipients, would seem to have primacy in ascribing valence to news. As was discussed earlier, however, it is the party closest to or who is the primary consequential figure who has a privileged position in this regard. Consider the situation in which someone has learned about an event-in-the-world and has oriented to this event independently of interaction with those whom the event most immediately affects. That can lead to *problematic presumptiveness* when the parties meet conversationally. In excerpt (28), Moira has called Leslie, a friend whose recent burglary she had just "heard" about. Moira employs a "my side" telling, which provides for Leslie to volunteer information about the burglary. As Pomerantz (1980: 194) observes, "A 'my side' telling is intended to be heard in terms of an unformulated event that is being treated as appropriately referred to in that manner, that is, as better unsaid." Indeed, Moira's telling is an expression of regret that avoids naming the event as she both offers her help and asks Leslie whether she would "rather not talk about it" (lines 1–5):

```
(28) H10B/Holt:X(C)2:1:9:1
    1   Moira:   . . . eh Le:s °hfhh Les I just wanted a'↓sa:y
    2            °hhhhh eh:m::: °t I'm sorry about what I hea::rd
    3            abou:t (.) an' I'm not being nosey is there
    4            anything I c'n do: or (.) can I help in any
    5            wa[y o::]r would you] rather not   ] talk about it.   ]
    6   Leslie:     [↑eh::]  h e h heh↑]  What about] the ↑bu::rgelar]
    7                    (0.2)
    8   Moira:   °t ↓Ye:s
    9                    (.)
   10   Leslie:  ↑Uhhh! °hh (.) ↓No:::. It's very kind of you: °h
   11            ↑No:::. °hh In fact (.) ↑we ↓thought it wz killingly
   12            funny really.
   13                    (0.4)
   14   Moira:   ↓Oh: good
```

It is Leslie who then formulates or names the referent event with "What, about the ↑bu::rgelar" (line 6). After Moira confirms this as the basis of her inquiry (line 8), Leslie at lines 10–11 shows appreciation for the offer of help and then, following a marker of contrast ("in fact," line 11), suggests that the event was "killingly funny really" (lines 11–12), whereupon after a brief wait (line 13) Moira says, "Oh: good." So the victim here denies the need for help and volunteers a positive feature of the event, which occasions a good news assessment from the recipient. Thus, Moira having learned of the burglary elsewhere shows an orientation to it that Leslie, the victim, does not share, and their interaction displays that events do not have an intrinsic value and that conversational evaluations therefore do not necessarily correlate with any abstractly imputed value. The burglary, not worked up as bad news but as a funny happening suggests that there is no necessary equivalence between the nature of events-in-the-world and how they are embodied in actual talk and interaction. Indeed, a stronger statement is that there is no nature of events-in-the-world except as they are so embodied.

In the NDS, recipients do regularly produce assessments that correspond to matters so far presented (Freese and Maynard 1998), but not in a passive, automatic, or mechanical fashion, according to some predetermined valence of the news. Assessment turns are carefully fitted not only to predecessor turns in the news delivery sequence but to prior inquiries and presequences. In general, interactional work regarding how news is to be assessed occurs at every point from the beginning to the end of its presentation. Consider Ellen's news to Jeff that she has decided to replace her adviser (below). This is special news; placing it in first topic position, Ellen had called Jeff with the purpose of telling him this news:

```
(29) EJ:1
    1   Ellen:  tch .hh Well I wanted to shar:e some news with you:,
    2           because you'll find it relevant to your particular::
    3           (.) situati[on      ]
    4   Jeff:              [Whoo]ps. Okay hold on, let me turn off the
    5           radio hhh
    6   Ellen:  Okay.
    7               (2.6)
    8   Jeff:   .hhhh Okay lay it on me.=
    9   Ellen:  =And this news has to do with our beloved (0.2)
    10          advisor.
    11  Jeff:   I- I wouldna gue↑ssed.
    12  Ellen:  tch .hh Ye(hh)ah I knew-, I knew you wouldn't
    13          .h[hhhhhhhhhhh]
    14  Jeff:     [Well  I  hope] it's not bad news?
    15  Ellen:  Oh no, it actually is pretty good news.
    16  Jeff:   ↑OH ↑GOO:D.
    17  Ellen:  I mean (0.4) well I think it's kinda good news.
    18          [.hhhh]
    19  Jeff:   [↑Tell] me.
    20  Ellen:  Um, I decided (.) tha:t (1.0) uhm I wanted to oust
    21          him.
    22                  (0.6)
    23  Ellen:  And I decided I need to find out whadidit (.) is I
```

```
24          have to do.
25   Jeff:  hyehrh kidding:. He's not going to be yer advisor?=
26   Ellen: =No.
27                (0.6)
28   Jeff:  °h::oh my gosh.°
29   Ellen: An::d I:=
30   Jeff:  =°Wo::[:w°]
31   Ellen:       [Um] tch .h [if::-        ]
32   Jeff:                    [GOODFER] YOU:::.=
33   Ellen: =It hit me last- tha(h) (h)nks. .hh
34   Jeff:  No seriously, good fer you. That took gu:ts.
35          I'[m- ] hope I'm inspired by you.
36   Ellen: [No-]
37   Ellen: hhnh Tha↑nks hhh .hhh uh:m it hit me . . .
```

Ellen's preannouncement at lines 1–3 proposes the relevance to Jeff of the news. In response, at lines 4–5, Jeff asks Ellen to "hold on" while he turns off the radio. After Jeff returns from turning off the radio and requests the news at line 8, Ellen produces a prefacing utterance at lines 9–10. In an ironic way, she identifies a figure in the news ("our beloved advisor"), which occasions a side sequence of sarcastic humor in lines 11–13. In line 14 Jeff solicits the news in a way that prefers "good" rather than bad news.[19] Ellen produces the preferred response in line 15, indicating good news to come. Jeff then produces a positive assessment at line 16 with heightened volume and intonation. Next, Ellen proposes to downgrade the "goodness" of the news by showing the assessment to be perspectival ("I think") and suggesting that the news is "kinda good" (line 17). Then, Jeff strongly solicits and almost implores Ellen for the news in line 19, and Ellen goes on to deliver it at lines 20–24.

However, it appears to take effort for Jeff to gather what the news is. Subsequent to Ellen's first formulation—that she has "decided" to "oust" the advisor—there is lack of uptake (line 22). Then, Ellen revises her announcement in a partially escalated manner, displaying resolve to carry out the announced decision (lines 23–24). Following this, Jeff produces a candidate elaboration (line 25), which Ellen confirms (line 26), and resulting in a co-produced elaboration. Then he shows appreciation of the news (lines 28, 30, 32, and 34–35).

While the news in this episode emerges as good and also special in that it was the reason for the call rather than something that merely came up in the developing course of a conversation, Ellen seeks to play down the status of the news, and to align her recipient to it in a particular way. According to her response to Jeff's line 16 preassessment of the news, for instance, Jeff may have overreacted to how good the news might be. That is, Ellen's line 17 ("well I think it's kinda good news") is a slight modification of her previous characterization ("actually is pretty good news") and reaffirms a sense of her having medium and not spectacularly good news. While Jeff's subsequent assessments (lines 28, 30) are appreciative, they are quieted relative to the preceding one (line 16), which he speaks with elevated volume.

Following his receipts of the news (lines 28, 30), Jeff goes on to congratulate and compliment Ellen. She exhibits reluctance in accepting his praise,[20] and this feature of the episode, along with Jeff's perseverance in getting her to accept the compliments, reproduce another pattern. As the participants move through anticipation, delivery, receipt, and official assessment of news, they accord it a valence in slightly disparate although compatible ways. It is not only that assessment of the news transpires across preliminary and announcing turns, then. When applying categories such as "good" and "bad" to deliveries of news, emphasis should be placed on the relativity of these categories, and the nuance with which participants work out just how good or bad some news is. Here, according to the deliverer and main figure, the news, although being special enough to prompt a call to Jeff, is only "kinda" good, and the achievement she reported, according to her hesitating and light acceptance, perhaps only marginally worthy of the excited reaction and compliments her recipient nevertheless urged upon her.

Conclusion

In and through interactionally contingent and emergent practices, participants achieve a mutual sense of some event-in-the-world as good or bad news. Having been asked, or having preannounced, or in pursuing an initial or shifted topic, one announces with an intended valence some event and the other reciprocates with gestures marking the announced information as news and assessing it positively or negatively, usually but not always in accord with displayed anticipations. That is, through produced structures of sequential organization, participants collaboratively achieve accountable (mutually visible and oriented-to) good or bad news.

I have analyzed a news delivery sequence consisting of an announcement, response, elaboration, and assessment. This sequence occurs in both reduced form (when a news receipt, for example, helps curtail further delivery) and expanded versions (when newsmarks, elaborations, and assessments continue the delivery). These sequences are not structural *vehicles* by which information about events-in-the-world becomes news, however. As *produced* forms, they represent participants' work to display the conditions that allow for events and information to become news-of-a-particular-kind. Such conditions include the routine or special nature of the event, knowledge of and accessibility to the event, its consequential figures, how worthy the reported event is for elaboration, whether it deserves abstract or particularized assessment, the degree to which deliverer and recipient, according to what they know, pronounce the news singly or collaboratively, just how good or bad the news is, and other matters.

These conditions, displayed in and as an actual telling, accord each conversational news delivery a particularity that represents participants' moment-by-moment interactional work. Bad and good news do not represent something fixed and existing objectively in the outside world. Rather, in progressive increments of interactively produced talk, in and as their methods-in-detail[21] of informing and responding, participants accord events-in-the-world their in situ newsworthy status and their in vivo valence as good or bad.

Coda: In the Clinic

As the joke in the epigraph to this chapter illustrates, procedures of informing do not envelop, for delivery and receipt, preconstituted, already-valenced news. Consider an example showing that my argument applies to the specialized medical setting as well as to more mundane conversational interaction. The patient, Ms. E, in talk that occurs both before and after excerpt (30), expressed a concern to leave her present job, either through qualifying for disability or by taking a medical leave of absence. Prior to this visit, Ms. E had been referred to two specialists, one in psychiatry for a possible diagnosis of depression, and one in cardiology for a potential heart condition. Dr. D, a general internist and the patient's personal physician, so far had a report from the psychiatrist but not the cardiologist, and the patient's line 1 question is in regard to the psychiatrist's report:

(30) DP6,2:P2:57
```
 1  Ms. E:  W'll what did Doctor Huntington tell you?
 2  Dr. D:  We:ll? He said- (.) in the letter pretty much: (.)
 3          what you told me. He: (.) he had a chance to look over
 4          your medical records (1.3) before he wrote the letter.
 5          (1.0) .hh (0.5) and he does not think that(hh) ah
 6          depression is an important part of your illness right
 7          now.
 8                          (1.5)
 9  Dr. D:  I think that's good news.
10                          (1.5)
11  Dr. D:  >I mean< if he's right.
12                          (2.5)
13  Dr. D:  °If he's right.° It's good news. .hh And he's pretty
```

```
14          goo:d at (1.5) figuring [these things] out.=
15  Ms. E:                      [Y'well-     ]
16  Dr. D:  =I think.
17  Ms. E:  Obviously I've been having::: occasional:: (0.5)
18          periods of depression but whether they're (2.5)
19          whether they're cau:sed by the: (1.0) jumpy legs and
20          the sleeplessness [or whether]
21  Dr. D:                    [Er:right    ]
22                            (0.8)
23  Ms. E:  it's:- (.) the depression that er:: (1.3) is causing:
24                            (0.5)
25  Dr. D:  Yes::::. an: that's what ↑he was concerned with.
26                            (1.3)
27  Dr. D:  He doesn't think you hav::e a consistent major
28          depression as- psychiatrists ordinarily think of it.
29  Ms. E:  °Hm°
```

After Dr. D delivers the news that the psychiatrist disconfirmed a diagnosis of depression (lines 2–7), the patient is silent (line 8). The doctor then proposes an assessment of "good news" (line 9), and again the patient is silent (line 10). Subsequently, Dr. D suggests a contingency ("if he's right," line 11) to his good news assessment. Yet another silence occurs (line 12), followed by the doctor's repeating the contingency and characterizing the specialist's competence, although in qualified fashion (lines 13–14, 16). Finally, at lines 15, 17–20 and 23, Ms. E asserts having experienced depression, and then exhibits a vacillating stance about whether it was cause or consequence of "jumpy legs and the sleeplessness." Dr. D, at lines 21 and 25, acknowledges the psychiatrist's concern with this issue and, at lines 27–28 redelivers the news that this doctor does not think the patient has a "consistent major depression." At this point, the patient produces a most quiet and minimal acknowledgment.

Excerpt (30) illustrates how there may be disjunctiveness in medical clinics when, in the course of diagnosis, something is proposed as news and as news of a particular kind. Dr. D's delivery, that is, appears as an instance involving problematic presumptiveness. Though she asked what the psychiatrist had told the doctor, Ms. E appears not to accept that report and claims to have depression after the psychiatrist is quoted as saying that depression is not an "important part" of her illness. Nor does Ms. E affiliate with the doctor's characterizations that the report was "good news," perhaps because she was very anxious to "get out" of her job, and the psychiatrist's report would mean that she does not have a diagnosable condition to justify disability or leave. Whatever the reasons, Ms. E's silences and talk indicate strong although subtle resistance to the psychiatrist's report and Dr. D's interpretations. Whether the psychiatrist's report is to be accepted and just what kind of news it represents are left interactionally unsettled.[22]

Episodes in which participants are contentious about the newsworthiness of some report and/or whether it is good or bad news are rare although far from absent in my data.[23] When news is good from a clinical perspective, however, the problem may not be contentiousness between doctor and patient. Rather, because of the clinical logic of ruling out candidate diagnoses for a patient's ailment, often a "symptom residue" remains after a doctors inform patients of the "good news" that a particular disease is not present (Maynard and Frankel forthcoming). When a diagnostic possibility is ruled out, that is, persistent medical complaints go unexplained.

FIVE

Whose News Is This?
Social Relationships in Bad and Good News

A 40-year-old woman had extensive Hodgkin's disease which was fully explained to her and her husband by the medical registrar. "I sat there and I could see him talking but I couldn't take anything in. When I got home I burst into tears, but afterwards I calmed down and my husband explained all that had been said." [1]

The restrained way in which a patient receives bad news, like the woman who is unable to "take anything in" when told of her Hodgkin's disease, is a common occurrence. As such, this response to bad news — characteristically *stoic* — is a device to help contain the impulse to "flood out" (Goffman 1961: 55) or display strong affect, such as crying. That is, the stoic response is often *paired* with emotionality in various ways. As we shall see later in this chapter, there can be emotional "leakage" in an otherwise stoic response, which often merely delays an episode of crying, as in the example in the epigraph.[2] At other times a recipient of bad news may fluctuate between restraint and flooding out. After the judge announced that Lionel Tate, a 14-year-old found guilty of first degree murder for battering a 6-year-old girl to death when he was 12, would be sentenced to life in prison, a reporter observed, "His mother Kathleen Grossett-Tate, was at times stoic, at times weeping" (Canedy 2001). Still other times, the stoic and emotional responses may be spread across bodies, so to speak — as in clinics, when one spouse breaks down, while the other holds things together (see chapter 3, the "Donald Riccio" case). This spreading across bodies is evident in an account of how, in the U.S. presidential election in 2000, candidate Al Gore and family heard that the television networks, who initially put Florida in his victory column, had rescinded this judgment and, at 1:15 A.M., were calling the election for George Bush: "Mr. and Mrs. Gore were stoic, but some of the Gore children could not contain the tears, several advisers said" (Sack and Brun 2000). And finally, a display of emotion may simply break through or supplant any effort at restraint, as when a young woman learned from her internist that she was HIV-positive, and immediately began crying and sobbing (Quill 1991).

If an *un*impassioned response is paired in these ways with an impassioned one, nevertheless stoicism is the more predominant reaction, and it is a source of puzzlement to clinical researchers and practitioners,[3] who tend to emphasize the psychological impact that bad news has on recipients. One physician, discussing the problem of the bereaving patient, suggests:

(1) **Burgess and Lazare 1975**
The initial response to the news of the death of a loved one (or to any loss) is shock, disbelief, and numbness, especially when the loss is unexpected. The verbal response of the bereaved may be, "It's impossible," "You're joking," "I just don't believe it," or "This must be happening to someone else."

In discussing the "response to the news" the authors pay no attention to how the news gets packaged or delivered in the first place. In this chapter, I approach the enigma of the stoic response as an interactional and not just psychological phenomenon. Deliverers, we shall see, sometimes intentionally, often inadvertently, encourage stoicism on the part of their recipients.

Beyond the manner of delivery, we need to understand that the stoic response is characteristic mainly when the tidings are bad and are presented to a person who is of central consequence in the news. Other kinds of news deliveries do not so regularly involve stoicism on the part of a recipient. To the contrary, upon hearing news that is mainly about others, or that is good news about oneself, recipients usually assess the news verbally in relatively unrestrained strong terms.

To put the matter technically, deliveries of bad and good news display participants' orientation that the news is about or concerns various parties. In referential terms, the news may concern the deliverer (first party to the telling), the recipient (second party), or some third party who usually is not present during the delivery and receipt. Second-party bad news is the kind which regularly elicits stoic responses. Recipients treat first- and third-party bad and good news with an overt evaluative term of some kind, as they do when receiving good tidings about themselves. Of course, putting the matter so categorically simplifies most episodes, because news often affects not just one, but two, or even all three of these parties, whom I call the *consequential figures*. As consequential figures, first, second, and third parties are socially related to one another, and I will analyze how participants in conversation produce the visibility of these relationships. In the social science literature, investigators often view relationships as lying behind and influencing how people talk and act together, which accords relationships a kind of ethereal status, an existence outside of time and space. However, it is also possible to see how people constitute relationships in and as their talk and social interactions. This is to say that relationships are not behind anything; they are on the surface, in our overt doings and sayings. As a new world comes into being through an episode of news, participants to the presentation ineluctably build or rebuild particular forms of affiliation with one another.

To grasp the stoic response as an interactional phenomenon, then, necessitates consideration in detail of just how bad and good news involve and enact social relationships. I will explore this matter in three stages, first considering how conversational practices give life to normative features — rights and obligations — concerning the conveyance of bad and good news. Next, I will show how deliverers and recipients of bad and good news, through the use of reference terms such as names and pronouns, display aspects of their relationships with others who figure in the news. Then, I will analyze structural matters: how in the sequencing of talk, participants demonstrate the effects of the news for its consequential figures. The sequential analysis will enable a movement beyond relying on reference terms for understanding "whose news" some tidings are, and it will return us to the phenomenon of the stoic response as an interactional phenomenon.

Enacting Relationships: Offering and Asking for News

In my conversational data, participants are friends and in some cases relatives of one another. Gans's (1962: 77–79) observation (reported in chapter 1) bears repeating: The exchange of news among friends and kin on various topics from births to weddings to (presumably) deaths and many things in between "defines or redefines the place of the reporter and his audience in this large group."[4] Not exchanging news has, in fact, the potential for causing a breach in relationships:

(2) **Landers 2000**

Dear Ann Landers: I hope you will help me with an etiquette question. My sister and I are currently not on speaking terms. She recently became engaged. My mother called me and said, "Mary wants to know why you have not phoned to congratulate her on her engagement." I replied that Mary has a telephone and that it is *her* responsibility to call and tell me about her engagement. . . . *Bewildered in Westchester, Ill.*

Dear Be: You were not remiss for failing to offer congratulations. It is incumbent on the person whose celebration it is to notify family members and friends. Laying the blame on you is a cop-out. Don't buy it.

Sharing news is obligatory; when bearers of bad or good news come into the presence of kin or others who have a right to it, they should present it then and there or risk complaint (Sacks 1992a: 702). Accordingly, Button and Casey (1985: 29) demonstrate that when an open-ended *topic initial elicitor* such as

"How are things?," "What's doin'?," or "What's new?," draws nothing from a co-participant who is known to have news, the asker may follow the no-news response with a query (see arrow below) that has an *accusatory* character to it:

(3) HG:II:1 (Button and Casey 1985: 29)

```
1   Nancy:     What's doin
2                    (.)
3     Hyla:    aAh;, noth[in:,        ]
4   Nancy:  →          [Y'didn't g]o meet Graham?
5     Hyla:    ,pt .hhhhahh'Well, I got ho::me,=
6   Nancy:    =u-hu:h?
7                    (.)
8     Hyla:    Ayu::n:: .hh he hadn' called yet 'n there weren't any
9              messages'r . . .
```

Here, Nancy follows up on her initial elicitor (line 1) and Hyla's no-news response (line 3) with a query claiming that a meeting was to have occurred between Hyla and Graham, which can suggest that a report is due to Nancy about it. Hyla then (lines 5, 8–9) produces an account for her not having any news.

Indeed, at times the acquisition of some bad or good news can motivate a get-together (if only a telephone call) in the first place, particularly when the bearer of news has a sense of responsibility toward someone and perceives a "need to know."[5] Sacks (1992b) expands on his point about the obligatoriness of conveying bad and good news:

> if someone has some very large news that would involve having sorrow or joy about it, then it's their business to call others up while they still have the sorrow or joy. And it's not only their business to call others up while they still have the sorrow or joy, but they should tell it to them right off. And furthermore, if you're called up and you have a sorrow or joy to tell, then you should tell it right off. (472)

My suggestion is that presenting and hearing news in conversation is *reflexive* to the relationship of involved parties. As participants observe peer (kinship, friendship) rights and obligations for letting each other know the latest news, they are, *in their practices,* behaviorally accomplishing or achieving the visibility of those relations. That is, when potential deliverers *offer* news, they partially signify in that offering the very relation that obligates their telling. Also, when potential recipients *ask* for news, they are, in their attentiveness, performing particular concerns and enacting a social connection with their interlocutor. For example, the following excerpt is from a call in which Leslie has called Joyce to ask about Joyce's husband, Lord Geoff. Leslie asks a series of solicitous questions (lines 2, 9–10, 12–13, 17, and 19).

(4) H4G/Holt:M88:1:2:2
```
 1  Joyce:   Hello:?
 2  Leslie:  ehHello: how did Lo::rd (.) Geoff: get on.=
 3  Joyce:   =Oh hn: not ↓too bad:d not too ba:d,
 4  Leslie:  ˙hhhh-
 5           (.)
 6  Joyce:   They got im home alright abou(.)t uh:m::[:: one=
 7  Leslie:                                          [˙hhhh
 8  Joyce:   =o'clock I spoze (     [        )
 9  Leslie:                      [Oh ↓goo:d. He made good ↓time
10           the[n.
11  Joyce:      [↑Ye:s he di[:d.      [(
12  Leslie:                 [°hhh 'N[is he feeling better now a
13           little bit?=
14  Joyce:   =Mrwm, not really no:,=
15  Leslie:  =No: Poor chap.hh[hh         [hhhhhhe:ahhhhhhhh]hh
16  Joyce:                   [No eez not [feeling very well]
17  Leslie:  hAh↓:.[Still it's all: ↓over with h[n eh Will ↑he=
18  Joyce:        [Mm:;,                         [Ye:h (      )
19  Leslie:  =ha-:ve= the resu:lt yet,
```

Leslie displays prior knowledge of whatever the situation is in which Lord Geoff and Joyce are embedded, and with the call and this question series, she performs her concern for Lord Geoff and for Joyce, this performance being an aspect of methodically enacting a relationship of friendship with them.

Hence, in examining how announcements of news portray and display relationships, it must be understood that conversational episodes of bad and good news are, in a bearer's sheer selection of whom and when to tell, or in a hearer's decisions about when and how to solicit such news, already imbued with relational implications and doings. Henceforth, my analysis will assume this reflexivity and will concentrate less on (while not abandoning) the methods by which participants offer and ask for news and attend more to *overt* displays of relationship and sequentially positioned claims about consequences, which can be various in nature. Table 5.1 summarizes patterns to the delivery and receipt of bad and good news according to the displayed relationships of consequential figures. My analysis follows the ordering depicted there. I will begin by analyzing third-party news, then first-party (deliverer's) news, and, finally, second-party episodes, or those in which recipients are the primary figure.

Any schematic is going to severely gloss the details of how participants give and receive good and bad news. Table 5.1 suggests that the predominant mode for displaying a primary consequential figure is, in an announcing utterance, to refer to that figure in grammatical subject position and to predicate something

Table 5.1 Good and Bad News: Patterns of Delivery and Receipt according to Displays of Consequential Figures

	Primary Consequential Figure					
	(A) Third Party is primary figure		(B) First Party (Deliverer) is primary figure		(C) Second Party (Recipient) is primary figure	
	Delivery	Receipt	Delivery	Receipt	Delivery	Receipt
Kind of News						
Good	(Preannounce or preface) + 3rd party reference + did or has something good[1]	(Go ahead or blocking move) + Assessment and/or claim of "pleased," "happy," etc.	(Preannounce or preface) + 1st party reference + did or has something good[3]	(Go ahead or blocking move) + Assessment and/or claim of "pleased" and/or congratulations	(Preannounce or preface) + 1st-party reference + did or has something good for 2nd party reference	(Go ahead or blocking move) + Assessment and/or appreciation to deliverer
Bad	3rd party reference + did or has something bad[2]	Assessment and/or declaration of "sorry," etc.	1st party reference + did or has someting bad[4]	Assessment and/or declaration of "sorry," etc.	Reporting circumstances, giving reasons for unstated bad new upshot[5]	Stoic response, or "flooding out"
Examples	[1]"She's completely clear [of cancer] . . ." [2]"He died suddenly this week . . ." (Complication: news between "monitors" of an intimate's plight may be devoid of reference to consequential figures.)		[3]"I gotta raise . . ." [4]"I didn't pass my driving test . . ."		[5]"I found your ring . . ." [6]"She decided to go away this weekend . . . I don't have a place to stay."	

good or bad as having happened. While such a *subject-predicating* format often does reference the primary figure in that way, we will also see that there are considerable complications. Referencing of consequential figures is by no means a straightforward matter. For example, to show how "self" is a consequential figure in news about another (third party), a deliverer may embed the news in a developing narrative rather than in a forthright announcement. Or, when participants are closely monitoring the circumstances of a third party, deliveries of news may contain no reference to the party or parties whom deliverer and recipient nevertheless know to be the consequential figure(s). Still another complication is that, with second-party *good* news (recipient is the primary figure), the grammatical subject in an announcement may be the deliverer, who works to claim at least partial credit for the recipient's good news. Consequently, the news recipient and main figure of the news, in particular tellings, may be the grammatical object. Finally, with second-party *bad* news, the deliverer may engage in reporting circumstances or evidence implying an unstated upshot. Sometimes the grammatical subject in the announcement is a third party who may have caused the bad news for the recipient, and other times (as in clinics) the deliverer may simply tell the results of a test; in either case, the primary figure and recipient of the news is not mentioned.[6]

Announcements of Third-Party News: Displays of Relationship

Announcements of third-party news are in the format [third-party reference + did or has something (bad or good)], or in slight variations to this format.[7] In excerpt (5), Carrie preannounces some news (line 1 below) in a way that also presents the source of that projected news. Then, following Skip's go-ahead (line 2), Carrie reaffirms her source (the "letter"), produces an assessment ("well over eighty now, she's marvelous"), and reports a past "operation for cancer" before announcing the good news (arrow, line 8). This announcement, depending on the prefacing report, is in the regular format ("she's + completely clear").

(5) H17G
```
1   Carrie:  We ↑got a letter↑ fr'm Rhonda Griffen?
2    Skip:  ·hh ↑hOh[ y  e : s  ?  ]
3   Carrie:           [(I heard) fr'm] ↓he:r
4               (0.6) ((clattering))
5   Carrie:  an:d had a ↓letter from ↑her ·hh Because she:'s well
6            over eighty now, she's marv'lous. ·hh She had a big
7            operation for cancer about three or four years ago,
8        →   ·hh and she's: completely clea:r.
9               (0.2)
```

```
10     Skip:   ˙tlkOh goo:d. Goo:d. Oh that's g[rea:t.
11   Carrie:                                [(     ) got to see a
12             specialist agai:n? She's now moved into another
13             bungalow . . .
```

Skip assesses the news at line 10 with standardized terms, directed to an evaluation of the medical situation in which Rhonda Griffen is the primary figure. Subsequent talk preserves reference to Rhonda, as Carrie elaborates on her seeing a specialist, moving, and (in talk not in the excerpt) doing other things.

Now, how does Carrie's referencing of Rhonda Griffen denote relationship? First, between Carrie and Rhonda, the relationship is portrayed as one of informal correspondence and by extension a friendship. Beyond this, conversational practices for referencing third-party figures embody indications of relationship. As Sacks and Schegloff (1979) demonstrate, when reference is made to persons in conversation, there are two operative preferences. One is for speakers to minimize referencing by use of a single form, even though on any occasion of referencing there may be a large set of forms that, singly or in combination, can do the job. As examples, Sacks and Schegloff mention that "he, Joe, my uncle, someone, Harry's cousin, the dentist, the man who came to dinner, et cetera" (17), can all refer to the same person, but a speaker usually would, if possible, use only one of these when talking about the person. The other preference is to use *recognitionals,* or forms that invite and allow a recipient to recover the identity of the referent. These two preferences are compatible; when speakers refer to a person by naming, and use a first name (as in "Joe came by the other night"), they are doing minimal reference and assuming that a single form is adequate for recipients' recognition of the referent. But Sacks and Schegloff also observe that when the preferences compete — that is, when recognition cannot be achieved through a minimal form — the orientation to minimization is relaxed in favor of achieving recognition.

In excerpt (5), the reference form is first and last name — a slight relaxation of minimal reference — which would indicate Carrie's inference that first name alone might not work for Skip's recognition of the subject. Also, Carrie gives upward intonation to Rhonda Griffen's name, which is a way of *asking* for a display of recognition and shows that Carrie does not *assume* Skip's ability to know who the referent is even with her use of both names. At line 2, Skip does show recognition of the referenced party, so it is apparent that no further referencing is necessary. Nevertheless, because of the reference form and recognition work, Skip would appear to be relatively distanced in relationship from this party.

Where excerpt (5) involves good news, our next excerpt allows examination of referencing practices in an episode of *bad* news. Leslie announces that

Mrs. Cole is very ill (line 1). The formal way of referencing this party is an initial indication of a distanced relationship between these participants and the primary figure. Furthermore, the initial reference to "Mrs. Cole," elaborated by calling her "old," is also extended through Leslie's use of a try-marker ("d' you 'member," lines 1–2) and initiation of an insertion sequence whose first part seems to pose "Carol" (by virtue of first-name usage) as the party closest to Leslie and also best known by Mum; it is the husband of this party whom Leslie asks Mum to remember. The second part of the insertion sequence is a display of recognition ("Oh yes?") at line 3. The second "yes" at line 4 promotes a return to the news announcement, suggesting that the recollection of Philip Cole is also enough for Mum to recognize the reference to Mrs. Cole.

(6) **H4Ba/Holt:X(C)1:1:1:2**

```
 1   Leslie:   OH: uh:m: (0.6) ↑Old Missiz Co:le is very ill d'you
 2             'member Philip Co:le, Carol's: (.) husba:n[d?
 3   Mum:                                              [↑Oh ↓ye:s?
 4             Ye-:s,
 5                              (.)
 6   Leslie:   She had a stroke in Cary last wee[k.
 7   Mum:                                       [↑Oh: ↓dea-:r.
 8   Leslie:   And she seems t'be faili:ng
 9   (Mum):    ° ° (          ) ° °
10                            (0.7)
11   Mum:      She's ↑(quite'n) old lady wasn't she.
```

After Leslie completes her announcement (line 6), Mum receives and assesses the news with a standardized assessment ("oh dear," at line 7). With the complicated way in which identification and recognition are achieved, then, Mum is exhibited as socially related to the primary figure in only a distanced way.

Participants deliver third-party news using a format that informs on a primary figure by putting them in subject position in an announcing utterance and predicating what the figure did or experienced (Table 5.1). These are not just any third parties, however, but are, through acquaintance or friendship, in a relationship of relative propinquity to the deliverer of the news as well as the recipient. In that it is deliverer who has knowledge of whatever condition of the third party is reported on, the third party is shown to be socially more proximate to the deliverer. It is as if the deliverer mediates between the third party and the news recipient, but beyond this, when announcing their news, deliverers' referencing practices further define a relationship between the third party and recipient of the news. The longer or more complex the referencing identification, the more social distance there appears to be between the third party and the news recipient.

Third-Party News: Consequential Figures

Even if primarily about other parties, bad and good news can be consequential for deliverer and recipient in a range of ways as well. Excerpts (5) and (6) are minimally consequential in the sense that neither deliverer nor recipient makes any strong claim of concern over the situation of the third party.[8] At times, the participants to a news delivery do make such claims.

Third-Party News That Concerns Teller

News deliverers sometimes have news about a third party and also show themselves to be a figure in the situation. For example, a bearer of death news may lead into this news by telling her recipient that she is "going to a funeral on Tuesday" (chapter 4, excerpt (18)). As a kind of headline, this turn obtains an alignment from the recipient that allows for the elaboration that Philip Cole's mother "died." Another device whereby a deliverer can portray herself as a consequential figure is to render news in a narrative fashion, as in excerpt (7) below. Recall that Leslie had called to find out how Joyce's husband, Lord Geoff, who had undergone some medical testing, was doing. Joyce replied that he was "not too bad" but that he was not feeling very well. Now, Leslie asks about the tests (line 1 below), and obtains Joyce's good news (lines 22, 24, 26, 28, 31–32):

(7) **(Excerpt 4 continued)**
```
20   Leslie:  Will ↑he ha-:ve the resu:lt yet.
21                    (0.5)
22   Joyce:   Yes we saw Mister Williams:.
23   Leslie:  [Yes ]
24   Joyce:   [an:'] um: °p I went t'pick im up
25                    (.)
26   Joyce:   Mister Williams came in 'n said °hhh you'll be glad
27            to know I checked him and °hhh a:-nd uh it's uh (0.3)
28            ↑clear:: as a whistle 'e [said,
29   Leslie:                           [°hhhh Oh ↑that's
30            ↓mar[v'lous.]
31   Joyce:       [N o : :] No problems at ↓all, 'e said aren't ya
32            plea:sed? I said yes::?
33   Leslie:  Oh ↓good.
```

In the narrative, Joyce herself appears as either one of the recipients or perhaps the only recipient in an informing scene, to which she has access because she went to pick up her husband. In the focal part of Joyce's narrative (lines 26–28), the doctor, Mr. Williams, arrives at this scene, and then is quoted as announcing his findings. As will be seen when we consider second-party (recipients') good

news, the doctor's quoted delivery is a way "claiming credit"—of showing himself to have done something to bring about the good news. After Leslie hears the
quoted announcement (lines 26–28), she produces an assessment at lines 29–
30. The positioning of this assessment just subsequent to the Lord Geoff reference targets him and his "clear as a whistle" status.

Now it becomes clear how Joyce herself is part of that situation. At lines 31–
32, Joyce, overlapping Leslie's assessment, continues her narrative by quoting a
second version of the doctor's news ("N̲o problems at ↓all"). This reaffirms the
first clear-as-a-whistle diagnosis, and can propose to finalize the informing about
test results. To this, Joyce adds that the doctor inquired ("aren't ya plea:sed?")
about her own reaction. The doctor's "you" references Joyce; he is shown to observe that the news directly concerns his recipient, or second party, as well as the
third party, her husband. And she depicts herself as answering the doctor by having agreed with the proposal in his question. This quoted question–answer sequence,[9] within the narrative, is now sequentially implicative for Leslie's next
turn of talk. When Leslie produces a subsequent assessment, "Oh good" (line
33), it therefore evaluates both the husband's news and his wife's reaction to it.
In other words, Leslie appears to be commenting that it's good that there are
"no problems" for the husband *and* that Joyce herself is pleased.

This example permits us to further define terms that have already been used.
Joyce gives the good news about Lord Geoff in a way that from the outset shows
herself as a secondary figure in the news delivery situation (she is a recipient of
the news) about another party, her husband. In the narrative, it is her husband
(third party) who is primary; news about him is first presented and assessed. The
delivery eventuates in a demonstration of just how she also figures in that situation (she is one who is pleasurably affected by the news). Accordingly, a device
for displaying how a third-party's news is consequential for a deliverer (self) is
to render the news in a narrative fashion and to portray self as a consequential
figure within the narrative. Another example, from chapter 4, involves bad
news:

(8) **H08B/Holt:X(C)1:2:7:7**
```
 1  Leslie:  ˙hh Well I've ↑written to you in the letter
 2           K̲atharine's: ↓f̲ace is still hurting he:r?
 3               (.)
 4    Mum:   ↑Oh ↓dea̲:r.=
 5  Leslie:  =S̲o uhm: she's g̲oing t'see our d̲octor when she comes
 6           ho[me.
 7  (Mum):     [(        )
 8               (0.3)
```

    9   Leslie: ˙hh An' I'll gẹt her fịxed up with a dẹ:ntist toọ:,
   10   (0.7)
   11   Mum: Oh w't a ↓nuisance ịsn't ↓it. Is ịt ↓ey:e teẹ:th?

After a preface informing mum that her forthcoming news is in a letter,[10] Leslie's announcement at lines 1–2 refers to her daughter Katharine's "face" as "hurting he:r?". Mum's "↑Oh ↓dea:r" at line 4 therefore hearably evaluates Katharine's situation. Then, elaborating on the news, Leslie at lines 5–6 reports a consequential action of Katharine that affects Leslie in the bad news situation, albeit in a passive way: Katharine will see "our" doctor after coming "home." A second consequence (notice the connective, "An' . . . ," line 9) depicts Leslie in a more active role; she will fix Katharine up with a dentist. Then, Mum's "oh w't a nuisance" (line 11) can be assessing Leslie's secondary involvement as well as Katharine's primary predicament.

   In a variety of ways, deliverers claim to be affected by third-party news. They may start their bad news by reporting the consequences of this news for themselves. Or they may produce an announcement by narrating how they (as tellers) experienced something as a consequence of what happened to the third party. If the initial announcement references only the third party, then after the announcement response, an elaboration may employ a narrative form that exhibits the teller as a consequential, secondary figure. Thus, although the deliverer may be in an abstractly close relationship to the third party by virtue of being a wife (excerpt (7)), mother (8), or other relative, this may say little about the concreteness of the relationship. That third-party news can be taken to affect the news deliverer derives not so much from the categorical relationship between deliverer and the third party as it does from the practices whereby deliverer inserts self into the news situation, experiencing the situation because of what happened to the primary figure. The kinds of consequences may range from the more subjective (being "pleased," for example) to the more practical (having to support or help someone).

Third-party News That Concerns Recipient

   Either deliverer, or recipient, or both can demonstrate in their talk whether or how some third-party news concerns the recipient. However, deliverer and recipient do so according to their positions in producing the news delivery sequence. A deliverer *proposes* third-party news to concern a recipient in a preannouncement or other type of preface to the news announcement. Recipients *claim* how news is consequential for them in turns subsequent to the news announcement.

In an example involving bad news, at lines 1–3 in excerpt (9), Betty, who is from out of town and is paying a visit to her son, has called Fanny. They discuss the possibility of getting together, and then Betty indicates that she has held off telling her recipient, Fanny, some "terrible" news because, during a previous opportunity, Fanny was with "company." In discussing the obligation to tell news to friends and relatives, Sacks (1992a) remarks on the "further obligations *not* to announce something even if someone whom you ought to tell it to is present, when others who ought not to hear it are also present" (703). On Betty's part, the effect of such an obligation here is a display of concern for Fanny, in a turn precedent to the delivery of the news. The excerpt is also an example of how the recipient of the bad news, by virtue of the clues that she is given, is herself able to pronounce the news.[11]

(9) **Death Announcement**
```
 1    Betty:  I: uh::: I did wanna tell you en I didn'wanna tell
 2            you uh::::::: uh:: las'ni:ght. Uh:: because you had
 3            entuht-uh:: company I, I-I had something (.) terrible
 4            t'tell you.=
 5    Betty:  =So[ u h: ]
 6    Fanny:     [How t]errible[is  it .]
 7    Betty:                   [.hhhhh]
 8            (.)
 9    Betty:  Uh: ez worse it could be:.
10            (0.7)
11    Fanny:  W'y'mean Eva?
12            (.)
13    Betty:  Uh yah .hh=
14    Fanny:  =Wud she do die:?,=
15    Betty:  =Mm:hm,
16            (.)
17    Fanny:  When did she die,
18            (0.2)
19    Betty:  Abou:t uh:::(v) (.) four weeks ago.
20            (.)
21    Fanny:  °Oh how horrible.
```

After Fanny guesses the news (line 14), it is confirmed (line 15), and the timing of the event is established (lines 17–19), Fanny produces an oh-prefaced assessment at line 21 ("oh how horrible") that deals with the death situation and does so in a way that fits with Betty's preannouncing characterization of "terrible."

Such an assessment is somewhat distanced from its object; it evaluates the bad-news event but does not *personalize* it. While Betty has proposed that the news concerns Fanny specifically, Fanny does not display, at least here, how the news may affect her. Subsequent talk is occupied with a discussion of the circumstances of the death, and Eva's "wanting" to die, her unhappiness, and other matters. Later in the conversation, after the discussion of the death of another acquaintance's husband, and others who have died in "that generation," Betty suggests, as a way of moving toward closing the call, that the news about Eva was why she called Fanny:

(10) **Sequel to Death Announcement**
```
1    Betty:  =Th[at's why I ca:lledju Fa[nny I]thought thatchu would=
2    Fanny:      [(And)                [(   )]
3    Betty:  =want t'know.
4                        (.)
5    Betty:  [.hhhhhhhhh]
6    Fanny:  [We:ll I em]a:wflly sorry that's all I c'n sa:y.
```

So Betty further proposes that the news is consequential for Betty ("I thought thatchu would want t'know") and that it was the reason for the call. Moreover, Fanny does finally claim how the news is consequential for her: she's "a:wflly sorry." This personal-state marker ratifies Betty's proposal about the news affecting Fanny and collaborates in the display of Fanny as a secondary consequential figure.

Recipients can and do show news to be consequential to themselves more immediately, for example, just after a news delivery sequence assessment turn:[12]

(11) **R2G/Rahman I:8**
```
1    Jenny:  . . . cuz she said she wouldn' be going if Milly wz going
2            t'thaht keep fit thing.
3    Vera:   uRight yeh °hh Oh I met Milly:, eh:::m yestihday en
4            she'd hahdda foh:rm from the Age Concehrn about thaht
5            jo:b.h=
6    Jenny:  =<Oh=she=hahs?>
7    Vera:   So: eh she wz sending the foh:rm bahck
8            [the:n you]   know]
9    Jenny:  [Oh she di-] aOH w]'l thaht's goo:d ah'm s- ↓pleased
10           she applie:d,
```

At lines 9–10, Jenny displays a change of state ("OH") and produces a standardized assessment "w'l thaht's goo:d," which comments on Milly's situation. Then Jenny says "ah'm s- ↓pleased she applie:d." Briefly and succinctly, Jenny appends to her assessment a claim about the consequences the news has for her. Although Vera neither shows it to be the reason for the call nor introduces it by formulating its particular relevance for Jenny, the latter treats Vera's introduction of the news as virtually having proposed that relevance. Jenny both assesses the news and personalizes it.

Sequential structure and consequential figures. Beyond using reference forms that indicate relationship, deliverers have ways of showing that third-party news is consequential for them. As well, deliverers, recipients, or both can indicate that some third-party news particularly concerns the recipient. Deliverers may show themselves to be consequential figures by headlining their focal news, or through a narrative rendering of their tidings. Otherwise, when deliverers or recipients emerge as secondary consequential figures, it is by way what they do before and after the focal news delivery sequence in which some third party is referenced and something good or bad is predicated as happening to that party. These preceding and succeeding declarations of consequence for deliverer or recipient transform what might otherwise be only or *solely* third party tidings — news that does not officially affect the participants to a news delivery, as in the excerpts concerning "Rhonda Griffen" (5) and "Mrs. Cole" (6) — into an event that has more local and intimate consequences, as in excerpts (8) through (11). In declaring the effects of third-party news for themselves, deliverers and recipients exhibit their relationship to that third party to be relatively close, at least as compared to news deliveries in which deliverers and recipients make no such declarations. Positioning these declarations before or after the focal news that references a third party effectively places a membrane around the news and its receipt that helps constitute a third party as the primary figure and the deliverer and/or recipient as secondary consequential figures.

Refraining from Reference in the Delivery and Receipt of Third-Party News

Through seeking to tell others or asking others for some news, through referencing, and through proposals and claims about its consequences, participants not only inaugurate a new social world. They simultaneously render particular interrelations among various figures as constituent and visible features of that new world. Paradoxically, at times, neither deliverers nor recipients may demonstrate in their talk how news is consequential for them, although it manifestly involves either or both very strongly. This matter, a complication noted at the bottom of column A in table 5.1, returns us to the phenomenon of the reflexive relation between news and the relationship of parties who share it. When a mother is about to give birth, or someone is gravely ill, for instance, those who are relationally close to that third party may monitor the situation with such regularity that the news can be conveyed trenchantly and succinctly, without verbalizing how it affects deliverer or recipient or both. (Per chapter 4, these birth, death, or other announcements may motivate telephone contact and, as the "reason for the call" mark the informing episode as a special one as compared to the more routine kind that arises in the course of interaction between regular conversants.) The urgency with which the news is conveyed and the compactness of the announcement index an affinity among the consequential figures as participants to the informing share the news in a *pithy* manner and thereby weave further strands in the web of their interrelationships.

In an ethnographic study of a small community in a Tampa, Florida apartment building for single people with AIDS, Cherry (1996) explores how the illness and death of one resident, Mike Farano, affected members of this community. Toward the end, those who were closest to Farano visited him in his room and kept one another apprised of his physical and psychological state. The members of this community had become close to Mike's mother and, just before his death, decided to make a plaque that would express their appreciation for her role in taking care of Mike during his last few weeks. Mike died on the very day that the group had planned to present the plaque to his mother.

(12) **Cherry 1996: 63**

> After my classes end at noon, I stop home to take a short nap. This has been a very long week. The phone rings at 1:40 p.m.
> "Hello."
> "Keith?"
> "Hi — Marshall. How's it going?"
> "Fine."
> Not fine. His voice is straining.
> "Mikey died at 1:20."
> "Well, do you still want to do this?"
> "Yeah. We wanna do it, but we wanna wait until the body's out of the apartment."

Marshall, the caller in this recollected conversation, and Keith, the call recipient, are among Mike's close friends, and both are part of the group that has been keeping watch over his health and planning the plaque ceremony for his mother. Whereas when news announcements occur in the course of an ongoing conversation, and participants do not mark the news as consequential for themselves, it may indicate a distanced relationship from the third party, here the opposite is the case. Neither deliverer or recipient declares, in this remembered version of their talk, how the news affects them, except with a paralinguistic leakage on the part of the deliverer whose strained voice allows the recipient's inference that things are "not fine." Otherwise, Marshall rather bluntly tells the news and Keith does not comment on or assess the news, instead taking a practical stance and asking about the plaque ceremony.

The very intensity of monitoring relationships allows for consequences to be

understood without being stated. Carolyn Ellis's (1993) narrative of how she
learned of her brother's death in a plane crash is a further illustration. This is a
scene when, after having heard about the crash (but not yet knowing whether
her brother was a survivor), Ellis's partner, Gene, arrives home, and she rushes
to the door:

(13) **Ellis 1993: 714**

> "What's wrong, honey?" Gene asks as he steps through the door, drops his pack-
> ages to the floor, and embraces me. Quietly and desperately, I say, "My brother's
> plane crashed." "Oh, my God," he says calmly. Do something, I want to yell,
> Make it okay. But I say nothing. His body quivers; his embrace tightens. It feels
> good to be held and to have told someone.

As a face-to-face rather than telephone encounter, it illustrates how a terse delivery and receipt of news can be connected to an embrace or other gestures that
demonstrate an understanding of the effect of the news on a consequential figure
without verbalizing that effect.

In both of these examples, despite how the news intimately affects both the
deliverer and recipient, there is no explicit reference to either. However, in both
there is reference to the third party as primary figure. Marshall uses first-name
reference in telling Keith about Mike, and Carolyn Ellis refers to "my brother"
in reporting the plane crash to Gene. Just as it is possible to refrain from referencing profoundly affected secondary figures (deliverer and recipient), reference
to that primary figure can be avoided too. Excerpt (14) is from a conversation
between a father and son:[13]

(14) **SDCL:malignancy I (Beach/SDSU)**

```
 1   Son:   What's up.
 2                 (0.4)
 3   Dad:   .hhhhh (.) They ca:me back with thee::: hh (0.2)
 4          needle b[iop]sy results or at least in: (.) part.
 5 (Son):            [( )]
 6                 (.)
 7   Son:   Mm [hm. ]
 8   Dad:      [.hhh]hh the tumor::, that is thee:: adrenal gland
 9          tumor tests positive, it is: malignant,
10   Son:   O:kay?
11   Dad:   .hhh uh::m=
12   Son:   =That's the one above her kidney?
13   Dad:   Yeah. tch
14                 (0.3)
15   Son:   °pt° Okay:, ah gee I didn't even re:alize there was a
```

```
16          tu:mor there, I knew sh[e had a problem] I [thought=
17   Dad:                        [We::ll okay     ]  [.hhh:::
18   Son:  =it w[as-  ]
19   Dad:       [may-] maybe I'm not sayin' it right. .hhh There
20          is- I don't kno:w that there is a tumor there. They:
21          nee:dle biopsied thee adrenal gla:::nd.=
22   Son:  =O[kay.  ]
23   Dad:     [I gues]s that's what I should say .hhh and that one
24          came back testing positive.
25   Son:  Mm:ka:y.
26   Dad:  .hhh They: di::d uh:: (.) double: needle biopsy:: of:
27          thee: (.) lu:ng .hhh that one they do not have the
28          results on.
29                 (0.6)
30   Son:  °Jee[sus°]
31   Dad:       [.hhh]h So:: the doctor was in there tonight . . .
```

The person whose "needle biopsy results" (lines 3, 4) were "positive" and "malignant" (line 9) is the wife of Dad and the mother of Son (and, consistent with the transcription identities, I shall call her "Mom"), but no reference is made to her as Dad announces the news here by way of "citing the evidence" (Maynard 1991) rather than predicating a condition of the primary figure in a more assertive manner. The first references to this figure are at line 12 when Son mentions "her kidney," and at 16 when he reports knowing "she had a problem." Son's use of these indexical or contextually embedded terms exhibits his understanding that Dad's initial reference to the biopsy and test results invoke Mom's situation. In other words, Dad's way of announcing the news "historicalizes" this conversation relative to past conversations and understandings (Sacks 1992b: 193) and can be a way of doing "being intimate."[14] Son, as well as Dad, were well aware of Mom's previous history with cancer, knew that Mom was undergoing a new biopsy, and that the results were imminent (Beach 2002).

To the extent that bad news about mother to her son is consequential for him, and to the extent that this news, from the man who is her wife, is also consequential for *him,* then this is an episode in which deliverer and recipient make no reference either to the third party as primary figure or themselves as secondary consequential figures. Instead the episode shows that a nonreferential mode of delivery can index the close relations among all the parties. In other words, an event-in-the-world may mean a catastrophic change for some primary figure. As secondary figures transmit news about this event to one another, they may intimately share the changed social world augured in the news, precisely as its presentation and reception lack overt mention about who is affected and how.

Announcements of First-Party (Deliverer's) News

First-party news is that in which the deliverer is the primary figure. In its consequences, it sometimes appears as this party's own news, because no consequences are proposed or claimed for the second party (the news recipient). At other times, the news is portrayed as also affecting or having consequences for the recipient.

Solely First-Party News

Here are two excerpts involving good news; the announcement and its response are arrowed in each instance.

```
(15)  R9G/Rah:B:1:VMJ(10):2
    1    Vera:      An' then Alan en:s °eh:m (.) Norma came round jis °we
    2               jis ghot in las' ni: [ght,°
    3    Jenny:                         [Ooo well wasn'thaht lucky
    4               thetchu went whe[n you did] then.=
    5    Vera:                      [Y e : s,]
    6    Vera:   1→ =ahnd oh we hadda smashing ni:ght.
    7    Jenny:  2→ Yih ↑di:d oh thaht's goo:[d then. ]
    8    Vera:                               [Y e : s.]
    9    Vera:      Buu:t Valerie said the same tuh me: by: Gud she looks
    10              olduh th'n me she sai(hd)d.

(16)  NB6G/NB:II:2:R
    1    Emma:      ˙hh How you ↑doin.
    2    Nancy:  1→ ˙t hhh Pretty good. I gutta rai:se.h °hh[hh
    3    Emma:   2→                                        [Kuu: [ud
    4    Nancy:  3→                                              [↑Yeh
    5               two dollars a week.h
```

In a fashion similar to solely third-party news, the announcement refers to a party (here, the speaker) about whom something good is predicated (see table 5.1, column B). That is, the deliverer reports something good having happened to self or that self did. The recipient may mark the announcement as news (excerpt (15), "yih↑d:id," line 7) and, in any case, produces a positive assessment.[15] The assessment turn may be followed by a confirmation and topic change (15, line 9) or elaboration concerning the first-party's news, as in excerpt (16), lines 4–5).

First-party bad news is similarly done in a predicating format, and may be part of an overall troubles-telling sequence. Jefferson (1988: 420) has described a "series of recurrent elements" in conversations in which participants talk about troubles; the announcement of the first-party's or teller's bad news and a recipi-

ent's responses occur as part of an order of surrounding activities that, according to contingently developing sequences, allow for the troubles to be told and
handled in particular ways. For example, there often is a segmental approach to
the news, followed by exposition, work-up, close-implicature matters, and exit.
Here, I concentrate only on the news delivery and receipt, which occupy the
mid-portion of the overall troubles-telling sequence. At lines 1, 2, 4, and 6–7 below, Dana announces her eye trouble, following which Gordon produces a
standardized oh-prefaced assessment (line 8).

(17) **H19B/Holt:88U:1:4:3**
```
 1     Dana:  1→ But um (0.7) all mu- this morning (0.3)
 2                → uh[:m (0.5) I: (0.2) my eye's been=
 3   Gordon:          ['k h-h-h h h h h h h
 4     Dana:  → =really [itching badly=
 5   Gordon:              [°h h h h h h
 6     Dana:  → ='n .hh we've been (0.2) throwing boiling water in it
 7               'n stuff ['n it (.)] [itches a lot. .hh         ]
 8   Gordon:  2→        [Oh dear] [hhhhhhhhhhhhhhhhhh]
 9                          (0.3)
10     Dana:  So um (0.4) at's really nice an' um (0.2) las' night
11             I got off the phone . . .
```

After Dana's announcement and after Gordon's assessment is a place where
Gordon might further align as a troubles recipient, for example with a solicitous
inquiry. Instead, there is a silence (line 9), subsequent to which Dana produces
an apparently ironic comment and then changes topic (lines 10–11), in a pose
of troubles-resistance.

  Another instance of troubles resistance is reproduced below. Ann announces
that she's "in a pig sty" because of getting only one mattress with two beds that
had arrived (lines 1–3, 6–7):

(18) **R3B/Rah:B:1:JA(11):3**
```
 1     Ann:  1→ Oh:. No w'l ah'm absolutely in a pig sty c'z the two
 2                → beds'v come this mohrning.the new be:ds. °hhhh An:d
 3                → uh b't o[nly one
 4   Jenny:              [>(Don't you think) that wz< quick that wz
 5             quick them coming,
 6     Ann:  → Not too bahd. B't thez only one mahtress with it.
 7             → They don't know where the othuh mattress is.
 8   Jenny: 2→ Oh: no:.
 9     Ann:  So anyway weh- it'll tuhrn up I expect.
```

Jenny, who at first takes Ann's partial delivery of news in an upbeat manner (lines
4–5), after Ann's contrasting completion of the announcement responds with a

denying or negative newsmark (line 8), and Ann then produces an "optimistic projection" (line 9). As Jefferson (1988: 427) remarks about this excerpt, the "Oh: no:" is especially "troubles receptive" but the missing mattress turns out to be only "one of several aspects of a multi-faceted trouble." Displaying troubles resistance here is a way of closing down attention to the mattress in favor of developing further facets of the trouble.

These two excerpts suggest that deliverers can enter the news announcement part of a troubles telling without proposing that their news has consequences for their recipients. In showing troubles resistance, and sensitivity to the response accorded their announcement, they may constitute the bad news as just their own and not as particularly consequential for their recipients. However, a complexity here is that, by offering to tell their troubles, speakers are, per my earlier discussion of the reflexivity of relationships to selections of whom to inform, enacting a presumptive consanguinity. That the deliverers' news is proposed to have consequences for their recipients may be a matter that exists, in the first place, in these practices of seeking or availing oneself of particular others for the telling of troubles and bad news. Otherwise, the proposal of consequences remains unspoken. Then, similarly, recipients demonstrate how consequential the news is for them not necessarily through a verbal claim but according to how strongly they align to teller's announcement of bad news in terms of demonstrating receptiveness to hearing more about the trouble. In other words, they may perform how affected they are through intoned sympathetic assessments and other ways of allowing the speaker to reveal more about the bad news and the trouble it represents.

First-Party News with Explicit Consequences for Recipient

Instead of, or in addition to, these relational performances, participants in an episode of first-party news may overtly propose or claim that it has consequences for the recipient. As with third-party news that concerns the recipient, this may implicate a reciprocal claim by the recipient that the news does have consequences for him or her.

Deliverers' displays of recipient-consequential first-party news. As an example of how a deliverer may work to propose consequences for her recipient, recall (from chapter 4) how Carrie prefaces her good news to Leslie about a new granddaughter with "I: thought you'd like to know" (lines 4–5):

(19) **H13G (Holt:1988:2:4:1)**
```
1   Leslie:  Hello↑?h
2   Carrie:  Oh Les↑lie it's Carrie.
```

```
 3   Leslie:  °t hOh: ↑Carrie: ↑Yes he↑llo[:.hh °hh hh
 4   Carrie:                              [I: thought you'd like to
 5            know I've got a little gran'daughter
 6   Leslie:  °thlk ↑Oh: how love↓ly.
 7   Carrie:  ↓Ye:s bo:rn th's <early hours'v this ↓morning.
 8   Leslie:  °k↑Oh: joll[y goo:d, [h
 9   Carrie:            [↓Ye:s  [↑Christi:ne ↓Ru[th.
10   Leslie:                              [°hhhhh ↑hOh:: that's
             ↓ni::ce:.h What a nice name. eh ↑hhah[↑heh hu °hhhhh
12   Carrie:                                      [(Yeh'v ↑cou:rse.)
13   Leslie:  Ye:s. hheh he he °hhhhhhh
```

Carrie's announcement is in the form [first-party reference + have something good], and Leslie assesses this information in positive fashion (line 6).

With third-party news, I've suggested that a deliverer's proposal of consequences for a recipient exhibits a relationship of concern for that person and an orientation to his or her interests. However, when the deliverer is the primary figure and proposes consequences for a recipient, the matter of relationship is slightly different. Carrie's "I thought you'd like to know" may be *summoning forth* a feature of her relationship with Leslie that is not or cannot be presumed, namely that Leslie actually would like to know her news. A perhaps stronger example of such summoning forth is the following. Recall, from chapter 4, how Ellen calls Jeff to tell him that she has decided to "oust" the academic advisor they share:

(20) EJ:1
```
 1    Jeff:   Hello.
 2    Ellen:  Hi Jeff, this is Ellen
 3                  (0.4)
 4    Jeff:   Hi::, what's up.
 5    Ellen:  Do you have a few minutes?
 6    Jeff:   Yea:::h I sure do.
 7    Ellen:  tch .hh Well I wanted to shar:e some news with you:,
 8            because you'll find it relevant to your particular::
 9            (.) situati[on    ]
10    Jeff:             [Whoo]ps. Okay hold on, let me turn off the
11            radio hhh
12    Ellen:  Okay.
13                  (2.6)
14    Jeff:   .hhhh Okay lay it on me.=
```

In asking if Jeff has "a few minutes" (line 5), which is a way of requesting his time, Ellen displays a concern not to intrude. After Jeff accedes to the request (line 6), she preannounces her news at line 7 with a proposal that it is "relevant" to Jeff's "particular situation." This kind of news-sharing is different from the obligatory; the relationship between Jeff and Ellen appears to be one in which a prospective conveyance is neither strongly compelled nor expected and needs to be justified. Deliverers who *assert* relevance to or interest from their recipients, it seems, cannot fully depend on it.[16] In other words, first-party (and possibly other) news deliveries with assertions about thinking or wanting to share news, including (19) and (20), contrast with those first-party deliveries lacking such assertions, and in which deliverers presume relevance and interest.

Certainly, when one party *asks* how the other is doing, as Emma does in excerpt (16), she thereby can be taken as projecting alignment as an "interested" recipient to a delivery of news. When the deliverer has not been asked, and simply offers news without asserting its relevance, that involves a stronger form of presumptiveness on the deliverer's part. Or a deliverer may precede an announcement with a relatively simple assertion that it is the recipient's due. When Andi (at lines 3, 5) preannounces to Betty her news about being pregnant, she characterizes it as "for you":

(21) **ARL3:18**
```
 1   Andi:    .hhh well: speaking of bot↑toms are you sitting down?
 2   Betty:   Ye↑ah.
 3   Andi:  → Well we have some news for you.
 4   Betty:   What?
 5   Andi:    .hhh that may come as a bit of a surprise ehhh!
 6   Betty:   I see- what are you telling me?
 7   Andi:    hhhh! Bob and I are going to have a baby.
```

The prefacing phrases in excerpt (19) ("*I: thought* you'd like to know") and (20) ("*I wanted to shar:e* some news with you, because you'll find it relevant to your particular:: situation") mitigate the proposals of recipient interest and/or relevance. Here, without such a preface, Andi's line 3 utterance presumes relevance and depends on the recipient's interest in a more forceful way.

As with first-party *good* news, deliverers who are the primary figure in what may be anticipated to be *bad* news may, in various ways, propose its relevance to recipients. In my narrative data, here is a young man's recollection of how he told his parents that he was gay (recall excerpt (4), chapter 2):

(22) **Edgar 1994:231**
> I prepared for months in advance, reading books, talking with friends, and even went to a counselor for several weeks before telling my parents in order to practice role playing the actual event. At dinner one night during Christmas break, I said, "There is something that I want to tell you two, and I want you to be an active part of my life, and feel that without telling, you won't be. It's that I'm gay."

In preannouncing the news, he proposes that sharing it was critical to their being part of his life. Another instance of gay self-disclosure is similar:

(23) **Edgar 1994:230**

> I stated to her (my ex-fiancee), "I can't stand seeing you hurt like this. . . . I think I'm hurting myself, too." Holding her hand while both of us were crying, I said, "I need for you to help me end this pain for both of us. I love you an awful lot, but I'm gay."

Preceding the announcement, this man suggests that his disclosure may remedy both his recipient's and his own "hurting." Beforehand, he also claims needing his recipient's help.

These examples suggest that deliverers' preceding displays of how their bad news also concerns their recipients may be similar to good news. That is, proposing consequences for recipients appears to summon forth the relationship. Indeed, in these instances, preannouncements and prefaces may work to *restore* a relationship that has become precarious. Consider this story about a man who found out that he was HIV-positive:

(24) **Schmalz 1992**

> Mr. Stoddard, a gay-rights lawyer in Manhattan, decided last December to tell his parents, who live in Texas. But after he told his mother, she pleaded with him not to tell his father, who has cancer and is in his late 70s. Eventually, Mr. Stoddard, 44, decided that *if he and his father were to be part of each other's lives, the older man had to know.* Mr. Stoddard took his father to Paris, where, over lunch on the Champs Elysees, he told the elder Mr. Stoddard of his HIV. infection. "I said, 'Dad, there's something you should know.' He didn't seem alarmed; he seemed disappointed. I think because he's ill, too, my father sensed the optimism I felt." (Emphasis added)

I interpret Mr. Stoddard's "optimism" as referring to the positive possibilities for relationship between him and his father. The compulsion to tell one's own bad news, and to propose its relevance to a particular recipient, may thus derive not from a relationship as it is but as one might like it to be. Of course, the successful summoning forth — restoring — of a relationship is contingent on a receipt fitted to the afflicted party's telling of the news. In (24), a basis for his mother's objection to Mr. Stoddard's conveyance to his father may have been a fear that the bad news would incapacitate the father.[17] Instead, the son infers that the father was merely "disappointed" and, because of his own illness, was in fact able to identify with the son's experience.

Deliverer's ex post facto display of recipient consequence. Proposals of relevance, assertions of relevance, and relationship formulation as precedent to news deliveries are practices by which deliverers suggest their news to be consequential for their recipients. Another practice returns us yet again to the reflexivity involved in bringing news to a particular recipient. Rather than employing introductory proposals, assertions, formulations, or other displays that news is consequential for a recipient, deliverers may somehow demonstrate the relational relevance of the news as part of the emerging *course of talk* and virtually in an ex post facto manner.

In the conversation from which excerpt (26) is taken, Susan had called Gordon to ask if he was "free this evening." In reply to this pre-invitation, Gordon says, "Uh not this evening, no," because he has another arrangement. Then, after Susan proposes closure (line 1 below) to the pre-invitation and reply sequence, Gordon (line 3) asks for an account or explanation related to the pre-invitation:

(25) **H22B/Holt:SO88:1:5:2 (modified transcript)**

```
 1    Susan:   Okay,hh well 'at's all I wanted to know,
 2             (0.2)
 3    Gordon:  .k.k Why's that.
 4             (0.6)
 5    Gordon:  .mp[t
 6    Susan:      [Um::::: (.) nothing, h[h
 7    Gordon:                            [.t.hhh
 8             (0.5)
 9    Gordon:  Yee[jih(p) (.) bo:red[hmhhhhhh[h
10    Susan:      [hhheh          [-(0.7)-   [m:No::,hh .hh-
11             (0.4)
12    Susan:   Well I didn't pass my driving test.
13    Gordon:  ˙kl ↓Ah-:-:-:-:.h (.) (˙k) (.) Oh that's a pity (.)
14             wz it today.
15             (0.5)
16    Susan:   No it wz yesterday.
17             (1.0)
18    Susan:   [(              feel)] sorry for myself yesterday so that=
19    Gordon:  [Commiserations.]
20    Susan:   =I I might do tonight.
21             (0.5)
22    Susan:   °I [(        ) °
23    Gordon:     [hh-hh-hh ˙klk I see:.
24             (0.4)
25    Gordon:  ˙hh ˙t ˙hhhhh hEh:m ˙mp (0.7) ˙mp gnThat's really
26             sa↓:d. That's a real shame.
27             (0.3)
28    Susan:   Tis isn't it.
29             (0.2)
30    Gordon:  Yea:h
```

At first, Susan declines to give an account (line 6) for the pre-invitation. Gordon follows this by proposing a candidate account himself, that Susan is "bored" (line 9). She rejects this (line 10), hesitates (lines 10–11), and then announces her bad news at line 12 as a correction of his candidate account. Coming after Gordon's request for an account *and* after his own offering of an account, the news is conveyed *reluctantly*. Additionally, by being produced in response to two requests from the recipient, it is locally, demonstrably relevant to him: he has displayed himself as *wanting* to know. Subsequent to Gordon's assessment of the news (line 13) and query about when it happened (line 14), Susan, in overlap with Gordon's offering of "commiserations" (line 19), indicates that she had felt sorry for herself "yesterday" and is ready to "do tonight" (lines 18, 20).

As Susan reveals it, the upshot of her pre-invitation to Gordon for going out that evening is that it was motivated by the bad news. Gordon is someone with whom the primary figure wishes to spend time in the aftermath of the original event. This revelation evinces consequences of the news for her recipient that are relationally firm but differently so than in other first-party deliveries of news. Susan, having experienced a bad news situation, and then only reluctantly delivering the news to Gordon, exerts a claim on him as one with whom she can share an after-the-fact distraction. Gordon is someone with whom she potentially can drown the sorrow in whatever way "doing tonight" implies.

Recipients' displays in relation to first-party news. After Gordon assesses Susan's news by offering commiserations to Susan, he further submits (lines 25–26) that it is "sa↓d" and a "real shame." These are clear offers of sympathy but it is noteworthy that he does not say how he himself may be affected by the news. By contrast, excerpt (26) is an instance in which, after the news, the recipient demonstrates how the news concerns her:

(26) NB3B/NB:II:4:R

```
 1   Emma:  HI: HONEY HOW ARE y[uh.
 2   Nancy:                    [Fine how'r you.
 3   Emma:  .kh.hh.hh.hahh AOH: AH'M PRETTY GOO::D I HADDA LIDDLE
 4          O:P'ration on my toe this week I had t'have (0.2)
 5          toenail TAKEN O:FF,hh
 6          (.)
 7   Nancy: Why[:
 8   Emma:     [.hhh.hh Oh:: [I have a fungus 'n I: had'n inf::↓ECtion,
 9   Nancy:                  [(What wuhhh)
10          (.)
11   Emma:  'T's a [hell of a]
12   Nancy:        [O h ::: ]::: E:m↓mah[:.
13   Emma:                              [I'n that aw:fuh
```

```
14   Nancy:   ° .hh.hh.hh° [↑W'l w: [at a sh:↑ame=
15   Emma:                   [.hhhhh [.hhh
16   Nancy:   =Didjih haft'ko in the hospi↑t'[l?
17   Emma:                               [n:No::: I jist hadda lo:c'l
18          dea:l en:nuh id wud'n any fu:n but I'm BETTER I wz: lying
19          on: the cou:ch out'n [fron t]
20   Nancy:                      [e-Oh:]:: I: 'm ↓sorr[y E:m]ma:h, hh
21   Emma:                                    [AH::.]
22          ↓I AM TOO WHYNCHE COME'N SEE me.
```

Subsequent to her delivery of bad news (lines 3–5, 8), Emma appears to start an
assessment of the situation (line 11), but at line 12 Nancy intercepts that with
an oh-token whose stretching and intonational contour works sympathetically
to assess the news and Emma's situation (Goodwin 1986b). At least, Emma evidently takes Nancy's turn that way by producing "awful" as an assessment (line
13) that is designed in an agreeing fashion and that Nancy, with "w:at a
sh:↑ame" (line 14), confirms. Then there is a question-answer sequence regarding where the operation was performed (lines 16, 17–18), following which
Emma claims being better (lines 18–19) and reports being "on: the cou:ch out'n
front." In response (line 20), Nancy produces an "I:'m ↓sorry" utterance, indicating her own negatively valenced state in relation to Emma's news and in that
way further offering condolences or sympathy. This is like third-party bad news,
in which expressions of regret are prototypical devices through which recipients
can personalize their receipt of news by showing how other parties' bad news
also concerns or has consequences for them.

As with bad news, when a deliverer's news is good and has been proposed to
be relevant to a recipient, that party can elect to claim or not claim that it has consequences for them. That is, recipients may or may not personalize the news.
Consider our familiar instance of Andi's tidings about her pregnancy:

(27) **(Continuation of 21)**
```
 7   Andi:   hhhh! Bob and I are going to have a baby.
 8   Betty:  Oh my goodness↑ hhow- (1.0) did you have a reversal-
 9          he have a reversal?
10   Andi:   Yea:h.
11                  (1.0)
12   Andi:   .hhh[:::::::::  ]
13   Betty:      [whe::↑n.]
14   Andi:   tch eyup. Last Mar↑ch.
15                  (0.4)
16   Andi:   .mhhh ((sniff))
17   Betty:  OH [MY G:OOD]↑NESS:
18   Andi:      [And  (ituh)]
```

```
19   Andi:  It was [very successful,] (very quickly] hh::h .hhh
20   Betty:        [OH    I'M    SO] [↑HAPPY.    ]
```

Betty's assessment at line 17 exhibits surprise and excitement, partly through it's
elevated volume and pitch, in a fashion consistent with how the news was preannounced (it "may come as a bit of a surprise," excerpt (21)). Furthermore, in
a continuation of the assessment, Betty claims being happy (line 20), thereby
stating how the news has affected her.[18] Similarly, after Ellen, who has suggested
that her news is "relevant" to Jeff (excerpt 20), tells Jeff that she has decided to
"oust" their advisor, and after he assesses the news and congratulates her, Jeff
says, "I hope I'm inspired by you" (chapter 4, excerpt 29). This claim of being
affected may be equivocal but it personalizes the news nonetheless. By contrast,
above in excerpt (19), although Leslie is unabashedly positive in her assessment
of Carrie's news about her new granddaughter, and eventually produces a kind
of congratulatory comment ("Oh well done") just subsequent to the excerpt,
she never says how *she,* Leslie, is affected by the news, never says she is happy or
glad for Carrie, or that she is glad to know the news. She does not, in other
words, personalize the news in the way it was proposed to be consequential for
her. If such expressions are not noticeably absent, they may be systematically absent (see Schegloff 1996), being nonresponsive to the way in which the news is
introduced and keeping it at some distance from the recipient personally.

We have seen that first-party or deliverers' news involves an announcement
that predicates something that the deliverer did or did not do, something that
the deliverer has or does not have, or something that happened or did not happen to the deliverer. At times, such news appears as solely affecting the first party,
but deliverers, in a preannouncement or preface to the announcement, can propose that their own first-party news has consequences for the recipient. Deliverers also do this in relationally reflexive ways, by seeking a recipient to whom they
can tell their troubles or with whom they simply want to get together in the aftermath of a news experience. And, in assessment turns after the announcement,
recipients can show that the deliverers' news has consequences for them, indicating their own personal state as evoked by the news. When a deliverer
proposes the news as having consequences for the recipient, it often signifies a
relatively precarious relationship, which the deliverer works to restore by way of
offering the good or bad news. Sometimes, however, deliverers' proposals of
consequences for a recipient are strongly assertive and appear to presume rather
than recover a closeness of relationship. When deliverers propose or otherwise
demonstrate that their news is consequential for a recipient, a recipient may rat-
ify the proposal by claiming to be affected in particular ways. These displays

exhibit the recipient's co-involvement in the new social world of the deliverer in a more intimate fashion than when no such displays are present.

Announcements of Second-Party News

Second-party news is that in which the recipient is the primary figure. In third-party and first-party episodes, delivery devices are regular across instances of good and bad news, except when there are narrative renderings of news announcements, or when practices of monitoring the primary figure's situation are involved. Otherwise, when reference is made to the primary figure, the teller predicates something bad or good as having happened to that party. Devices for delivery to a recipient who is the primary figure are distinctive, compared to third-party (others') and first-party (deliverer's) news. When the primary figure is the recipient, devices for presentation also differ according to whether the news is good or bad.

Second-Party Good News

A regular pattern in good news to recipients who are the primary figure is for deliverers, in an announcing utterance, to refer to themselves as having done something that has brought about the situation that is good news for the recipient. Grammatically, the primary figure appears in the predicate of an announcing utterance, and in response to the news the recipient may direct some form of appreciation to the deliverer. In chapter 7, I explore at length the pattern of a deliverer claiming and receiving credit for a recipient's good-news situation. Here, it simply can be noted that, because of this pattern, an announcement of good news in which a recipient is the primary figure departs from the regular [reference to primary figure + did or has something good] format. Instead, per table 5.1 (column C), the format is [reference to deliverer + did or has something good for + 2nd party (primary figure) reference].

Second-Party Bad News

Bad news in which the recipient is the primary figure is different still—not only from third-party and first-party news, but also from announcements of good news for recipients. As table 5.1 shows, delivery of recipient-consequential bad news involves *reporting circumstances* or using other devices that provide for an unstated bad news upshot, and the second party and primary consequential figure may not be referenced at all. In turn, although recipients may flood out immediately by crying and sobbing, they more often produce a restrained or stoic response.

In excerpt (28), Leslie's line 1 announcement is about her adult daughter

Katharine, who has returned from Leslie's home elsewhere in England to York. Trevor appears to have called Leslie's home and left a message that he wanted to talk to Katharine. Leslie now has called Trevor and line 1 is at the beginning of the call in first topic, reason-for-the-call position.

```
(28) H12B/Holt:J86:1:1:1
  1  Leslie:  'hh Well: I'm afraid Kathrine's back in Yo:rk
  2           ↓Trevor.
  3                 (0.2)
  4  Trevor:  Oh you're jo:↓king.
  5                   (.)
  6  Leslie:  ↓No-:,
  7  Trevor:  Oh when d'she go ba↓:ck.
  8  Leslie:  T'da:y?
  9                 (0.5)
 10  Trevor:  °Oh Go: [d°
 11  Leslie:          [She'll be ↑back by now if you ring her I
 12           expect she'll be there: (.) uh b't I should ring her
 13           after six.
 14  Trevor:  When did she ring me: .=Cz I've been away as we:ll. (e)
 15  Leslie:  'hhh Oh: .hhhh About two days ago.
```

Leslie's announcement is marked as bad news with "I'm afraid," and has Katharine in the grammatical subject position. However, she is not the primary consequential figure in this episode. That party is Trevor, insofar as Leslie may be engaged in what Drew (1984) describes as "reporting something without providing the upshot or import" (128), and is allowing for Trevor to find the implications of her line 1 announcement. The two interactants come to treat Katharine's return to York as primarily consequential for Trevor, the upshot being that she is unavailable for him locally. At line 4, Trevor requests confirmation through an ironic joke proposal, a ritualized assertion of disbelief, to paraphrase Heritage (1984a: 339). Then Leslie confirms the news (line 6), they establish the timing of Katharine's leaving the locality (lines 7–8), and, as a way of assessing the news, Trevor produces an "Oh God" expletive at line 10, a "response cry" in Goffman's terms.[19] Speaking softly, he does not produce any lexical assessment, such that his response is relatively restrained. After this, Leslie proposes a remedy: Trevor can call Katharine in York.

Earlier, I observed that previous attention to stoic responses has mostly considered the psychological aspects of this phenomenon.[20] In a way, Trevor's disbelieving receipt evinces rejection and denial. But we also need to appreciate that the manner of delivery — the reporting device by which a bearer presents tidings to the primary figure — can *encourage* such a response. This is even more evident

in the next excerpt. Charlie has called Ilene, and his news is in first-topic, reason-
for-the-call position:

(29) Trip to Syracuse

```
 1      Ilene:   Hullo:,
 2               (0.3)
 3    Charlie:   hHello is eh::m:: (0.2) .hh-.hh Ilene there?
 4      Ilene:   Ya::h, this is Ile:[ne,
 5    Charlie:                      [.hh Oh hi this's Charlie about
 6               th'trip the Syracuse?
 7      Ilene:   Ye:a:h, Hi (k-ch)
 8    Charlie:   Hi howuh you doin.
 9      Ilene:   Goo::[d,
10    Charlie:        [hhhe:h heh .hhhh I wuz uh:m: (·) .hh I wen'
11               ah:- (0.3) I spoke the the gi:r- I spoke tih Karen.
12  (Charlie):   (.hhh) / (0.4)
13    Charlie:   And u:m:: (·) ih wz rea:lly ba:d because she decided
14               of a:ll weekends fuh this one tih go awa:y
15               (0.6)
16      Ilene:   Wha:t?
17               (0.4)
18    Charlie:   She decidih tih go away this weekend.
19      Ilene:   Yea:h,
20    Charlie:   .hhhh=
21    (Ilene):   =.kh[h
22    Charlie:       [So tha:[:t
23    (Ilene):             [k-khhh
24    Charlie:   Yihknow I really don't have a place tuh sta:y.
25      Ilene:   .hh Oh:::::: .hh
26               (0.2)
27      Ilene:   .hhh So yih not g'nna go up this weeken'?
28       ( ):    (hhh)/(0.2)
29    Charlie:   Nu::h I don't think so.
30      Ilene:   How about the following weekend.
31               (0.8)
32    Charlie:   .hh Dat's the vacation isn'it?
33      Ilene:   .hhhhh Oh:. .hh ALright so:- no ha:ssle,
34               (·)
35      Ilene:   S[o-
36    Charlie:    [Ye:h,
37      Ilene:   Yihkno:w::
38       ( ):    .hhh
39      Ilene:   So we'll make it fer another ti:me then.
40               (0.5)
41      Ilene:   Yihknow jis let me know when yer g'nna go:.
42    Charlie:   .hh Sure .hh
```

```
43    Ilene:   yihknow that- that's awl, whenever you have
44             intentions'v going .hh let me know.
45  Charlie:   Ri:ght.
46    Ilene:   Oka::y?
47  Charlie:   Okay,=
48    Ilene:   =Thanks inneh- e- than:ks: anyway Charlie,
```

Charlie displays that he has news by characterizing the reason for the call as "about the trip to Syracuse" (lines 5–6). Then, prepackaging that news as something he learned by having "spoke . . . tih Karen" (lines 10–11), and as "rea:lly ba:d" (line 13), he announces that Karen has "decided . . . tih go awa:y" (line 14, 18). After Ilene's receipt (line 19), which provides for continuation rather than marking the initial announcement as complete, and treats this report as "background" to what follows (Heritage 1984a: 307),[21] Charlie (in lines 22, 24) suggests a consequence of Karen's going away, which is a consequence for him—he does not have a place to stay. Ilene responds to this with a change-of-state token (line 25) and proposes an upshot, that he's "not g'nna go up this weeken'" (line 27). After receiving confirmation (line 29), Ilene inquires (line 30) about the next weekend. Line 32, a detailing of circumstance tied to Ilene's temporal formulation, indicates a negative answer to this inquiry.

Next, Ilene at line 33 produces another "oh" token and a "no problem," restrained acknowledgment to this news: "AlRight so:- no ha:ssle" (line 33). She also suggests a formulaic remedy, making it for another time (lines 35, 37, 39). With these utterances, as Drew (1984: 130) argues, Ilene treats her proposal for the following weekend as having been rejected. Accordingly, it is here shown that Ilene figures as the primary figure in the news. If we track matters, what is "bad" is that Karen has decided to go away, that Charlie does not have a place to stay and is not going to "go up" this weekend, and as a result, that Ilene then does not have transportation to Syracuse. As the primary consequential figure in this bad news, however, Ilene is never referenced in the deliverer's announcing utterances.

A remarkable, even dramatic, contrast therefore exists between second-party bad news, in which the recipient is the primary consequential figure, and most other kinds of good and bad news. Instead of a subject-predicating format ("you cannot presently talk to Katharine"; "you no longer have transport to Syracuse"), the deliverer engages in reporting circumstances or giving of reasons for some unstated bad news upshot. This is a very cautious way of delivering the news, and it is factual and abstract. It should be no small wonder, then, that recipients are reciprocally detached-seeming or restrained in their manner of receiving the news.[22]

The stoic response as traversing a line between detachment and self-absorption. Beyond the way that a stoic response may mirror a deliverer's cautious presentation of bad tidings are other interactional matters. The stoic response is in stark contrast to immediate flooding out that bad news can occasion and also reflects recipients' refraining from lexical assessment (the use of "how awful," "terrible," "horrible," and other evaluative terms). And this stoicism is linked to proposals of remedy. The preferred form for a remedy is for the deliverer to offer it, as when Leslie suggests that Trevor can call Katharine in York. Its dispreferred form is for a recipient to request it,[23] as Ilene does for the trip to Syracuse. In either case, stoic responses on the part of recipients *indicate coorientation to the recipient's embeddedness in a course of action that requires relatively immediate amelioration*. In their interactional dealings with the bad news, that is, participants regard the transformed social world of the recipient as one that urgently needs betterment. From this standpoint, recipients' devices for assessing bad news involving other primary figures — "how horrible," "that's awful," "what a shame," and the like — appear as *too* detached; they neither immediately provide nor occasion remedial talk. Like evaluations of good news, they often occasion assessment sequences or topical detailings that reaffirm the type of news that has been delivered. When the primary figure in some bad news is the first-party or deliverer, a recipient's assessment can occasion further troubles talk that specifically avoids the provision of solutions (Jefferson and Lee 1981), and when the primary figure is a third party, assessments can occasion gossip or other evaluative talk concerning that figure. Although stoicism exhibits restraint, in comparison to assessments and topical detailings of the bad news, it is less detached, for it indicates a pressing alertness to possibilities for abatement and redress.

Besides the assessment, another device whereby, upon hearing about a third party's bad situation or a deliverer's own dire circumstances, recipients show that the situation or circumstances also affect them, is the claim to be "sorry," or "sad," or otherwise (through intonation, for example) exhibiting sympathy. This device is also withheld in recipients' response to bad news about themselves, and for good interactional reasons. Personal-state expressions are a way of affiliating to the nature of another party's situation and indicate that the recipient is also personally affected. Used in relation to one's own state, however, such expressions may be redundant, since the parties already orient to the recipient as the primary consequential figure. Additionally, *claiming* to be sorry or sad may border on self-pity. As Pomerantz (1978) has demonstrated about self-praise, which, interactionally, is to be avoided, self-pity is also something that participants apparently are to eschew.[24]

The restraint exhibited in stoic responses to bad news, in short, traverses a line between being too removed from the news on the one side and being inappropriately self-absorbed by the news on the other. Furthermore, the response that is paired with the stoic response and sometimes entirely supplants it — flooding out by crying and sobbing — is not the same as self-pity. Flooding out is a response that marks just how overwhelming some new world can be for the primary figure who enters it. In Katz's (1999: 191) terms, "the person in crying is making an emphatically embodied statement" about *loss*, attempting to reconcile "two worlds that cannot share a language." In responding to bad news by flooding out into crying or sobbing, the recipient exhibits the precise discomfiture that Garfinkel (1967: 49) suggests is the concomitant of experiencing disruption to the perceived normality of one's everyday world. It is as if an old world has been lost, and a new world has been opened with recipients of the news invited to enter, but they lack the words, symbols, and other resources to do so in a meaningful way. Commonly, deliverers who encounter crying and sobbing offer comfort in various verbal and nonverbal ways, consistent with how they handle the stoic response. They produce formulas for abatement and redress, thereby working to remedy what the bad news portends for a particular recipient.

Coda: In the Clinic

Ethnographic research on bad news takes an abstract approach to the relationships involved, viewing the categorical class, occupational, and other identities of participants as influencing how the news is delivered and received. There may be correlations between categorical identities and conversational enactments, but an approach is needed that examines the full detail of informing episodes and examines how participants, in the concreteness of their actual practices and in ongoing talk and social interaction, display their relations to others and others' relations to them. Participants enact relationships of distance and closeness in and through choosing to inquire after or offer information about their lifeworld experiences. They also enact these relationships according to how, if they have chosen to request or offer news, they articulate an ensuing news delivery sequence. In presequences to the NDS, in the NDS itself, and in succeeding turns of talk, participants exhibit who the primary and secondary consequential figures are. When news is primarily about others, deliverers and recipients can show whether and how they are also personally affected.

In clinics, patients or family members (when patients are by age or affliction regarded as interactionally incompetent) are the primary consequential figures. In this situation, as in ordinary conversation, the stoic response rears its head as the regular way for receiving bad news. I have recurrently witnessed physicians and other experts from internal medicine, oncology,[25] developmental disability, and HIV clinics present the tidings to patients or family members, who say nothing or, if they say something, it is very little and spoken in a resigned way.[26] Patients and family members also do nothing, sitting rather rigidly in their chairs. As with the Hodgkin's patient quoted in the epigraph to this chapter, there are often reports about *later* breaking down emotionally, which is one way that the stoic response is *paired* with an emotional reaction.

I have said that medical and other literatures approach the stoic response with a focus on the patient and family and the psychological impact bad news has. A lesson from my analysis is that delivers *and* recipients contribute to its manifestation. That is, clinical deliveries of bad diagnostic news are similar, in generic ways, to deliveries of news in more casual or informal settings. Clinicians who deliver bad news often do so in a factual and abstract way that encourages a reciprocating, emotionally distanced response. And in other ways, because recipients appear to traverse a fine line between detachment and involvement, the stoic response reflects interactional matters, particularly a shared orientation toward remedying the bad-news situation. Sometimes, however, a recipient, upon acknowledging bad news, displays a strong emotional response. Then, deliverers produce further forms of remedial talk that help contain and move away from such affective displays.

An informing interview from the developmental disabilities clinic where I spent time amply illustrates these patterns. A mother, accompanied by her sister, brought a five-year-old girl, "Sara," for testing and diagnosis to the clinic. Specialists in psychology, pediatric medicine, speech and hearing, occupational therapy, special education and other areas examined her over a two-day period and, by comparing and consolidating their findings, decided upon a diagnosis of severe mental retardation. The clinicians all met with the mother (Ms. M) and aunt (Ms. S) and officials from the daughter's school to present their findings and the diagnosis. The psychologist who was in charge of the case, Dr. P, asked the various clinicians to report their test results to the mother and aunt. After the others gave their reports, Dr. P, in the segment below, presented the diagnosis. Frames from the videotape of this meeting illustrate both the stoic response and a delayed flooding out when the mother eventually releases a small sob or cry (see figures 5.1 and 5.2).

In his delivery of diagnosis, Dr. P employs what we have termed a "syllogistic" delivery of bad news (Gill and Maynard 1995). During this talk (preceding the excerpt and through line 1 below), Dr. P is gazing at Ms. M, who has her hand to her mouth and is returning his gaze. However, at lines 2–3, she shifts her gaze down and toward the table (figure 5.1a), where it stays except briefly.

a. Dr. P: ". . . everything . . . is pretty consistent in a on:::e to two year level of functioning." [excerpt (30), lines 2–3.]

b. Ms. M's stoic pose during silence [excerpt (31), line 29] after Dr. P's statement "that's all that mental retardation means."

Figure 5.1 Left to right: Ms. M (the mother), Ms. M's sister, Dr. P (the psychologist). Partially visible on the left are other clinicians and, on the right, school personnel.

In the syllogistic delivery, a *particular* premise consists of initially citing or reciting testing evidence. Dr. P suggests that, in Sara's case, "everything" has been "pretty consistent" in finding a low "level of functioning" (lines 2–3). A slow rate of learning (lines 6–7) is also present.

(30) Case H:detail
```
1   Dr. P:  Everything seems ta be delayed, some more than others,
2           but everything .hhh uh:: is pretty consistent (0.6) in a
3           on:::e ta two year level of functioning. hh .hhh so that-
4           s- that's of concern.
```

a. Ms. M emits a sob and reaches for tissue [excerpt (31), lines 30–31].

b. Ms. M dabs eyes, Dr. P puts hand to face [excerpt (31), line 32], before he
proceeds: "Let me uhin (1.2) . . . not try to ah- I- I don't wanta .hhh s::oft coat
that . . ." (lines 33–34).

Figure 5.2 Left to right: Ms. M (the mother), Ms. M's sister, Dr. P (the psychologist). Partially visible on the left are other clinicians and, on the right,
school personnel.

```
 5              (0.4)
 6  Dr. P:  tch .hhhh uh:: rate of lear::ning .hhh is hard ta tell
 7          but it obviously uh (0.2) uh has been slow.
 8              (2.2)
 9  Dr. P:  And I don't see at this point .hhh uh people are- are
10          still looking but it doesn't loo::k like they're any
11          obvious .hhh cau::ses which we could tre:at ta try ta
12          reverse the way things are going.
13              (1.0) ((Ms. M nods slightly))
```

```
14   Dr. P:  I think they're- are .hhh uh:: :m .h many many many
15           things that can be done ta help her lear:n up ta her
16           potential .hhhh but I really do fear that uh: that what
17           we're talking about is a- (0.4) is- ta some extent a
18           permanent disability.
```

After a silence at line 8, Dr. P slightly hedges about whether there are "obvious cau::ses" whose treatment could reverse things (lines 9–12) but largely discounts this. Here, Ms. M produces a slight nod (line 13) and then (lines 14–16), Dr. P suggests an optimistic projection (Jefferson 1988), again formulating a contrasting proposal about the permanence of her "disability" (lines 16–18).

Next, Ms. M glances at Dr. P (lines 19–20), who offers a *general* syllogistic premise (lines 21–24):

(31) Case H:detail; (Excerpt 30 continued)

```
19               (2.6) ((Ms. M raises head, glances at Dr.
20               P, returns gaze to table))
21   Dr. P:  Now. (1.0) .hhhh when a kid is- (0.2) delayed (0.2)
22           significantly an' when there's pretty good reason ta
23           believe that the delays are gonna be permanent .hhh
24           that's what we call mental retardation.
25               (2.6) ((Ms. M continues to gaze at table))
26   Dr. P:  Slo:w learning. (1.0) with (0.1) an indication that it's
27           going to be a long term kind of problem. That- that's all
28           that mental retardation means.
29               (20.0) ((Ms. M continues to gaze at table))
30   Ms. M:  ((sobs:)) .hhhhhhh hhhhhhhh .hhhhhh ((Ms. M moves forward
31           and grabs tissue, sits back down))
32               (2.5) ((Ms. M dabs eyes; Dr. P moves hand to face))
33   Dr. P:  Let me uhin (1.2) not try to ah- I- I don't wanta .hhh
34           s::oft coat that because I mean that- that's a serious
35           (.) diagnosis and I don't wanna make a jo:ke or make
36           light of that. (0.2) Ih ih it's serious and ya have right
37           ta- (0.2) and good reason ta be real upset .hhhh uh: I
38           think it's also though- (0.1) uhin .hhhh mental
39           retardation does n:ot mean .hhhh uh:: that the child
40           won't learn, (0.2) cause the child (0.2) will learn.
41               (0.6)
42   Dr. P:  Uhh::m (1.2) it'll:: be a struggle 'n .hhhhh it also .hhh
43           doesn't mean that she can't live a happy (0.4) uh::: and
44           even productive life.
45               (1.4)
46   Dr. P:  Whe[n:   ]
47   Ms. M:      [Tha]t's all I'm looking for, I jus:::- I want her ta
48           talk .hhhh
49   Dr. P:  Yeah
```

That is, abstractly referring to "a kid," Dr. P produces a definition of "mental retardation" (lines 21–24) that includes the characteristics that have been found in Sara's case and just previously reported to the parents. The conclusion, that Sara is mentally retarded, is a logically implied but unstated upshot and diagnosis. Mrs. M, as recipient, is silent (line 25). Dr. P, offering an interpretation of the silence as indicating a lack of understanding (Pomerantz 1984b), rephrases what he has stated about the rate of learning and permanence of the disability (lines 26–27). He goes on with a mitigating proposal about the mental retardation term (lines 27–28).

In a powerful display of the stoic response, for fully 20 seconds Ms. M continues gazing down at the table (line 29, and figure 5.1b). The room, with its many professional participants besides Ms. M and her sister (who looks at Dr. P during this time), is void of talk and almost all activity, until Ms. M emits a sobbing kind of inbreath-outbreath-inbreath and moves forward from her chair and reaches to grab a tissue from a box on the table (lines 30–31, figure 5.2a). She then sits back down and dabs at her eyes with the tissue (figure 5.2b). Having just offered his mitigating proposal, and having observed the contained response and brief show of emotion on Ms. M's part, Dr. P now suggests the seriousness of the diagnosis and the "good reason" for Ms. M "ta be real upset" (lines 33–37). He also continues with a *good-news exit* from the bad news,[27] offering the remedies that "the child (0.2) w<u>ill</u> learn" (lines 38–40), and, after another, brief silence (line 41) and an acknowledgment of the "struggle," that Sara can live a "happy," "prod<u>u</u>ctive life" (lines 43–44). Subsequently, Ms. M for the first time demonstrates a partial alignment (lines 47–48) with what Dr. P has said. In subsequent talk (not in the excerpt), she elicits from Dr. P a suggestion that her daughter will learn to talk, whereupon Ms. M says, "thank you," laughs in a way that occasions laughter from others in the room, and adds, "that's all I wanted to hear." The restrained discharge of a sob (line 30) not only has been confined to a fleeting moment within a more extended exhibit of stoicism but is transcended by the laughter.

As an interactional phenomenon in the clinic, the stoic response partakes of structures we observed in ordinary conversation. When someone has second-party bad news, they may deliver it as a "reporting," by citing and reciting evidence for an upshot about a condition affecting the recipient that goes officially unstated. Reporting circumstances and citing evidence, because they are about *facts* pertaining to an affected person rather than about a condition that person may be said to possess,[28] provide for restraint on the part of recipients, whose feelings may nevertheless bubble to the surface in a delayed fashion. In our example, acknowledging the emotion — the mother's "right" to be "real upset" —

the clinician quickly proposes a kind of remedy concerning the child's ability to learn. The mother, as well, is oriented to remedy: she wants her daughter to "talk," and obtains the clinician's agreeing prognosis that she will. Stoicism as well as flooding out function to make remedy proposals relevant in the sequencing of talk.

Not only in the instance above does a psychologist, after syllogistically telling a mother that her child is mentally retarded, and after witnessing her sobbing grab for a tissue, propose that her child "will learn." In another clinic, in a geographically separate part of the United States, nearly 15 years earlier, a pediatrician told a different mother that her child, a boy, was mentally retarded. This was the Donald Riccio case (chapter 3). When Mrs. Riccio sobbed loudly and denied the news, the pediatrician remarked to her, "he can learn, and he is learning." These episodes, otherwise so disparate in time and space, demonstrate the strength of interactional patterns surrounding the delivery and receipt of diagnostic and other kinds of news. One pattern is the pairing of stoic and flooding out responses (in the Riccio case, this pairing was between the father and mother). Another strong pattern, embodied in part through the regular use of good-news exits from bad news, is the *asymmetry* we maintain between bad and good news.

Shrouding Bad News, Exposing Good News: The Benign Order of Everyday Life

While the good news of finding no cancer is welcome any time and any place, bad news should be withheld until it can be conveyed with the good news that there are treatments to be offered.[1]

"Of all the formula tales," Abrahams (1963) writes, "perhaps the most enduring is the 'that's good, that's bad' story." In folklore inventories, the following instance is listed as "The House Is Burned Down":

> Two men, who had not seen one another for a great while, meeting by chance, one asked the other how he did. He replied, he was not very well, and had been married since he saw him. "That's good news, indeed," said he. "Nay, not such good news, neither," replied the other; "for I married a shrew." "That was bad," said the friend. "Not so bad, neither," said the man; "for I had two thousand pounds with her." "That's well again," said the other. "Not so well, neither," said the man; "for I laid it out in sheep, and they all died of the rot." "That was hard, indeed," says his friend. "Not so hard," says the husband; "for I sold the skins for more than the sheep cost." "That made you amends," said the other. "Not so much amends neither; for I laid out my money in a house, and it was burnt." "That was a great loss, indeed." "Nay, not so great a loss, neither; for my wife was burnt in it."[2]

Among other things, the historical and cross-cultural presence of this story type suggests that the pairing of bad and good news in particular ways is a universal tendency. For this reason, it is surprising that investigators have concentrated so much on bad news and not much studied its relation to good news. Although experimental studies of the "mum" effect have proliferated,[3] ethnographic and, until recently, other naturalistic research systematically concerned with both bad *and* good news in real social settings has been slim.[4]

A prominent feature of bad news, as compared with good news, is that the former is interactionally covered or shrouded in particular ways. Another formula tale gives further evidence of this and leads into analysis of the conversational tactics whereby participants protectively envelop bad news and expose good news. This tale is called "The Climax of Horrors,"[5] and it shows that even "no news" may be more esteemed than bad news, at least from a deliverer's point of view.

A wealthy man was ordered by his physician to go away to the mountains for a rest. He went home, told the members of his family what the doctor had said, and told them, "While I'm away I don't wish to be annoyed by letters or telegrams. In fact I don't want to receive any news of any kind. So he went away and was gone about six weeks. He returned to the city very much improved in health, and very anxious for some news from home. He got off the train at the depot, was met by his servant, and the following conversation ensued.

"Well Henry, how is everything at home? Is there any news?"

"No sir, there ain't no news sir. Everything is just about the same as when you went away. There ain't no news."

"Well you know I'm just dying for some word from home now. You can tell me any little thing, no matter how trifling."

"No sir, there ain't no news. There ain't nothin' to tell you sir. Except uh, there's just one little thing. Since you went away your dog died."

"Oh my dog died eh? Well that's too bad. What killed the dog?"

"Well sir the dog ate some burnt horse flesh, and that's what killed the dog."

"Ate burnt horseflesh! Where did he get burnt horseflesh to eat?"

"Well sir you know your barn burned down, burnt up all the cows and horses, and after the fire had cooled off, the dog went in and ate some of the burnt horseflesh and that's what killed the dog."

"Oh, my barn burned down eh? How did the barn catch fire?"

"Well sir, you see the spark from the house flew over, caught onto the barn, burned the barn down, burnt up all the cows and the horses. And after the fire cooled off, the dog went in and ate some of the burnt horseflesh and that's what killed the dog."

"Oh then my house burned too, eh? Well how did the house catch fire?"

"Well sir, they had some candles burning in the house, and one of the candles caught onto the curtain. And the curtains caught onto the roof, and sparks flew over, and caught onto the barn, and burned the barn down, burnt up all the cows and the horses. And after the fire cooled off, the dog went in and ate some of the burnt horseflesh and that's what killed the dog."

"They had candles burning in the house, where I have gas and electricity? I never knew there was a candle in the place."

"Oh yessir, they had the candles there. They had the candles burnin' all around the coffin."

"The coffin? Who's dead?"

"Oh yessir, that's another thing I overlooked. Since you've been away, your mother-in-law died."

"Oh my mother-in-law died eh?"

"Yessir, she's dead all right. You needn't worry about that."

"Well what killed my mother-in-law?"

"Well sir, I don't know exactly what killed her sir. But around the neighborhood, they say it was from the shock of your wife runnin' away with the chauffeur. But outside of that sir why there ain't no news."

Surely the bad news here was forecasted, in that the wealthy man's servant, rather than his chauffeur, showed up at the train station, which may have prompted the man's insistent inquiry for news despite the servant's denials that there is any. Accordingly, instead of the news being volunteered, the bad news arrives as answers to questions, with each answer giving hint of worse yet to come, until the servant is prodded into laying out the penultimate tidings. Finally, in a prototypical way of ending a story, the servant returns to his pre-story characterization, "there ain't no news," and thereby also continues to minimize the series of horrors as well as the climax that has just been reached. Found in British, Hungarian, Indian, Lithuanian, Russian, Serbocroatian, and Spanish folktale collections, this story along with its "House Is Burned Down" cousin thematize a relation among different kinds of news. Both tale types make visible a *benign* rather than *malign* social world. The first man's house burned, but with his shrew of a wife in it,[6] and the second man lost his dog, livestock, barn, house, mother-in-law, house, and wife, but otherwise "there ain't no news." As serious and bad as things are, they could be more momentous and much worse.

If these tales appear in varied cultural settings, and resonate humorously today, then the issues they awaken about the handling of diverse kinds of news are common and general. Storytelling, after all, is intimately involved in the constitution of social life and, among other things, provides "cognitive and emotional coherence" to collective experience (Bauman 1986). The stories illustrate a theme to be developed from empirical study of everyday talk and social interaction. Over and over again in their talk, participants organize the relationship between bad and good news as an asymmetric one in which good news is, in a variety of ways, privileged over bad news. Participants' asymmetric workings with bad and good news result in a practical everyday (and not just storied) world that has the interactionally produced sense of being a benign rather than malign one.

Shrouding Bad News and Exposing Good News

The "Climax of Horrors" tale identifies a device for covering or shrouding bad news, which is for a deliverer to exhibit reluctance by withholding the news and producing it only in response to inquiry rather than as an offered announcement. Recall excerpt (25) in chapter 5, where Susan tells Gordon that she failed her driving test. This news is delivered after she telephones and asks him if he is free that evening, after he reports other plans and queries her about why she's asking, after she demurs with "Um nothing," and after he offers a candidate account, "you just bored?" She disconfirms this candidate, and then announces after a silence and as a kind of reluctant correction, "Well I didn't pass my driving test." The bad news arrives in guarded fashion, only as an answer to Gordon's probing questions. I will examine a roughly similar example below; excerpt (1) involves Pete having bad news about being out of work, which is buried in Pete's rather elaborate glosses, and is solicited through questioning by the recipient, Marvin. In contrast, an episode of good news in excerpt (2), delayed in its delivery, nevertheless involves more immediate exposure of the valence and substance of the tidings.

Delay in the Delivery of Bad News: Covering and Reluctance

Pete's job-loss news is not the reason for the call between him and Marvin; rather, Marvin calls Pete to remind him of a meeting and the news comes up later in the call, prefigured at line 5 of the excerpt when Pete answers Marvin's "How'r you" with "pretty good?" Jefferson (1980) calls this a "downgraded conventional response" (the conventional one being "fine"). There are two main features to such downgraded or *qualified* responses.[7] The first is its premonitory one. Jefferson argues that "pretty good" and like objects, while not projecting an immediate report on a trouble, "may nevertheless mark the presence of a trouble." That trouble is reported later, often as bad news. A second feature of these responses is that their use "can be invoking and managing the dual relevance of attending to a trouble and attending to business as usual" (163). Indeed, after Pete's line 5 qualified response, Marvin initiates the first topic in line 6 with talk about the upcoming meeting. This discussion, as indicated at line 7, occupies 39 lines of transcript.

(1) Jefferson 1980:158–59

```
 1     Pete:   How'r you:.
 2    Marvin:  I':m great,
 3     Pete:   Goo:d.
 4    Marvin:  How'r you.
 5     Pete:   Pretty good?
 6    Marvin:  Hey we're havin a meetin:g Tuesday ni:ght,
 7             [[approximately 39 lines omitted]]
 8     Pete:   Okay Mar[vin,]
 9    Marvin:          [How:]'r things goin.
10     Pete:   Aw::::: nothin doin,
11    Marvin:  Nothin doin u[h
12     Pete:                 [No: how's it with YOU:.
```

```
13   Marvin:  ˙t˙khh (          ) everything's gr:eat, h[avin a good=
14     Pete:                                                [Is it?
15   Marvin:  =time'nd (.) °h e[n j's wunnerful.
16     Pete:                    [( )-
17     Pete:  Yeh well that's goo:d. I'm glad somebody's enjoyin
18             it,
19   Marvin:  ih hih hha hh[eh
20     Pete:              [Je:sus I've had a hell of a ti:me.=
21   Marvin:  =hih u- Have you?
22                  (0.3)
23   Marvin:  [Wuh
24     Pete:  [Since the ei:ghth of O:cTOber,
25                  (0.2)
26   Marvin:  Wuh uWhat's 'a:t.
27                  (0.2)
28     Pete:  We:ll ah nothin t'DO:.
29                  (0.3)
30   Marvin:  Oh you mean you're not worki[n?
31     Pete:                              [nNo::.
32   Marvin:  °Ooh I didn't know that,°
33                  (0.3)
34     Pete:  I went over'n got fou:r, four days in la:st week and
35             the week uh the week before one da:y,
36                  (0.2)
37   Marvin:  Aw::: Jesus.
```

In answering Marvin, at line 10, Pete produces a response different from his earlier one that is, nevertheless, another qualified and equivocal *gloss*. "Most roughly," Jefferson (1985: 436) has said, "a gloss can be a 'generalization' and/or somewhat inaccurate and/or incomplete and/or a masking or covering-up of 'what really happened.'" And she argues further that, depending on the occurrence of an "auspicious" environment, glosses may become "unpackaged." When Marvin repeats the gloss at line 11, this may invite unpackaging; it could be taken as a *repeat request* for clarification. However, Pete simply confirms (line 12, "No"), then inquires back and gets Marvin's upbeat answers (lines 13, 15).

Now, Pete produces an agreeing assessment of Marvin's situation ("Yeh well that's goo:d") and adds a personal state evaluation ("I'm glad somebody's enjoyin it," lines 17–18), suggesting Marvin to be a member of a *category* ("somebody") that is "enjoying" things. Marvin takes this as an apparent joking or otherwise humorous comment, as he offers laughter at line 19, which Pete rejects by intersecting the laughter with a serious complaint (line 20). This complaint also, retrospectively at least, constitutes lines 17–18 as the first half of a "compound" turn constructional unit or TCU (Lerner 1991: 44).[8] Pete's utterance at line 20 serves to complete the compound turn in a way that deletes the offer of laughter at line 19 and further glosses Pete's situation as one that contrasts with Marvin's, the stress in "I've had hell of a ti:me" being a way to mark by intonation a tie to and divergence from "somebody's enjoyin it."

The issue can be raised as to why Pete takes this tack *now* (Schegloff and Sacks 1973). In other words, he has twice been asked how he is (lines 4, 9), and been offered a virtual third opportunity to elaborate when Marvin repeats Pete's second answer with "Nothin' doin uh" (line 11). The simple matter may be that Marvin's unabashed positive responses (lines 13, 15) to Pete's "how's it with YOU:?" are *upgraded* conventional responses, glosses themselves that are implicative of further talk (Sacks 1975; Schegloff 1986: 129). If so, the alternative to Pete's artfully interjected complaint at lines 17 and 20 may be elaboration of why Marvin is doing so "great," which would veer topical talk in a direction that would remove altogether the relevance of Pete's bad news and troubles (Sacks 1992b: 358). This juncture in the talk after line 15, therefore, may represent a no-later-than, last-resort auspicious environment for Pete's bad news to become unpackaged from the glosses he has so far offered.

Here (lines 17–18, 20), Pete's reference in his compound TCU to having a "hell of a ti:me" yet appears as an incomplete version, again retrospectively, of what eventually emerges. It is followed by Marvin's further inquiry (line 21), a temporal formulation (line 24), and still another question (line 26). The latter occasions a more complete but not, for Marvin, full version of Pete's trouble — "nothin t'DO:" at line 28 expands on "nothin doin" at line 10 — and Marvin next produces a candidate rendering, "Oh you mean you're not workin?" (line 30). After Pete confirms (line 31), Marvin produces a quieted exhibit of receiving news (line 32). In short, although strongly cued by Pete's counter to his own upbeat response to a how-are-you inquiry (Schegloff 1986), Marvin has now provided an auspicious environment for Pete's troubles talk. He does so by the practice of inquiring into Pete's glosses with a series of questions — "Have you?", "Wuh uWhat's 'a:t," and "Oh you mean you're not workin?" — that finally elicit and collaboratively help specify the bad news.

The effect of Pete's glossing and show of reluctance (occasioning of questions) is that when his news arrives, it is not because it has been offered but because it has been asked for. But withholding one's news is a risky venture. It may be a way of enacting the news bearer's reluctance to tell, but it also may mislead a recipient and result in talk that moves away from the relevance of reporting the bad news. Nevertheless, shrouding the news with qualified responses and glosses can result in the occasioning of inquiries that officially *extract* the bad news from its covering.

Delay in the Telling of Good News: Anticipatory Leakage

Through the use of qualified conventional responses and attending to business as usual, the bearer of bad news in excerpt (1) delays telling it. Bearers of good news also may delay the delivery, but this appears to serve different ends than with bad news. Whereas delays are an embedded part of shrouding and covering bad news, they often leak the nature of good news and heighten its anticipation. Sudnow (1967) observes that in hospitals, when surgeons emerge from behind doors with a solemn appearance, they carry bad news. However,

> In instances where news is favorable, announcers are known quickly to indicate that fact in their approach to recipients: they walk very rapidly towards them, attempting to shorten the amount of time when the recipient will be unduly worried. Surgeons have been observed to leave the operating with broad smiles on their faces, and begin talking long before they get within usual conversation distance. (121)

This pattern operates in the details of talk and interaction. Excerpt (2) involves Andi, the newly pregnant woman we previously have seen delivering the news to Betty, now with her husband Bob calling another couple, Lucy and Rich, to tell them. Lucy and Rich have been out of the United States on sabbatical. Rich answers the phone initially. Following a brief chat about how Rich is helping his daughter with homework, Bob asks if Lucy "is around tonight too?" Answering affirmatively, Rich offers to "get her on the phone" and Pete says, "Yeah, maybe she'd want to be." So Rich briefly leaves the phone, and returns with Lucy (on an extension) who trades greetings with Bob and Andi (lines 1–3 below), and then asks "How're ↑you::.." (line 4). Notice Bob's qualified response (arrowed), after which he immediately queries Lucy about her present activities.

```
(2a)  ARL IB
   1  Lucy:    Hello::!
   2  Bob:     [Hi Lu]cy
   3  Andi:    [Hi::: ]
   4  Lucy:    How're ↑you::..
   5  Bob:  →  Oh: pretty ↑goo:d, what're we tearing you away from
   6           tonight heh [heh
   7  Lucy:                [Oh::: not much?
   8  Bob:     Not much? H[uh:?]
   9  Lucy:                [No::]: I'm just actually I just got a real
  10           pottery catalog and I was looking at it.
```

Bob's query offers an exaggerated version of their having summoned Lucy to the phone and he also adds two laughter tokens (line 6), thereby offering a kind of apologetic but light or humorous approach to the intrusion. At first, Lucy downplays her previous involvement (line 7) and then, in response to Bob's questioning repeat (line 8), says what she was doing. Subsequently, Andi welcomes her "back to the U.S.," and asks how it feels to be "back to normal" (not shown on transcript).

These queries of Bob and Andi occupy the initial part of a series of questions to Lucy and Rich about their respective work situations, the children, sabbatical, and the state of their house after it had been sublet during the sabbatical. Their answers comprise topical talk that occupies six-and-a-half minutes. Although this is not business as usual in the sense of making arrangements to meet or get together, Bob and Andi jointly show an orientation to catching up on the others' circumstances before moves are made to discuss their own:

```
(2b) ARL IB
    1   Lucy:  What are you all up to in (.) in Midtown?=
    2   Rich:  =I'm waitin' fer some big new::s of some kind=
    3   Bob:   =Big [news:: hu::h? ]   [okay:::      ]         [hih]
    4   Andi:        [eh heh heh heh] [hih .hih .hih] .hhh    [You] ↑ar::e
    5          ehh heh heh [.hhhhhh eh ]
    6   Bob:                       [Arright well] we got some big changes goin' on
    7          around he::re.
    8   Rich:  [(        )    ]
    9   Andi:  [Are you sit]tin' down?
   10   Rich:  What?
   11   Andi:  Are you sitting down:?
   12   Lucy:  Yea::h?
   13   Andi:  ehh::!
   14                   (0.8)
   15   Bob:   Go ahead A[ndi       ]
   16   Lucy:            [When ar]e you moving.
   17   Andi:  Go ahead Bob heh [heh   ]       [heh ]
   18   Lucy:                   [ehhh!]        [    ]
   19   Bob:                                 [Well] we're expecting a
   20          baby in March.=
   21   Rich:  =Well::: my::: ↑goodness.
   22   Andi:  [eh heh h[eh heh]
   23   Bob:   [eh heh h[eh heh]
   24   Lucy:          [What! ]
   25   Rich:  [(Make [sure     we're) sitting dow(heh)n hh
   26   Bob:         [WHA(h)T [heh heh heh heh heh
   27   Lucy:               [↑What?
   28   Bob:   [heh heh]
   29   Lucy:  [I- I-     ] expecting? (0.3) as in having it yourse::lf?=
```

```
30   Bob:  Ha::[ving it oursel(h)ves] ye(heh) (heh)s .hih
31   Andi:      [eh heh heh heh heh ]
32   Bob:  That traditio(h)nal way [heh [heh heh heh
33   Andi:                          [eh heh heh [.hhh
34   Lucy:                                      [Yes [it's a=
35   Andi:                                           [.hhh
36   Lucy:  =good [thing we're sitt(h)ing dow(heh) [(heh) (heh)n
37   Andi:       [heh                              [
38   Bob:                                [sitt(h)ing dow(h)n
39          [heh yes]=
40   Andi: [heh heh]=
41   Bob:  =[heh heh heh [heh heh]
42   Andi: =[Heh heh heh [heh heh] .hhh hhh
43   Lucy:               [Two people who claimed they weren't gonna to
44          do this [(I hope ya know)
45   Bob:          [Hy:: kno::w heh .hh
46   Lucy: heh heh!
47                  (0.4)
48   Bob:  So:: this is:, as I've been tellin' folks a: reversal in
49          .hhh thought as well as pro(h) [ce(h)ss heh heh=
50   Andi:                                 [hhhhhh
51   Bob:  =[heh heh heh] heh heh [.hhhh
52   Lucy: =[ehh heh heh]         [
53   Rich:                        [Well uh it's-
54                  (0.4)
55   Lucy: Congratula[tions]
56   Rich:           [Yea::]:: well wonder[ful    ]
57   Lucy:                                [That's] good ↑new::s.
58   Bob:  Nnnanks
59   Lucy: hheh!
60   Bob:  Well we're re:al excited about it so::=
61   Lucy: =Goo:d!
```

Lucy's question to Bob and Andi is about what they are "up to," after which
Rich says, "I'm waitin' fer some big new::s." The call recipients thereby exhibit
an expectation that the call involves more than their callers' interest in the recipients' own affairs, given their recent return from sabbatical. Such expectations
can be responsive to several cues: this being a long-distance call, Bob's accepting Rich's offer to get Lucy on the phone, and Bob's "pretty good" response to
Lucy's how-are-you. "Pretty good," in other words, may be produced and heard
with the two features of premonitoring news while allowing also for attention
to business as usual (in this case, hearing about the others' circumstances).

As a qualified conventional response, "pretty good" in the context of excerpt
(2b) premonitors prosperity talk (see note 7). And whereas bearers, once a re-

turn from business as usual is occasioned, continue to exhibit reluctance in producing bad news/troubles talk, that is not the case with good news/prosperity talk. In excerpt (2b), to be sure, there are further delays following the solicitation of Andi and Bob's news, but these delays are occupied with laughter at the "big news" formulation and at Rich's having to wait for it (lines 3–5). That is, Bob (line 3) repeats Rich's phrase about "big news," which can be a way of retrieving an item from previous talk for joking appreciation (see Schegloff 1987a: 213). Andi at line 4 and in overlap with the latter part of Bob's utterance, responds with laughter, taking an inbreath when the overlap stops. At that point, Bob offers a laughter token (line 3), while Andi produces a questioning repeat and adds more laughter (lines 4–5). After this, the news is further delayed when Bob preannounces "big changes" (line 6–7) and Andi injects a readiness check, asking if their recipients are "sitting down" (lines 9, 11). Positioned after the joking and laughter, these postponing moves are not protectively covering the forthcoming good news so much as proffering jesting prefaces that dramatize its favorable status.

Subsequent to Andi's readiness check is talk occupied with establishing who of the Bob–Andi unit will make the announcement. Bob suggests that Andi should "go ahead" (line 15), and overlapping this Lucy interjects a guess as to the news, proposing that they are "moving" (line 16). Andi next (line 17) tells Bob to "go ahead," thereby declining Bob's invitation to her, and she appends laughter tokens to this utterance. Notice that Lucy, having offered a guess as to the news, and having it disattended by Andi's return invitation to Bob, produces a laughter exclamation token (line 18), which aligns to the exchange between Bob and Andi concerning who is going to do the announcement. When Bob delivers the news (at lines 19–20), there is a preceding token ("Well"), which may work to absorb the last laughter particle in Andi's previous "go ahead" turn. Otherwise, the news is fronted within and is the sole occupant of Bob's announcing turn at talk. Once the announcement is implicated through its preannouncements and the recipients' go-ahead signals, then, there is no hinting or clueing, no glossing, no solicitation of further requests for the news, nor is Lucy's guess officially recognized.[9] Rather than being shrouded in exhibits of reluctance, the news is exposed by being forthrightly delivered. And its bearers convey the positive valence from the very outset of their having been asked what they are "up to" and what their possible "big news" is.

Without analyzing in detail the rest of the fragment, it can be noted that Rich (line 21) and Lucy (line 24) initially receive the news with markers of surprise, while Andi and Bob continue to offer laughter (lines 22–23). Subsequently, both Rich (at line 25) and Lucy (lines 34, 36) acknowledge with laughter Andi's

having asked about their "sitting down." Lucy's latter turn implicates a new series of joking and laughter on this topic (lines 38–42), after which Lucy proposes an ironic comment on Bob and Andi's previous decision not to have children (lines 43–44) to which Bob responds with a "knowing" laugh (line 45).
Thus, the light tone that was augured as far back as when Lucy initially got on
the phone, and was more strongly promoted as Lucy and Rich solicited and Bob
and Andi preannounced their news, is preserved throughout the delivery, its receipt, and the interactional sequelae (including lines 46–61).

Premonitoring Bad versus Good News

When a co-participant produces a qualified conventional response to "how
are you," it can premonitor either bad or good news, and allow for attention to
business or a display of orientation to the potential news recipient's own situation. And just as news bearers in holding off bad news exhibit "troubles-
resistance," bearers who hold off good news may be demonstrating their
"prosperity-resistance." In either case, news bearers show that they are not
so overwhelmed by their own circumstances as to necessitate indulging in immediate revelation. Beyond this, similarities in the delaying of bad news and postponing of good news dissipate. After business as usual, preannouncements of
bad news may require not just regular go-ahead signals but further queries from
a recipient that help unpackage the tidings, whereas the delivery of good news
is advanced rather than hindered. Moreover, good news may be staged by joking, laughter, and other devices that cue recipients as to a positive valence while
keeping the exact substance in check. Accordingly, an aspect of the asymmetry
between bad and good news is the differential restraints on *flooding out* (Goffman 1961: 55)—"under certain circumstances the individual may allow his
manner to be inundated by a flow of affect that he no longer makes a show of
concealing." The affective correlates of good news, such as laughter, are less constrained than the correlates of bad news, such as crying and sobbing.

Disciplining the Inquiry into Asymmetries

Dealing with the phenomenon of asymmetries between good and bad news
is more difficult than a first glance might reveal, because each episode of bad or
good news can be unique in its produced orderliness. Thus, in excerpt (1), the
party with the bad news is the called party rather than the caller, and his news is
therefore not the reason for the call, whereas in the good-news call, in excerpts
(2a) and (2b), this news is the reason for the call. In addition, the bad-news call
involves only two parties, whereas the good-news call has four parties, bifur-

cated into two sets of couples. Also different is the subject matter of the calls. More generally, episodes differ not only according to what the news is about, but in terms of the nature of the news or what I call the *intensity* of the valence—how good or bad the news is. They differ in terms of the relationship between the parties who give and receive the news. Just considering the "who" variable, or the primary figure of the news, chapter 5 showed that it can be about the deliverer, the recipient, or some third party. If the news is about a third party, then analytically there is the relationship to the third party for both deliverer and recipient to appraise. Ethnomethodologically, we can recognize that all of these features—the subject matter, the nature of the news, the intensity of the valence, who the primary figure is, the relationships between involved parties, and other features as well—accord each episode a particularity and singularity that can make any blanket comparative strategy go far off the mark analytically.

Nevertheless, if there is universality to how members of social worlds configure their experiences with bad and good news, then interactional patterns and structures correspondingly traverse through these episodes, representing generic practices for handling bad and good news and relating them to one another. To appreciate these practices, comparisons between bad and good news can be disciplined by attempting to hold constant as many features of these episodes as possible. For example, despite other differences, both the excerpts above involve first-party bad or good news. I will now compare two examples on the basis of a kind of binary relationship—they are at opposite ends of the birth–death spectrum. Excerpt (3) involves the good news of birth in the family, and excerpt (4) represents bad news of death in the family. Excerpt (3) is the familiar example of good news in which Carrie has called Leslie about her new granddaughter, and she presents her news in first-party fashion ("I've got a little gran'daughter"). In excerpt (4) the bearer of the news presents it as third-party news ("Miriam died this morning"). Despite this difference in the format for delivery, in both examples there are consequential figures closer than the teller. In each case, these figures are the parents of the child, whose reactions are reported and examined in later parts of the conversations not included in the transcripts reproduced below. Another common feature is that the deliverer telephones the recipient and the news she bears, again in each case, is the reason for the call.

By representing a binary comparison of news deliveries, excerpts (3) and (4) also permit analysis of how reception reinforces the asymmetry of shrouding versus exposure. In excerpt (3), when Carrie announces the news about a granddaughter (lines 4–5), it can be noticed that she preempts specific opening moves such as a return greeting to Leslie's line 3 hello and how-are-you sequences.

(3) H13G (Holt:1988:2:4:1)
```
 1   Leslie:  Hello↑?h
 2   Carrie:  Oh Les↑lie it's Carrie.
 3   Leslie:  °t hOh: ↑Carrie: ↑Yes he↑llo[:.hh °hh hh
 4   Carrie:                            [I: thought you'd like to
 5            know I've got a little gran'daughter
 6   Leslie:  °thlk ↑Oh: how love↓ly.
 7   Carrie:  ↓Ye:s bo:rn th's <early hours'v this ↓morning.
 8   Leslie:  ˙k↑Oh: joll[y goo:d, [h
 9   Carrie:             [↓Ye:s  [↑Christi:ne ↓Ru[th.
10   Leslie:                                  [°hhhhh ↑hOh:: that's
11            ↓ni::ce:.h What a nice name. eh ↑hhah[↑heh hu °hhhhh
12   Carrie:                                      [(Yeh'v ↑cou:rse.)
13   Leslie:  Ye:s. hheh he he °hhhhhhhh
```

In this announcement, Carrie first proposes the relevance to Leslie of her news and also indicates its valence (at lines 4–5 with "I thought you'd like to know"); Carrie then gives the news about the granddaughter right away. Colloquially, she is *eager* with her news, and Leslie, at line 6, immediately oh-receipts this delivery with a positive assessment, following which Carrie gives two additional components to the news (lines 7, 9). After each, Leslie juxtaposes positive assessments (lines 8, 10–11), and the two parties follow that by displaying agreement on the "nice name" (lines 12–13).

Matters are different in excerpt (4) concerning death. Fay's niece has died, and she has called to tell Judy. Having identified her call recipient (lines 3–4), Fay not only inquires as to whether she has awakened her (line 5), but also initiates a how-are-you sequence (lines 7–8), which Judy reciprocates (line 8). Fay's answer ("pretty good," line 9) to Judy's inquiry is a qualified conventional response.

(4) UTCL A38.027
```
 1   Judy:  Hello?
 2                  (0.3)
 3   Fay:   Judy?
 4   Judy:  ↑Yes.
 5   Fay:   Were you asleep?
 6   Judy:  No, huh uh I'm gettin ready to go to ↑work
 7   Fay:   Oh:: how's it goin.
 8   Judy:  ↑Fine. How'r you doin[:.
 9   Fay:                        [Pretty goo::d.
10                  (0.2)
11   Fay:   .hhhh I tried callin you the other night, and you weren't
12          ho::me.
13   Judy:  Oh really?
```

```
14   Fay:   Yea:[:h,
15   Judy:       [What night was that.
16   Fay:   Oh:: it musta been: Monday or Tuesday
17   Judy:  O:h ye[ah. ]
18   Fay:          [May]be Wednesday.
19               (0.3)
20   Judy:  Monday I work u::h late. Tuesday I was off though.
21               (0.7)
22   Judy:  [(I:::-)              ]
23   Fay:   [Wonder what I-] see when was: it.
24   Judy:  I dunno, I went to the doctor on Tuesday and I 'n't- (0.4)
25          I got home 'bout four thirty.
26   Fay:   No it was in the e::veni:ng.
27               (0.8)
28   Fay:   .hhh So anywa:y.
29               (0.2)
30   Fay:   Well I just called to tell you, Miriam died this ↓morning
31               (0.6)
32   Judy:  Yo:ur kid[din:g.]
33   Fay:             [No::, ] she died at four thirty.
34               (0.8)
35   Judy:  °You'r:e kidding°
36               (0.2)
37   Fay:   So:
38               (0.4)
39   Fay:   She had a real rough two days:
```

Instead of producing her bad news, Fay hesitates (line 10) and, with a "my side telling" (Pomerantz 1980) about having "tried callin" Judy (line 11), implicates a series of turns concerned with when Fay had tried calling and where Judy was. While these matters never get resolved, of interactional importance may be the indication that Fay had attempted to connect earlier, and therefore had something to report. Coupled with Fay's initial qualified conventional response to a how-are-you inquiry, which is otherwise equivocal as to whether there is trouble, this can be a stronger way of occasioning or soliciting the co-participant's inquiry. That Fay may be waiting for such inquiry also appears evident at line 27, where there is a silence after "no it was in the e::veni:ng," and at line 29, after her upshot indicator ("hhh So anywa:y," line 28). Both are points of completion where Judy appears to avoid turn transition and, specifically, asking why Fay had called and is calling now.[10] At line 30, Fay proffers the reason for her call on the way to announcing her bad news. Overall, then, Fay may be working in a number of ways to do this announcing in response to inquiry rather than through her own initiation. If so, the attempt does not work here, but it fits with the pattern in which participants with troubles and bad news may fashion collaboration in its uncovering. In contrast, the good news of Carrie's grand-daughter was rather unilaterally offered and thereby exposed.

Finally, notice how Judy's announcement response (line 32), the ritualized disbelief token, is delayed (line 31), as is her quieted repeat (line 35) of this response, after Fay's line 33 elaboration. By virtue of its sequential positioning, in the fourth slot of the news delivery sequence, the repeat may be withholding assessment as such and simply displaying further surprise or astonishment. Again in contrast with excerpt (3) and how Leslie receives the news of Carrie's grand-daughter, the responses here are measured and restrained, suggesting that recipients of third-party news, as when recipients or second parties are the primary figure, may exhibit stoicism.

To frame the matter informally, deliverers *and* recipients exhibit eagerness with respect to good news, and reluctance in relation to bad news.[11] Deliverers produce good news forcefully in the sense of placing its valence and often its substance forthrightly into a developing conversation, and likewise recipients respond strongly and immediately. Deliverers present bad news in a more hesitating manner, and recipients are restrained in their acknowledging and assessing turns.

The Sequelae to Good and Bad News

So far, we have been examining patterns and practices exhibited internally to the organization of preannouncement and announcement sequences, and observing the overwhelming if not invariant asymmetries between bad and good news.[12] A related matter is how participants talk *after* a news delivery. Once again, we will see an asymmetry between bad news and good news, where bad news gets buffered much more than good news. In three episodes discussed below, all concerning pregnant dogs, good news is exposed and bad news is shrouded in the news delivery sequence. In addition, there is a buffering of the bad news after completion of the NDS and before participants move to a next topic or phase of the conversation. Good news does not get such treatment.

Good News about Forthcoming Puppies

Two examples of good news illustrate ways in which, subsequent to good news, there can be relatively immediate movement to shift or change topic or to close the conversation.

Topic shifting. In excerpt (11), Marge's first utterance is a complimenting comment on a picture card she has received from Ellen, who is a proud dog owner:

Shrouding Bad News, Exposing Good News   175

(5) JH6G/Heritage:I:6:3

```
 1   Marge:        Th'dogs er a:bsolutely lovel[y.
 2   Ellen:  1→                                    [Oh good. I'm hoping
 3                 fuh'nothuh littuh shortly
 4                       (0.2)
 5   Marge:  2→ Ah::[(ha  [           ).
 6   Ellen:  3→       [Uh:: [Tessa wuh (.) Tessa wz mated about uh:m
 7                 °tch °h two weeks ago:.
 8                       (0.3)
 9   Marge:  4→ Oh: ↓love[ly.
10   Ellen:                    [So: if it's taken they should be heuh in
11                 about six weeks b't I ↓dont' know yet've course you
12                 cahn't tell, (.) until, °hh
13   Marge:        O[h h o w r e a]lly lovely.=
14   Ellen:         [about a month,
15   Marge:        =°hh Ez a matter've fact I was going to ↓ah:sk you,
16                 °p°hhh eh:m (.) (.) is there anyone very reliable
17                 thet does clipping . . .
```

This excerpt follows the prototype news delivery sequence, with a headlining announcement about expecting a litter (arrow 1), recipient's encouraging news-mark (arrow 2), and an elaboration of the news (arrow 3), after which the recipient produces an assessment (arrow 4). Following this at lines 10–12, is a further elaboration of the news in regard to the timing of the focal event; this occasions Marge's accentuated assessment at line 13 (in overlap with the completion of Ellen's turn, line 14). Then, when Marge finishes her assessment, she changes topic to ask about "anyone" who does "clipping" (lines 15–17). That is, in an immediate post-assessment shift of topic, she inquires of Ellen where she might get her own dog groomed.

Conversational closing. In the next example, Ellen's husband Edward, talking in a later phone call to Ronnie, who had called him about a business transaction, also introduces the good news about the dogs being pregnant. His announcement is late in the call and tied to Ronnie's response to a conversational close-offering from Edward (lines 1–3 below). Ronnie returns a closing component (lines 4–5) with good wishes for Edward's wife ("the lady mayoress" — Edward is mayor of his town), but, instead of initiating the successor to a closing sequence — a terminal sequence — Edward takes the opportunity to report on his wife's present activities (lines 6, 8, 10–11). In other words, he makes a movement out of closing (Button 1987; Schegloff and Sacks 1973):

(6) JH1G/Heritage:OIII:1:Call 5:Excerpt (retranscribed)

```
 1   Edward:       Awright Ronnie well we: we look fohwuhd t' seeeing
 2                 you the:n en fuhrthuhmohr f'm both'v us many thanks
```

```
 3                          fuh calling?
 4    Ronnie:               Nawt eh taw:ll en det uh give the lady mayoress a big
 5                          hug from me enna kiss will you?
 6    Edward:               Ah'll do [the:t yes? yes ye]he she's verry busy ahm
 7    Ronnie:                        [°hh hh heh heh heh]
 8    Edward:               °hh She's veddy busy et the mo:m'nt,
 9    Ronnie:               Ah'll b[et she i]s.
10    Edward:                      [u h dih]dishing u:p (0.4) uh fohr the do:gs
11                          incident'ly?
12    Ronnie:               Oh:: ye:ss::
13    Edward:   1→          Ye:s she's got uh she's got two bitches hopefully
14              →           producing puppies, uh::ah:::=
15    Ronnie:   2→          =[(Oh good.)]
16    Edward:   3→          =[in    about] a month's time.
17    Ronnie:   4→          W'thet's mahv'lous. °hhhh Well anyway v-ehm ehm uhm
18                          Edward I had tih ring you up bec'z I'm so deˇlighted
19                          . . . ((referring to business deal))
```

After Ronnie at line 12 acknowledges Edward's report on his wife's activities, Edward goes on to announce that "two bitches" are pregnant (arrow 1). Thus, the report on Ellen's activities comes to serve as a bridge to this announcement. Continuing with "uh::ah:::" (line 14), Edward holds his turn and, just as he starts to elaborate on the timing of delivery (arrow 3), Ronnie, in overlap, marks and assesses the news (arrow 2), with an item ("Oh good") that (if the transcription of sound is correct) is regularly sequence- or topically terminal (Heritage 1984a: 303–5).[13] However, Edward finishes his overlapped turn and elaboration, after which Ronnie (arrow 4) assesses the news strongly. He then breathes in, produces a possible preclosing "Well anyway," and changes topic to the reason for the call, which eventuates in a return to closing and terminal sequences for the conversation. This move toward closings may have been augured in the topically discouraging "Oh good" news receipt at line 16, and Ronnie's "W'thet's mahv'lous" works to finalize the news delivery as closings promptly ensue.

Sequelae to Bad News

After the delivery and receipt of good news in conversation, participants allow and initiate direct movement to shift or change topic or bring the conversation to a close. As in excerpts (5) and (6), it is often the recipient who proposes the transition, whatever it may be. Similar patterns are found in interactional data involving patients and family members meeting with cancer information specialists, support group leaders, or family therapists. Jones (1997) shows that these professionals, upon receiving and assessing news from their clients as "good," can within the same turn offer further information or advice. That is, although on-topic questions or formulations also occur, topic shifting is immediately permissible. Exit from bad news is differently configured. The sequelae to bad news in conversation suggest that it is impermissible to make a transition from such deliveries to other types of talk without first putting a positive face on the bad news. When participants shift or change topic, or move into closings they regularly produce one of three sequence types that I call *good news exits* from the bad news. They use (1) remedy announcements, (2) bright-side sequences, and (3) optimistic projections.

Remedy announcements. A first category of good-news exit from bad news is the remedial proposal sequence. Often it contains an idiomatic expression that offers some more-or-less concrete resolution to the problem that bad news adumbrates, and the remedial sequence may, as in excerpt (7), follow troubles talk into which the bad news has segued. The proposal of remedy and its acknowledgment permit movement away from the news, such as the shift to a closing of the conversation. This bad-news excerpt is related to the two previous excerpts about the pregnant bitches of Edward and Ellen. One of the dogs has subsequently given birth to her pups and they died. (Just prior to Alfred's line 1 inquiry, he and Edward had been discussing investments.)

(7) JH3B/Heritage:IV:2:Call 4:Ex:2

```
 1    Alfred:        Edith wz asking how th'dogs wuh
 2                   (0.3)
 3    Edward:  1→    °h Oh well uh:m uhm uh:m: it it's a chapter'v
 4                   accid'nts I'm afrai:d,
 5    Alfred:  2→    °Ohh.°
 6    Edward:  3→    mghhm We lost all th'm: she had sev'n.
 7                   (0.2)
 8    Alfred:        Ye:s I kn[ew  s  h  e  w ' z ]
 9    Edward:   →             [An'they wuhr a:ll] prematua:h,
10    Alfred:        I knew [she w' feeding     ] one,
11    Edward:   →           [°An'they were all°]
12    Edward:   →    Yeh very sma:ll ye[s yes]    [ukkhh! ((cough))
13    Alfred:  4→                      [Ye:s ] ah[:: sohhrry to heah that.
14    Edward:  3r→   ukhh! No they uh °hh lahst one die:d,
15    Alfred:  4r→   Oh:: I'm sorry[t'°hear that°]
16    Edward:                      [A:nd u h : :]m uhm E-ellen wz very
17                   distressed [by it °hhh
18    Alfred:                   [I bet she was.
19    Edward:        Uh::m: she- she's (.) she's got oll huhr ffam'ly
20                   °ˇheu:h° ovuh heah fuh th'weekee:nnd so:: ah got (.)
21                   so much on huhr plate. °h she cahn't think about it
22                   but pohr little uh::::: pohr li=th'pohr little dah:g
```

```
23                   Tessa.
24    Alfred:        Yeh
25    Edward:        She's pining.
26    Alfred:        Yes::=
27    Edward:        =en she won't eat,
28    Alfred:        No=
29    Edward:        =ah:: end a'course °that gets Ellen moh wuhrried.°
30    Alfred:        °I'll bet it does.°
31    Edward:        So uh:m anyway,hh uh,hh thea:hr ther ih ti:s,
32    Alfred:        M[mh
33    Edward:  ⇒       [uh:: jus'g'nna haftuh s- uh try agay:n nex'time.
34    Alfred:        Yes
35                        (0.2)
36    Alfred:        °°Oh yes°° °hhhh enny case Edward eokay so w'l
37                   [leave th]e arrangements' they ah:re,
38    Edward:        [A'right. ]
39    Edward:        Yahp
40    Alfred:        If I hear anything diffrent you'll ring me.
```

Before we consider the exit from the bad news, it is worth noticing the shrouding entrance to it. Edward, in response to Alfred's question about the dogs (line 1), headlines his news by saying that "it's a chapter'v accid'nts" (arrow 1) and, after Alfred's response, pronounces the loss of puppies in an elaboration turn (arrow 3). This use of an announcing turn to forecast the news, and delaying of the focal news until the elaboration part of the news delivery sequence, is not invariant with bad news, but it does happen regularly. In contrast, when Ellen and Edward each announced the pregnancy to their respective friends, they placed the news in turn 1, unabashedly exposing it. It is as if bad news *requires* forecasting, while good news does not.

Having pronounced the death news, Edward proceeds to make a series of further elaborations (arrows following 3) about losing the dogs, how many there were, their prematurity and small size. Alfred intersperses displays of some knowledge at lines 8 and 10 and subsequently aligns to Edward's details with a sympathetic assessment (arrow 4), which could serve to terminate the news delivery. However, Edward adds an utterance that, with a finalizing report (the "lahst one die:d", arrow 3r) possibly configured to Alfred's claims of knowing that Tessa was "feeding one," recompletes this news delivery. Alfred, for a second time, offers a sympathetic assessment (arrow 4r). Now, rather than this marking the end of the news, Edward, having received Alfred's affiliative alignment, "lets go" with further troubles talk (Jefferson 1988: 428). He reports about how the situation affected Ellen (lines 16–17, 19–21) and the dog Tessa (lines 22–23, 25, 27), and how the dog's "pining" further "wuhrried" Ellen (line

29). Along the way, Alfred aligns to this telling with tokens of receipt, regret, sympathy, and the like, until Edgerton produces an abstracted summary (line 31) and then proposes a formulaic remedy (arrow, line 33) about trying "agay:n." Alfred responds to this proposal with tokens of agreement ("yes," and "oh yes," lines 34, 36), and then, after an inbreath, proposes closings (line 36). The pattern here is one that Drew and Holt (1998) have described, wherein the news teller suggests a figurative summary with which the recipient agrees; this makes closings relevant. Overall in this segment, after the bad news is troubles talk related to it, a summary, and finally a remedy proposal sequence before a thematic transition is made.

Bright-side sequences. In a study of death announcements as one type of bad news, Holt analyzed a "bright side" sequence. Subsequent to the news of a death and its negative assessment, participants describe and evaluate the deceased person's life prior to death and/or manner of dying in a way that provides for positively assessing the news. Recall the excerpt from chapter 4 concerning the death of "Philip Cole's" mother; excerpt (8) continues the transcript after the death announcement (line 10) and has a prototypical bright-side sequence.

```
(8)  H7B/Holt:X(C)1:1:6:15
  1   Leslie:  Well I'm I'm s:- (.) proba'ly going to a funeral on
  2            Tuesday,
  3                 (0.4)
  4    Mum:    ↑O[h ↓dea:[r.
  5   Leslie:     [°t      [°ukhhh-hu °p°thh D'you 'member- You know
  6            Philip Cole you ↑know 'e had this u-very: good °hhhh
  7            very busy little mother that wz al[ways
  8    Mum:                                       [↑Oh:: ↓ye[s.
  9   Leslie:                                                [busy
 10            doing thin:gs 'nd, (.) She die:d.
 11    Mum:    Ah↓:::.
 12                 (0.2)
 13   Leslie:  eh-in the week ↑very peace↓fully:
 14    Mum:    Yes.
 15   Leslie:  °p°hh She jus' didn't recover from a stro:ke, she
 16            ju[s:t sort'v fell asleep.
 17    Mum:    [Oh:.
 18                 (1.0)
 19   Leslie:  A:[nd u h ]
 20    Mum:      [Well tha]t's a nice ↓way t'go↓ [isn't it]
 21   Leslie:                                     [Y e : s]=
 22            =tha[t's right]
 23    Mum:        [(     ] ),
 24                 (0.6)
```

```
25   Leslie:  An' an' ↑people had a chance to say cheerio t[o he:r 'n=
26   Mum:                                                      [Yes
27   Leslie:  =the vicar came 'n °hhh you know 'n i- it wz all very
28            peaceful.
29   Mum:     Yes, (.) How nice
30                    (0.3)
31   Leslie:  So they're ↑not g'nna have a: dis↓mal funeral↓ they said
32            th[ey're goin't' have a r::eally a thansgiving for her=
33   Mum:      [Tha:t's )
34   Leslie:  =li:[fe.
35   Mum:         [for her ↓life. Yes that's -[right. ]
36   Leslie:                                 [M m:.]
37                    (0.5)
38   Mum:     ↑Hm: (0.6) That's ni:ce
39                    (0.2)
40   Leslie:  Yes.
41   (Mum:)   (      )
42                    (0.9)
43   Mum:     That's all then ↑love
44                    (0.4)
45     Les:   Uh:m how's things the↑:re?
46                    (0.3)
47   Mum:     ↑Mm:m, everything seems t'be alri:ght
```

Leslie at lines 13 and 15–16 produces a positive characterization of the way that Mrs. Cole died, to which Mum responds with a fitted assessment (lines 17, 20). Leslie agrees with this (lines 21–22) and goes on with further components to the bright side (lines 25, 27–28), after which Mum (line 29) provides a further mildly upbeat assessment, "How nice" (line 29). Finally, at lines 31–32 and 34, Leslie puts yet another positive face on the matter, formulating the postmortem ceremony with contrasting components—"not a dismal funeral/thanksgiving for her life"—to which Mum aligns by demonstrating agreement (line 35) and producing a further positive assessment (line 38). There is next an agreement from Leslie (line 40), and from Mum something inaudible to the transcriber (line 41). Mum then initiates termination of the conversation at line 43; her possible preclosing, however meets with Leslie's query (line 45), which reopens the conversation. After a death announcement, Holt (1993: 203) observes, evaluations become increasingly positive as the participants collaboratively move away from the bad news.[14] The bright-side sequence mediates between the death announcement and the possible closing or movement to next topic.

Optimistic projections. A third good-news exit is one that, in the context of discussing how participants bring closure to troubles talk, Jefferson (1988) calls the "optimistic projection." Regularly, such projections involve formulaic, idiomatic expressions, such as "it'll all come right in the end," "it'll iron itself out," which Drew and Holt (1998) have shown to occur regularly in the context of topic transition in conversation. While they use such expressions in relation to many other topics, participants often exit the delivery and receipt of bad news with them, as when, in one conversation (see excerpt (18) in chapter 5), Ann tells Jenny that her new beds have arrived, but with only "one mattress." Jenny responds with "Oh no," and then Ann exits this news telling with "So anyway . . . it'll turn up I expect" before reengaging the topic of rearranging her bedroom.

In addition, a particular way of making optimistic projections in the context of bad news is with a statement or statements of hopefulness. In one conversation, Joyce informs Leslie about her neighbor Helen having cancer. There are several components to the telling. It starts with Joyce's noting that Helen had developed a lump in her neck, had had it removed, developed a second lump, and had been having chemotherapy since. Now here is a second component of the news:

(9a) H27B/Holt:088:1:8:6
```
 1   Joyce:  . . . she looks desperate but uhm °p°hh she went t'see
 2           the specialist last week 'n °t°hh he says you know::
 3           gi- December the fouth come'n see me, you've °hhhhh
 4           (.) had your las'treatment n::ow yo know h-all you
 5           c'n do is keep y'r fingers crossed
 6   Leslie: Oh: dear dear dea:r.
 7                   (0.5)
 8   Leslie: [Hm::::.
 9   Joyce:  [So I do hope she survives °hh=
10   Leslie: =[H u : h .]
11   Joyce:  =[It's very] sad cuz . . .
```

After Leslie's standardized but accentuated oh-prefaced assessment (line 6), Joyce produces a hopeful optimistic projection (line 9), which serves as a preface to further characterizations of Helen's situation (starting at line 10 and continuing in talk not reproduced here). Joyce mentions Helen having an unhappy first marriage, and then meeting and marrying another divorced teacher, Ron, suggesting "they're so happy." And she goes on with other upbeat versions of Helen's situation:

(9b) H27B/Holt:088:1:8:7
```
 1   Joyce:  A:n:d uh even the kids she said're so happy with Ron
 2           you know=
 3   Leslie: =Aoh::.
 4                   (.)
```

```
 5   Joyce:  They look such a nice family they w'r in church this
 6           mornin:[g
 7   Leslie:       [Ah::.
 8   Joyce:  °tch°hhh[hh
 9   Leslie:        [Oh I ↑hope she'll be alri:ght, [hh
10   Joyce:                                        [Oh: e-yeh so
11           do I [°hhh
12   Leslie:      [Hm:.
13   Joyce:  But going back to Nancy she pho:ned . . .
```

In the context of the bad news about cancer, however, Leslie treats these informings regarding Helen's felicitous family situation as further components of the bad news. For instance, to the item about how happy the remarried couple are, Leslie had said "Oh what a shame." Here, Leslie produces downward intoned sympathetic tokens (lines 3, 7) in response to reports of how "happy" the kids are "with Ron" (lines 1–2) and how the family looks "nice" in church (lines 5–6). Then, at line 9, Leslie, as recipient, produces the hopeful projection, after which the news deliverer, Joyce, agrees (line 10–11) before then changing topic (line 13). Thus, it is a completed hope-announcement sequence—that is, a hopeful proposal in one turn and agreement in a next turn—that occasions exit from the bad news topic.

The Benign Order of Everyday Life

A major theme of this investigation is that bad news and good news, as natural disruptions to the familiar social world, render it as strange and permit exposure to the usually unseen practices whose routine employment gives organization to the world. Comparing bad and good news demonstrates that, and shows how participants in interaction structure the social world as a relatively benign one. Just as biases against bad news and toward good news figure in folklore collections of jokes and stories, and earmark a universal tendency, such biases are overwhelmingly present in the concreteness of participants' real-time talk and social interaction.

Ethnomethodological studies, investigating trouble spots in otherwise familiar environments, establish that the world is, in practical terms, objective and real for its participants, owing to their taken-for-granted and therefore largely unseen efforts (Zimmerman and Pollner 1970). The *mundane reality* participants experience derives from how, on every occasion of inquiry into the nature of the world, they effortfully infuse it with qualities of coherence, determinateness, and noncontradiction (Pollner 1987: 26–27). When participants entertain contradictory observations about the world—"reality disjunctures"—they do not doubt the possibility of an objective, unitary world. Instead, participants question the adequacy of the *observations* or the *observers*. For example, when a defendant in traffic court claims to have been traveling at 68 miles per hour and a police officer has charged that the defendant was going 78 mph, the court does not entertain a possibility that both versions could be right. It is presumed that the defendant was going just one speed, and parties to the dispute search for ways to discredit one or the other version. If, the defendant claims that his speedometer was in error and can provide evidence of that, then there is an explanation for the discrepant versions that resides in the adequacy of measurement. In dismissing the defendant's charge, and using this faulty observation as a reason, a judge sustains the objectivity of the world. The defendant was going but one verifiable speed.

Beyond its produced character as real, the social world is also an *ordinary* one, by way of participants indicating themselves to be *ordinary people*. "That is to say," Sacks (1984b) writes, "what you *look* for is to see how any scene you are in can be made an ordinary scene, a usual scene, and that is what that scene is" (416). For instance, recall from chapter 2 Sacks' discussion of the "at first I thought" syndrome whereby, when confronted with catastrophic events, people first react with normalizing interpretations of them. Participants' default stance, in the face of the extraordinary, is to hold onto the customary and prosaic. Or, having witnessed an exceptional scene, like a car crash, people report it in ways to make of the accident that it was just "another" accident. As Sacks puts it, the witness cannot claim "to have seen God in it. You cannot have a nervous breakdown because you happened to see an automobile accident. You cannot make much more of it than what anybody would make of it" (427). Others will sanction the person who tries to assemble it as something beyond just an unusual or uncommon event. In a myriad of ways, participants "do" being ordinary.

Inasmuch as the everyday social world is achieved as externally real and ordinary, it also has an accomplished benign structure. As interactively constituted, disclosures that transform the world for participants exhibit strong asymmetries between bad and good news. With respect both to its delivery and receipt, participants, in their practices of talk and social interaction, shroud bad news while exposing good news. They delay and withhold the telling of bad news, and are more immediate and forthcoming with good news. After its delivery and receipt, good news can stand on its own as transition is made to other topics and activities, but bad news invariably obtains some kind of mediating good-news exit, whether it is a remedy proposal, a bright-side sequence, or some kind of optimistic projection. This suggests that, just as bearers carefully protect bad news before its delivery and, in collaboration with recipients, carefully unwrap it, after its presentation both parties, in one way or another, auspiciously rewrap the tidings before moving to new topics and other activities. Good news, however, remains exposed; parties to the delivery and receipt handle the news forthrightly and then allow for unmediated topical and activity departure from the news. Put differently, bad news needs and mostly gets an anodyne or palliative relief in the form of good-news exits from it, whereas good news seems to serve as its own palliative.

In theoretical discussions, prominent sociologists have recognized participants' asymmetrical treatment of bad news and good news, but, in my view, too easily invoke the impositions of status and culture to explain it. For example, Gouldner (1975: 6) writes that "people do press us for good news and wish to avoid hearing the bad, and indeed, such people are often located at the top and have power over us." And Parsons (1951: 443–44) remarks on an "optimistic bias" inherent in American culture that results in a propensity for denial and a bias toward the belief that "things will be all right." My analysis suggests more universality to the asymmetry between bad and good news. The asymmetry is, to use Goffman's (1983) term, a phenomenon of the *interaction order*, a matter of how participants structure their direct relations independent of external rankings and particular national, subnational, or other groupings. In their relations with one another, status superiors and inferiors, and those equal in rank, collaborate in producing the asymmetry, as do individuals within many different cultures and societies. Certainly there may be variation in how shrouding and exposing occurs in particular cases,[15] which implies a call for comparative research, but otherwise we confront something that is more robust and impermeable than what status and culture can impose. Solidarity among participants—the possibility of acting in concerted ways—may depend upon having an objective world, an ordinary world, and a benign one as well.

It is conversational, interactional practice that sustains the asymmetry, and it happens not in a volitional way. In fact, it may be that parties to good news need and want to explore the other side, and parties to bad news may have feelings of depression and grief as accompaniments to the disclosure that resist a good-news exit. Even in the face of such individual wishes and experiences, in and through the praxis of actual interaction, participants work to sustain an asymmetry in which good news is celebrated and not diminished, while bad news and the accompanying feelings are cushioned and countered.[16] It is in this sense that participants render the socially sanctioned world of everyday life as a benign one rather than a malign one. In local circumstances of normal societies, in other words, a produced benign order prevails with piercing force.[17]

Coda: In the Clinic

I have suggested that holding constant the features of bad and good news episodes is an important way to discipline their analytic comparison. A convenient and strong way of doing this is to examine the delivery and reception of diagnostic news in clinical settings. Of course, each episode will have its specific character and particularities, but many things, including the clinical setting, the particular disorder under consideration, clinicians' professional training and expertise, recipients' lay status, the consultative nature of the interaction, and other aspects of the encounter, are similar, and permit relatively straightforward comparison. Therefore, I will review some interaction-based clinical studies that advance the analysis of patterned asymmetries between bad and good news.

Analysis of asymmetry is one matter. It is another matter to consider why bad news is shrouded and covered while good news is exposed. Exploring this question is aided by my ethnographic experience in, and recorded data from, an HIV-antibody testing clinic. Practices in this clinic are partially anomalous in that, while clients receive bad and good news asymmetrically, clinicians' deliveries of both kinds of tidings are more symmetrical than usual. This anomalous or "deviant" case allows for probing, in social organizational terms, why the asymmetries may otherwise exist.

Clinical Studies of Bad and Good News

The studies I will review include three in medical offices for humans and one veterinary clinic. In the veterinary context, Stivers (1998) came upon the phenomenon of "online commentary," or talk by clinicians describing what they see, feel, or hear during a physical exam. Veterinarians, while examining animals, also may explain medical procedures or evaluate what they see in a way that projects diagnosis. In performing this online commentary, Stivers found, veterinarians present bad news in a "mitigated" fashion. They use markers of uncertainty, rhetorical forms such as the litotes ("She's *not right* in her nervous system"), and prefacing modifiers ("quite a little racket" precedes a diagnosis of "deep bronchitis"). With good news, however, veterinarians are more likely to give the diagnosis in an unmitigated fashion ("No hernias, looks good").

In another study of online commentary involving physicians in pediatric consultations and adult primary care practice, Heritage and Stivers (1999) describe two configurations related to bad and good news. In the first, physicians who find significant evidence of illness during examinations remain silent, but produce online commentaries when signs of disease are mild or absent. This is a way of offering reassurance to patients or parents. In the second configuration, and paradoxically, when evidence of illness is minimal or lacking, physicians engage in online commentary to forecast what may be bad news for patients or parents. The bad news they forecast is that, although the patient is seeking relief for a symptom, a "no problem" diagnosis is on its way, and the physician cannot prescribe medication to alleviate the condition. In short, as a device for conveying diagnostic information, online commentary is not uniformly associated with good or bad news. But if clinicians employ the device contingently and as a "flexible resource" (Heritage and Stivers 1999: 1507), they consistently shroud bad news by silence or forecasting.

Probing the conveyance of diagnosis in a primary care or internal medicine clinic, we found that physicians produce bad news about blood pressure and other minor conditions very cautiously, while they are more forthright with good news (Maynard and Frankel forthcoming). Such asymmetry held when the conditions were more serious, as in conveying diagnoses concerning cancer and heart disease. A facet of the asymmetry is that physicians deliver and patients receive diagnostic good news using semantically positive terms, but handle bad news in a semantically neutral fashion. Per the findings of chapter 5, furthermore, patients are most often stoic when they receive bad news. Nonvocally, parties to a good news episode may maintain mutual gaze for long periods and their bodies frequently are aligned to one another, each participant sitting upright on a chair and squarely facing the other. In episodes of bad news, doctor and patient may avert eye gaze and face-to-face confrontation.

Finally, studying how nurses in Sweden give blood pressure, pulse, and blood sugar results to patients, Leppänen (1998: 149–66) discovered that they may forecast bad readings through markers or question–answer sequences that refer back to earlier unfavorable results, feelings of stress, or other reminders that can be used to anticipate the upcoming news. As well, nurses may delay the news with inbreaths and pauses, "soften" the delivery ([a glucose reading] *"lies a little high,* thirteen point five"), and account for or attempt to explain the results. When readings are good, however, nurses regularly provide a straightforward statement of the numerical value, except in circumstances where patients may not understand the value. Then, nurses precede or succeed the number with a positive assessment ("your blood sugar is six today, so it is completely normal").

Besides analyzing the different modes for presenting bad and good news, Leppänen studied how patients responded (166–81). After hearing bad test results, patients may utter exclamations but otherwise, in line with the findings of chapter 5, appear to be stoic. When they receive good outcomes, patients utter positive assessments, after which nurses agree:[18]

Nurse: One hundred and sixty over eighty-five,
Patient: .hhh but that was you know absolutely excellent
Nurse: Oh yes, it is. (Leppänen 1998: 167, English translation)

The patterns varied slightly when patients did not indicate that they understood the numerical values. Then, in cases of both bad and good results, nurses would first offer the respective assessment.

A "Deviant" Case: Bad News and Good News in HIV Counseling

Using data from HIV-antibody testing clinics (hereafter "HIV clinics"), I will build on these studies of bad and good news in clinics involving veterinarians, nurses, and physicians. In this clinic, although clients' receptiveness to bad and good news fits the asymmetric responses identified in the other clinics, the delivery of bad news departs from the asymmetries — counselors were often as direct and forthright in their conveyance of bad news as they were with good news. With reference to this "deviant" case,[19] it is possible to argue that ordinary shrouding of bad news guards against the release of anticipated affective responses from recipients, whose stoicism contributes to and is virtually synonymous with the restraint on emotion. If one *does not feel* particularly emotional on hearing bad news, the stoic response further averts such feeling, and if one *does feel* the emotion, stoicism forestalls its display. Exposing good news, on the other hand, can also potentiate affective responses and displays in the moment. The ultimate difference is that participants embrace experiences and displays of positive affect, such as smiling and laughing, because they are perceived to enhance social relationships, but avoid experiences and displays of negative affect, such as crying and sobbing, because in many social contexts they are deemed to threaten social relationships.

HIV clinics, like other medical environments, offer an advantage of permitting disciplined comparisons of diagnostic news involving favorable and unfavorable test results. When my clinical data were collected, the testing procedure involved clients arriving at the clinic for an appointment, or else simply "dropping in." Depending on how busy the clinic was, they waited very briefly or for as long as half an hour for a counselor, who called clients individually into an office and began the session by asking clients what their risk for infection was, making suggestions or giving advice about safer sex practices (Kinnell and Maynard 1996; Silverman 1997). As the interview came to a close, counselors drew a blood sample from the client and prepared it for sending to a state-sponsored laboratory for testing. After two weeks, the results were ready, and clients returned to the clinic to obtain them. Although sometimes indeterminate, results usually were either negative (good news) or positive (bad news) for the presence of the HIV-antibody.

HIV good news. As might be anticipated, when a client's test was negative for HIV antibody, counselors regularly delivered the news by stating the "results" forthrightly in their announcing turns. Excerpt (10) is an instance, and the delivery begins just after the counselor (CO) preannounces the news (line 1) and identifies the client (CL) at lines 1–3 by code (this was an anonymous testing clinic):

(10) B1B1:1:1
```
 1   CO:  I'll give you your results? hh Lemme just verify your co:de
 2        is 123456ABC.
 3   CL:  right
 4   CO:  Okay. .hhh the results came back non↑reactive. hh negative.
 5        hh
 6   CL:  Wonderful.
 7                       (2.6)
 8   CO:  .hhh Any questions: about what it means:: what it doesn't
 9        mean::
10                         (1.0)
11   CL:  U::::hm hh not really I this is my::::: (1.8) this is
12        the sixth time I've been tested . . .
```

After the identification sequence, the counselor presents the results as "nonreactive" and goes on to define what this means ("negative"; line 4). Then almost immediately, the client responds to the news with a positive assessment (line 6).

In Excerpt (11), the client, encouraged by the counselor, is more expansive.

(11) B6A1:1:1
```
 1   CO:  Ah: your code was: (2.0) 444555MNO, right? okay.
 2                (0.4)
 3   CO:  Result came back n:o:n reactive.
 4                (.)
 5   CL:  [.hhhhhhh]
 6   CO:  [which is ] negative.
 7   CL:  whhhhhhhh [.hhhhhhhhhh]
 8   CO:           [take a deep] breath
 9   CL:  hhh .hhhhhhhhhhhh (0.2) ahhhhhhhh .hhh hh
10                (0.2)
11   CO:  More people cry: at a negative than they do at a
12        PAHs[itive.]
13   CL:      [oh ye] ah heh heh hih
14                (0.6)
15   CL:  I'm not gonna cry. hhhh
16                (0.4)
17   CL:  .hh I'm jes' happy.
```

With no prelude other than identifying the client, the counselor delivers the good news at line 3. This is followed by a "beat" or micropause at line 4. Then, in overlap with the counselor defining "nonreactive" (line 3) as "negative" (line 6), the client starts an episode of huge sighing (lines 5, 7) in the midst of which, at line 8, the counselor proposes permission for the deep breathing. CL goes on with two more such sighs (line 9). And while CO then also suggests the occurrence of crying as a relevant response (lines 11–12), CL produces an agreeing utterance with post-utterance laughter (line 13) and then replies (lines 15, 17) that the sighing was not a prelude to crying but an expression of his happiness.

Another session also has a client who sighs loudly at the news of his negative test. This session shows another way in which a counselor may deliver the news, and that is in the assertive format (Maynard 1991a; Peräkylä 1998), where HIV is predicated as an absent condition for the client:

(12) B7A1:1

```
 1   CO:  Okay. .hhhhh the result came back no:n reactive, which
 2        means you (0.1) they did not find any antibodies in your
 3        blood stream.
 4             (0.1)
 5   CO:  Oka::y?
 6             (0.1)
 7   CO:  And I know we're going to h[ave  lots  of  discussio]n=
 8   CL:                             [whhhhhhhhhhhhhhhhhhhhhh]
 9   CO:  around that toni(h) (h)ght and figure out what's goin' on::
10        an- an why that ↑is. .hhhhh but they did not find any
11        antibodies at this point, so you're negative.
12             (2.0)
13   CL:  mhhhhhhhh
```

At lines 1–2, after announcing "the result," CO provides a lay definition of "nonreactive." The brief pause at line 4 indicates no audible response from the client, and CO next solicits one (line 5). Still getting no response (line 6), CO goes on to suggest a subsequent agenda (lines 7, 9); in the midst (line 8), CL releases an elongated sigh. CO, having suggested the agenda, at lines 10–11 draws an inbreath and repeats the earlier definition of the laboratory not finding "any antibodies," and now produces the "plain assertion" (Peräkylä 1998) or upshot at line 11, "so you're negative." Following a silence (line 12), CL again expresses a long sigh.

The use of the assertive format appears related to the reticence of the client: the counselor uses that device coupled to a repeated lay definition of the results after the client's silent way of receiving the diagnostic results and after he has sighed, but given no verbal receipt. This "subsequent version" (Davidson

1984), by offering more clarity, may be "pursuing a response"—a more expanded or verbal display of understanding (Pomerantz 1984b: 153–55) from the client.

HIV bad news. When HIV-antibody tests emerge as positive, it is bad news, and in this clinic counselors were almost as likely to expose the bad news as they were the good news. Counselors, in other words, regardless of whether the result was positive or negative, straightforwardly "cited the evidence" in a fashion consistent with the pattern Peräkylä (1998) finds to be associated with situations in which there is temporal distance between testing and diagnostic news delivery.[20] For example, the counselor in excerpt (13) announces his client's bad-news positive results at line 6 in a way that is very similar to how the counselors in excerpts (10) and (11) presented good news:

```
(13) B52A1:1:6
    1  CO:   A:nd your code i:s: hhh .hhh (0.4) thirteen fifteen sixty
    2        two?=
    3  CL:   =Mm hmm=
    4  CO:   =dee ay ef?
    5  CL:   Yes.
    6  CO: → .hh Okay your results came back positive.
    7  CL:   Okay
    8                    (1.0) ((moving papers))
    9  CO:   °Okay°
   10                    (0.5)
   11  CO:   Was this something you were expecting::? er[: : ]
   12  CL:                                            [Oh] sure.
   13  ( ):   (    )
   14  CL:   I'd a ben more surprised if it ha:dn't.
   15                    (2.1) ((still moving papers))
   16  CO:   °Okay.° .hhh they did the elizha test?
   17  CL:   Mm hmm.
   18  CO:   .hh a:n:d they:: (0.1) backed it up with another test
   19        called the western bloṭ.
   20  CL:   Righ:t.
   21  CO:   .hh which is a confirmatory type of test. It's more
   22        concise.
   23                    (5.8) ((moving papers))
```

After the news delivery, the client produces a simple "okay" (line 7) and then is silent (line 8). The counselor follows this with a quiet "okay" (line 9), and, apparently working to obtain a more expansive receipt, asks if this was an expected result (line 11). After the client answers that he was not surprised (lines 12, 14), and subsequent to another silence as he evidently prepares to refer to the two specific tests (line 15), CO names these tests in reciting the procedure (lines 16,

18–19, 21–22).[21] Accordingly, while the counselor here exposes the bad news, the client is stoic.

In excerpt (14), such stoicism is problematic for the counselor, who works in several ways to probe the client's restrained response:

```
(14) B68A1:1
  1   CO:  Okay. .hhh they did the resa- the te::st. .h and on the
  2        elisa (0.3) it did come back reactive or positive, okay?
  3               (0.4)
  4   CO:  They then did the western blot (0.3) and that also came
  5        back reactive.
  6               (.)
  7   CO:  Okay so that's the confirmatory. .hhhhh I didn't do your
  8        pretest, were you expecting this?
  9               (1.2)
 10   CL:  Yea::h. hhh
 11   CO:  What made you expect it.
 12               (0.2)
 13   CL:  Lumps on the neck.
 14   CO:  Okay. How long have they been there.
 15               (1.0)
 16   CL:  Couple months.
 17   CO:  Where (0.1) in the neck. in the back?
 18   CL:  Yea::h.
 19   CO:  (    )
 20               (5.5) ((CO may check CL's neck))
 21   CO:  ↑kay yeah, okay
 22               (1.7)
 23   CO:  .hhh is the first time you've ever been tested?
 24               (2.5)
 25   CO:  °what d'ya thinking.°
 26               (2.6)
 27   CL:  I donno. Mh hhh
```

Having identified the client by code (not on transcript), the counselor pre-announces his news (line 1), and, without any verbal go ahead nevertheless straightforwardly proceeds to deliver the news in two components. The first is at lines 1–2 and is a report of the ELISA test. And even though CO asks for a response with "okay?" (line 2), there is no verbal return from the client, as indicated by the silence at line 3. The second component of the delivery, involving the "western blot," is at lines 4–5. After this, which is a "transition-relevance place" and point where CL also could take a turn of talk (Sacks, Schegloff, and Jefferson, 1974), he doesn't. CO proceeds in line 7, as a way of completing the news delivery, to characterize the test as "confirmatory," and takes an inbreath at another point of possible turn transition before next asking whether the client expected them (lines 7–8). After CL's confirmation (line 10), and reference to "lumps on the neck" (line 13), CO asks about (lines 14, 17), and may inspect them (lines 19–20). He then queries about whether this is CL's first test (line 23). Even though syntactically a "yes/no" question, this utterance may be a way of soliciting from the client an expression of how surprised he may have been. When the client does not answer (line 24), CO in a quiet, gentle fashion asks CL what he is "thinking" (line 25), as a subsequent version of the question and more exacerbated way of asking CL to embellish his response. To this, CL answers that he doesn't know (line 27).

Across a series of opportunities and requests to talk, then, the client is controlled in his response to the bad news.[22] His restraint accords with what others have found in clinics for HIV counseling. "Addressing dreaded issues" is the phrase researchers give to the problem of eliciting clients' talk about "loss, disfigurement, death and dying" (Bor and Miller 1988; Peräkylä 1995: 233). In the clinic studied by Peräkylä, counselors working with HIV-infected individuals and families would arduously deploy a three- or four-step strategy — a series of questions that built on one another — to evoke clients' talk about a potentially "hostile" future that their HIV-positive diagnosis projected.

Additionally, the client's restraint fits the pattern of stoicism by which recipients deal with various kinds of bad news in which they are the primary figure. And this response is in contrast to the way in which recipients generally react to good news, including that which is about negative HIV status (with positive assessments and other exhibits of its favorable nature). In other words, a client's stoicism in the face of hearing about his HIV infection fits the pattern of *asymmetry* between bad and good news. Now, however, because the stoic response to HIV bad news is a problem for counselors in the clinic, it contributes a clue to the anomalous *symmetry* in the devices for delivering bad and good HIV-antibody testing results. Counselors, through exposing bad diagnostic news, *preemptively seek to penetrate and shatter the anticipated stoic responses of their clients.*

"Cracking the Emotional Nut"

To develop my argument, I draw on participant observation in the HIV clinic and employ what I call the "limited affinity" between conversation analysis and ethnography. Starting with excerpt (15), from another HIV informing, I analyze the excerpt on its own terms, and also in light of material gathered ethnographically in the clinic, including a joint interview with two counselors, "Roger" and "Tony." Roger was the counselor who conveys the positive result in excerpt (15), and his discussion with me helps to explicate the strategy he employed for conducting the session. Furthermore, Tony and Roger, with the latter taking the lead, had told a client that he tested positive. (As the client declined my request to have this session recorded, I do not have a tape or transcript of it.) The counselors' reports to me concerning that interview are also revelatory about excerpt (15). Other interviews and a written counseling guide supplement these reports.

In excerpt (15), Roger deploys a version of the perspective display series for conveying the diagnosis that his client is infected with HIV. In chapter 2, I described how the PDS can be a way of forecasting bad news. This is particularly true when clinicians, before giving a diagnosis, use a "marked" perspective display invitation and ask their recipients what they think is "wrong" or what a "problem" is, thereby signaling the possibility of forthcoming adverse diagnostic tidings since reference to a difficulty has already been made. When counselors ask for recipients' perspectives employing "unmarked" queries,[23] which do not refer to any problem, the effect can be very different. In excerpt (15), lines 2–3, Roger, who holds the test results, gives them to the client, whose pseudonym is Dell.

(15) B49A1:1
```
 1  CO:  Okay. .hhhh want you to::: (1.4) ((flipping of pages)) give
 2         this a rea:::d and tell me what you can make out of it
 3         hhhhh.
 4              (25.9) ((opening and closing of drawers))
 5  CO:  °An I'll be right back.°
 6              (58.2)
 7  CO:  °Okay I'm back.° hhh .hhhh (0.2) what do you make out of
 8         this:::.
 9              (2.1)
10  CL:  That my test came back reactive.
11  CO:  R::ight. kay. .hh and that tchu were reactive hhh .hh not
12         only on the elisa test. (0.7) .hh but also on the
13         confirmatory test the western b:lo:t.
14  CL:  I don- I'm not sure bout- I don't know the difference . . .
```

Roger does not mark his perspective display query to Dell at lines 2–3 with any indication of what the news is. After producing this query, Roger opens and closes drawers of the desk at which he sits (line 4), takes leave (line 5), and goes out of the room for nearly a minute (line 6).[24] Upon returning, he asks Dell to report what he has made "out of" the documents he had left in Dell's hands (lines 7–8). Following a silence, Dell suggests an interpretation, that his "test came back reactive," and Roger is then able to confirm this and to explicate it by referring to both tests that were performed (lines 11–13).

When I later asked Roger about his strategies for delivering bad news, he replied,

> . . . let's face it. When you're getting results like this, you mostly feel incredibly alone in the world right?
>
> DM: Right
>
> Roger: Nobody's been to this movie before. . . . By turning a person to finally look inside is what frequently I find cracks the nut—the emotional nut. Once that nut is cracked, then you can make progress, you can joke, you can laugh, you can hold hands, you can talk about medical referrals, you can do a lot of real good positive—and positive I mean moving forward—kind of referral work. (Interview, 3/27/91, p. 5)

Roger not only suggests that his primary aim was to elicit an emotional response.[25] He also articulates a general belief at this clinic: that testing positive, whether expected or not, is a major change of status. In terms I used in chapter 1, it is as if these counselors, who know that client's experiential, everyday world is suffering major change, consider the informing event to encompass a noetic crisis of large proportions. They also believe that, *until* the client deals with the transformation emotionally, he will avoid carrying out healthcare regimens necessary to the prolongation of health and life.[26] Early in my interview with Roger, he said,

> I'll skip way ahead. If I had to make one recommendation to anyone doing a positive test, it's that if you can get that person to have an emotional release, in most instances, cry, you've gone a long way. . . . Until they can start verbalizing where I am, how I'm feeling, what this means, nothing else happens. (Interview, 3/27/91, p. 1)

Roger's rationale for his strategy of asking the client to read his own results thus piggybacked on his belief that nothing can happen until he obtains an "emotional response":

> So for me rather than trying to shelter or blunt the blow or make nice or take care of or nurture an individual, I come at it much more face to face, much more bluntly. 'Here's a piece of paper that you need to read. Now read it and tell me what you make out of it. And then out of your own mouth in your words, you tell me what that means.' Verbalization of that is the number one step, and then of course we almost always go into emotional overload. (Interview, 3/27/91, p. 6)

By inviting the client to read his own testing outcomes, Roger means to confront the client "bluntly," and he hopes that this will jump-start a needed catharsis.

As we have seen, however, clients often appear resolute in withholding any display of affect when they first receive the bad news. Interactionally of notice is that counselors, even in their relatively blunt delivery, still employ the tactic of citing the evidence — giving test results — rather than predicating HIV disease in an assertive format such as "you are HIV-positive" or "you have the AIDS antibody."[27] In the analysis in chapter 5, citing the evidence in the case of bad news is associated with stoic responses. So counselors are not, by any means, fully incautious when they bluntly deliver bad HIV news.[28] Still, they may doggedly pursue the emotional outburst. Such an outburst never did occur in the session from which excerpt (15) is taken. However, I asked Roger and Tony about the other session in which they told a client that he was HIV-positive and did succeed in eliciting an emotional response. Roger reported using the same strategy of giving the client his results to read and following the patient's pronouncement with his confirming declaration of testing results. The client had lost his lover to AIDS three months previous to his own diagnosis, and was "a very smart man," according to Roger, but he "had great difficulty reading the results and understanding that in fact he'd tested HIV positive" (Interview, 3/27/91, p. 1). Consequently, Roger probed him with query after query about how he was feeling.

> Roger: Now I repeated this question probably a dozen times using different
> words and basically he kept on saying he didn't know how he felt.
> DM: And the question you were asking was?
> Roger: "Where are you at?"
> DM: Okay.
> Roger: "How are you?"
> DM: Okay.
> Roger: "What are you feeling?" "What are you thinking now?" Okay, continuously bringing it back to the client. (Interview, 3/27/91, p. 3)

According to Tony, who was observing the exchange, Roger finally asked, "What are you going to do tonight?," and as the client replied, "I'm gonna go home and toss and turn some more," he also began to cry.

Extrapolating from Roger's account, any exposed form of delivering bad news may be seeking an emotional response from its recipient. Therefore, not only his own way of thrusting reports of testing results into the client's hands, but other straightforward ways of presenting bad news, as in excerpts (13) and (14), are working on behalf of "cracking the emotional nut," when it is believed that doing so is necessary to "move forward" in the therapeutic process. If relatively blunt deliveries are not successful in doing this because recipients remain stoic, then deliverers may produce a series of postinforming queries—again as in excerpts (13) and (14)—that are partly disguised ways of pursuing an affective display. One counselor at the clinic, if unsuccessful during early parts of a session in evoking an emotional response from an HIV-positive client, would hug him at the apparent end of the session:

> Some people who go into a stoic mode and [say] "I've expected this, it's okay, I've dealt with it, da ta da ta da," once you get into a hug situation they decompensate a little bit, they start crying, and I can really find out more information about where they're really at. And then the real interviewing begins. You know, so initially it's the ending of the interview but many times it's just the start. (Interview, 9/18/90)

Orientation to the importance of clients' emotional displays was part of the subculture of the clinic, and counselors exhibited an array of devices for evoking them.

Affect and Social Relationships

As energetically as counselors try to elicit a crying response from their clients in the HIV clinic, they are not always successful, whereas with good news, claims and displays of positive affect are abundant and profuse.[29] This goes against theorists like Goffman who have treated crying and laughter as *equivalent* forms of flooding out. "Whether the individual bursts out crying or laughing," Goffman remarks, "he radically alters his general support of the interaction; he is momentarily 'out of play'" (1961: 54).

In other words, laughing presentations of good news, like the pregnancy announcement in excerpt (2b), and emotional displays such as sighing in the HIV excerpt (11) are produced and heard as *in-play* ways of handling such good news. It is with bad news that fear of the recipient going "out of play" appears to be prominent. In hospitals, when emergency room physicians have told relatives about a patient's death, a temporary state of mutual disattention occurs:

> While the informed relative is actively engaged in crying, weeping, sobbing, or moaning, the doctor maintains as passive a stance as the fact of his presence will allow. He looks away, or downwardly, and says nothing. Occasionally physicians employ the procedure of turning around, leaving their backs to the crying relative. (Sudnow 1967: 141)

From the bereaved's point of view, they may deemphasize their feelings of loss, "out of respect for the difficulties of interaction facing those less intimately involved in the death than themselves" (140). Indeed, any emotional display can present a difficulty for the physician, because

> he cannot remove himself from the setting and still accomplish other tasks, e.g., instructing relatives regarding funeral obligations, obtaining an autopsy permit (in hospital patient deaths) and generally controlling the encounter so that it doesn't generate into an explosive scene. (142)

A male patient, for example, who was told he had a severe form of cancer (Maynard and Frankel forthcoming) responded with a series of expletives and other "response cries" that indicate a propensity for loss of emotional control (Goffman 1978). The patient was almost writhing in his chair, and then got up and began pacing away from the physician, who remained seated and urged his patient, "Stay with me, Clint," attempting to summon him back to his chair so they could discuss the meaning of the diagnosis and the course of treatment. In an internal medicine clinic, when a physician had to tell his patient that she had AIDS, she began to cry and sob intensively. The physician writes,

> This patient wanted to flee and began pacing around the small examination room, unable to sit still. I wanted to give her room to pace, but I was also fearful that if she fled she might harm herself or find herself completely alone without any direction when the high energy state wore off. (Quill 1991: 466)

Given the potential for a recipient's emotion-charged leaving the scene, practices for shrouding bad news are directed not just to the containment of emotions such as crying and sobbing but to preserving social order and relationships.[30]

When deliverers expose rather than cover bad news, as in the anomalous case of the HIV clinic, it is a strategic effort to garner an emotional response from their recipients. Although their practices depart from the usual asymmetry in which bad news is shrouded and only good news exposed, the stripping of bad news can be on the same social organizational plain. Just as deliverers who shroud bad news do so to maintain interactional order, those who actively seek a display of affect from clients or other recipients regard such responses as facilitating the further flow of interaction. *After* the evoked display of affect they can talk about a host of things including the needs of the individual and his relation to the community and its services. In the HIV clinic, this includes pharmacological and other forms of therapy, support networks for the person, integration into systems of referral, and so on.

In the clinic's view, bluntly delivering the bad news of HIV infection is an efficient way of getting to address ancillary matters. In other clinics, such as those concerned with developmental disabilities, professionals may share the orientation to evoke a recipient's emotion as a way of moving beyond anticipated stoicism and related responses. In chapter 3 we examined an instance of a pediatrician, Dr. Davidson, who made use of a direct, assertive format to inform the parents of Donald that "he is retarded," whereupon his mother, Mrs. Riccio, cried and sobbed while denying it. If that pediatrician was at all like our HIV counselors, she purposefully worked to rouse this response in order to confront the mother's denial and move toward consideration of how to place her son in what would be, in the clinical view at least, an appropriate treatment and educational environment.

The Benign Order of the Clinic

Practices for delivering bad news in the HIV clinic may depart from strong tendencies elsewhere to envelop such news by a variety of delaying and withholding tactics, but after the news is delivered patterns are similar to other settings. That is, in the HIV clinic, when the news is good because there is no evidence of infection, clinical encounters are of brief duration (often less than five minutes, with some clients leaving almost immediately). This is unmediated transition to next activity. By contrast, when the news is bad because the client's tests show the presence of antibodies to the HIV virus, counselors engage in good-news exits. They produce optimistic projections, such as "Being HIV positive is not a death sentence. It does not mean that you're gonna come down with AIDS. The statistics right now are in your favor of staying healthy." Counselors also offer remedies of various kinds, such as (in the same interview), "You can do some things for yourself that . . . actually can increase the odds of staying healthy . . . reasonable diet, getting enough sleep, exercise, uh staying away from things that further stress the body."[31] Discussions, of course, are more extended than these statements and the sessions are often very lengthy (one to two hours) as a consequence.[32] Such patterns occur with less consequential conditions. Nurses who have successfully communicated good blood pressure or blood sugar results to patients "move to ancillary matters or to other activities," according to Leppänen (1998: 170). After they announce bad test results, however, "longer stretches of talk follow in which nurses attempt to *calm* the patients" (Leppänen 1998: 181).

The benign order is operative in a variety of clinics and has potentially large consequences.[33] For example, the editorial quoted in the epigraph to this chapter, and proposing that physicians with bad news about a malignancy should delay the tidings until there is good news about treatment,[34] probably captures what is already practiced. In his ethnographic study of an oncology ward,

McIntosh writes that physicians never "bluntly" tell patients, "Yes, you have cancer." Instead, says McIntosh (1977: 63–64), "The news was always qualified by an accompanying statement stressing the more hopeful aspects of their condition."[35] The consequences from this effort on behalf of a benign world reside in patients' and family members' sometimes distorted understanding of the illness. Research on disclosure to patients with end-stage cancer finds that many physicians favor withholding prognosis altogether. When they would disclose, physicians first overestimate privately how long patients have to live and, second, convey assessments even more favorable than their private ones in their intended communications to patients (Christakis and Lamont 2000; Lamont and Christakis 2001). "These stepwise optimistic prognoses," Lamont and Christakis (2001: 1102) argue, "may cause patients to become twice removed from their actual survival." A too rosy picture is not entirely due to physician practices, however; terminal patients themselves evince optimism until the end and actively solicit it from their doctors (Kutner et al. 1999: 1349).[36] This evidence accords with my argument that the quotidian, benign order is ongoing, even morally required, in social interaction. As a collaborative achievement, it imposes itself in an enormous range of mundane encounters, occurs in a variety of ordinary and institutional settings that house such encounters, and profoundly affects how participants in those settings organize — perceive, portray, project, and experience by way of talk and social interaction — the everyday world.

SEVEN

Praising or Blaming the Messenger: Moral
Issues in Deliveries of Good and Bad News

Diplomatic immunity essentially started as a practical matter. If one society, one tribal group, one nation wished to communicate with another, the communications weren't going to be very effective if the messengers got killed when the message was an unpleasant one. So, there grew up a common understanding that messengers were not to be mistreated because you didn't like what they had to tell you.[1]

That diplomatic immunity, a matter of inter*national* relations, developed as a protection against blaming the messenger, attests to the powerful inter*actional* effects that bad news can have. Conversationally, therefore, it is not surprising that bad news is something for which deliverers seek to avoid blame. However, to continue a theme of the last chapter, there is an asymmetric converse to this. Good news is something for which deliverers work to claim credit. In relation to each kind of news, furthermore, recipients support or resist the deliverer's stance in particular ways. With bad news, recipients may accept deliverer's blame avoidance, or, conversely, blame the messenger. With good news, recipients regularly offer congratulations and gratuities that acknowledge and honor the deliverer's agency.

Conversational patterns involved in blaming and crediting messengers raise another theme from chapter 6 having to do with the moral stature of events in the everyday world. Morality, in Garfinkel's (1963) suggestive work, refers to ways that members of society "trust" the world of everyday life through adherence to a set of reciprocally binding assumptions, the Attitude of Daily Life (chapter 1). Bad news and good news events, because they violate that sense of trust, are deeply moral disruptions and shake the foundations of the perceivedly normal character of everyday life.[2] According to Garfinkel, a possible feature of perceived normality is the "causal texture" of quotidian events — their relation to something that or someone who conditions, effects, or precipitates their occurrence. Put differently, the causal texture of mundane reality is an aspect of *proto-morality,* or the substructure, as Bergmann (1998) calls it, that is the precondition for the particular substance of a society's overtly communicated meanings. That causal texturing is a moral feature for participants becomes evident when their lifeworld undergoes alteration. Because everyday informing events — deliveries of news about lifeworld occurrences — constitute at the same time as they are taken to reflect such alteration, these events can bring to the fore issues of what or who caused the worlds' objects and events to have the new contents they have. Participants during the delivery and receipt of news display their concerns with agency or with who is responsible for originating or bringing about reported changes in mundane circumstances. To put the matter succinctly, as bad and good news exhibit the morality of everyday life they also bring "moral discourse" (Bergmann 1998; Linell and Rommetveit 1998) to the fore. However, conversational episodes are patterned such that claiming or assigning responsibility for good news occurs relatively immediately in its delivery and receipt, while claiming or assigning responsibility for bad news is delayed. Accordingly, crediting messengers appears to be a "preferred" or structurally valued conversational activity, while blaming them is "dispreferred" or devalued.[3]

Crediting and Blaming in Conversation

As I have mentioned, when bearers of good news deliver that news in conversation, they may work to present it as their own accomplishment, and/or recipients may attribute agency to the deliverer. In this way, good news can redound to the credit of the bearer. If that happens, then after the good-news delivery, there is a compliment sequence. Bad news is a different matter. When the event reported in the news is potentially due to a deliverer's agency, the deliverer produces accounts that seem designed to avoid the attribution of their own agency, because bad news can be *discrediting*.

Good News and Agency

Prior to excerpt (1), Leslie and Robbie had been discussing some photographs that Robbie had and making arrangements for Leslie to "pick them up" or for Robbie to "drop them in" to Leslie. As that topic wound down, Leslie introduces the question in line 1 below:

(1) **H5G/Holt:M88:1:5:12**

1	Leslie:	↑Did um (.) °tch (.) uh you get that ↓book back?
2	Robbie:	↓I've got <u>two</u> books f'you:.
3	Leslie:	Have ↑↑<u>YOU:</u> [<u>g</u>oohhd
4	Robbie:	[And
5	Robbie:	An' I've got th'm in my basket 'n they are <u>ho</u>:me. I
6		didn't l<u>e</u>ave th'm at school in case you w<u>a</u>nted them.
7	Leslie:	<u>Oh</u>:. <u>right</u>.
8	Robbie:	That al↑<u>ri</u>:ght,
9	Leslie:	Yes fine what are ↓they. The ↑House on the Str<u>a</u>:nd,
10	Robbie:	Ye<u>:</u>[s,
11	Leslie:	[°hh<u>hhh</u> <u>a</u>:nd <u>e</u>hm[:

```
12   Robbie:                    [(Univers[ity   [Hi:ll.)
13    Leslie:                             [°tch [Ye:s:. Yes[:.
14   Robbie:                                                    [I've
15           got ↑th'm ↓both.
16    Leslie:  Oh you are kind I never expected to ↑see The ↓House
17           on the Strand agai:[n
18   Robbie:                    [Oh: ↑yes, ye[s it's been ↓fou]nd.
19    Leslie:                                [O:h  I o v e↓ly.]
20    Leslie:  Oh well ↓done.
21   Robbie:  So, I've ↑got those two safely at ho:[me
22    Leslie:                                      [hThank you very
23           mu[ch.
24   Robbie:  [a plea↑sure
25    Leslie:  e↑You're at home now yourse:lf aren't you?
```

Leslie's question asks about an action of Robbie, and Robbie's reply at line 2 incorporates the linguistic form of the inquiry by replacing "did you get" with "I've got." Thus, in preserving reference to herself and reporting her own action, Robbie depicts herself as an "actor-agent" performing a praiseworthy action (Pomerantz 1978b), doing a favor for her news recipient.

Indeed, that Robbie may be actively working to take and receive credit for the reported happy upshot here is evident in further features of the interaction. After Leslie marks and assesses the news (line 3), Robbie (in lines 5–6) reports on the books being at her home and portrays this as resulting from her other-oriented action. Initially, Leslie merely acknowledges this state of affairs (line 7), which occasions Robbie's checking whether that is "al↑ri:ght" (line 8); again Leslie produces a rather flat acknowledgment ("Yes fine," line 9), subsequently asking and hearing (lines 9–13) what the books are. At lines 14–15, Robbie again reports having "th'm ↓both." Now Leslie praises Robbie as "kind" and, in the same turn, exhibits as a basis for her appreciation "never" expecting to see the book called *The House on the Strand* (lines 16–17). Robbie next reconfirms the presence of the book ("Oh:↑yes, yes," line 18), which occasions a positive assessment from Leslie at line 19, while, in overlap, Robbie once more reports an action that produced the result ("it's been ↓found," line 18). Subsequent to this, Leslie produces another form of appreciation ("Oh well ↓done," line 20). Robbie's following utterance is a positively framed report of her action ("So, I've ↑got those two safely at ho:me," line 21), a rerun and possibly summarizing version of what she started with ("they are ho:me," line 5), but with the interjection of her own actor-agency once again. Finally, Leslie thanks her (lines 22–23) and Robbie accepts the expression of gratitude (lines 24).

In all, Robbie produces four reports of action (lines 5–6, 14–15, 18, and 21), three of which refer to herself as subject-agent of the action that produced the good news result, at least in the sense that she squired the books from school to home for Leslie. The exception to this pattern, in which Robbie produces a report by way of a passive linguistic construction with an unspecified agent ("it's been ↓found," line 18), exhibits a contrasting means for announcing the news. Otherwise, then, she *claims credit* for the good news, and provides a basis for the positive evaluation in the form of gratuities that follow. Without assigning any intention to Robbie — e.g., that she was "seeking" approbation — it is clear that she takes responsibility for actions involved in the good news result, and that she delivers this news in a way that eventuates in and possibly provides for or solicits praise and an expression of gratitude. My argument is that anticipation of such a sequel can enter into the structuring of the news report in the first place. In exhibiting her agency or her responsibility for the good news, Robbie may be *prospecting* for compliments.[4]

Of course, because the use of first-person reference in excerpt (1) reflects the way that Leslie inquired after the books, it could be that Robbie's assumption of agency is contingently related to this inquiry. However, good news that is offered rather than requested appears to be done similarly:

(2) **Maynard A:452**

```
 1    Carl:  Oh you know what? h
 2    Betty: Wha:t.
 3    Carl:  Spea(h)k(h)ing .hh
 4    Betty: Spea(h)king of being a slob
 5    Carl:  Speaking of irony
 6    Betty: [(Yeah)]
 7    Carl:  [Okay?]
 8                    (1.5)
 9    Carl:  You're gonn[a b]e (.) greatly relieved.
10    Betty:            [( )]
11                    (1.0)
12    Carl:  I looked, behind the campho↑phenic ↑bottle today? And
13           I found your ring. eh heh heh .hih
14           h[ih    hih    hih ]
15    Betty:  [↑Did ↓you ↑real]ly?=
16    Carl:  =Yeah.
17                    (0.2)
18    Betty: I:::'m ↑so re↓lie↑::ved?
```

Carl preannounces his news (line 1), then projects, for Betty, a reaction to the news (lines 3, 5, 9), displaying that the upcoming news has consequences for her and proposing just how it does. Next, in his announcement (lines 12–13), Carl depicts the finding of Betty's ring as due to his efforts, his looking. Betty produces a newsmarking request for confirmation (line 15), and when Carl does confirm (line 16), she then assesses the news (line 18) by reporting a feeling state in accord with what Carl projected.

Regularly, in good news episodes in which a recipient is a primary figure, deliverers portray their agency in producing the good news result. Their announcements thereby contain at least two possible foci. One is the deliverer's own action, and the other is the result of that action. Accordingly, if deliverers are prospecting for compliments, they do so in a partially disguised manner. While the deliverer *takes* credit for the good news result, it is permissible for a recipient to observe and display appreciation for only that result, as in excerpt (2). Of course, while Betty's assessment at line 18 accords with Carl's projection, when she first responds to the announcement, her newsmark (Did you really?," line 15) references Carl's agency. Other times, deliverers not only have their agency referenced but *receive* credit in the form of praise, as in excerpt (1).

Parties with good news do not always blatantly display their agency and solicit compliments. Rather, there may be considerable subtlety and maneuvering, such that the party with good news avoids the attribution of being engaged in self-praise (Pomerantz 1978a). As Bergmann (1998) points out, there is an "inbuilt reflexivity" to moral activities, such as assuming responsibility for some social outcome. Such activities themselves can be subject to moral evaluation. Claiming credit for a good-news outcome may be of particular concern when it is first-party news—that is, when the deliverer, rather than a third party or recipient, is the primary consequential figure. Whereas our previous two examples contained news that was mainly consequential for the recipient, the next two examples will involve news in which the deliverer announces news about "self" as the principal beneficiary. The first episode is the one involving Ellen's announced ousting of her adviser (chapter 4). It will be remembered that she initially formulates her reason for calling Jeff as something "relevant" to him and his "situation" (lines 1–3):

(3) EJ:1
```
 1    Ellen:  tch. hh Well I wanted to shar:e some news with you:,
 2            because you'll find it relevant to your particular::
 3            (.) situati[on      ]
 4    Jeff:           [Whoo]ps. Okay hold on, let me turn off
 5            the radio hhh
 6    Ellen:  Okay.
 7                    (2.6)
 8    Jeff:   .hhhh Okay lay it on me.=
 9    Ellen:  =And this news has to do with our beloved (0.2)
10            advisor.
```

```
11    Jeff:  I- I wouldna gue↑ssed.
12    Ellen: tch .hh Ye(hh)ah I knew-, I knew you wouldn't
13           .h[hhhhhhhhhhh]
14    Jeff:    [Well I hope] it's not bad news?
15    Ellen: Oh no, it actually is pretty good news.
16    Jeff:  ↑OH ↑GOO:D.
17    Ellen: I mean (0.4) well I think it's kinda good news.
18           [.hhhh]
19    Jeff:  [↑Tell] me.
20    Ellen: Um, I decided (.) tha:t (1.0) uhm I wanted to oust
21           him.
22                   (0.6)
23    Ellen: And I decided I need to find out whadidit (.) is I
24           have to do.
25    Jeff:  hyehrh kidding:. He's not going to be yer advisor?=
26    Ellen: =No.
27                   (0.6)
28    Jeff:  °h::oh my gosh.°
29    Ellen: An::d I:=
30    Jeff:  =°Wo::[:w°]
31    Ellen:       [Um ] tch .h [if::-        ]
32    Jeff:                     [GOODFER] YOU::::.=
33    Ellen: =It hit me last- tha(h)(h)nks. .hh
34    Jeff:  No seriously, good fer you. That took gu:ts.
35           I'[m- ] hope I'm inspired by you.
36    Ellen: [No-]
37    Ellen: hhnh Tha↑nks hhh .hhh uh:m it hit me . . .
```

Even as this news is "for" Jeff and "about" their advisor (lines 9–10), when Ellen arrives at a position for announcing her news, she interjects herself as the agent and implied primary beneficiary of what has happened. Her initial formulation (lines 20–21) is that she has "decided" to "oust" the advisor. Then, after a silence (line 22) Ellen revises her announcement in a partially escalated manner, displaying resolve to carry out the announced decision ("And I decided I need to find out," lines 23–24). Following this, Jeff produces a candidate elaboration (line 25), which Ellen confirms (line 26), and then he assesses the news (lines 28, 30) with whispered displays of appreciation.

After his initial hushed appreciation, Jeff responds to the news in a way that recognizes Ellen's agency: he goes on to congratulate and compliment Ellen. As he does this initially (line 32), she is pursuing a shading of the topic, a possible account for her decision ("if::- it hit me last-," lines 31, 33), but Ellen abandons that move and receives the congratulatory utterance with a laughing "tha(h)(h)nks" (line 33). Jeff at lines 34–35 counters her laughter tokens with "No seriously," a repeat of the congratulations ("good fer you"), praise ("that took gu̲:ts"), and a display of the consequences for him ("I hope I'm inspired by you"). This time Ellen produces a solid or nonlaughing "tha↑nks" at line 37, after which she manages to produce her topic-shading utterance in the clear. Thus, Jeff's congratulations and compliments to Ellen occur as a trajectory that is competitive with Ellen's stepwise topical movement, and he perseveres with those actions to obtain her serious acceptance. In *exhibiting reluctance* in her receipt of his compliments, Ellen may be observing the constraint to avoid and downgrade praise and compliments (Pomerantz 1978a). In a conversational sense, nevertheless, she appears to have *earned* such praise in the way that she involved herself as an agent in bringing off the good news she reports to Jeff.

Hence, if deliverers prospect for compliments in bearing good news about self, they often do so in a way not to be seen as such or engaging in self-praise. A tension between prospecting for compliments and averting being seen to praise self therefore exists, and also appears in the next episode. Ida, who has been doing regular exercises, had been urging the benefits of this routine on Jenny. They joked about this, and then Ida broached a close to the conversation, announcing that she had to "go" and that she would be "seeing" Jenny soon. Jenny's return in line 1 below, a flattering projection, occasions some good news about Ida's weight loss. (This news is initially stated in British units; line 3's "nine fi̲:ive" refers to *stones*, and is approximately 135 pounds.)

(4) R7G/Rahman: II:21

```
 1   Jenny:  I'll be s̲eeing you: uahs a new:: us̲ylphlike fi̲g̲guh soon
 2           E̲:[y?
 3   Ida:      [Okh E̲y̲: I'm nine fi̲:i̲ve,
 4                 (.)
 5   Ida:    I wz nine nin̲e yihknow Jen̲n̲y̲?
 6   Jenny:  Su you've ↑lo̲st foh [pounds.=
 7   Ida:                         [(     )
 8   Ida:    =Ah'v ah ni̲:ne I wz ni̲:ne nine y- a w̲eek ahftih
 9           C̲hrissmiss. Ah kn̲o:w thaht fuh sure.coz °hh I: wz te̲lling
10           you ah wz getteen as̲ha:med jih kno:w,
11   Jenny:  iYe:s,
12   Ida:    An- mi̲:nd ah'v c̲ut ou'c̲hoc'lates'n things b't you d̲o put
13           o:n aftih Chrissmiss d̲o:n' we.
14                 (0.2)
15   Jenny:  Oh uh [(i̲n this weathuh)] yes.]
16   Ida:          [Well  I'm  d̲own n]ow, ] °hh I'm nine fi̲:ve this
17           mohrnin:g.
18   Jenny:  °h T̲haht's very goo̲:d?=
19   Ida:    =So[:
20   Jenny:     [Smas̲hing y'haftih kee[p that (u̲[p) t h e n]
21   Ida:                              [B't    [ah ↑d̲oon't] lo̲ok i̲:t,
```

```
22          Ah dohn' I don'know where aa p't hh:::[khh hih]
23  Jenny:                                      [hOh: g]o on
```

Ida's announcement at lines 3–5 is a self-report; Jenny's response at line 6 proffers an "upshot" of Ida's report that also potentially *attributes* agency to Ida. "You've lost four pounds," while observing the difference between "nine five" and "nine nine," can also suggest that Ida did something to lose the weight. After this receipt, Ida produces a narrative about her prior weight, her feelings of shame, and removing chocolates from her diet (lines 8–10, 12–13). Accordingly, in having "cut ou'choc'lates'n things," Ida claims agency and involvement in producing the weight loss as an outcome. Then (after an ambiguously co-implicative proposal about how the weight was put on, lines 12–13, and Jenny's agreement, line 15), Ida submits another version of the news (lines 16–17). Coming after the narrative, this version of the weight-loss event explicitly can be heard as invoking Ida's own accomplishment. Accordingly, when Jenny assesses the news positively (line 18), and then upgrades her assessment and encourages Ida (line 20), it also compliments her. That is, positive assessments that follow announcements of accomplishments not only deal with the news as news but can indicate praise toward the achiever. The deliverer's response here displays such an analysis of the assessments according to the pattern that Pomerantz (1978a: 98) has described; the recipient of a compliment in some fashion disagrees (lines 21–22), thereby avoiding self-praise.[5]

Bad News and Agency

Deliverers of good news, in a partially disguised fashion — by depicting themselves as having brought about the news they report and thereby providing at least two foci for recipient response — may prospect for compliments. If they receive such compliments, they may, in the avoidance of self-praise, contest these compliments or their presentation. When news is bad, the interactional situation is very different. What is avoided is the issue of responsibility itself. Such avoidance takes work, because being forthright in reporting bad news can occasion an immediate attribution of blame, as Pomerantz (1978b) has shown. That is, when a report is *unembellished*,[6] and without designation of actor-agents, a recipient's response may treat that event as a consequence of actions and initiate the attribution of responsibility for those actions.

(5) Pomerantz 1978b: 117
```
1  N:  My f:face hurts,=          ←unembellished report
2  H:  =°W't-
3          (.)
4  H:  Oh what'd'e do tih you.    ←attribution of responsibility
```

(6) Pomerantz 1978b: 117

```
1   A:  It blew up.                    ←unembellished report
2   R:  Didju really?
3           (Silence)
4   R:  Whadju do to it?               ←attribution of responsibility
```

Sometimes, the attribution may be to another or third party, as in (5), but blame may also redound to the messenger, as in (6).

For a messenger to deflect blame involves embellishment, and/or other practices on the part of the recipient. Previous to excerpt (7), Leslie and Robbie had been discussing a friend and her allergies.[7] Leslie's "this ↑is eh why I'm not ↑quite ↓so well" in line 1 invokes the earlier discussion, projects the upcoming reference to allergies (line 3), and prefaces an announcement about a rash (lines 3–4). Saying that she "came out" in the rash embellishes the announcement by depicting it as a reaction that had no human agency.

(7) H15B/Holt:M88:1:5:28

```
 1   Leslie:  Well: th:this ↑is eh why I'm not ↑quite ↓so well at
 2            th'moment I'd thought I'd got t'the: bottom a'my
 3            ↑allergies but I came out'n most ↑terr↓ible rash last
 4            week, °hhhh[hh
 5   Robbie:            [↑Oh:[↓:
 6   Leslie:                 [An' I wz telling th'm all at school how
 7            m'ch better I wa:s but I: ↑think it might've been: um
 8            primulas I touched.
 9              (.)
10   Robbie:  ↑Oh you poor ↑↑thi::ng.
```

After Robbie's line 5 newsmark, Leslie elaborates on the news and includes an attribution that the specific allergic source was "primulas [she] touched" (line 8). Leslie's touching of the primulas could imply her agency in bringing about the allergic reaction, but raising that issue in a turn position posterior to the announcement of her disappointment ("I thought I'd got t'the: bottom a'my ↑allergies") and the description of her suffering (the rash) minimizes the issue. Furthermore, the emphasis here is on the primulas; they are mentioned almost immediately after her "might've been" formulation that tentatively proposes to *link* her condition to some source (Gill 1998) and Leslie places stress on the word "primulas" such that "I touched" audibly recedes as the utterance ends. Robbie's line 10 assessment targets neither the explanation nor Leslie's agency and instead deals with Leslie and her condition, which can constitute an "empathetic" alignment as a troubles-talk recipient (Jefferson 1988: 425). The two parties appear to collaborate in refraining from blaming the messenger.

Excerpt (8) shares features with (7). As in (7), Susan's announcement of bad news arrives as an account or explanation. She has called Gordon to see if he is free for the evening and after saying that he was busy, he asked why she was asking. Reluctantly, she reports on her driving test.[8] There is a collaborative turning away from the deliverer as agent in the bad news result and toward the deliverer as *victim*. That is, Susan mounts no claim of responsibility for the result, and Gordon avoids blaming the deliverer by offering sympathy.

(8) **H22B/Holt:SO88:1:5:2 (modified)**

```
 1    Susan:   Well I didn't pass my driving test.
 2    Gordon:  ˙kl ↓Ah-:-:-:-:.h (.) (˙k) (.) Oh that's a pity (.) wz it
 3             today.
 4                 (0.5)
 5    Susan:   No it wz yesterday.
 6                 (1.0)
 7    Susan:   ( [            feel) ] sorry for myself yesterday so=
 8    Gordon:     [Commiserations.]
 9    Susan:   =that I might do tonight.
10                 (0.5)
11    Susan:   °I [(        )°
12    Gordon:     [hh-hh-hh ˙klk I see:.
13                 (0.4)
14    Gordon:  ˙hh˙t˙hhhhh hEh:m ˙mp (0.7) ˙mp gnThat's really sa↓:d.
15             That's a real shame
16                 (0.3)
17    Susan:   Tis isn'tit.
18                 (0.2)
19    Gordon:  Yea:h
```

At first, after Susan's delivery of the bad news (line 1), Gordon assesses it as a "pity" (line 2). Slightly later, he offers "commiserations" (line 8), as Susan explains how she handled and plans to handle the situation (lines 7, 9). Next, Susan adds something that is indecipherable on the tape (line 11); Gordon receives that (line 12) and further assesses the news at 14–15 in a way consistent with his "commiserations," whereupon Susan agrees with his assessments at line 17. Overall, the two parties display orientations to the pitiable, shameful *situation* in a way that suggests sympathy for Susan's involvement in it but not responsibility for it.

Nevertheless, the issue of Susan's responsibility eventually emerges in the conversation. When later Susan re-initiates discussion of the event (after some intervening talk that centers on Gordon), she offers to explain the bad news result:

(9) H23B/Holt:SO88:1:5:5 (modified)
```
1    Susan:  I wz juh I wz js really nervous in my test I think, an'
2            my nerves js took over.
3                    (0.2)
4    Susan:  .hhh I think (.) that's something which really ha:ppens
5            when you're taking the firs' time=
6    Gordon: =Did you think that (.) you were gunna fail.=at the end
```

However, her account suggests not that she did something in particular but that her "nerves took over" (line 2). Susan proposes that this is something that just "happens" (lines 4–5) and, invoking the categorical "you" and thereby a generic "first time," also suggests that it is anyone's fate during such a time, thereby deflecting full claim to personal responsibility for the event. Gordon's question at line 6 re-invokes Susan's exam in particular and occasions talk about what happened during the test.

As Susan tells the story (in talk not reproduced here), it turns out that she had not been able to figure out what a "traffic warden" was doing where some road work was going on. Accordingly, in narrating the matter, she does explain what she did that resulted in the failure (and reports the examiner citing her for "not looking at the traffic warden"). The positioning of this story and explanation indicates that *after* delivering bad news, *after* a sympathetic response, and *after* portraying the matter as something out of her control, a subject if invited by recipient to talk about the event, may begin to acknowledge her own responsibility for the result. Structurally, because the deliverer offers it in a position well after the news delivery, rather than in response to an accusation or blaming in its immediate environs, this acknowledgment is like an admission or confession.

The pattern of admitting blame for bad news in a post-delivery, post-receipt position is illustrated in an episode involving weight gain. Excerpt (10) forms a convenient contrast with excerpt (4), in which Ida reports a weight *loss* to Jenny, who receives the news by attributing agency to Ida, "So you've lost four pounds." A speaker's weight gain, if undesired, has intrinsic possibilities for attributing responsibility to the gainer, but in the episode below, the recipient of the weight-gain news denies the news. Jenny, after a shopping trip, had called Ann to see whether "perhaps it was a bit late to come round for coffee." Ann replied, "No," and after brief discussion of the shopping trip, Jenny initiated a closing of the conversation with "Okay then I'll pop round if you're ready." Indicating that coffee or tea would be available, Ann said "You can have whichever you like, just tell me in advance," and this ensues:

(10) R2B/Rah:A:2:JSA(9):3

```
 1  Jenny:  Eh- wahtuh plea:se,=
 2   Ann:   =Are you- you sur[:e:
 3  Jenny:               [Oh: e-ye- ey list'n l:'m d<I went on
 4          the scale yestee I'm> ten stone now,
 5              (0.5)
 6   Ann:   Well now y[ou don't look it]
 7  Jenny:            [T e n s t o: ]ne:.
 8   Ann:   Y'don't look it Jen ah must be honest.
 9  Jenny:  Ah well ah mean t'say when you consider thet I should be
10          what izzit ei:ght'n a hahlf.=
11   Ann:   [O h g o 'w a y :]
12  Jenny:  [(°l-) I think thah]t's [(how 'tis)°
13   Ann:                          [(I think that half) that
14          (magazine on ( ))
15  Jenny:  ehhhh heh huh [huh °ehhh] So I've got a stone enna hahlf
16   Ann:                [(heh heh)]
17  Jenny:  tih lose someweah heh
```

Jenny's reply to Ann's offer is a request for water (line 1), and after Ann asks for confirmation (line 2), Jenny produces an account for this request that announces her weight (lines 3–4). A feature of this announcement is that it reports *how* she knows her weight—she "went on the scale"–and suggests that the weight is a recent attainment ("ten stone now") but does not propose any source for this attainment. After a brief silence, Ann denies the news (line 6) while in overlap Jenny emphasizes the gain by repeating the weight (line 7). Then Ann self-retrieves her denial (line 8), and Jenny reports her proper weight (lines 9–10), occasioning yet another denial by Ann (line 11).

In a way, there is contestation over whether there is any news here, and it is only through Jenny's perseverance in the face of Ann's denials that her proposal about weight gain achieves a sort of implicativeness in the talk. Jenny produces a joke at lines 13–14, and after laughing, Jenny claims responsibility for what should be done to remedy the situation (lines 15, 17). This can imply her fault for having gained weight in the first place. Admitting fault, besides being in a position posterior to her announcement, is tacitly embedded in the remedy proposal.

Recipient as primary figure. So far we have examined instances of bad news in which the deliverer is the primary figure. When bad news is directly consequential for the recipient, the pattern is similar. Deliverers are interactively cautious in their presentations, and, in terms of responsibility for the bad-news event, provide for third-party or impersonal attribution rather than self-attribution. In the excerpt involving Charlie and Ilene and "the trip to Syracuse"[9] Charlie reports having "spoken to Karen" and learned that she is "going away," which leads to a consequence for him — he doesn't "have a place to stay." Ilene gathers the upshot that he's "not [going] up this weekend," which is also bad news for her, since she does not have a ride. Of interest in relation to the deliverer's agency is that "the speaker is officially responsible only for the reporting" (Drew 1984: 137), and not for *what* is reported. Deliverers giving an account for the bad news upshot, in other words, may not only avoid stating the upshot; they cleanse the report of any formulation regarding their own agency. Indeed, if anything, a deliverer may portray himself as someone for whom the bad news is consequential and who is victimized similarly to the news recipient. Put briefly, in initiating his telling with the news that Karen has decided to go away, Charlie provides for this third party as an agent bringing about consequences for both himself and Ilene, and thereby embodies a "no-fault-of-mine" delivery of the bad news. This represents a radical contrast with recipient-consequential good news, in which deliverers may work to claim credit for the good news upshot, thereby prospecting for compliments or gratuities. In giving good news, deliverers also usually name or formulate the news rather than allow it to go unstated.

Asymmetry in Moral Discourse

Because everyday informing episodes — deliveries of news about lifeworld occurrences — constitute at the same time as they are taken to reflect alteration in participants' lifeworlds, these episodes can bring to the fore issues of what or who caused the worlds' objects and events to have the new contents they have. However, according to indications in this chapter, moral discourse or ways in which participants, in their communicative acts, approach agency and responsibility differ depending on whether, for example, something has been lost or found, weight has been gained or lost, a test has been passed or failed, a diagnosis has been confirmed or disconfirmed, or negotiations for the sale of a desired house have been blocked or consummated. The structure of moral discourse differs, in other words, according to whether the concertedly achieved valence of the news is good or bad. Most regularly, in the focused moment when participants come to an altered everyday world through the actions of announcing and receiving news, their accounts regularly deny a deliverer's responsibility if the new world is "bad," and attribute responsibility to a deliverer if the new world is "good."[10] It is as if bad new worlds just happen, while good new worlds are something we achieve.

Coda: In the Clinic and Other Professional Settings
Bad News

Ethnographers have afforded a large amount of attention to giving bad news in various institutional settings, especially legal (law enforcement) and medical ones. They describe how official or professional messengers often feel guilty and/or worry about being blamed, employing various exculpatory devices for delivering the news.

Physicians, for example, may use an "elaborate" presentation to family members that explains how an individual's death occurred (Clark and LaBeff 1982), which is meant to assure them that both the physician and the family did everything they could for the deceased. One such elaborate way of presenting news is to cast the news as a "logical sequence of progressive events" that leads to an inevitable conclusion (374). This logical pattern is evident in the more casual arena of Charlie telling Ilene about the canceled trip to Syracuse.

Syllogism in the clinic. In the more formal setting of a clinic for developmental disabilities, this logical pattern may be embodied in the "syllogistic" delivery of bad diagnostic news (Gill and Maynard 1995). We saw an example of this at the end of chapter 5, and in the excerpt below, the same psychologist, Dr. M, similarly informs the parents of a five-year-old boy that their child is mentally retarded. He defines what mental retardation is in such a way that the parents, both of whom are present in this interview, can draw the conclusion about their son's retardation. In previous talk, Dr. M, on the basis of his and other clinical examinations, has cited the evidence by reporting test results to the effect that Ken has a significant, pervasive, untreatable brain abnormality, which is permanent. Mr. and Mrs. D had acknowledged these assessments. That Ken has these problems is the *particular premise* of the syllogism. Now, Dr. M, at lines 1–2, 4, and 7–11, which lead up to the diagnostic announcement (line 14), re-references the clinical findings. In other words, he is *reciting* the evidence:

(11) L 45:17

```
1      Dr. M:  When:- when you put a:ll these things together. When
2              there are [dela:y]s,=
3   Mrs. D:           [°M hm°]
4      Dr. M:  =When they're significant, and it looks like there's no:
5              (0.8)
6  (Mrs. D):  °m°
7      Dr. M:  clear treatable cau:se. .hhh uh- ta fix: (.) the problem
8              up. .hh uh:: (.) a:n when it looks like this has been
9              going on for a long period of ti::me, .hh (0.5) an:::d
```

```
10              (0.5) projecting ahead you're:: not optimistic that the
11              kid's going to catch up, [.hh uh]=
12  Mrs. D:                             [°M hm°]=
13   Dr. M:  =that's what we call mental retardation.
14                  (1.5)
15  Mrs. D:  And this is what it is.
16                  (0.5)
17   Dr. M:  °M hm.°=
18  Mrs. D:  =°Okay.°=
19   Dr. M:  =°Yeah.° Almost certainly.
```

In reciting the evidence and relating it to mental retardation, Dr. M has presented the general premise of the syllogism: problems that are significant, untreatable, of unclear causation, and long-term, are called mental retardation. The particular premise (Ken has clinically identifiable problems) and general premise (these same problems are what "we call mental retardation") suggest a diagnostic conclusion: Ken has mental retardation. Ken's mother deduces the upshot, completing the syllogism (see line 15), although using indexical or what linguists call deictic expressions ("this," "what," "it") for the condition and not referencing her son at all. Dr. M confirms her deduction at lines 17 and 19.

As with the "trip to Syracuse" excerpt, citing and reciting evidence is one way of accounting for bad news and, in a logical or progressive fashion, presenting that account to invite a recipient's inference or deduction and perhaps even pronouncement of the bad news. Here, the evidentiary and logical presentation is probative for the diagnosis, and the deliverer's agency in obtaining, or responsibility for, the diagnosis need not be questioned. Reciting evidence and being logical, accordingly, appear as practices that deflect the issue of a deliverer's responsibility.

Blaming another. To avoid imputations about their own agency, deliverers can propose putting the blame for bad news elsewhere. An excerpt that illustrates this is from a phone call in which Miss Ryan, who has a house to sell, calls and talks to Irma, a mother whose adult son is attempting to buy the house. On behalf of her son, Irma has just visited Jones and Company, who apparently has a contractual relationship with Miss Ryan to handle the selling of the house. Meanwhile Miss Ryan has just gotten off the phone with the company. Previously, there had been negotiations directly between the son and Miss Ryan, but Miss Ryan now informs Irma about the company phone call and in response to Irma's query about her "puhsition" (line 1), announces that she accepts the company's "a:rgument" (lines 3–4):

(12) JH6B/Heritage:0I:1:1
```
 1   Irma:  No:w what's th'puhsition ez far e you:'re ↓c'ncuhr:ned.
 2   Ryan:  Wul ez ↑far ez I'm c'n:cuh:rned i:t's: thet um I'll haf
 3          to ecce:pt Jones'n Co's a:rgument thet (0.3) yohr son wz
 4          introduced t'th'propity via them.=
 5   Irma:  =Ye:s well no:w °h obviously one's going tuh haftuh do
 6          that but I ken assu:re you: °hh thet he wz ↓not.
 7              (.)
 8   Irma:  .hhh We've checked now on all the paypiz ↓e ↑has an'
 9          Mann'n Comp'ny said they wuh sent through the pos', we
10          have had n:nothing fr'm Mann'n Comp'ny ↓through the post.
11             (0.3)
12   Irma:  Anyway, (.) tha:t's th- uh you know you c'm(b) (.) ahrgue
13          ih it's like (.) ↓uh:[m
14   Ryan:                       [Well
15             (.)
16   Irma:  banging y'r head against a [brick wa:ll.]
17   Ryan:                             [Ez fahr ez] I'm c'ncerned
18          on this situa:tion, oll private negotiations between us
19          mus' cea:se.
20             (0.2)
21   Ryan:  °hh
22   Irma:  °M[m↓hm°
23   Ryan:    [Ah:nd (.) any c-negotia:tion:s you: wish to enter in on
24          th' propity you haftih go vla Jones'n Co.
25   Irma:  °↓Mm:.°
26   Ryan:  °hh I bin on t'th's'licitih (he thowt thet) yihknow give
27          me s'm: legal gui:dan[ce
28   Irma:                       [Yeah:. Yah.
29   Ryan:  Ah::nd I'm really lef' between th'devil'n deep blue sea:
30          I have nno ohption BAH↓T.h (0.2) tuh re↓vuhrt tih ↓that.
31             (.)
```

Notice how, when making the announcement, Miss Ryan portrays her position as one that she is compelled to accept, and as one that is Jones and Company's argument. In Goffman's (1979) terms, she is taking a "footing" here in which she is the mere "animator" of a position "authored" by somebody else. Irma acknowledges the position ("ye:s," line 5) and agrees that "one" has to "do that," exhibiting an understanding of Miss Ryan's abstract footing.

From the outset of delivering what emerges as a series of bad news announcements, Miss Ryan manages to avoid responsibility for what she reports. Irma disputes Miss Ryan's adopted position, avowing a counterposition (lines 5–6) and, after no uptake at turn-completion, reporting evidence for that position (lines 8–10). The silence at line 11 indicates a further withholding on

Miss Ryan's part, and Irma goes on to assert an idiom (lines 12–13, 16) as a way of making complaint. As Drew and Holt (1988: 405–6) show, idiomatic complaining occurs in sequential contexts where speakers cannot rely upon recipients to affiliate. Furthermore, while idiomatic complaining regularly operates to bring closure to a sequence, here Miss Ryan interrupts the complaint (line 17) to add components to her initial announcement. After the first additional component (lines 17–19), Irma delays and speaks an acknowledgement very softly (line 22). In response to the second component (23–24), she produces a minimal and very quiet acknowledgment (line 25). Thus, Irma appears to continue resisting the news. At lines 26–27, Miss Ryan suggests that she is following a solicitor's guidance, and following the tokens at line 28, she formulates her own idiomatic complaint ("lef' between th'devil'n deep blue sea," lines 29–30), and proposes that she had "no option" in regard to her position. Once more, she has attributed that position to an outside source, and portrayed herself as compelled rather than having agency in the matter. As the talk goes on (not in transcript), Irma continues resisting Miss Ryan's account and then initiates a topic change. In short, Miss Ryan holds to her position, and works to avoid blame for it. She is at least minimally successful in that, while Irma disputes the validity of the position, she neither contests the messenger's avowals of being compelled to adopt that position nor accuses her of being responsible for it.

Good News

Whereas the literature on informing interviews in professional settings discusses the concern that deliverers have about being blamed for bad news, this literature is mute about good news and therefore about whether and how a deliverer's agency may play a role in its presentation. As in ordinary conversation, the evidence suggests that professionals giving good news may display their agency in generating the result they announce. One piece of evidence derives from the good news narrative that Joyce produces when Leslie had called to find out how Joyce's husband, Lord Geoff, who had undergone some medical testing, was doing.[11] Joyce replied that he was "not too bad" but that he was not feeling very well. Now, Leslie asks about the tests (line 1 below), and obtains Joyce's good news (lines 3, 5, 7–9, 12–13), conveyed in a story about seeing the doctor, "Mister Williams":

(13) **H4G/Holt:M88:1:2:2**
```
    1   Leslie:  Will ↑he ha-:ve the resu:lt yet.
    2                 (0.5)
    3   Joyce:   Yes we saw Mister Williams:,
```

```
 4   Leslie:  [Yes ]
 5   Joyce:   [an:'] um: °p I went t'pick im up
 6                 (.)
 7   Joyce:   Mister Williams came in 'n said °hhh you'll be glad to
 8            know I checked him and °hhh a:-nd uh it's uh (0.3)
 9            ↑clear:: as a whistle 'e [said,
10   Leslie:                          [°hhhh Oh ↑that's
11            ↓mar[v'lous.]
12   Joyce:       [N o : :] No problems at ↓all, 'e said aren't ya
13            plea:sed? I said yes::?
14   Leslie:  Oh ↓good.
```

The news is delivered by way of depicting the doctor's as having come in and announced the news. Of interest is how Joyce quotes the doctor as having, after a fashion, claimed credit: "I checked him." If Mr. Williams actually delivered the news in this way, then he showed himself to have turned up the good results. He performed the act that brought about the good news.

Deliverers who have good news for recipients regularly interject their own agency in a way that, as argued earlier, solicits the recipients' displays of appreciation. As an example, we can observe a later development involving the house that Irma's son Gary was seeking above in excerpt (12). A newly involved agent, Miss Ness, managed to arrange its sale to Gary through contacting a party in Germany who was connected to the house, thus apparently bypassing both Miss Ryan and Mann and Company. So she calls Gary with the good news:

(14) Heritage:0I:Call 7

```
 1   Ness:  I jus got through tuh Germ'ny?
 2                          (0.3)
 3   Gary:  Yes?
 4   Ness:  We ahr going through with it you en I: t'gethuh an' this
 5          guh:rl? I've got huhr Germany phone numbah? °hhh
 6          [hh
 7   Gary:  [Oh really?
 8   Ness:  She's given up wuhr:k?hh°hh An' she w'come over en take
 9          the deal o:ver en do the rest of it an' we'll fihget
10          about Miss Ryan.
11   Gary:  Fantastic.
12                          (0.2)
13   Ness:  [°So:.° ]uh]
14   Gary:  [Gr::ea:]t. ] That's (0.2) that's n-really good n- (0.9)
15          good news then and so thehr's this other (0.2) she'll (.)
16          take it out'v °hh°hh hu-u-u-u-out of Mann'n Compny's
17          hands th'n
18   Ness:  I:'m doing it furs'thing Mondee mohrning . . .
```

Miss Ness begins her announcement by showing her role — she "got through to Germany." Then, after Gary provides for continuation (line 3), she involves both herself and Gary in the good news situation (lines 4–6). After Gary's newsmark (line 7), Miss Ness elaborates on how the "deal" will get taken over from Miss Ryan (lines 8–10), whereupon Gary evaluates the report as "fantastic" (line 11), "great," and as "good news" (lines 14–15). This excerpt is dramatically different from Miss Ryan's earlier delivery of bad news about the property to Gary's mother. From the outset, for example, Miss Ness displays her agency in arranging the upcoming deal.

Then, after answering Gary's question (lines 15–17) about taking it "out of Mann and Company's hands" (this answer starts at line 18 above but is not reproduced in full), Miss Ness recounts her conversation with the girl in Germany, which includes quoting herself, below (lines 1, 3, 5–6):

(15) Heritage:01:7:2

```
 1   Ness:  And I said you reahhly des:p'r'ly wanted that place?
 2   Gary:  Ye[:s?
 3   Ness:      ['hhh An' you (.) have no (.) problems not tuh get it?
 4   Gary:  Right,
 5   Ness:  An' she said tuh me,hh (0.7) f'heav'n sake geo ahead an'
 6          please jus sell it t'Mis'uh Steph'n.
 7                  (.)
 8   Gary:  Oh: (.) ↓good well that's v- (.) that's v:- (.) really
 9          good.
10                  (.)
11   Ness:  [eO:kay?   ]
12   Gary:  [Good en u]very (0.4) very gllad'n
13                  (.)
14   Ness:  Well it'l[l: help]
15   Gary:            [gla:d ]
16   Ness:  It'll [help y ' r ]
17   Gary:        [You've done] this Missiz Ness en it's
18   Ness:  It'l[l help yer C]hristmas
19   Gary:      [v e r y kind]
```

In this quoting, Mrs. Ness depicts the seller's permission to "go ahead" (line 5) as a response to her own talk to this seller (quoting herself in lines 1, 3), and thereby as something induced by that talk. Next, Gary positively assesses this report (lines 8–9, 12), and claims a "glad" state (lines 12, 15). Then, Mrs. Ness portrays the accomplishment as oriented to her recipient's situation (lines 11, 14, 16, 18), thus shifting reference away from herself at the precise point where Gary's assessment (lines 8–9) could be heard as praising and complimentary to Mrs. Ness, whose move may operate to avert any official exhibit of self-praise.

Nevertheless, overlapping Mrs. Ness's talk and competing for turn space (lines 12, 15, 17, 19), Gary appears to pursue a line that proposes to credit her (line 17) and show his appreciation (line 19). Later, after Mrs. Ness relates more of her conversation and gives the German party's phone number to Gary, and as several approaches to closing the conversation transpire, he also thanks her each time.

What happens in professional settings may reflect how, as Schegloff (1988: 455) writes, "Members of society first learn to be competent interactionists, and then shape or adapt their practices to the contingencies . . . of professional practice." Having experienced bad and good news as competent conversational members of society, professionals may already know how to anticipate interactional ramifications of their news and, with regard to the issue of agency, design their announcing actions accordingly. Comparing excerpts (12), (14), and (15), it can be said that professionals who deliver bad news appear to eviscerate displays of their agency and responsibility, thus avoiding blame for the news. Professionals with good news work to display their agency and to claim responsibility, thereby prospecting for and often receiving compliments, praise, and other exhibits of appreciation. They do this, however, in a fashion that avoids possible attributions of self-praise.

"Blame Negotiations" and Courses of Action

As deliverers of bad news work to eviscerate displays of their agency so as to avoid being blamed, this reflects an orientation to potentials on the horizon of the informing. Evidence that participants anticipate forthcoming accusatory actions exists in Atkinson and Drew's (1979) investigation of justifications in cross-examination, where witnesses discern not-yet-stated blame in the questions of legal counsel, and fashion exculpatory answers, for example by minimizing the seriousness of events about which they are being questioned. We will see that a similar pattern is present in another interactional environment. However, the present concern is not with responses to questions about "bad" events, but with practices for announcing those events in the first place. Delivering their news, professionals may work to suggest a course of remedial action and to blame someone else, often the primary figure, as part of building the case for that course of action. By the same token, a recipient's blaming the messenger is not necessarily an end in itself. Rather, it can be laying the grounds for a course of remedial action different from that which the deliverer implies or comes to espouse.

Bad news about Spanish class. In a telephone conversation between an eighth-grade Spanish 1 teacher (Mrs. Stewart) and the Mother of a student (John), the teacher presents the bad news that John is currently earning a "D" in the class. Talk comes to center on an explanation for John's poor performance, and a multifaceted moral discourse emerges. In Watson's (1978: 110) terms, there are "blame-negotiations," and the apparent effort of the bad news recipient (Mother) is to portray the deliverer (Mrs. Stewart, the teacher) as a blame-worthy "feature of the circumstances" described in the news.

At the beginning of her call to John's mother, Mrs. Stewart (the teacher) told her, "I'm calling a few parents tonight of kids who seem to not be having such a great start here in second semester." The bad news follows at lines 4–5 below. Notice that Mrs. Stewart leads up to this information by citing the evidence–reporting the grades she has "in the book." No actor-agents are referenced in this reporting; the grades are something that Mrs. Stewart does "have" (line 1), but her delivery is agnostic about responsibility for them.

```
(16) LS 1:2:2
    1    Mrs. S:   Uh:m (.) I have (.) f:our gr↑ades:↓ in the book hh so
    2              far:.hh two fer each wee:k a:n: one is a hundred .hhh
    3              a::n: eghh ↑two are: h (0.2) uh below (.) passing and one
    4              is a Cee. .hhh so:: that puts it- the av'rage at uh::
    5              (0.4) at a Dee right no::w.
    6              (1.0)
    7    ( ):     [(  )]
    8    Mother:  [Ah::] you know, one <o' th'things> that's rea↑lly
    9              concer:ning me:: about, John's performance in ge↑n'ral in
   10              Spanish↓ .hhh is that I think he's qu↑ite ↑ca:pable of
   11              getting Bee's: and A:ays:
   12    Mrs. S:   Mm [hmm]
   13    Mother:      [as  ] far as his (.) .hh ↑language ski:ll: abilities=
   14    Mrs. S:   =Mm hm=
   15    Mother:   =uh:, go. .hh An' I'm wondering why: he's getting such
   16              low scores: .hh period. Just across the boar:d, and what
   17              it is::: because=
   18    Mrs. S:   =.hhh[h
   19    Mother:        [uh he's always been e- not in written↓ language
   20              expression .hh but he's always been adept in lan↑guage.
```

In the context here, which is ripe for some blame attribution, Mrs. Stewart delivers her news (lines 1–5) by citing the evidence and as a "my side telling" (Pomerantz 1980) that operates as an "information elicitor" (Bergmann, 1992) inviting a recipient to volunteer *her* side. John's mother delays in responding (line 6), and gives her side by claiming a concern about "John's performance" and characterizing him as capable of getting B's and A's (lines 8–11) in relation to his "language skill abilities" (line 13). Then, Mother launches a search for the cause of John's "low scores" (lines 15–17), "wondering why" and "what it is" when he has "always been a̲dept in lan↑guage" (lines 19–20).

The student as a locus of the problem. In answering the mother's question, Mrs. Stewart (in talk not reproduced here) tells her that most of the grade comes from written worksheets and quizzes. Then Mother asks about the quizzes (lines 1–2):

(17) LS 1:2:3 (normalized)

1	Mother:	Now are these things pretty much things that need to be
2		studied for in order to do well
3	Stewart:	Oh yes
4	Mother:	And so you think it's a matter of just not study- I- what
5		is the problem with the worksheets? or quizzes?

At line 4, Mother's displayed understanding of Mrs. Stewart's answer-so-far to her question of causality is that the problem may be John's studying. However, mother abandons that line to query about the "worksheets" and "quizzes" (line 5). Hence John as a possible locus of responsibility is only momentarily referenced. Next (but not in the transcript here), Mother asks, in a way that shifts the focus from John to the way in which the class is taught, "And he certainly knows when a quiz is going to be right?" To this, Mrs. Stewart responds that there cannot be "any mistaking it," since she announces the quiz several days in advance "in English" and reminds them the day before it.

Mother also asks about whether John was "attentive" in the class. After answering in the affirmative, and commenting that his spelling is a particular problem, Mrs. Stewart goes on to say that she had talked to John about the "possibility of repeating Spanish 1" when he enters high school the next year. John's mother objects to this proposal, saying "I react STRONGLY to the idea that he is doing so poorly that he should repeat a year of Spanish." Mrs. Stewart's response is to tell a story about her own failure to pass her first driver's test, concluding that she "was not mature enough to handle it . . . it wasn't my fault." Thus, by analogy, she disavows faulting John in terms of his development, which can be something biological, but she still implicates him as a locus of the problem — he needs to mature. Hence, the original news delivery, which is agnostic about agency in relation to the bad grades, can be a backdrop for this later suggestion, retrospectively being informed by it: there are bad grades in the book because John is not mature enough for the work, and needs to repeat Spanish 1 to catch up. Mrs. Stewart goes on to raise the possibility that if he is "frustrated" and "angry," John might "give up" on Spanish altogether rather than completing three or four years during his high school career.

Blaming the messenger by praising a predecessor. In her next turn after

Mrs. Stewart's story about her driver's test, and her posing the possibility of John's giving up on Spanish, Mother says, "It sounds like to me you're saying he's not doing very well at all. What you're talking to me about is a very poor performance." She announces that she had "been promoting very strongly that he take Spanish and that he continue in it" and that this was "an area he ought to excel in." Then:

(18) LS 1:2:3

```
 1   Mother:  Now I'm sitting her:e, and I'm listening, ta someone tell
 2            me::, that they think that he ought to repea::t, it, in a
 3            very stro::ng sort of ↑wa:y. .hhh an I guess I'm r::eally
 4            concerned about that, a lot.
 5   Stewart: Okay=
 6   Mother:  =An' I'm ↑al↓so concerned, because I:-, I- a:n' an' that
 7            has nothing ta ya know say: .hh but you know he h::a:d a
 8            very good start with Missus Anderson.
 9   Stewart: Mm hmm=
10   Mother:  =A:n: I'm not ya know co:mmenting on the teaching?
11            because I I have na- absolutely no ide↑a .hhh but he was
12            very happy with her, h[e liked    ] her a lot,=
13   Stewart:                       [Mm hmm]
14   Mother:  =an I was r:eally ve:ry very much hoping .hh that he
15            would've had her this year. .hhh and that's not saying
16            anything, you know, negative about you:. It was just that
17            we had a very fi:ne experience, [with he]r=
18   Stewart:                                 [Right. ]
19   Stewart: =.hhh We[ll    ]
20   Mother:          [An'] I I hav:e to::, ya know I'm sitting in the
21            back o' my mind saying now .h would this be going on with
22            Mrs. Anderson's class.
23   Stewart: .hh[hh    ]
24   Mother:     [An' I ] have ta be honest with you. Because that's
25            exactly what I'm thinking.=
26   Stewart: =Right and that's v[ery natural]
27   Mother:                     [And I:'m:   ] real concerned and I-
28            it's like I want Mrs. Anderson's, ya know comment. Uh why
29            why hasn't she been with him all year:, ya know .hhh an'
30            an' [I just  ] .hhh aga:in=
31   Stewart:     [.hh m-]
32   Mother:  I'm I I'm (.) talking ta you very up front, very
33            straightforward .hhh an' I'm not try:ing ta sa::y,
34            anything against your tea↑ching because I don't ↑kno:w
35            you. [An'  I  don't  know  you[r teaching (style)]
36   Stewart:      [.hhhhhhhhhhhhhhhhhhhhhh[Well::             ] I have
37            been teaching the same curriculum:, eghhm that (.) Julie
```

```
38                    has been tea[ching.]=
39    Mother:                      [Right.]=
40    Mother:    =[I un] [d e r s t a n d that.]
41    Stewart:   =[.hhh] [for years: and I have] been supplementing .hhh
42                    tha::t with some work out of the textbook that's
43                    available to us::, m:ostly because uh:: .hhh she has been
44                    teaching her curriculum fer years and it's kind
45                    of hard to step into someone else's curriculum.
```

In lines 1–5, Mother formulates what she has heard from Mrs. Stewart, and then reports her reaction — being "r::eally concerned" about the proposal for John to repeat Spanish 1. Following Mrs. Stewart's "okay" (line 5), she goes on to indicate another concern. She starts with a partially-formed denial: ". . . an that has nothing ta ya know say . . . ," and proceeds with a contrast marker ("but," line 7) and a display of appreciation (7–8) for John's former Spanish teacher, Mrs. Anderson. Subsequent to this display, and Mrs. Stewart's continuer, Mother appears to revise and complete the denial; she is "not co:mmenting on the teaching" (line 10). Then, she again proposes a contrast (with "but"), displays more appreciation for the former teacher (lines 11–12; 14–15), and produces another denial that this says "anything . . . negative" (lines 15–16) about Mrs. Stewart. Mother completes her turn by reverting to a further display of appreciation for Mrs. Anderson (lines 16–17).

In overlap with the completion of this utterance, Mrs. Stewart produces an agreement token (line 18) and (partially in the clear) a contrast marker (line 19), which together suggest impending disaffiliation from or disagreement with Mother's line of talk (Pomerantz 1984a). However, Mother, with an "An" token building a next turn of talk to be a continuation with her last, and by raising a rhetorical question (lines 20–22) shows appreciation yet again for the former teacher. And this time, instead of countering a possible interpretation that this is critical of Mrs. Stewart, Mother stakes a claim to being "honest" because she has revealed "exactly" what she's "thinking" (lines 24–25). When Mrs. Stewart exhibits agreement with and support for this stance (line 26), Mother, in overlap with the end of that turn, once more states being "real concerned," and goes on with still another appreciative comment about Mrs. Anderson (professing to want the latter teacher's "comment" and to know why she wasn't "with" John this year, lines 27–30). Mother next refreshes both her claim to honesty (lines 30, 32–33) and her denial that she is thereby saying "anything" about Mrs. Stewart's teaching (lines 33–35).

Citing evidence for a bad news upshot in a "my side" telling, by inviting the recipient's side of the story as in excerpt (16), may be a deliverer's way of testing

the waters before issuing further proposals that suggest a particular course of
action to remedy the situation, especially when those proposals will implicate
someone other than the messenger herself. In this case, that someone is the primary figure, who is the son of the recipient. Recipients of bad news, on the other
hand, have devices for pursuing a different course of action or resolution where
blaming the messenger is part of that pursuit. In a way that may propose to "set
the record straight" (Mandelbaum 1993: 262) about John's difficulties, Mother
does not overtly criticize her son's teacher and co-interactant. Rather, she
demonstrates appreciation for his former teacher (Mrs. Anderson), while denying that this comments negatively on Mrs. Stewart. Although Mother overtly
exhibits regard for her son's previous teacher, by her denials she also demonstrates an understanding that such praise and appreciation could be heard as saying something "negative" about John's present teacher, Mrs. Stewart. Hence,
the initial public availability of possibly *blaming* Mrs. Stewart for John's poor
performance is reflexive to these very statements of denial. The device here is
covertly blaming the messenger for bad news by praising a predecessor who had
the position that the messenger now occupies. A further device is to interject,
between the shows of appreciation and denials, a claim to being honest and
straightforward. Purporting straightforwardness may bid to justify and mitigate
the open praise and the related but unstated potential criticism and blaming of
her co-interactant.

That Mother's praise of Mrs. Anderson can be heard to blame Mrs. Stewart
for John's problems in Spanish 1 is also apparent in Mrs. Stewart's eventual response to Mother's line of talk. Mrs. Stewart treats Mother's reference to her
"teaching" and "teaching style" (excerpt (18), lines 34–35) *defensively;* she explains and justifies herself by linking her teaching methods to the "same curriculum" as Mrs. Anderson ("Julie," lines 36–38) uses. Mrs. Stewart also reports
that she supplements this curriculum with other work (lines 41–43).[12] Without
offering a gloss that would characterize her own style as "good" (and therefore
engaging in self-praise), the teacher's detailing can support such an upshot
tacitly (Drew 1992: 491–95). Then, Mrs. Stewart gives a reason for supple-
mentation (lines 44–45), mentioning how "hard" it is to "step into someone
else's curriculum." In all, Mrs. Stewart exhibits anticipation that Mother's
"concerned" report of her reaction, which takes no stance on the teacher's style,
could question that style; that is, that there could be an overt blame sequence
to which the previous talk could be leading. Beyond the excerpt reproduced,
Mrs. Stewart further explains her teaching, reporting that she consults daily with
Mrs. Anderson. Mother says, "I guess I'd just like to get to the bottom of why
he's not doing well," brings up John's written and oral language skills, argues

that it is only in written exercises that he has problems, and suggests that these should be monitored closely for the rest of the year.[13] Finally, she announces, "He is going to sign up for the Spanish 2 class," and Mrs. Stewart responds, "Okay that's fine."

The moral risk in being a bearer of bad news. Explaining John's record and dealing with the recommendation to have John repeat Spanish 1 occupy a major part of the talk subsequent to Mrs. Stewart delivering the bad news to Mother about his poor performance. As the excerpts above indicate, after an initial focus on John and his habits of study and attending in class, discussion about Mrs. Stewart's own role and responsibility for this performance comes to occupy a significant moment in the talk. This discussion carries forward as a feature of subsequent interaction: as Mother argues about the classroom emphasis on written work and requirements for such things as proper spelling, she seems to be commenting on Mrs. Stewart's teaching style and role in John's performance in a covert way. Finally, just as implicating John—if only in terms of his maturity—can justify retention in Spanish 1, blaming Mrs. Stewart for her son's poor performance can service Mother's later proposal for John to move to Spanish 2. Although both the deliverer and the recipient of the bad news—the student's teacher and parent, respectively—are circumspect about allocating blame, each one has a version of where it belongs. In professional settings, like ordinary conversation, bearers of news are not just the conduits of information; their own agency can figure heavily in the interaction and moral discourse surrounding the news. Little wonder that individuals may gear their career decisions because of this, sometimes avoiding, as chapter 1 showed, occupations in which having to disclose bad tidings is an all too regular responsibility.

EIGHT

Sociopolitical Implications: Everyday Rationality in Public Decision Making

"Everyday things represent the most overlooked knowledge. . . . Quotidian things. If they weren't important, we wouldn't use such a gorgeous Latinate word. Say it," he said.
"Quotidian."
"An extraordinary word that suggests the depth and reach of the commonplace."[1]

Bad and good news, in interaction, reveal taken-for-granted structures of everyday or "quotidian" life. Heretofore, my investigation has centered on relatively private and secluded conversational and clinical encounters. Now I wish to turn to larger arenas, to propose that inquiry concerning the quotidian structure of everyday life, because of the "depth" and "reach" of this structure, may help make sense of more public and political behavior. That is, my study of the concrete endogenous ordering of interaction offers the potential for analyzing and understanding specific features of major and sometimes massively consequential social events. That conversational behavior and organization may have this import seems to go against something that the interaction order theorist Goffman (1983: 9) once wrote:

> When your broker informs you that he has to sell you out or when your employer or your spouse informs you that your services are no longer required, the bad news can be delivered through a sequestered talk that gently and delicately humanizes the occasion. Such considerateness belongs to the resources of the interaction order. At the time of their use you may be very grateful for them. But the next morning what does it matter if you had gotten the word from a wire margin call, a computer readout, a blue slip at the time clock, or a terse note left on the bureau? How delicately or indelicately one is treated during the moment in which bad news is delivered does not speak to the structural significance of the news itself.

The important point, with which I agree, is that the interaction order and macrosociological structures often have separate existences, neither one necessarily being reducible to the other. My investigations have centered on orderliness and organization at the level of interaction, and I argue that the practices for delivering and receiving news are consonant with features of local social worlds. And if these worlds and social structures are not reducible one to the other, in-

226

teraction in some circumstances nevertheless does make contact with and influence features of societies that house it. One point of contact, Goffman (1983: 8) himself claims, occurs as an outcome of the transmission of information and decision making in organizational and institutional settings. Because they often require the immediacy of talk and social interaction, transmitting facts and deciding what to do render organizations and societies in which these processes occur "vulnerable" to interaction-order effects.[2] As I draw this book to a close, I can only give brief glimpses of this possibility in the case of bad and good news. Interactional practices involving such news condition whether, how, and how appropriately participants perceive and handle events in the larger world. It is a cliché of the researcher, yet true in this instance: others will need to do more extensive research on the interactional effects on public and political decision making of the produced orderliness involved in news deliveries. I will summarize events that are complex historical and social occurrences.

Public Manipulations of Bad and Good News

In the direct relations through which they share tidings about social worlds undergoing profound transformation, participants collaboratively assemble and experience as objective the attributes those worlds come to have. By now, I hope this proposition is robustly demonstrated in the communications we have seen in ordinary conversation and between parties operating in institutional or organizational settings including clinics. To see whether the proposition is also valid about the patterning of public and political events — social structures that affect people more massively — I will rely heavily on anecdotal evidence, but draw on our knowledge about the organization of interaction. I will argue that, in contrast to perspectives emphasizing cognitive appraisals and participants' utilitarian "rational choice" decision making, we need to consider the *everyday rationality* of choices made in public and political and other official arenas. While touching on other events, I will spotlight a controversy surrounding the contamination of the U.S. blood supply with HIV-virus in the early 1980s.

The Political Arena and Public Consequences

A quick glance at the political arena provides initial purchase on bad and good news as a feature of public life. Time and again, major governmental figures may have news that potentially enhances or devastates their images, their campaigns, their agendas, their tenure in office, and local, national, and international interests. Keeping things in hand is pejoratively called "spin control," a particularly egregious admission to which cost the finance minister of Brazil his job in 1994. When Rubens Ricupero, the minister, was helping campaign for a centrist candidate for president, he began talking to what he thought was a limited number of people about economic indicators. Unaware that a live microphone was nearby, he let a comment slip: "I have no scruples. What is good, we take advantage of. What is bad we hide." Because of the uproar his comments generated, Mr. Ricupero shortly thereafter had to resign his position. His remarks indicate once again an asymmetric stance toward bad and good news and, more to the point here, that politicians attempt to calculate and orchestrate the effects of such news.

The media, if not the public, are aware of such manipulative tactics. Writing in the midst of the Monica Lewinsky scandal surrounding then President Bill Clinton, the journalist Joe Klein recounted that three days before Clinton gave testimony to Congress in August 1998, a headline appeared in the *New York Times:* "President Weighs Admitting He Had Sexual Contacts."

(1) **Klein 1998: 48**

> The media's first impression was that this was business as usual, the beginning of a new spin cycle — that it was a controlled leak, with the White House taking charge of the Lewinsky story and preparing the public, so that the President's revised testimony wouldn't come as a complete shock.

To the extent that such imputations are true,[3] they suggest that public figures work to forecast bad news with the hope of the exact effects described in chapter 2. Recipients — the public, in this case — having been prepared, will be more receptive to the news when it is delivered. But politicians don't always attempt to shroud bad news. Just after he was elected as president, George W. Bush was accused of accentuating bad news about the economy, with the purpose of blaming the previous administration and also to justify his plans for a tax cut (Rosenbaum 2001). As a result, the public, as well as the Congress, knowing that bad news needs remediation, would be more willing to entertain these controversial plans. We can say of these actors on the national scene that they exploit their knowledge of interactional structure for large-scale political ends.

Chemical Exposure during the Iraqi War

Political manipulations of bad and good news are pervasive and hint at another public feature, which is the contention involved in the conveyance of such news. In the mid-1990s in the U.S., a controversy bubbled into the press regarding whether and to what extent U.S. soldiers had been exposed to chemical weapons during the 1991 war with Iraq. Despite claims that there were many exposures, the Pentagon has officially acknowledged only one.[4] This itself may be a shrouding of bad news, and more features of bad and good news present themselves when we examine a particular instance of American troop exposure. This moves us in the direction of considering consequences for the public (in this case, soldiers) from the shrouding of bad news. On the second day of the Iraqi war, Czech chemical weapons specialists, with sophisticated equipment for detection, measured chemical agents in the northern Saudi desert. The Czechs sounded the alarm to their own troops in the area, who, within sight of American soldiers, quickly put on gas masks and chemical warfare suits.

In contrast, when Czech officers told American commanders about the problem, the Americans decided to do nothing. For two immediate reasons, they not only refrained from ordering troops to don any protection but did not inform them at all of any risk of exposure. One reason was that officers regarded the level of exposure as very low. Another was that American officials adhered to a theory that exposure would cause immediate and lethal symptoms, and these were not happening (McGovern 1997: xiii).[5] At more distance, a reason for the American resistance may have been the responsibility the United States bore for the bombings that released the chemicals and, in earlier years, for having made available to the Iraqis the munitions containing the Iraqi chemical weapons (Eddington 1997: 253–55).

Cognitive Risk Assessment

Assuming that Vacek was correct about American officers' underestimating the problem of chemical exposure, scholarly investigations of risk assessment meant to correct straightforward rational choice models of decision making go a long ways in explaining how the officials in this case may have miscalculated the dangers. For example, Tversky and Kahneman (1974) propose that a "representativeness" heuristic can affect judgments of risk in that people often use associational principles and stereotypes to determine the likelihood of an event rather than facts about frequencies, distributions, or other patterns of occurrence. When American officials claimed to notice no symptoms among their troops, and concluded that nothing was wrong in the environment, this could reflect ignorance or eschewal of facts about the latent dangers involved. In their minds was this stereotype, possibly learned from acute cases, that chemical exposure should have relatively prompt effects.[6] In addition, according to Vaclav Hlavac, a chief warrant officer in the Czech army at the time, at least one American officer "decided not to alert the troops under his command because he did not want to create a 'panic'" (Shenon 1996). Sociological treatments of risk assessment stress the importance of actors' (in this case, officers') involvement in organizations and organizational routines that put the organizations' interests ahead of other considerations, such as the well-being of persons affected by official decisions (Douglas 1986; Heimer 1988: 511–13). Although his views are subject to dispute, Eddington (1997) argues forcefully that the U.S. government and military had strong institutional reasons for suppressing news about the Iraqi chemical exposures.

Accordingly, many factors may explain the reluctance of American officials to say anything to the troops, but analytically we have to *infer* how they may have perceived the situation and weighed risks. Theory and research about risk assessment develops abstractions about how subjects and actors *think*—the ways they more or less rationally weigh costs and benefits—and how their thinking affects action.[7] As a consequence, such theory and research says little about what subjects and actors concretely *do* in the world of conduct as they perceive, transmit, and receive information about social events. Studies of actual interaction take the opposite tack, attempting to avert what Ryle (1949) calls dogma about the "ghost in the machine" (a mind separate from and directing body), and therefore refraining from inferences about what goes on in people's heads. Ethnomethodology and conversation analysis discover structure-in-action in the realm of *practices*. For example, while I have discussed the phenomenon of "realization," by this term I refer not so much to a cognitive or psychological event as to perceptions of social worlds that are exhibited in the concrete methods whereby participants speak and act together. My recommendation, however, is far from claiming that studies of actual interaction can explain all the complexities to public disasters. More modestly, I do believe they can help make sense of how people *perform* in interaction with one another when making choices involving risk. That is, it is important to consider the organization of direct relations among the parties who concertedly present information and draw conclusions that are sometimes consequential, even life threatening, for large numbers of people.

To hone the analysis of everyday rationality, a first step is briefly to review the writings of Schutz on the constitutive phenomenology of everyday life and Garfinkel on ethnomethodology. For Schutz (1962), when participants act rationally they adhere to presumptions that form the "attitude of daily life" (see chapter 1), and fashion their conduct together in terms of *recipes* and *typifications* that the presumptions make real and relevant for *courses of action*. The analyst needs to grasp the actors' point of view to know what these recipes, typifications, and courses of action are. Altering the Schutzean preoccupation with participants' presumptive and typified *conceptual* apparatus, Garfinkel (1967: chap. 8), locates rationality in *activity*—in what participants say and do when competently engaging one another about decisions to be made. Both Schutz and Garfinkel attempt to deflect attention from utilitarian rational-choice models, but not because they are invalid depictions of thought processes. Rather, in positing abstract cost-benefit analyses on the part of participants, investigators use such models as yardsticks with which to appraise and assess real human behavior. Even in the correctives that Tversky and Kahneman (1974, 1981) advance in their heuristic critique of rational choice is a strong element of irony toward how people actually operate.[8] And, as we will see, a government panel reviewing the 1980s blood supply contamination attributes it to faulty cost-benefit analysis on the part of major decision-makers, who were purportedly computing advantages and disadvantages, some more erroneously than others. By reviewing this case, I hope to show something different. While much can be learned by considering how participants cognitively sort the costs and benefits of pursuing particular paths, until we pay attention to everyday rationality — commonsense decision making — we will not know anything about how, in interaction, one set of participants who has information that involves risk to others can communicate this information effectively.

The Conveyance of Information as a Site of Contention

A reminder is due at this point: participants talking about events-in-the-world manage the information according to the actions the talk implements. The character of an event-in-the world, we saw in chapter 4, is not inherent, which means that when information is somehow communicated from one party to another, the transaction can be a *site of contention* as to whether the information is news and what sort of news it is. If contention about information occurs in private, informal situations, it emerges in larger more public arenas as well. For the Czechs involved in the Iraq war, their measurements indicating a release of gas were bad news; for American officers these measurements were not news, or at least not bad news, and no actions were necessary.

Finding chemical agents in the field, Czech personnel took preventative action not only by ordering troops to don gas masks and suits, but by telling the news to their American counterparts, and expecting similar actions from them. This sequence of actions is one example of how delivering bad news may be a device for requesting remedial action on the part of recipients. In this situation of chemical exposure, the primary consequential figures in the bad news were *third* parties — the American soldiers. *First* parties, or deliverers as primary figure, also use the device to request help, which suggests that bad news and remedies are regularly paired or coupled in a variety of circumstances.[9] Exemplary instances of both kinds of bad news — third party and first party — and their pairing with remedies occur in 911 emergency telephone calls to dispatch centers. Callers have their own or others' bad news to report, and in forming their bad news as a complaint, *explicitly* ask for help. Call takers, if they discern an actionable situation, offer remedy by dispatching police, fire, or medical assistance (Whalen, Zimmerman, and Whalen 1988; Zimmerman 1992). In less formal situations, deliverers may use bad news as an *inexplicit* request for remedy, and a recipient may grant the request in the next turn. Thus, in data where Melissa calls George at her place of work with the "bad news" that she will, because of an illness in her family, be unavailable for her next shift and that she needs to "tell somebody," George offers a type of help by responding, "Oh I can handle that," implying that he will let their supervisor know.

In relation to potential public catastrophes, recipients of explicit or inexplicit requests that deliverers package as bad news also may grant these requests straightforwardly, as when Czech soldiers responded to warnings about chemical pollution in the Saudi desert. Declining such requests is more interactionally complicated. As a conversational illustration, consider what happens when an individual, Donny, is stranded on his way to work (Mandelbaum and Pomerantz 1991; Schegloff 1996). Donny telephones a friend, Marcia, and comes immediately to the point. "My car is stalled and I'm up here in the Glen," he says. This potentially represents bad news and implicates an offer of remedy or help from Marcia (Schegloff 1996: 15). Marcia, however, registers this utterance only with the change-of-state token, "Oh." That is, she accepts his report as news, but avoids attending to it as bad news and as a complaint for her to help resolve. As Donny continues, he produces several items further soliciting her help, including a report that imparts the urgency of his predicament — he has to "open up the bank in Brentwood." Still, Marcia is not at all forthcoming, ultimately stating that she has "to leave in about five minutes." She thereby "declines to offer help, without ever saying 'no'" (18).[10]

Marcia's trajectory toward, and veiled ways of declining to help, then, are set in motion by her abstemious response to Donny's purported bad news. In other words, she responds to his news as "just news" rather than as something serious enough to involve abandoning her present course of action. The analytical upshot is that, as an interactional matter, when reasons exist for recipients to decline participation in remedy, it may condition the way in which adumbrated bad news is received in the first place. Rather than first dealing with news and its projected valence as a matter apart from what the news projects in terms of remedial action, *recipients embed their positions on remedy in the very way that they react to the news.*[11] Simply put, a recipient works to disrupt the sequential pairing (bad news delivery + proposals for remediation) by discounting the first half of the pair.

This returns us to the premise that the difficulty of bad news is its association with a changed social world. For recipients to acknowledge such a new world may mean abandoning their previous worlds, as comprising whatever courses of action in which they are currently engaged, and becoming part of the new world in the very direct sense of working to mitigate its impact. Hearing about Donny's predicament, Marcia is unwilling to take such a route — she is not to be dislodged from "having to leave in about five minutes." In more public arenas, commitments to ongoing courses of action are institutionalized, as when American officials may have discounted news about Iraqi war chemical exposure because of sensitive political issues.

The potential for recipients to disconnect the bad-news remediation pairing suggests that, for those who want to have their information taken seriously as bad news, correctly or accurately imparting this information requires prior assessment of how engaging in remedy will affect their recipients as occupants of particular lifeworlds. The deliverer's news, that is, needs to be tailored to an understanding of their recipients' present courses of action, especially in situations where altering those courses of action involves high risk.

Bad News and Blood: HIV Infects Individuals with Hemophilia

The coupling of bad-news with proposals for remediation pervades a variety of socially and politically significant arenas. In terms of the social organization of direct interaction, and with a slight transformation, it helps make sense of the Iraqi war situation in which American troops were dangerously exposed to chemical gases. Here, the news to American commanders, if accepted as such and as bad news, while not requiring remedial action to help the Czechs who delivered the news, could have meant movement to inform American soldiers and to command protective measures for them. We need not speculate about how the American officers engaged in cognitive risk assessment. As they became determined not to take action, officers firmly resisted what the Czechs purported to be bad news. According to the pattern identified in our conversational episodes, they sought to rupture the bad-news remediation pair by discounting its first half and not regarding the information in the way the Czechs intended. Other social and political situations exhibit this same pattern.

Contamination of Blood Supplies with the HIV Virus

In the early 1980s, supplies of Factor VIII, the blood clotting substance also known as antihemophilic factor or AHF, became contaminated with HIV virus and massively infected human populations around the world who had the disease of hemophilia. In the United States, when officials at the Center for Disease Control (CDC) in Atlanta became aware of the possibility of contamination, they attempted to inform officials at agencies and firms who were in charge of the nation's supply of Factor VIII, but to no immediate avail. Not until about 1985, more than two years after initial warnings were sounded, did the nation act to cleanse the blood supply on any systematic basis. By then, the supply was so contaminated that within two more years, according to CDC estimates from 1987, approximately 9,465 or 63 percent of the estimated 15,500 people with hemophilia in the United States were infected with HIV (Leveton, Sox, and Stoto 1995: 21).

The story, a complicated one as told and retold in various accounts,[12] illustrates how those in a position to anticipate and take early countermeasures against a major national and international health threat did not do so. My argument is that this phenomenon is partly due to the produced orderliness of direction interaction involving bad and good news. To make this argument, I will reverse my usual approach of considering the clinical issues in a chapter's coda. Instead, I take an immediate look at what happened in hemophilia clinics. From the clinic and doctor–patient relationships, I will extrapolate to suggest that familiar interactional patterns were also manifest in more public arenas involving institutional actors charged with monitoring and organizing hemophilia treatment in the wider population.

In the Clinic

Physicians treating hemophiliac individuals in the 1980s suffered greatly with the specter of bad news about blood and HIV infection. Although early on, officials from the National Hemophilia Foundation (NHF) decided against allowing much flow of information regarding blood contamination to go forth to clinicians who, with their patients, could have decided the risks (Leveton, Sox, and Stoto 1995: 195), some clinicians who *were* positioned to know about the situation were still extremely cautious. For example, Regina Butler was chair of the NHF Nursing Committee, and heard about the contamination at a meeting of the NHF's Medical and Scientific Advisory Council in October of 1982, when officials from the Center for Disease Control reported on several hemophiliac individuals who had contracted HIV apparently by using contaminated blood. She reacted to the report at that meeting by thinking, "This is a horrible thing, and it's going to kill our patients." In an interview with Resnik (1999), she recalled, "at that moment, at that talk, listening to him, I thought, 'This is it. From now on it's never going to be the same.' I just had a profound feeling, a sense of doom that this is really major stuff" (122). But she did not express this reaction openly at the October 1982 meeting and then delayed conveying the news to the Hemophilia Treatment Center in Philadelphia, where she worked. Only after parents had called a meeting, invited Butler as the Center's director, and asked her what was going on, did she disclose the news and begin instituting measures to counteract possible contamination (122–23).

Still, compared to other clinicians, Butler was ahead of the game. Later, when knowledge about the contamination was more widespread, physician specialists remained closemouthed with their patients:

> one of the case studies revealed that physicians often responded to the initial questions of patients with reassurances that the risk was not serious, that the patient was overreacting, that "there are always risks," and that patients and doctors should wait and see what happens . . . Or, the physician conveyed the impression that the risk was a problem associated with homosexual behavior and therefore not a problem for individuals with hemophilia. . . . In addition, physicians downplayed the size of the risk, saying, for example, "only one percent of hemophiliacs were contracting the disease." (Leveton, Sox, and Stoto 1995: 195–96)

Interactionally, the pattern is the one we saw in chapter 6: physicians *shrouding* the bad news and, in contrast exposing good news in their talk to patients. In this case, the good news was about the benefits of Factor VIII or AHF concentrate as they existed prior to the HIV contamination.

> The Committee also found that some physicians were reluctant to discuss bad news, including a prognosis with dire implications, once symptoms of AIDS began to occur in their patients. Even when confronted with initial symptoms of AIDS, the physician's message to his patient sometimes was not to worry. (199).

An interviewee suggested to a National Academy of Sciences (NAS) review committee that when AIDS appeared in a previously healthy person with hemophilia, the experience was "frightening" for physicians, who were "uncomfortable" discussing the infection and its implications with patients (ibid.). And when physicians *were* communicative, at least some patients and families themselves were unwilling to change their use of AHF because this felt like going back to an era of less-effective treatment strategies (2002–01), whereas by the early 1980s and before the HIV outbreak, those involved in hemophilia treatment considered themselves to be in a kind of golden age (discussed below). Once more, the asymmetry in which bad news gets shrouded and good news exposed, is co-produced, not something entirely imposed upon recipients. Also collaborative is professional and lay participants' clinging to a former social world. On either side of the tidings — delivery and receipt — comprehending a new world can be perversely difficult.

In Public or Governmental Settings

Moving to larger arenas and the dawning awareness among federal and private groups concerned with the national blood supply that something was seriously amiss, I will emphasize a crucial conference taking place in Atlanta in January 1983, at which CDC officials presented their bad news about contamination of the blood supply and discussed a set of remedial actions, only to be rebuffed by most parties in attendance. The story begins in 1982, when Dr. Bruce Evatt, a specialist in hemophilia at the CDC, became aware of three hemophiliac individuals, in different parts of the country, who had become ill with conditions that appeared to be like GRID (gay-related immunodeficiency disease), as the disease of AIDS then was known. However, these patients did not fit the profiles of any groups, including intravenous drug users, Haitian immigrants, and male homosexuals, known to be at risk for the disease. In fact, the only commonality among hemophiliacs was their disease and use of Factor VIII to treat it, but this was enough for Evatt and colleagues at the CDC, going by the record of how GRID rapidly emerged to infect hundreds of Americans, to project a similar epidemic among people with hemophilia. CDC officials energetically began a campaign to tell medical groups what was happening and to suggest measures that could contain the outbreak.

On 4 January 1983, two hundred people were assembled at the behest of the U.S. public health service at CDC headquarters in Atlanta. In attendance were representatives from the CDC, Federal Drug Administration (FDA), National Institutes of Health (NIH), National Hemophilia Foundation, American Red Cross, American Association of Bloodbanks, National Gay Task Force, and Pharmaceutical Manufacturers Association (on behalf of plasma manufacturing companies). At this point, there were eight known hemophilia AIDS cases in the nation and suspicions about two more. In addition, a baby had died of AIDS in San Francisco after receiving blood transfusions. From the perspective of officials at the CDC, the evidence was by now even stronger than it had been weeks or months earlier that, through HIV transmission in blood products, an AIDS epidemic was descending on the hemophiliac community.[13]

Given this evidence of an impending outbreak, officials from the CDC entertained ideas of remediation, seeing two main ways of dealing with the threat. One involved screening potential donors according to their membership in "at risk" groups, especially male homosexuals who were frequent blood donors. Another remedy derived from an apparent correlation between HIV infection and Hepatitis B. Because at that time there was no test for HIV but there was a test for the presence of Hepatitis B antibodies, the latter test could be used as a

"surrogate" method for discerning the presence HIV in a person. So CDC officials felt that despite their bad news, they had two effective countermeasures to
enact. As Donald Francis, one of Evatt's colleagues at the CDC, put it, "not only
did we present the data to them, but we really laid it on a silver platter what to
do about it, in the least costly way" (quoted in Starr 1998: 336). Evatt himself
recalls going "into that meeting expecting it to be a snap. How could anybody
doubt the data we'd accumulated, the *trends?* We thought it was a no-brainer"
(ibid., 271). To the CDC officials' utter surprise, they found consensus "impossible to achieve" (Leveton, Sox, and Stoto 1995: 116).

That the 200 attenders did not agree with the dire news or proposed solutions was extremely surprising and shocking to the CDC officials (Resnik 1999:
271; Starr 1998: 127). Immediately, a question confronts us as to why CDC
officials, so sure of their message, encountered strenuous opposition and failed
in their goal of achieving consensus about what to do.[14]

Accepting the News and Taking Countermeasures

I would argue that the potential bad news about HIV in the blood supply
encountered a countervailing force — the interactional pressure to maintain the
social world as a benign one, even in the face of signs, if not firm evidence, that
the world had already been changed radically in a malignant direction. Often we
represent such predicaments in terms of a resistance to change and an investment in the status quo (Leveton, Sox, and Stoto 1995: 201), but these handy
phrases suggest a simple rigidity to human psychology and action, and fail to
capture the dynamic quality of lived social experience. In confronting a socially
produced asymmetry that puts bad news in a disadvantaged position, disclosures about HIV contamination unleashed actions associated with bad news —
blaming the messenger, emotional discomfiture, and, in particular, an effort to
disconnect the bad-news remediation pairing.

Before exploring these dynamics, let us consider one other answer to the
question about why CDC officials met opposition. It might be that in 1983 no
one of the potential recipients of the news was equipped to apprehend it or do
anything about it. In fact, at each stage of development, there were those who
almost immediately did realize the threat. They responded to the CDC's information as bad news, regarded the contamination of the blood supply as real, and
decided that remedial action was in order. For example, Starr (1998) reports this
early (fall 1982) reaction to CDC findings: "Tom Drees, president of Alpha at
the time, said he was 'knocked off [his] chair' when Evatt addressed a group of
fractionators. He immediately made plans to exclude high-risk donor groups,
despite charges of discrimination" (267). By the time of the January 1983

meeting in Atlanta, plasma companies (fractionators) had already been exclud-
ing gays, Haitians, and drug users from their donor pools. They reacted favorably
to the CDC's recommendations and accepted their news and projections of a
possible epidemic.[15]

Nevertheless, winning the day collectively was what observers of the scene,
as well as the actors they interviewed, repeatedly call "denial." "'I think they
were listening, but I just don't think they wanted to believe it,' Evatt reflected.
'The implications were so catastrophic for the whole industry they just wanted
it to go away'" (273). Denial is a regular response to bad news and can be evidence of, or a defense against, the cognitive disorientation occurring when the
social world of some participant is a candidate for transformation. However, as
a largely psychological construct it does not offer an explanation according to
the social processes in which it may be embedded. Before more fully exploring
the interactional dynamics, I will review two other social processes: rational
choice and the negotiated information order.

Rational Choice and Negotiated Information Orders

The NAS committee review of the HIV—blood supply crisis (Leveton, Sox,
and Stoto 1995: 122) adopts a rational-choice approach to the way in which the
January 1983 meeting transpired, arguing that a first-order "absence of consensus [on] matters of epidemiology led to second-order disagreements about the
costs and benefits of alternative actions." The authors continue:

> Indeed, the committee suspects that many of those arguing alternative views
> would have been surprised and uncomfortable if told they were actually engaged
> in a dispute over cost-benefit calculations. However, as they projected the scenar-
> ios about what would happen if they undertook one strategy or another (e.g., the
> implementation of a screening test, the deferral of a high-risk group) and drew
> conclusions about the desirability of those scenarios, they were, in effect, tallying
> advantages and disadvantages of alternative courses of actions and reaching sums
> and totals that diverged from those advocating other approaches.

Disputing such a straightforward analysis, Healy (1999: 540–41) insists that
risk management by organizations and individuals is more complex, that *constituencies, exchange relations, organizational ties,* and structural *interests* of actors
involved in a decision process all need to be taken into account.

Thus, another approach to the denial of a blood supply crisis involves the
concept of a "negotiated information order" (Heimer 1985) and associated
ideas about the management of uncertainty and risk. Particularly important

when organizational actors make risky decisions are the exchange relations between providers and their constituencies. Those who accepted the CDC perspective and took immediate action were as mentioned, mostly representatives of plasma companies, motivated to safeguard the *recipients* of, or customers for their products (Healy 1999). This group was much smaller than the population of suppliers. The companies' interests, in other words, revolved around protecting the market for their product, and this meant that taking steps to remove possible sources of contamination made sense. In contrast, blood banks and the Red Cross, who were in a "gift-giving" relationship with the population of hemophiliac individuals, were more concerned about maintaining a stock of blood products and about their *suppliers*. They had, as Healy suggests, "a hard time finding and keeping donors, but they had plenty of recipients for these gifts at the other end" (541). Different constituencies and organizational ties for the blood banks as compared with the plasma companies, and disparate kinds of exchange (gift-giving as opposed to market-pricing relations), meant specific and distinct interests to protect.

Interactional Dynamics: Breaching the Social World of Hemophilia Treatment

As percipient as rational choice theory and the negotiated information order approaches to risk assessment may be about cognition, they are silent about *how*, in interaction, participants present and receive information that purports crisis and bad news. We need to consider actors' interests, constituencies, exchange relationships, and organizational ties not only as factors that somehow influence abstract thinking, but as courses of action in which decision-makers are solidly and concretely embedded. In this way, interests, constituencies, relationships, and ties may be a feature of interaction that is consequential for the actual sequencing of talk and social interaction, especially when some bad news and proposals for remediation breach the social world formed by participants' ordinary routines. In the blood supply case, information about HIV contamination threatened to create deep fissures in the world of hemophilia treatment, and this affected the actual reception of this information. Although, by one standard or another, actors may have engaged in suboptimal reasoning,[16] their conduct exhibited an *everyday* competence and rationality.

In the early 1980s, CDC officials were up against a world of hemophilia treatment known as the "Golden Age," when freeze-dried pooled plasma concentrates of Factor VIII had fully revolutionized therapy (Resnik 1999). As recently as the 1950s and 1960s, the main way of treating hemophilia was by hospitalizing patients for weeks at a time and giving them whole blood transfusions, a highly inefficient process that only slowly stopped the bleeding, after which painful swelling and debilitation of joints (including arthritis) might linger. Then, in the mid-1960s, researchers discovered cryoprecipitate, the frozen residue of blood plasma that contained high concentrations of Factor VIII. Safer, less expensive, and much more effective than whole blood transfusions, cryoprecipitate was a breakthrough for hemophilia treatment in its own right (ibid., 41). But in the late 1960s and early 1970s, an even more revolutionary development combined cryoprecipitation with procedures known as *fractionation* for concentrating plasma from larger donor pools. Whereas cryoprecipitate needed special refrigeration and was difficult to administer, fractionated Factor VIII concentrate was more stable and potent, easier to inject because it required smaller dosages and less time, thereby facilitating self-administration and home treatment. All in all, it improved patients' lifestyles exponentially and increased the life span dramatically.

Along with the development of fractionation, the 1970s saw an increased organization of the hemophilia community, which helped in obtaining federal legislation in 1975 authorizing grants to local hemophilia treatment centers, and the emergence of a "team" approach to treatment that involved a number of professionals besides physicians. For hemophiliac individuals, all of this promoted a new and wonderful sense of mastery and control over their illness and their lives.[17] In the 1970s, federal officials and directors of treatment centers, and in turn the hemophilia community, were able to be strongly optimistic about prospects for at least the young, mostly male population with the condition:

> These boys, who had access to comprehensive care, including home care education and concentrates, could look forward to a relatively normal childhood and a normal life span. This transformed version of childhood included a relatively pain-free existence, normal school attendance, participation in selected athletic activities, and summer fun and camaraderie at one of the growing number of "hemophilia camps." (90)

Operating from within this Golden Age, blood bank physicians naturally would worry about their gift relationship with hemophiliac patients (Healy 1999). If they were to impose surrogate testing and screening, donor attrition could skyrocket and they would not be able to meet demand for the life-enhancing and life-saving product.[18] The Golden Age also affected even the plasma companies who, although newly willing to screen and test their donors, did not withdraw from the market already-contaminated plasma products, including Factor VIII concentrate, because of its otherwise indisputable benefits.[19]

The Effects: Informing Episodes as Orderly Bad News Productions

However actors arrive at decisions about risk, a question that has mostly gone unasked and unanswered is what the communicative environment surrounding risk assessment comprises. I am suggesting that presenters' information is often purportedly bad news and that recipients may react to it as such. Analysis that grasps communications as involving patterns intrinsic to the delivery and receipt of bad news can make social-organizational sense of facets and details in the environment. For example, participants in a threatened social world, to refuse taking remedial action without being seen as negligent, are initially prone to contest and reject purported bad news. At the 1983 meeting about blood supply contamination in Atlanta, indeed, contention was the order of the day. Even though Evatt "tried to explain that when a disease appears suddenly and spreads rapidly it meant that they were witnessing the birth of an epidemic" (Starr 1998: 273), various parties charged CDC officials with "overstating the facts" and using "very soft" evidence ("only a handful of cases") (Resnik 1999; Shilts 1987: 220). Simply rejecting the CDC's presentation of evidence out of hand, representatives of the blood banks remained dubious about the possibility of blood-transmitted AIDS, and officials from the FDA stated a lack of conviction that AIDS even existed. By this contention, representatives and officials were able utterly to rupture the bad-news remediation pair. Lack of alignment to purported bad news undermines the relevance of corrective actions. The blood banks, following their resistance to the CDC's news, eschewed any changes to how they collected and dispersed Factor VIII.

In such a contentious context, when a messenger says the world has changed, recipients are prone to blame that messenger. In fact, FDA officials made comments "indicating a lack of confidence in the scientific capabilities of some of the CDC personnel" (Leveton, Sox, and Stoto 1995: 125). An official at the American Red Cross, which as late as June 1983 was on record as against donor screening and other measures advocated by the CDC,[20] wrote in a memo after the January meeting:

> CDC is likely to continue to play up AIDS — it has long been noted that CDC increasingly needs a major epidemic to justify its existence. This is especially true in light of the Federal funding cuts and fact that AIDS probably played some positive role in CDC's successful battle with OMB to fund a new $15,000,000 virology lab." (287)

In an interview with Resnik (1999: 121), Evatt of the CDC noted his perception that, in a context where it was known that CDC had to cut its budget by 15 percent, "people thought we were making this disease up just to generate increased funding."

Further connected to the changing of social worlds is the matter of affect. As participants pay heed to the attitude of daily life and its recipes, typifications, and courses of action, it involves a moral commitment and emotional investment. If a participant's world is breached, it can mean anomic experience and unleash displays of affect that are ordinarily held in abeyance. Indeed, as CDC officials attempted to share their projection of an impending HIV outbreak in the blood supply, the emotion of all participants at the 1983 meeting became salient. Representatives of blood banks became angry and engaged in ridicule. CDC officials themselves became affectively unhinged:

> Don Francis pounded the table with his fist. . . . "How many people have to die?" shouted Francis, his fist hitting the table again. "How many deaths do you need? Give us the threshold of death that you need in order to believe that this is happening, and we'll meet at that time and we can start doing something." (Shilts 1987: 220)[21]

It was as if CDC officials, having come to realize that the nation's blood supply was dangerously contaminated, had already entered a new world, and wanted to usher other actors, including the potentially ultimate sufferers — people with hemophilia — into that self-same world, so that preventative measures could be taken. When very few went along with those officials, it roused their indignation as deliverers of the news. Hence, the stability of emotional experience becomes threatened not only for recipients of news as they are potentially extricated from their old world, but also for participants in a new world who, in telling about it, cannot obtain intersubjective accord with their audiences that this new world is the real world.

Everyday Rationality

In some fashion, participants who heard the CDC's case must have weighed the costs and benefits associated with taking preventative actions. If so, literatures on rational choice theory, the heuristics of risk assessment, and negotiated information orders, because they can explain how actors sometimes perform in suboptimal ways, are relevant. Particularly important are the paths by which interests, exchange relations, and organizational ties may affect decisional processes. Mostly, however, because of their emphasis on psychology and cognition, these approaches disregard how decisions, whatever they are and however induced cognitively, are enacted in participants' direct relations and practices with one another. It is not the mere emphasis on cognition that leads away from the actuality of communication, however. When economic rationality and heuristic strategies for risk assessment are used as abstract instruments to measure actors' performances, these performances must often appear deficient or incompetent. Appreciating how decision-making during crises and disasters exhibits an everyday or quotidian rationality, on the other hand, brings the concreteness of talk and social interaction and the *competence* involved in producing local orderliness to the fore. Everyday actors acquire and use information and knowledge together — that is, with one another in the practices by which they present and react to news — according to morally required sense-making recipes and constructions embedded in actual courses of action.

Patterns found in conversational episodes of bad and good news may be generic enough to manifest themselves in the discourse of more public settings.[22] Of course, because the talk is part of "meetings" and "hearings," where officials may make rehearsed presentations and recipients are members of an audience, the discourse will be different from conversation, as the organization of turn-taking and other features of the talk are altered. What may be common, however, are the terms of everyday rationality. At the 1983 CDC meeting, blood bank representatives and other oppositional recipients of the CDC official's message about HIV contamination of the blood supply simply held fast to the perceived normal environment in which they were strongly embedded, and they worked to withstand, as any adherent to the routine order of everyday life would, potential breaches to that environment, even while suffering emotional distress at the prospective breaching. They did this in and through interactions with others at the meeting, exerting discursive efforts to maintain the benign order of everyday life — the golden age of hemophilia — when already a malignant virus was afoot that eventually undermined that order in a devastatingly tragic way, blaming the messengers for wanting to disrupt their benign world.

*

Approaching public crises like the blood supply contamination or the presence of chemical gases in the Gulf with resort to everyday rationality reflects a sociological understanding of these crises based on the organization and integrity of participants' actual orientations, actions, and interactions. The social practices involved are not explained by the calculation of participants and, although they may accommodate to such calculation, the practices independently constrain further endeavors. What other constraints exist as participants work concertedly in situations of change and crisis needs investigation, for the effectiveness of communicating news and of prompting needed correctives derives strongly from the organization of those practices.

We can only speculate as to what other tragedies would benefit from such investigation, and while I have a folder of examples at hand, I will mention just two. A co-pilot from a plane needing to land at Kennedy International Airport in New York in 1990, telling ground control that his plane was "running out of fuel" failed to obtain uptake on how extreme the emergency was. Air traffic controllers did not give the plane priority status for landing, and it crashed while circling, killing 73 people (Johnson 1990).[23] In 1999, during the conflict in the Balkans, a midlevel analyst at the Central Intelligence Agency tried to inform his superiors that the United States had targeted the wrong building for bombing in Belgrade. An American B-2 fighter ended up shelling the Chinese Embassy, creating a terrible diplomatic predicament that undermined U.S.–China relations and resulted in China's suspending negotiations on their entry to the World Trade Organization (Schmitt 1999). Whether this shelling really was an error has been questioned, but in the official report by the U.S. ambassador to China, the CIA analyst's attempt to inform about the wrong target is glossed as "a series of frustrating miscommunications — missed phone calls and lack of follow-up" and is listed as a factor in what the United States regarded as a series of horrible mistakes. In these examples we have two more instances in which recipients fail to register what deliverers mean to construct as bad news and as requests for remedial actions.

In my analysis, 'failures' like these are not due to incompetence or suboptimal reasoning. Rather, they are the outcome of the way participants competently and commonsensically organize their interactions — according to generic practices — when bad and good news are lurking. When outcomes affecting masses of people derive from how participants talk and behave in their close relations, it means that the interaction order is in need of urgent appreciation. Far from an occasionalist illusion, this is a recognition that the actual, local occasion and its produced orderliness may have tentacles that reach far into the outside society. Of course, these examples offer only the grossest indications of what needs extensive probing and analysis; how, in their interactions, deliverers and recipients of bad news do or do not jointly achieve the nature of the news, come to realize a changed social world that the news augers, and, if it is called for, put appropriate correctives in place. When the news is bad, and officials believe that something needs to be done, structures of interaction are particularly important to understand. Although analytical hindsight is one thing, and being there is different, we still can wonder how participants in the blood supply arena might have handled the crisis differently or better had *they* seen their task as one of conveying bad news rather than as simply presenting epidemiological facts and logical solutions fitted to projected objective trends. To an extent, that is, officials at the CDC believed that members of their audience consisted of rational actors in the economic sense who would be satisfied dealing with the abstractions inherent in statistical projections, instead of commonsense participants severely committed to particular courses of action in the everyday and concrete world of hemophilia treatment. As real-worldly commonsense actors, and as competent interactants, they could be expected to handle the CDC's proposed news in patterned ways according to discrete practices of talk and social interaction.

Would an approach appreciating everyday rationality have been more effective and convincing? Can official actors with bad *or* good news, not in a cynical or manipulative manner, and not for their own welfare but for the public welfare, take account of the interactional structures surrounding the conveyance of such news, and be more effective in obtaining needed remedial and other kinds of civic and governmental reactions? Is it possible for news bearers, before reporting their dire statistics and other findings, to configure their disclosures according to how their recipients, embedded in particular social worlds, see things? Is it possible to anticipate disruptions to the bad-news remediation pairing, surmount the pressure toward maintaining a benign social world, avoid tendencies toward crediting or blaming the messenger, and overcome other practices that participants deploy in the disclosure process, all of which may inhibit the appreciation of what deliverers intend to convey?

We can take a lesson from Wittgenstein's proposal (1953: ¶109) for "arranging what we have always known," which I understand to mean that research can give us *discursive* knowledge about our commonsense practices–what we tacitly know how to do but do not necessarily formulate expressively. Surely an understanding of language use in everyday life additionally offers the potential for *rearranging* what we have always known, perhaps substituting one set of practices for another, so that, in particular settings, we do things better than we have. My investigation has observed regularities in how participants, with their emotional involvements, and in talking to one another, can and do journey from one social world to another across the bridge of news delivery and receipt. Analyzing these regularities contributes to the sociology of interaction, and, because the analysis derives from how participants themselves do things, it represents a kind of collective wisdom that can be reflected back to those who are immersed in worlds undergoing more or less radical change and who want or need to grasp and share this fact with one another. Jointly comprehending the full ramifications of bad and good news is beneficial for parties in immediate co-presence. Collectively comprehending such news when it affects large groups is good for public dialogue and the structure of society as a whole.

How to Tell the News

With my research, I have advocated for attending to the details of language use and social interaction. Now, in staking out recommendations for how to deliver news effectively, I will depart from such detail and ascend to a general and abstract level, for the brief list of procedures and the rubric below are meant to be useful to professionals in medicine, law, religion, law enforcement, social welfare, business and other fields.[1] If I abandon detail, nevertheless my overall recommendation is for professionals themselves to pay attention to the particularities of interactions when engaged in delivering news.

Several matters are preliminary to my procedural recommendations. A first one is a reminder about something said in chapter 1: the bearer of news is a messenger *in* the lifeworld and *of* the lifeworld. In the lifeworld, messengers are in a precarious position. They have their own noetic crisis — changed world — to experience almost at the same time as, in sharing the news, they bring such a crisis to their recipients. Recall from chapter 2 how, in calling his wife, Jackie, with the news of Martin Luther King Jr.'s death, Jesse Jackson had to repeat the message to her. In Jackie's view, this was because he had "to make himself understand it." Things may be different in professional settings, where news that is a *crisis* for recipients is *routine* for its deliverers (Hughes 1951: 320), who sometimes have to give certain tidings over and over again. Many times, however, bearers of news have extremes of emotional reaction that run parallel with their recipients. They suffer greatly with bad news, and may even find good news overwhelming. Thus, as it was in Jesse Jackson's experience, the problem of *realization* may be almost as acute for professionals as it is for their recipients.

While this chapter is meant for professionals and others who, by virtue of occupation, may have a surfeit of experiences involving the conveyance of consequential tidings to tell their patients, clients, parishioners, or others, we need to remember a second matter that this book accentuates. The delivery of news is an interactive event, whose outcome reflects many circumstances of social life, including how recipients react to what they hear. Consequently, the communicative effectiveness of bearers, beyond how they present the news in the first place, is contingent on these circumstances and the actions of recipients. There is, in other words, no sure-fire method of delivery for the professional that guarantees "success" (however that might be measured) across the board. Nevertheless, there are procedures that can enhance the probability of success. In medicine, it is well recognized that, as one set of investigators (Chisholm, Pappas, and Sharp 1997) put it, news recipients "are able to respond both to the news itself and to the manner in which it is told."

Investigators, probing *bad* news, have recognized the importance of manner. At the same time, they have almost completely neglected good news. In medicine, for example), at least two problems confound the delivery of good diagnostic news. One is that, for a variety of reasons, what may be good news from a clinical viewpoint is not always so from a patient's perspective (see the coda to chapter 4). Surely, this divergence of perspective inhabits other professional domains as well. The other problem is what we call the "symptom residue" (Maynard and Frankel forthcoming). When some condition is ruled out medically (good news), a patient may still experience symptoms that then go unexplained. Elsewhere, this situation has its analogues whenever official conceptualizations fail to register residual signs of distress (Abbott 1988: 45), which means we need a protocol for professional settings that covers the giving of good *and* bad news, plus other kinds of news as well (uncertain, indeterminate, and so forth).

Then there is the matter of simplicity. While strategies like the procedures listed below can enhance the conveyance of news, it is difficult for professionals to read or remember such a list on every occasion. However, if these procedures are made habitual,[2] then it is possible to remember a simpler rubric for handling the inherent contingencies of particular occasions. After the list of procedures, I will discuss such a rubric, which involves approaching news by asking questions.

A final matter. To each of the procedures listed and to the rubric should be added an "if appropriate" or "if relevant" clause. Neither the rubric nor all procedures are appropriate or relevant for every situation. Remember the epigraph to chapter 2 concerning how one brother told bad tidings to the other. Having learned a device whereby he could have conveyed the death of the cat, he tried to use the device for imparting the news that their mother had died. Skilled and competent use of procedures is not mechanical; it requires exquisite commonsense because no two situations are completely alike.[3]

Procedures for Delivering Bad or Good News

1. *Prepare oneself.* As persons in the world, deliverers may have their own elation (good news) or grieving (bad news) to experience, and it pays to be aware of and deal with these emotions beforehand so as to be sensitive to recipients when actually conveying the news.

• Remember that news, no matter how minor or major the condition or experience it involves, means a changed world for the recipient. It should be delivered *carefully* — that is, in a way that communicates caring for the recipient. It is appropriate to begin an informing interview with questions about how recipients are doing.

• Bearing the news also may be world-changing or otherwise extremely difficult for deliverers. It is important to have the support of trusted colleagues and to be able to call on that support especially if difficulties are anticipated. Talking to a colleague before meeting with recipients can be enormously beneficial.

2. *Prepare the environment adequately.* Whenever possible, deliver news in person, not over the phone or by e-mail. This is especially important with bad news. I have collected many complaints about the impersonality of telephone or electronic mail conveyances of news, but have never seen a complaint about the proximity of face-to-face encounters. Also provide a comfortable and private setting — avoid hallways, corridors, reception areas, and the like. Determine who should be present by querying other staff and/or the primary recipient.

3. *Consider the relationship; prepare the recipient.* The quality of a news presentation is inseparable from the relationship between deliverer and recipient — whether, for example, the recipient is someone well known to the deliverer, or a stranger. No matter how close or distant, the quality of the relation is enacted in and through every initiative of the deliverer. Although deliverers cannot control recipients' responses, they literally can set the tone by how they speak and act (Freese and Maynard 1998). Forecasting the news through demeanor, talk, and gestures provides for mutuality between deliverer and recipient and enhances the likelihood of recipients' comprehending the news. Blunt disclosures (dropping the news on the recipient with no lead-in) and stalling (beating around the bush, giving lengthy accounts of circumstances, giving jargon-filled explanations, etc.) isolate a recipient and are more likely to entail misapprehension.

4. *If possible, elicit the recipient's perspective before delivering the news.* Ask recipients what they think, know, or believe about what is going on. Then, deliver the news forthrightly and by connecting it to what recipients say. This is using what I have called a perspective display series (PDS).[4]

"What do you think is going on?," "What have you learned so far?," and similar questions permit the professional not only to learn what recipients know and believe. Ultimately, such questions allow for producing the deliverer's version of things *in relation* to those beliefs and knowledge. For example, in an interview in the Developmental Disabilities clinic, Dr. Rogers, a pediatrician, asks Mr. and Mrs. Hanson for their views of their son, David: "Have you noticed any improvement since I saw him last, which was over three, four months ago?" The parents, with Mr. Hanson doing most of the talking, reply that David is now more "controlled" and less 'wild." Still, they have complaints. Mrs. Hanson says that "he won't listen," and Mr. Hanson adds, "You really have to yell at him, repeat, repeat, repeat."

> Mr. Hanson: You know I think basically the problem is as I also said to Ellen, that when you reach the age of about four or four and half you more or less stop maturing right there.
> Dr. Rogers: Okay. Well that kind of leads me into what we found. Uh essentially what we have found in David is that at a certain point his development HAS stopped.
> Mr. Hanson: Right.
> Dr. Rogers: And uh, when tested he then tends to look to us like a kid with retarded development.
> Mrs. Hanson: Mm hmm
> Mr. Hanson: Mmm
> Dr. Rogers: This is a kid who's reached a certain point and then he stopped.
> Mr. Hanson: Right.

By acknowledging and virtually repeating what the parents have said about David's maturation having "stopped," Dr. Rogers can move from this point to propose a diagnosis of "retarded development." He thereby works to align the clinical diagnosis with what the parents have said. Of course, while Mr. Hanson agrees with the characterization of "stopped," he and Mrs. Hanson provide only token acknowledgments ("Mm hmm" and "Mmm") to the label of retardation.

Often recipients will display resistance like this. Consequently, use of the PDS does not ensure complete and immediate accord. However, in the case above, the pediatrician learned what the parents thought about their son (that he does have some problems, for instance), which permitted articulating official diagnostic information with their perspective and terminology. He also *confirmed* what they knew and believed. Finally, Dr. Rogers reflected the parents' view of their child using their terminology — *affirming* the clinical version by reference to their perspective — and *co-implicating* their perspective in the diagnostic delivery.

Being blamed as messenger (chapter 7) is always on the horizon for a deliverer of *bad* news, and the PDS can help avoid this. With what may be *good* news from a professional perspective, use of the PDS elicits a sense of whether recipients share the official perspective. Interactional evidence suggests that use of the PDS maximizes the chance that recipients will understand and accept diagnostic or other official news.

  5. *After the news is delivered, stop, allow the recipient time to take it in; show em-*

pathy and concern. If the news is bad, recipients may appear stoic or may "flood out" with tears or other affective responses; if the news is good, recipients may also express their relief or other feelings effusively (chapter 5). In response, deliverers can do these things.

• Stay quiet. Silence on the part of the professional is appropriate particularly with bad news, for it gives recipients time to absorb the news and collect themselves (Frankel 2000), and the deliverer can observe how recipients are responding nonverbally. With good news as well, it may take some time for the recipient to adjust and feel ready to proceed with discussing other matters or with closing the interview.

• Be empathetic, which entails understanding a recipients' feelings and communicating your understanding of them (Suchman et al. 1997):

> "I know this must be very hard."
>
> "I can see that you are feeling very sad, and that is very natural."
>
> "You are right to be happy."
>
> "It's okay to laugh/cry, many people do when they get this kind of news."

Also relevant are empathetic questions (Lo, Quill, and Tulsky 1999):

> "You sound (or appear) distressed. What is the worst part of this news for you?"
>
> "What is concerning you most? What feels the most difficult?"
>
> "As you think about this news (or diagnosis), what do you project? As you think about the future, what is most important to you?"

• Without becoming overly sympathetic, or "underdistanced" in relation to one's own emotions so that they become salient or paramount to the interaction,[5] deliverers can let recipients know that and how they are affected by the news (chapter 5). "I am sad/happy about this news too" may be enough.

6. *Beware of the tendency to shroud bad news and expose good news. Keep things simple, and respond to recipients' cues regarding how and when to proceed.* Often the deliverer's own anxiety is so high in giving news that two things can happen. One is to minimize bad news or otherwise shroud it, and maximize or expose good news in a way that distorts a situation (chapter 6). Another tendency, whether the news is bad or good, is to perform what I call an "information dump"—telling the recipient much more than can be understood or absorbed in the immediate circumstances.

• Never take away hope but always be realistic and truthful. Initially, provide only the essential information, and be clear, forthright, and honest. If the news is bad, be careful not to cover it up quickly or allow recipients to do so by moving to the bright side. When the news is good, messages about caution may be in order.

• Ask whether recipients understand what has been said. In some circumstances, it is possible to ask them to repeat the news.

• Be aware of how inclined recipients are to resume, allowing them to indicate the timing and amount of information that is provided next. Moving ahead should not occur until recipients have understood what has been said so far, and want to continue. Again, deliverers can probe:

> "I have more information to give you about further testing. I can also say what we know about the prevention of/prognosis for this kind of disease/situation. Let me know when you want me to continue and how much you would like to discuss."

• Deliverers can respond to recipients' own difficult questions with further inquiry aimed to discover the basis for the recipients' questions.[6]

7. *Have a follow-up plan.*

• Determine what else recipients may be concerned about in addition to the just-discussed topic.

• If a recipient is alone, be sure that there is an environment of support to turn to, especially if the news is bad. Ask about what recipients will be doing next and with whom they will be sharing the news. Would they like to practice telling the news to others, or have a family meeting to discuss the news?

• Make arrangements to see recipients for further discussions and appropriate counseling. In the near future, be accessible by phone or in other ways to field questions and concerns that arise relatively immediately after the encounter.

A Rubric for Delivering Bad or Good News

It can be cumbersome to remember or consult written procedures every time the professional has news to convey to a patient, a client, or family members. As established ways of thinking and acting during clinical and other occupational encounters — as habit — these procedures do not need conscious reminder or reflection. Assuming good habits, I think that a single conscious rubric can cover many of the procedures and serve as a guide through the interpersonal and social contingencies of an actual delivery of news. Embodied in each of the procedures above, this rubric is: Before proceeding with the news, *ask questions.*

This rubric implies delivering information and news by inquiring rather than telling. Put differently, it is a stepwise way of telling the news that follows recipients' lead, gives them a degree of control, and particularizes the learning process. In delivering news, the method also can discover whether recipients want to have such control.

1. Deliverers begin by asking their recipients whether they would *like* to give input to an informing process or prefer the professional to lay things on the line.[7] If recipients want simply to listen, deliverers can respect that wish by proceeding directly to the news. Still, the deliverer should follow steps 3 and 4 below.

2. If a recipient does like to give as well as receive information, then the next question is a query about the recipient's perspective, to be followed by an aligning, co-implicating style of delivery.

3. Once the news has been delivered, and after a period of waiting, it is time for further, empathetic questions to discern what recipients have understood and when and how they would like to proceed.

4. The informing interview ends with questions about what recipients plan to do next and how deliverers can best follow up.

*

The poet Louise Glueck (quoted in chapter 1) has said, "The world was whole because it shattered." Telling the news may implicate messengers in the shattered social worlds of recipients, but being the messenger also means helping make the world differently whole again, to "know what it was," and now what it is. Beyond having a burden, bearers of news therefore have an *opportunity* to advance their recipients toward realization and all that it entails. Promoting such realization can be, as Buckman (1992) has stated, a two-way rather than unilateral process, one that draws upon and enhances a relationship instead of alienating the participants. Tellers, messengers, deliverers of news, in addition to being forthright and honest, perform best by being responsive to recipients and thereby bearing the news jointly and collaboratively.

Transcribing Conventions

1. Overlapping speech

A: Oh you do? R[eally   ]
B: [Um hmmm]

Left hand brackets mark a point of overlap, while right hand brackets indicate where overlapping talk ends.

2. Silences

A: I'm not use ta that.
(1.4)
B: Yeah me neither.

Numbers in parentheses indicate elapsed time in tenths of seconds.

3. Missing speech

A: Are they?
B: Yes because . . .

Ellipses indicate where part of an utterance is left out of the transcript.

4. Sound stretching

B: I did oka::y.

Colon(s) indicate the prior sound is prolonged. More colons, more stretching.

5. Volume

A: That's where I REALLY want to go.

Capital letters indicate increased volume.

6. Emphasis

A: I do not want it.

Underline indicates increased emphasis.

7. Breathing

A: You didn't have to worry about having the .hh hhh curtains closed.

The "h" indicates audible breathing. The more "h's" the longer the breath. A period placed before it indicates inbreath; no period indicates outbreath.

Adapted from Gail Jefferson, "Error Correction as an Interactional Resource," *Language in Society* 2 (1974): 181–99.

8. Laugh tokens
A: Tha(h)t was really neat.

The "h" within a word or sound indicates explosive aspirations; e.g., laughter, breathlessness, etc.

9. Explanatory material
A: Well ((cough)) I don't know

Materials in double parentheses indicate audible phenomena other than actual verbalization.

10. Candidate hearing
B: (Is that right?) (   )

Materials in single parentheses indicate that transcribers were not sure about spoken words. If no words are in parentheses, the talk was indecipherable.

11. Intonation.
A: It was unbelievable. I ↑had a three point six? I ↓think.
B: You did.

A period indicates fall in tone, a comma indicates continuing intonation, a question mark indicates increased tone. Up arrows (↑) or down arrows (↓) indicate marked rising and falling shifts in intonation immediately prior to the rise or fall.

12. Sound cut off
A: This- this is true

Dashes indicate an abrupt cutoff of sound.

13. Soft volume
A: °Yes.° That's true.

Material between degree signs is spoken more quietly than surrounding talk.

14. Latching
A: I am absolutely sure.=
B: =You are.

Equal signs indicate where there is no gap or interval between adjacent utterances.

A: This is one thing [that I=
B: [Yes?
A: =really want to do

Equal signs also link different parts of a speaker's utterance when that utterance carries over to another transcript line.

15. Speech pacing

A: What is it?

B: >I ain't tellin< you

Part of an utterance delivered at a pace faster than surrounding talk is enclosed between "greater than" and "less than" signs.

Some Conversation Analytic Precepts

Many readers, I presume, are already familiar with conversation analysis as an approach to studying language and social interaction. For those who are not, a number of excellent secondary sources on conversation analysis exist. Following on Heritage's (1984b) chapter 8 overview in *Garfinkel and Ethnomethodology,* other books include those by Duranti (1997: chap. 8), Hutchby and Wooffitt (1998), Levinson (1983), Psathas (1995), Silverman (1998), and ten Have (1999). Harvey Sacks' lectures (Sacks 1992a, b), which plowed and planted the field in which subsequent CA inquiries have blossomed, are the primary and penultimate source, and Schegloff's (1992a, b) introductions to the lectures provide an outstanding account of their intellectual, scientific background and reach. For obtaining a thorough overview of CA, any and all of these will be helpful. Drawing mostly on Zimmerman's (1988) succinct article-length treatment,[1] and as a technical aid for readers who do not have previous familiarity with conversation analysis, I discuss precepts that inform my inquiries. These precepts, used in the analysis of conversational excerpts, are covered thoroughly in the previous books and chapters on CA; I take the liberty of much repetition and therefore of not citing passages in other works that my discussions overlap.

1. *Talk and social interaction as an orderly domain.* Sacks (1984a) set the initial course for the investigation of conversational interaction not out of an interest in language per se, but because it is domain of social action that could be "captured, examined in detail, and be available for repeated inspection" (Zimmerman 1988: 406). Hence, it is possible to describe and analyze the orderly properties of conversational interaction as the achievements of participants, which Zimmerman calls an *organization principle.*

2. *Talk and social interaction as autonomous.* Rather than being a product of exogenous influence, processes of conversational interaction have their own internal constraints (Zimmerman 1988: 408). For instance, in taking turns at talk, Sacks, Schegloff, and Jefferson (1974) find that participants have three ordered options: (1) a current speaker may select the next speaker, (2) a next speaker may self-select, or (3) a current speaker may continue. With this system of turn-taking, participants have an *intrinsic* motivation for listening to one another, independent of other motivations including interest, deference, or politeness. Potential next speakers must listen to a current speaker to find out whether they have been selected to take the next turn, to discover when the current turn ends and it is appropriate to start speaking, and to know what they may be constrained to say next, given what has been said in the turn

of talk underway. This intrinsic motivation for listening, and other mechanisms of interaction including the organization of repair, mean that conversation is to a large extent self-governing with respect to the orderly achievement of mutual understanding. The orderliness of conversational interaction, in other words, is *locally determined*.

3. *The importance of detail*. To investigate the orderly achievement of mutual understanding as fully as possible, and because of the detail-eviscerating characteristic of abstraction, conversation analysts avoid initial considerations of how attributes like race, class, and gender affect conversational interaction (Zimmerman 1988: 408). Sacks turned to conversation and to the preservation of detail within it because of the sense that it was within this detail that social organization and orderliness were to be found. Thus one of Zimmerman's (1988: 415) "working principles" is, "No scale of detail, however fine, is exempt from interactional organization, and hence must be presumed to be orderly." This implies an interest not just in what participants say but also in silences, in overlapping talk, in sound stretches, breathing, and so on. Hence, conversation analysts transcribe tape recordings to show as many of these features as possible.

4. *Utterances as activities*. In one of his early lectures, Sacks proposes that the most banal and familiar conversational utterances are social objects that *do* actions and activities without necessarily formulating them as such. With "This is Mr. Smith," a call recipient can unofficially ask a caller to identify himself and to do so with the same mode of address. With "I was trying you all day and the line was busy for hours," a caller can "fish" for information as to her caller's whereabouts by giving her own version of things, which invites the recipient to tell hers (Pomerantz 1980). Conversation analysis represents the attempt to describe and analyze a host of ordinary activities — describing, criticizing, insulting, complaining, giving advice, describing, requesting, apologizing, joking, greeting, and many more. Of primary concern in this study are such activities as reporting, announcing, and assessing news. Not often is any activity identified by way of some semantic verb form or by the syntactic structure of an utterance; rather, *features of the social context,* most especially an utterance's place in an organized sequence of talk (Heritage 1984b: 245), contribute to its production and understanding as an action.

5. *Sequential organization and a "proof procedure" for analysis*. Accordingly, the fundamental framework for doing analysis of talk and social interaction is sequential organization. Because, as a feature of a turn of talk in conversation, a current speaker is required to display an understanding of the talk in previous turns, speakers can look to the next turn after their own to find an analysis of what they have just said. If the displayed understanding in that next turn does not align with speaker's own, then the *next* turn of speaker can be devoted to correcting the matter. By and large, *repair* of all kinds of conversational trouble exhibits sequentially systematic properties (Schegloff, Jefferson, and Sacks 1977), which means that conversation has inbuilt procedures for its maintenance as a mechanism of social action and interaction. This is *local determination;* as Zimmerman (1988: 423) puts it, "the course of con-

versational interaction is managed on a turn-by-turn or local basis." And because of the requirement that participants display their understanding on this local, turn-by-turn basis, analysts have a "proof criterion" and a "search procedure" for the analysis of any given turn: see how recipients construct their understanding of it. Heritage (1984b: 254) has called this sequence-based accomplishment of understanding an "architecture of intersubjectivity."

6. *Preference structure in conversation.* The concepts of "preference" and "preference structure" in conversation can be misleading if they are taken to suggest something about psychological attitudes or motivations of participants. Instead, in the literature on conversation analysis, when it is asserted that agreement is preferred over disagreement, acceptance is preferred over rejection, and being offered a favor is preferred over asking for it, these assertions relate to the produced orderliness in talk and social interaction. Even when participants may "want" to disagree with someone, or "desire" not to accept an invitation to a party, they often display their disagreements or declinations (respectively) in a *dispreferred* fashion. Thus, the term "preference" refers to structural properties of and systematic practices in conversation. Primary research in Sacks (1987) and Pomerantz (1984a) captures these properties and practices, and secondary discussions (Atkinson and Drew 1979: chap. 2; Duranti 1997; Heritage 1984b: 265–80; Levinson 1983: 332–45; Schegloff 1988) clarify the issues.

Schegloff (1988b) makes a distinction between two types of preference, "structure-based" or sequence-type and "practice based" or response-type. I will refer to these as "first pair-part" and "second-pair part" preferencing, respectively, but otherwise draw on Schegloff's distinctions and the work of Sacks (1987) and Pomerantz (1984a).

With *first pair-part preferencing*, Sacks (1987) observes that some "adjacency pairs" may be started with a turn that is marked to expect a particular type of answer. That is, as Schegloff (1988b) puts it, "some 'first pair part,' such as an invitation, an offer, a request, is said to have or 'project' some type of 'second pair part' as its preferred response, e.g., accept or grant, and others as dispreferred, e.g., decline or deny." For example, a yes-no question such as "You're going, aren't you?" is built to prefer a "yes" answer, while "You're not going, are you?" is built to prefer a "no." That participants orient to this preferencing is seen in how answerers, having heard the way a question is marked, will produce an expected answer, even when the "facts" depart from the answer:

A: That where you live? Florida?
B: That's where I was born. (Sacks 1987)

Questioners, on the other hand, after getting no response to an initial question, will reshape it in a way that elicits agreement:

A: They have a good cook there?
    ((pause))
A: Nothing special?
B: No everybody takes their turns. (Sacks 1987)

If questioners were only concerned with the "correctness" of an answer, Sacks points out, it would not be necessary for them to reshape the question in this fashion. In their design of questions as first-pair parts in two part sequences, then, interactants often engage in work whereby they can obtain agreement rather than disagreement with what the question proposes. The orientation by both speakers and recipients to obtaining agreement with adjacency pair first parts leads Schegloff (1988: 454) to characterize preference structure as inhering in particular *sequence types*.

With *second pair-part preferencing,* preference structure refers to how participants do or enact a responsive activity (see table A.2.1). A participant "is said to do some type of response, such as an acceptance or grant, *"as a* preferred," or some other response, such as a decline or a denial, *"as a* dispreferred" (Schegloff 1988: 453). Pomerantz (1984a), in an extensive study, observes that when one party proffers an initial assessment, agreement or disagreement is relevant in the next turn. *Agreement* turns regularly maximize the visibility of the agreeing components they embody, while *disagreement* turns minimize the visibility of disagreement.[2] When agreement is preferred, the agreeing components often occupy the entire next turn to an initial assessment, whereas speakers regularly preface disagreement with other components, including agreeing ones. Further, although they minimize between-turn gap when agreeing and package their agreement utterances in a single turn of talk, speakers regularly delay disagreement by pausing and/or producing the disagreement over a series of turns (Pomerantz 1984a: 65). Also very often, disagreements and other kinds of dispreferred responses are accompanied by accounts or explanations for them, whereas preferred responses such as agreements are stated baldly, with no explanation (see table A.2.1 for examples).

Table A.2.1 Examples of Agreement and Disagreement Showing Second-Pair Part or Practice-Based Preferencing

---

Agreements

(a) Pomerantz (1984: 59, extract 9)

A: Adeline's such a swell [gal

B: [Oh God, whada gal. You know it!

(b) Pomerantz (1984: 59, extract 10)

J: T's tsuh beautif day out isn't it?

L: Yeh it's jus' gorgeous

(c) Pomerantz (1984: 65, extract 18)

A: Isn't he cute

B: O::h he::s a::DORable

Disagreements

(a) Pomerantz (1984: 70, extract 22) [silence]

A: God izn it dreary.

   (0.6)

A: [Y'know I don't think-

B: [.hh It's warm though.

(b) Pomerantz (1984: 71, extract 37) [silence plus confirmation request]

A: . . . You sound very far away.

   (0.7)

B: I do?

A: Ymeahm.

B: mNo I'm no:t.

(c) Pomerantz (1984: 72, extract 40) [agreement prefaced disagreement]

C: . . . you've really both basically honestly gone your own ways.

D: Essentially, except we've hadd goed relationship et home.

C: .hhhh Ye:s, but I mean it's a relationship where

N O T E S

Chapter One

1. From Louise Glueck, "Formaggio," *Vita Nova,* 13 (Hopewell, NJ: Ecco Press), 1999.

2. A week after the World Trade Center attacks, William Hirst, a psychologist, was at work with research assistants surveying New York passersby on the street about where, when, and what they remember about the attacks, in order to investigate their flashbulb memories of the event and news about it (Parker 2001). A follow-up survey was planned for a year later in order to test the accuracy of the memories over time.

3. Regarding the neurology of the flashbulb memory (Livingston 1967), there is evidence that the experience of an emotionally arousing story activates β-adrenergic stress hormone systems in humans and enhances long-term memory for such an experience (Cahill et al. 1994). Nevertheless, definitional, conceptual, and methodological questions abound in regard to flashbulb memories, including whether they differ significantly from ordinary memory and how accurate they are. I make no claims as to the accuracy of flashbulb memories or the nature of neural structures that are said to provide for them, and am only interested in the flashbulb memory *account* (Wright and Gaskell 1995: 70–71) as narrative and as a conversational announcement.

4. Wright and Gaskell (1993: 136) argue that a "reconstructionist" explanation of flashbulb memory is better than a biological or other "special mechanism" hypothesis. That is, over time, people organize and reorganize the features of their memory. See especially Wooffitt's (1992: chap. 6) analysis of accounts of paranormal experiences, and the "I was just doing X, . . . when Y" format and related devices by which participants report such experiences. As Wooffitt (153) argues, telling tales of extraordinary experiences is sensitive to a variety of interactional features of the telling. Consequently, the organization of talk by which memory is rendered may structure the psychology of the memory. For a related discussion of how interactional concerns feature in the reporting of memory about discovering one's own possible illness see Halkowski (forthcoming).

5. Shibutani (1961: 130) defines social worlds as "culture areas" whose limits are set by "effective communication," and he includes *subcommunities, voluntary associations,* and *universes of special interest* as kinds of social worlds. This definition has been operative in the symbolic interactionist tradition and its concern with various segments of contemporary society, from little league baseball (Fine 1987) to courtrooms (Ulmer 1997), art (Becker 1982), and science (Fujimura 1996), to name just a few exemplary studies. By "social worlds," I mean something different and general, something more Schutzean (as I discuss below) in that social worlds can refer to members' situated sense of the taken-for-granted and known-in-common as achieved in any collective sphere of activity (Zimmerman and Pollner 1970). The Glaser and Strauss (1964) concept of "awareness contexts" approaches what I mean by social world, but their call for typologies of these contexts ("open," "closed," etc.) moves away from the concern, as I will describe it, with the concreteness and particularity of behavior.

6. In sociology, there are two major and venerable traditions that follow the "social construction of reality," each of which has made long-accepted contributions to social science. One tradition, with Spector and Kitsuse (1977) presenting an original statement, is in the social construction of social problems. More recent arguments are found in Holstein and Miller (1993) and Best (1995). The other tradition is in the sociology of scientific knowledge, and is known as "constructivism." For statements, see Latour and Woolgar (1979), Gieryn (1983, 1998), Knorr-Cetina and Mulkay (1983), and Woolgar (1988). For sociological criticisms of constructivism see Button and Sharrock (1993) and Lynch (1993: 90–107). My study differs from social-constructionist approaches, which tend to abstract from the detail of actual behavioral displays in the pursuit of historical processes, political actions, and other activities that transcend particular situations. While also concerned with the generic properties of human conduct, I believe such properties can be derived from and linked to real-time, in situ practices of embodied talk and social interaction.

7. A difference between specialists and the everyday participant, however, is that the philosopher (for example) is a "disinterested onlooker" (Husserl 1970b: 35), while the participant is a fully engaged actor who may range between despair and hope in anticipation of exiting the *epoche*. See, for example, McIntosh (1977: 302).

8. For discussion see Maynard and Clayman (1991: 390). Also see Anderson, Hughes, and Sharrock's (1985) explication of Garfinkel's methodological and heuristic regard for phenomenology.

9. The source of each narrative or transcript is denoted as follows. If the narrative is from a publication, a citation is provided. If it is from my own collection, a narrative number is given. If a transcript is displayed, the original publication source and/or conversational collection from which the transcript derives is included in the heading, along with page numbers or line numbers.

10. Eventually, Ms. Macrae's doctor tells her that cancer has metastasized to her lungs and neck. This bad news together with its prefiguring in what she overheard capture a dimension of the taken-for-granted world—our bodily engagement in it—that Merleau-Ponty (1962: 101) calls the "third term" in the figure-ground relation. That is, objects in the world stand out against a "double horizon" comprising both a backgrounded space—the figure-ground relation—*and* bodily space as a "matrix" of habitual ordinary action. Without apparent illness, our body is mostly out of awareness when we are engaged in worldly projects, such as opening a door, walking down a hall, driving an automobile, working at a computer, waiting in line, and so on. With potential or diagnosed illness, our body assumes a different value as we engage in everyday actions. The person's world is one in which the third term, the body, emerges at the forefront of awareness in ways that it does not ordinarily do. Whereas before diagnosis individuals may have ignored small pains, itches, twinges, spasms, and the like, they may now routinely and vigilantly attend to these minutiae (Kleinman 1988: 47, 58). See also Flaherty (1999: 94–95) on occasions for "stimulus complexity" and "density of experience" and their relation to the experience of time.

11. More than 30 years ago, Garfinkel (1967: 49) observed that the attitude of daily life played a large role in the "production, control, and recognition" of social affects, but that this area of emotions and perceived normality was "terra incognita" in the social sciences. Since then sociology, at least, has developed a large literature on emotions and formed a Sociology of Emotions section in the American Sociological Association. Over the years scholars have investigated "feeling rules" (Hochschild 1979) for the expression of emotion in social situations; "affect control," or the ways in which actors develop sentiments according to their definition

of the situation and construct events to confirm fundamental sentiments (Heise 1979); the relation between power and emotional states (Kemper 1981); the ritual or dramatic enactment that will allow for the safe and appropriate discharge of the emotions in social settings (Scheff 1979), and the social construction of emotions (Harre 1986). Despite these successful efforts to understand the social structuring of emotions, Garfinkel's observation about the relation between affects and the attitude of daily life still holds. We have not paid much attention to this particular relation.

12. As Garfinkel (1967: 182) puts it, "the society hides from its members its activities of organization and thus leads them to see its features as determinate and independent objects."

13. In her study of coroner's deputies strategies for announcing an individual's death to family members, Charmaz (1975: 303) writes, "Although deputies are more directly confronted with issues concerning death than most persons in everyday worlds, they disavow holding any unusual views or beliefs about the topic. Indeed, what is striking is the degree to which their views reflect typical cultural taboos. For the most part, deputies show an avoidance of death, discomfiture over the expression of grief by survivors, and an absence of personal philosophy about death in general or subjective views regarding their own deaths in particular."

14. See appendix 1 for transcribing conventions and discussion of transcription.

15. For example, Girgis and Sanson-Fisher (1995) searched the MEDLINE data base for the years 1973 to 1993 on the topic of bad news and culled over 300 citations. Using abstracts, they classified the reports and found that nearly two-thirds were letters, opinions, reviews, case reports, and "descriptive" papers. Some papers use surveys to assess the preferences of patients and providers for, respectively, receiving and telling bad news. Only four papers involve randomized control trials to test the effectiveness of various approaches to delivering bad news. Despite the lack of much firm outcome-based evidence about the informing process, these articles do not hesitate to make recommendations about how to break the bad news.

16. In so doing, newly diagnosed ill individuals engage a variety of risks, such as the possibility of being stigmatized, losing their autonomy, and having to deal with others' feelings (Charmaz 1991). Parents who learn of the developmental disability of a child, according to Darling (1983: 128), may postpone telling others, with the consequence of feeling increasingly isolated.

17. See discussions of this point in Heritage (1984b: 239–40) and Zimmerman and Boden (1991), who articulate positions with which I continue to align (e.g., Maynard (1984, 1991c). For critiques of these positions, see Hester and Francis (2000) and Watson (2000). This is not the place for a response to these critiques except to say that a central issue is whether there is a generic quality to conversational practices such that they can be deployed across casual conversation and in institutional or organizational settings. In my view, there is evidence for this generic quality; appreciating and analyzing practices of talk in institutions can incorporate the quiddity or "just-thisness" of such settings as well.

18. As Lind et al. (1989: 583) put it, "Physicians must depend primarily on personal experience and judgment, perhaps tempered by chance comments of colleagues or teachers in deciding how to approach an individual patient."

19. By highlighting lived experience, my research also excludes electronic conveyances of bad and good news. For informative statements and research comparing computer-mediated with telephonic and face-to-face communication of news see, for example, Sproull and Kiesler (1986) and Sussman and Sproull (1999).

20. For an extensive consideration of how the diagnoses of HIV and AIDS can affect the

construction of self see Rinken (1997), who suggests that there are two major modalities. In one, the person experiences transformation, a "new" self that is discontinuous with the "old." In the other, the person discovers aspects of the self not previously available to awareness, a "transformed" self that is otherwise continuous with the old. See also Davies's (1997) investigation of how an HIV diagnosis alters mundane assumptions about time; one adaptation toward "losing a future" is an expanded appreciation of the present.

21. For an analysis of the commonsense reasoning that connects one's sexual orientation to the conclusion, "I have no one to turn to," and possibly then to suicidal behavior, see the classic article by Sacks (1972).

22. There was a similar brouhaha in 1997 when John Robinson, the football coach at the University of Southern California, heard about his firing from the media rather than from either the athletic director or the USC president. Both the athletic director and the president came under criticism; the handling of the dismissal began to occupy the news as much as the dismissal itself. One sportswriter offered this opinion: "Garrett handled this about as poorly as humanly possible. It is difficult to fathom how Steven Sample, USC president, could call Robinson 'a great coach' and a 'personal friend' and yet not even speak to him when firing him" (Plashke 1997).

Chapter Two

1. Since good news may be forecasted as well, but differently from bad news, I postpone discussion of this topic until chapter 6 on the asymmetries between bad and good news.

2. The ethnographic literature on bad news has addressed what I call "forecasting" under a variety of other rubrics but has not fully explicated the phenomenon in a comparative way for its effects on recipients. For instance, Glaser and Strauss (1965: 147–48) examine "gradual" or "gentle" disclosure to families of dying patients, Clark and LaBeff (1982: 372–73) analyze the "oblique" delivery of death announcements, through which the deliverer aims to prepare the recipient with some kind of "lead in" or "gradual unfolding of the facts," McClenahen and Lofland (1976: 257) argue that disclosure's first stage is a "preparatory" one in which bearers "presage" their bad news, and Taylor (1988: 115–16) refers to a "preamble" with which surgeons gradually introduce terms such as "serious illness" before informing about breast cancer.

3. The compulsion of proximity derives from the "thickness" of information, including its flexibility and multidirectionality, that is available in co-presence (Boden and Molotch 1994). Hence, face-to-face contact is better than telephone contact, and telephone contact is better than letter-writing or e-mail. See also Heath's (1983: 212–13) discussion of how the working-class residents of Roadville, a textile-producing community in the southeastern United States, would never convey news to distant relatives of a family member's serious illness by letter; this would require telephone contact.

4. Often, a deliverer of bad news can manipulate the setting only in the grossest sense. Coroners' deputies, for instance, may have to tell family members of a death over the telephone or at home but cannot further manipulate the physical environment of the informing (Charmaz 1975). See also Clark and LaBeff (1982: 370).

5. On the avoidance tactics that nurses-in-the-know employ with cancer patients, see Quint (1965: 123). Physicians also use such tactics (Quint 1965: 129; Glaser and Strauss 1965: 142).

6. For an extended treatment of request refusals as a form of bad news see Izraeli and Jick (1986).

7. On the kinds of "jobs" that people can do within "utterance time," and the speed with which they can do them, see Sacks (1992a: 11, 1992b: 168).

8. See chap. 1, excerpt (3).

9. By "official" delivery, I refer to the point at which the deliverer either states the news or confirms the recipient's own statement.

10. More accurately, the doctor's tactic here seems to forecast the news for the wife, even though it is more of a misleading stall to the narrator. That a single tactic can operate variously depending on circumstances of and parties to an informing is considered below.

11. While catastrophic events may be their own blunt announcement, it can be noted that the narrators who experienced these events, by casting their stories in the "At first I thought it was X, then I realized it was Y" mode, engage in a type of forecasting to convey to others what happened. To the recipient of a such a story, that is, "At first I thought" may forecast the dire situation that is next to be depicted in the story with "then I realized. . . ."

12. As Good et al. (1990: 75) put it, "it seems likely that a cultural norm of avoiding disclosure is not based in a subversion of 'truth telling' but in different understandings of the nature of communications, as primarily relational rather than information conveying . . . and divergent cultural conceptualizations of the doctor–patient relationship." See, in particular, Surbone's (1997) discussion of the doctor–patient relationship in Italy.

13. Goffman (1974: 101) aptly terms the withholding of bad news from patients as a "paternal construction."

14. A bearer of bad news may stall the delivery of it for many reasons, either intentionally or unintentionally. In example (35), stalling may have been related to cultural values about how doctors should inform cancer patients. In some cultures, as we have seen, the tactic is thought to foster hope. Furthermore, among the chronically ill, Charmaz (1991: 110–19) found that avoiding disclosure can prevent undue (and sometimes stigmatizing) attention to the sufferer's health. Another reason for stalling, at least among physicians, is the lack of training in regard to the "how's" of presenting bad news (Maguire, Fairbaim, and Fletcher, 1986). Other professionals, such as nurses, are prohibited by formal and informal rules from being able to give bad news because it is their superiors' job (McIntosh 1977: 75; Quint 1965). Additionally, professionals may regard breaking bad news as the "dirty work" of their occupation and therefore entirely devalue the task (Davis 1963: 30). Then, although Davis observes that even when physicians gain sure knowledge of a disease like polio, they may *feign* uncertainty as a way of stalling (67), real uncertainly also does contribute to delays in delivery, particularly in cancer cases (McIntosh 1977: 45).

15. As Charmaz (1991: 30–31) has shown, *waiting* is often a component of seeking a medical opinion, and during this period, a person may *expect* good news, may *believe* that reassurance will be forthcoming that the "symptoms or earlier tests mean nothing":

> Joanne Dhakzak recalled being diagnosed with Hodgkin's disease: "I was in such a daze. I didn't believe that it was happening to me — because when I went to the doctor, I said, 'I don't know why I'm here. There's nothing wrong with me.' Maybe that's why it came as such a shock when the doctor said I had Hodgkin's."

Similarly, Fallowfield (1991: 40) found that women who experience an "extreme sense of shock when they hear the diagnosis" of cancer are those who were either unaware of the seriousness of their symptoms or denied their import. In these ways, she suggests, the women were "unprepared for the bad news."

16. In line with Mead (1934), Volosinov (1973), Vygotsky (1986), and others, the point is that social practices and interactional organization are implicated in individual cognition. Or, in Joas's (1985) terms, *practical intersubjectivity* provides for the individual actor's own perceptual formations.

17. This is a classic case of "asymmetry in dialogue." For a helpful discussion of the generic complexities here see Linell and Luckmann (1991); for a variety of empirical investigations see Marková and Foppa (1991).

18. Morality and its relation to ethnomethodology and conversation analysis is usefully explored in a variety of sources, on which I draw for this discussion. See especially Bergmann (1998), Garfinkel (1963), Heritage (1984: chap. 4), Hilbert (1992: chap. 3), and Linell and Rommetveit (1998).

Chapter Three

1. Sacks (1992: 469).

2. By the produced orderliness of everyday life, I mean that, to be intelligible to one another, participants in talk and social interaction collaboratively design utterances, silences, gestures, body movements, and other social mechanisms for direct action and communication. They do this in practical ways such that their interaction exhibits pattern and organization in the particularities of their interactive work. As Zimmerman (1988: 415) has put it, "No scale of detail, however fine, is exempt from interactional organization, and hence must be presumed to be orderly." On this point, and on the relation of transcription to ethnography, see West (1996).

3. The colleague is Bonnie Svarstad at the University of Wisconsin School of Pharmacy. With co-author Helene L. Lipton, she has published two excellent coding studies (Lipton and Svarstad 1977; Svarstad and Lipton 1977) about the effectiveness of diagnostic communication in this clinic.

4. My lack of familiarity with developmental disabilities facilitated this approach, which has parallels with the ethnographic strategy of "hanging out" (Dingwall 1997: 53) in a setting to experience the people and the social situation, avoiding prior questions and letting the situation pose its own questions. Although I was far from being physically in the setting, and could not attain the kind of "immersion" that ethnographers seek (Emerson, Fretz, and Shaw 1995: 22), I was present indirectly by way of what I could hear and read as real-time conversations on the tapes and transcripts.

5. In these tasks, I was ably and extensively assisted by Courtney Marlaire.

6. Much of this data was made available from collections of recorded telephone calls transcribed by Gail Jefferson and used by other conversation analysts. Additionally, students, friends, and colleagues recorded their home telephone encounters, which my research assistants and I transcribed.

7. My strategy for collecting data has parallels with what Glaser and Strauss (1967: chap. 5) call the "constant comparative method," which enables obtaining diverse instances of a phenomenon in order to develop an analysis that confronts the full complexity of that phenomenon.

8. As Pollner and Emerson (1999) point out, there is a tradition in ethnography of becoming a "practicing, competent member" in the research settings one studies. In ethnomethodology, this strategy has been articulated as the "unique adequacy requirement" (Gar-

finkel and Wieder 1992) and specifies that investigators become "vulgarly competent" in the professional or other orders of work in a particular setting.

9. Some ethnographers (Atkinson 1990; Clough 1992; Denzin 1991; Richardson 1991; van Maanen 1995) have supplemented traditional field methods with postmodern forms of inquiry, including various kinds and combinations of rhetorical, textual, discourse, and cinematic analyses.

10. Recordings and transcripts, although they are never an entirely complete rendering of any social scene (Grimshaw 1982), provide access to infinitesimally more particularities and minutia of conduct than ethnographic note-taking and interview data, which present stronger challenges for reconstruction and recall. Mechanical recordings, in other words, provide both "permanence" and "density" (Grimshaw 1989: 58–64) to interactional data and permit repeated inspection of those interactive bits that the recorder can capture (Sacks 1984a).

11. Sequential analysis involves dealing with utterances in relation to immediately preceding or succeeding turns of talk. "Adjacency pairs," such as greeting–greeting, question–answer, invitation–reply, and other two-turn couplets, are examples of tightly organized sequences. For detailed description of adjacency pairs see Schegloff and Sacks (1973: 295–96); for more general discussion of sequential analysis see Heritage (1984b: 245–46).

12. On the autonomous nature of conversation analytic inquiry see also Duranti (1988) and Zimmerman (1988).

13. As Pomerantz (1990/1991) observes, Moerman (1988) invokes notions of members' "orientations" and "concerns" and implies that ethnographers have privileged access to these features of conduct. Pomerantz suggests approaching these "mental" concepts as social and occasioned rather than as static backdrops to behavior. For a similar critique see Potter (1998).

14. See also the discussion of definitions of context by Tracy (1998) in her introduction to "Analyzing Context," a special issue of *Research on Language and Social Interaction*. This special issue arose from an all-day symposium at the Sixth International Conference on Language and Social Psychology in 1997 in Ottawa, part of which was devoted to questions of how "context" is used in discourse analysis.

15. Of these, participation frameworks, or ways in which speakers and recipients adopt different "footings" or stances in relation to utterances, have been most closely integrated with conversation analytic studies. See, for example, Clayman (1988), C. Goodwin (1986a), M. H. Goodwin (1990), Houtkoop-Steenstra (2000), and Maynard (1984, 1989).

16. For more thorough discussion of Goffman's frame analysis and Gumperz's contextualization cues see Corsaro (1981) and Maynard and Whalen (1995). Cicourel (1974) and Corsaro (1982) advocate the strategy of *triangulation* in which research subjects are asked to view videotapes of their own or others' interactions and to offer interpretations. This strategy adds to a project's interpretive base and helps to disambiguate obscure terms or phrases, but does not provide criteria for determining how social structure or other facets of context affect the course of interaction. For a wide-ranging discussion of the issues involved in social structure and interaction see Wilson (1991).

17. See Heritage and Greatbatch's (1991) general discussion of how turn-taking characteristics constitute talk as an institutional form of interaction. Their specific focus is the news interview; also see Atkinson and Drew (1979) for a treatment of courtroom turn-taking, Boden (1994) on turn-taking in business meetings, and Manzo (1996) on turn-taking in jury deliberations. Drew and Heritage (1992) have systematized Schegloff's (1987a) recommenda-

tions regarding procedural consequentiality to include, as sites of talk-in-interaction where this consequentiality may be expressed, lexical choice, turn design, sequence organization, overall structural organization, and "social epistemology" and "relations" (professional cautiousness, asymmetries in talk, and other matters).

18. In our study of repair sequences in the survey interview (Moore and Maynard 2002), we have shown that interviewers' strictures to ask questions in a standardized way results in systematic alteration of conversational mechanisms for the clarification of previous utterances. Interviewers regularly handle respondents' requests for clarification of a problematic question, not by rewording (as happens in response to conversational requests), but by repeating the question verbatim. Or, also in order to avoid rewording, they may tell the respondent who asks for interpretation of a question that it is "whatever it means to you." The effort on behalf of standardization, which follows the norms of a center and the survey research profession, may admirably screen such unmeasured influences as arbitrary alterations of stimulus questions from the conduct of the interview, but has procedural consequences in the talk for the usually simple or routine act of achieving mutual understanding.

19. While criticizing the field of linguistics for ignoring how speech is situated in society, Bourdieu himself neglects the study of practices as concrete productions in the here and now of actual talk and concerted activity. That is, Bourdieu (1991: 54–65) connects speech practices or "linguistic differences," introduced in his theorizing in an ad hoc manner, to systematic "social differences," and does not study interaction per se. The speech practices he identifies, meant to capture the subjective, embodied, and temporally contingent dimension to discourse, ultimately are generated and organized in accordance with external historical and social structural arrangements (Bourdieu, 1990). Similarly, when entering the realm of aesthetics (rather than language), Bourdieu (1984: 467–68) discusses "taste" as a system of classifications. Actors apprehend an everyday commonsense world of artistic appreciation from "internalized embodied schemes" or "cognitive structures" that are "constituted in the course of collective history." In short, needing investigation from the perspective of Bourdieu is the dynamic quality of classifying and other practices as they are lived interactively.

20. Different cultures, chapter 2 showed, may dictate whether, to whom, and how bad news should be presented. Studies in medical settings document how physicians, as high status professionals, may be accorded the exclusive task and obligation of disclosing bad diagnostic news, even when other personnel, such as nurses, are as fully in the know as the physicians (McIntosh 1977: 75). On a different note, according to anecdotal evidence, gender may be an element of social structure related to the giving and receiving of bad news. The humorist, Art Buchwald (1992), in a relatively serious moment, reports talking to a corporate headhunter who told him that when companies have bad news to deliver, male managers like to delegate the task to female spokespersons, because (according to the headhunter) "news delivered by female employees of a company sounds less ominous." A quick scan of my data from a developmental disabilities clinic shows that mothers are much more likely to be the recipients of the initial bad diagnostic news concerning children than are fathers. This implies that mothers may have the further burden of conveying the news to other family members. However much these distributional patterns may say about the organization of society in gross cultural, professional, gender, and other terms, my point is that they do not identify the *practices* by which deliverer and recipient, whoever they are, conduct their communications around bad and good news. If we come to know these practices, as embodied in the details of actual conduct, then it may be possible to say not only who takes or acquires responsibility for bearing news. It may open the

possibility for more rigorous comparisons of how (for example) professionals deal concretely with members of different cultures or, within a given culture, those who represent varied social categories such as gender, class, ethnicity, and the like.

21. A special speech-exchange system exists for trial-based discourse, and this system — in which questioning turns are preallocated to attorneys, and answering turns are preallocated to witnesses — provides a "structural position and resource" by which both attorneys and witnesses produce their talk and their competing versions of events (Drew 1992: 517).

22. In their critiquing CA studies of "institutional talk," Hester and Francis (2000), like Watson (1997), argue for a need to incorporate membership categorization analysis along with sequential analysis, a strategy that runs into this problem of regress and contradiction because there are no criteria for which "doings" or features of a setting should be put in the foreground for analysis. It can be argued that, when an analyst places some practices in the background and ethnographically presumes the relevance of particular identities, this is a kind of "privileged exemption" (Pollner 1987: 117–18) that follows what the participants themselves do when orienting to concrete activities underway.

23. See Meehan (1981) for a study of how doctors and patients, through their repair practices, display certain technical terms as "jargon."

24. See also the research of Heritage and Sefi (1992). They identify a "dilemma" that faces home health visitors in Britain, who are purveyors of advice that is frequently not well received by first-time mothers. The dilemma involves a "ticket of entry" problem, or how to justify their visits to homes. Heritage and Sefi describe this dilemma through ethnographic characterizations of the health visitor role and mothers' perceptions of it. The dilemma involves health visitors' need to make themselves useful in a situation where what they have to offer may not be needed or wanted.

25. Also see Gubrium's (1975) study of a nursing home and how the news of a death is disseminated (despite efforts of staff to contain it) from the dead person's room to staff, to other residents on the floor and, finally, throughout the entire home. On a different tack (a study in a work setting), but still relatively longitudinal, M. H. Goodwin (1996b) examines how personnel transmit the news of a landed plane to different divisions and areas of an airport (and the prosodic manipulations necessary to convey messages in a multifocused setting).

26. For general discussion see Silverman (1993: chap. 3). For recent empirical work see Lavin (2002) on parole hearings and Lutfey (2000) on compliance with medical regimens for diabetes. Particularly important for developing the CA-ethnography relation, per the discussion in Ten Have (1999: 57–60, 194–95) are studies of work settings (Heath and Luff 2000; Luff, Hindmarsh, and Heath 2000). And see Peräkylä's (1997: 203–5) proposals about how CA, in researching institutional settings, can incorporate the analysis of different "layers of the organization of interaction."

27. In the classification system for mental retardation, "mild" covers those with I.Q.'s of 50–70; Donald was tested at 54. "Moderate" retardation covers the 35–49 I.Q. range, "severe" refers to those in the 20–34 span, and "profound" is used for individuals with I.Q. scores below 20.

28. Clark and LaBeff (1982) compare the direct delivery of diagnosis to "oblique," "elaborate," "nonverbal," and "conditional" modes. Compare excerpt (1) to chap. 2, excerpt (36) from Darling's (1979) interview study of familial reactions to the birth of disabled children. In that excerpt, a mother recalls how her pediatrician "suggested" that her that her six-month-old daughter had cerebral palsy, whereupon she "just broke down completely in his office."

29. Van Dijk's remarks are part of an editorial lead-in to an exchange published in *Text* between Billig (1999) and Schegloff (1999) regarding CDA and CA. For additional discussion of CDA and CA see Wetherell (1998) and Schegloff (1998). For a broader statement regarding CDA see Fairclough and Wodak (1997). And for an effort to integrate a critical, Foucaudian discourse analysis with a conversation-analytic understanding of the organization of "troubles talk" (Jefferson 1988), see Miller and Silverman (1995).

30. This procedure—examining how participants themselves use categories and types—is parallel to what Emerson, Fretz, and Shaw (1995: 12–16) and other ethnographers advocate in regard to field research. Consequently, many ethnographers are in accord with conversation analysts, putting social structural matters in *brackets,* to use the phenomenological term, or out of play until participants themselves, *in the course of interaction,* bring these matters to bear on what they are doing. The impetus that ethnography shares with conversation analysis, in other words, is toward "thick description" (Geertz 1973). It is when ethnography or discourse analysis relies on prior categorizations, on narrative data, or other reconstructions, that social-structural matters may come to the fore and possibly distort what participants do in their practices. Interviews, for example, may characterize interactions in ways different from actual, detailed process (Emerson, Fretz, and Shaw 1995: 12–16).

31. An example of a prospective indexical is the term "problem," in the sentence "We definitely have a problem here on this jet bridge," said by a grounds crewman to an occupant of an airline's Operations Room at a large airport: "The sense of what constitutes the 'problem' is not yet available to recipients but is instead something that has to be discovered subsequently as the interaction proceeds" (Goodwin 1996). Similarly, the term "something" in the pediatrician's saying, "something that's very hard . . ." can be pointing toward what will define the "something." Unlike the example Goodwin shows, where the recipient of the utterance asks what the "problem" is, the recipients here are assembled in the first place (the event being called an "informing interview") to hear what the "something" is, and display their "recipiency" (Heath 1984) as the pediatrician continues on a hearable trajectory toward revealing the clinic's diagnosis.

32. Because this utterance (lines 9–10) is addressed to "Mrs. Riccio," Dr. Davidson may be suggesting the relevance of their identities as "mothers" and not just as "parents."

Chapter Four

1. Bor et al. (1993: 70) write, "News, of whatever kind, is information, whereas the idea that it is either *good* or *bad* is a belief, value-judgement or affective response from either the provider or the receiver of the information in a given context." This is as fine a definition of bad and good news as exists in the literature, and my purpose is to show how participants establish information-as-news and display an evaluation of it according to their own actions and responses during the course of delivery and receipt.

2. This should not imply that good and bad news deliveries are conversational equivalences. Chapter 6, I have noted, explores ways in which good news is privileged over bad news in conversational interaction.

3. When Emma later tells another person, Nancy, about these same matters, she starts with the news that Dan has "left to play golf," and follows this with the explanation:

NBII.2.R:page 2
```
1   Emma:   .hhh Yeah they: theh gun'tee off et twelve it's a comp'ny
2           dea:l so (.) th'couple wz spozetih come do:wn tuh (.) la:s'
```

```
 3              ni:ght'n yuhknow k-Harry en Kath'rn ther uh keh cz Harry wz
 4              gunnuh play k-
 5    Nancy:    Oh[:.
 6    Emma:        ['n comp'ny en then .hhh there wz a death in their fa:m'ly
 7              so: (.) [.hhh
 8    Nancy:              [Aww:::.
 9              (.)
10    Emma:     ↑THE:Y gosh uh this is really been a wee:k'ha:sn'it?=
11    Nancy:    =Oh:: it rilly ha:s.
```

Here, Nancy's "Aww:::.", with downward intonation, receives and assesses (Goodwin 1986b: 214) the information as bad news.

4. Since Leslie may already know about Geoff Haldan's gout, this may be marking as news not the existence of the condition per se but that his "sickness" (line 5) is the gout.

5. I draw on both Sacks' (1992b: 573) and Jefferson's (1980: 62–64) discussions of sequencing in the delivery of news.

6. As Freese and Maynard (1998: 213) observe, deliverers may be more influential than recipients in determining the *direction* of valence, but recipients, in their turns of talk, use more intense prosodic *indications* of that valence.

7. More sobering examples of this phenomenon occur in social contexts where one has bad news to report and doing so would put in the news bearer in real danger. For example, when fathers coerce daughters into incestuous relationships, daughters' attempts to tell can escalate the violence already being done to them. In her history of family violence, Gordon (1988: 234) writes, "The pressure for secrecy, often including threats of mayhem, was so great that victims often tried to disguise their hints so they could claim not to have violated their assailant's demand for secrecy. In trying to get agency help, one common mode was to make some other complaint . . . in the (perhaps unconscious) hope that the incest would be discovered without the victims taking responsibility for telling."

8. Bergmann (1993: 95) argues that preannouncements of news are the basis for gossip proposals; what distinguishes the latter is an implicit moral stance toward the gossip subject.

9. In subsequent talk, Sally and Judy continue to evaluate Vickie's situation with her mother as not so bad. Sally tells a story about a friend of Vickie's whose father collapsed from a brain tumor and "died the next day." Judy's response to this story is, "I mean there's reason to be upset on her part but there's also reason to feel very lucky." Then Sally suggests that Vickie's mother had done everything in life that she reasonably was "going to do." And so on. The continuing theme is Vickie's inappropriate response to the situation. That this mutually critical attitude toward Vickie evolves from a series of announcements that could be taken as bad news concerning the mother and Vickie's state may have to do with a feature of gossiping that Bergmann (1993) elucidates: gossip producers themselves are in a morally compromised position. Consequently, approaching gossip is something that is done ambivalently. Here, Sally's announcements allow for a sympathetic uptake as well as the skeptical one Judy employs. When Sally, having perhaps cued Judy that a skeptical stance is warranted (as through her lead-in at lines 3–4), also ratifies Judy's skepticism, movement is made toward a full-fledged gossip episode.

10. Recipients can help to develop something as news and as having a particular valence independently of their actual cognitive state or psychological attitude. For example, when the philosopher Ludwig Wittgenstein went through periods of intense religious devotion, he could be extremely remorseful. During such a period, one of the "sins" that Wittgenstein

confessed to friends involved a past counterfeit response to an announcement of an acquaintance's death. As Monk (1991: 369) reports, "Upon being told by a mutual friend of this death, Wittgenstein reacted in a way that was appropriate to hearing sorrowful news. This was disingenuous of him, because, in fact, it was not news to him at all; he had already heard of the death." This anecdote illustrates how interactional structure—the practices for assembling sequences and courses of action can supersede individual predisposition.

11. Others had already been announced: two beds had been delivered but only one mattress, and the new beds had caused some "overcrowding of furniture." See Jefferson's (1988: 427) discussion of the "mattress" excerpt.

12. At the risk of repetition, but for purposes of clarity, it can be succinctly observed that when "oh" is freestanding it operates as a curtailing newsmark and discourages further development (unless intoned in particular ways). So does "oh really." However, an "oh" plus partial repeat encourages elaboration of the news. Items such as "really?," "yer kidding," "did you," etc., are "assertions of ritualized disbelief" that systematically advance the news delivery. See Heritage (1984a: 339–41).

13. For further, detailed consideration of the distinctions drawn here, and especially explication of prosodic features distinguishing news receipts and newsmarks, see Local (1996). Also see Freese and Maynard (1998: 209).

14. As Goodwin (1986b: 214) observes, assessments can be done "with sounds such as 'Ah:::' whose main function seems to be the carrying of an appropriate intonation contour."

15. Similarly, Local (1996: 188–89) examines an excerpt in which a teller, following a good-news receipt (arrowed below), proposes to elaborate on her prior news announcement with an account:

Rah:B.2.JV(14):8
```
     Jenny:  I'm'nna do s'm spaghett'n: (     ) n-eh::meatballs
             f'teafuh this lot now,
      Vera:  Oh lovely.
     Jenny:  Cz they didn't have u they only had fish fingihs'n
             chips fih dinnuh,
      Vera:  °ee Yes.°
     Jenny:  B't thez no↑thing in to:wn.=
     Jenny:  =Mahrks'n S[pencihs shelves w'↑c l e a : u h ]
      Vera:              [Well they wouldn'stay fer a meal.]
```

Following the account, Vera produces a minimal response ("ee Yes.") and no further topical talk, thereby indicating "that her *Oh lovely* was indeed designed not to be a larger topic-extending turn" (Local 1996: 189).

16. See also Goodwin's (1986b: 214–15) discussion of the difference between continuers and assessments. Continuers attend to units of talk as being part of a not-yet-complete larger structure, while assessments comment on specific aspects of talk in progress and not as a prelude to subsequent talk. Assessments can mark the terminal point of an extended sequence.

17. And if the recipient of bad news concerning a close person does not ask "when," "how," and "why" questions, others make inferences. Famously, when O. J. Simpson was tried for the murder of his former wife, Nicole Brown Simpson, a police detective testified that Simpson was "strangely uncurious" during a telephone call informing Simpson of the death. The detective had called Simpson, introduced himself, and said, "I have some bad news for you: Your ex-wife Nicole Simpson has been killed." According to the detective, Simpson responded

by getting very upset and saying, "Oh my God, Nicole is killed. Oh, my God, she's dead." But subsequently, Simpson asked no questions:

> "Did Mr. Simpson ask you how she was killed?" Marcia Clark, the chief prosecutor, asked him.
> "No," the detective replied.
> "Did he ask you when she was killed?"
> "No."
> "Did he ask you if you had any idea who had done it?"
> "No."
> "Did he ask you where it had occurred?"
> "No."
> "Did he ask you anything about the circumstances of how his ex-wife had been killed?"
> "No." (Margolick 1995)

By revealing Simpson's lack of curiosity, prosecutors, as one report put it, "were trying to imply that Simpson already knew how his wife had been killed because he was the murderer" (Associated Press 1995).

18. Recipients may actively claim that something is "just news" as a way of counteracting the alternative of evaluating it. A newspaper story about Ward Connerly, the California businessman and University of California regent who led the charge against affirmative action, revealed that his father abandoned the family when Connerly was two years old. The reporter tracked the father down and then informed Connerly: "Ward Connerly was given the news by telephone. 'I did not know,' he responded sharply. 'I've had no contact with him.' He paused a few seconds, then, rather formally, as if issuing a statement, said, 'The fact that he's alive is news to me. It does not surprise me or delight me or disturb me. It's just news'" (Bearak 1997).

19. Jeff, in this utterance, employs what Schegloff (1988b: 453), following Sacks (1987), calls structure-based preferencing. He projects a preferred response, here through a construction that exhibits a hoped-for kind of news.

20. See further discussion of this part of the episode in chapter 7, excerpt (3).

21. For explication of what "detail" can mean see Garfinkel (1988). I mean that each turn in the news delivery sequence is the site of orderly, organized actions and interactions.

22. "Clinical experience highlights the value of waiting until the patient attaches meaning to the information," Bor et al. (1993: 71) say, "before defining it as either good or bad news." Similarly, in an extensive review of the medical literature on bad news, Ptacek and Eberhardt (1996: 496) comment: "Given the subjective nature of most bad news, it must be recognized that a medical diagnosis can be appraised as bad from the perspective of the giver, the receiver, or both. Such subjectivity may result in the physician and patient having differing views as to the meaning of the news, though this need not necessarily be the case."

23. See excerpts (11) and (28).

Chapter Five

1. Souhami (1978: 936).

2. Stoicism often appears in public, flooding out in private. For another example, Andrew Ramirez, the father of a son who went missing when part of NATO forces in Macedonia in 1999, recalls getting this news at home when an Army official arrived:

"We came to notify you that your son Andrew is missing in action with two other soldiers," the stranger said. It was not clear whether his boy was alive or dead. "I said,
'Thank you very much,'" Ramirez, 55, a shipping clerk recalled. "Then I went inside
and cried." (Schemo 1999)

3. For an example of the stoic response in an HIV clinic, and the counselor's difficulty with
it, see chapter 6, excerpt (14).

4. See also Goffman's (1983: 13) discussion of how the "obligation to update the other
regarding one's own circumstances" helps to "resuscitate relationships."

5. See Gagné, Tewksbury, and McGaughey (1997: 496–97) about how those undergoing
sex reassignment surgery structure their disclosures.

6. The complications here are reminiscent of linguists' attempts to define grammatical
subjects and predicates according to topic/comment, given/new, universal/particular, gram-
mar/logic, and other distinctions, when it was discovered that discrimination between subject
and predicate and other such pairs could only hold up under very limited circumstances (Lyons
1971: 334–44). The subject/predicate distinction, Lyons (1972) observes, "is universally and
clearly applicable only in sentences whose nuclei consist of one nominal expression and an in-
transitive predicate" (344). At the very least, pragmatic consideration to discourse deictics,
conversational implicatures, and so on, are required to disambiguate subjects from predicates,
topics from comments, given from new information, and so on (Levinson 1983: 88–89). My
analysis of language-in-use depends on understanding how participants co-produce and contingently understand the *action* an utterance performs. When the main action is announcing
news, the primary figure in the news may appear in different grammatical locations or even not
at all in the announcement turn, conditioned according to other actions that both deliverers
and recipients implement.

7. Variations include [third party's *feature* + did or has something (bad or good)]. See examples (7) and (8).

8. However, through prosody (pitch, intonation, loudness, speech rate), the deliverer in
excerpt (5) displays a kind of "delight" at Rhonda Griffen's being clear of cancer, and the deliverer in (6) shows a kind of "regret" at Mrs. Cole's having had a stroke (Freese and Maynard
1998). Accordingly, parties to a news delivery may portray concerns for the primary figure
through other means than their verbal claims.

9. Joyce's narrative contains direct reported speech (DRS; Coulmas 1986) of both the
doctor and Joyce herself. For explication of distinguishing design features of DRS in conversation see Holt (1996: 222–25). One function of DRS revealed in excerpt (7) is to *dramatize* an
event through its (reported) constituent utterances and the way they are spoken (235–36).

10. The maxim not to tell already-known news is discussed in Sacks (1992b), who suggests that this maxim is a feature of conversationalists' pervasive "orientation to co-participant"
(564). Leslie's prefacing "Well I've written to you in the letter" can be exhibiting this orientation, anticipating that when Mum receives her letter, the maxim will have been breached; the
letter will contain information that will already have been imparted by way of their current conversation. In Goffman's (1971: 129–48) terms, therefore, the preface may be offering to "remedy" the breach in advance of its occurrence.

11. See discussions of this practice in chapter 2, and of this excerpt in Schegloff (1988b)
and Maynard (1992).

12. This episode is analyzed according to the NDS in chap. 4, excerpt (22).

13. See Beach's (2002) analysis of this episode, which starts out with Dad and Son en-

gaging in efforts to talk in Spanish for the opening sequences of the call. I am indebted to Beach for providing a tape and transcript of this and other telephone calls in the "Malignancy Corpus," also described in Beach (2002).

14. I am drawing on Sacks' (1992b) remark, in the context of a discussion about interaction among otherwise strangers in public settings, that "if one can say to somebody 'How is he?' without a 'he' having been talked of, then that's a way of doing 'being intimate'" (196). It is not only that, eventually, references to "her" and "she" emerge without "her" and "she" having been named in excerpt (14). These references appear after an initial reference to "results" on an adrenal gland biopsy that can be heard as commonsensically invoking Mom as the site of this biopsy and providing for the understandability of subsequent uses of "her" and "she."

15. The assessment turn sometimes consists of a congratulations offered to the news deliverer:

Heritage 1984a: 342
```
    J:  Think we're gonna get a rai̲:se, first of next month.
    G:  You̲ are?
        ((pause))
    S:  We̲ are.
    G:  Congratul̲a̲tions.
```

16. As Sacks (1992a: 73–74) remarks, "at some point in some relationship, invitations are the proper way that activities get started, whereas a measure of intimacy between the persons is that they don't use invitations. The same seems to hold for accounts of phone calls. Persons who call up someone they are not intimate with, often construct accounts of how that came about . . . at a little later point in intimacy it seems that they don't. They just call up and say 'Hi, how are you.' And if you ask 'Why did you call?' they say 'No reason, just felt like calling.'"

17. Sacks (1972: 58, 65–66) has analyzed how a caller to a suicide prevention center, who reports having "no one to turn to," may arrive at that conclusion by anticipating dire consequences from telling infirm parents about his difficulties. That such anticipations are often correct is amply borne out in accounts of gay disclosure. Thus, in a Bloomington, Illinois newspaper article about "issues and emotions related to homosexuality," Johnson (1996) reports,

> In the course of the debate, many homosexuals in Bloomington have asserted their sexuality for the first time. At least two were teen-agers. In one case, a young man was kicked out of a house and told never to return.

> In another case, a mother said she "felt like my life was over" when her son revealed that he was gay. She called her parish priest, who told her, "He's the same sweet kid he was this morning."

> Another man, who also requested anonymity to protect his parents, said he wanted to avoid the nightmare experienced by a friend. "He came out to his mother, and two weeks later, she died of a stroke," he said. "He's convinced that he killed her by telling her."

The recurrence of such accounts is consistent with the suggestion that Western society is one of "heterosexual presumption." As David Aveline has argued, "Heterosexual interests are typically attributed to others by default, and permanently so until signs meaningful to the attributors indicate otherwise. . . . It follows that when a son tells his parents he is gay, they typically do not expect or anticipate such news. This event thus marks the end of their heterosexual presumption and suggests a state of anomie." In my terms, the event marks for parents the necessity of transition from one social world and view of a child, to another, radically different world and view. See Aveline (1998) for extensive research into the impact on parents of their sons' gay self-disclosure.

18. As with third-party news, recipients have ways of showing the consequences without being self-referential or producing a personal-state description. Rather, yet again they are reflexive to the behavioral enactments of participants. In the excerpt below, having received A's good news that "Angie's gonna have a baby," and congratulating the deliverer, B turns away from the phone conversation to report the news to another party:

Terasaki 1976, appendix III:3
```
    A:  Angie's gonna have a baby.
    B:  Oh really.
    A:  Yeah
    B:  Well, congratulations
    A:  Isn't that sump'n    [I didn't think she-
    B:  ((aside off phone)) [Angie's gonna have a baby.
```

A means for exhibiting the impact of news is to make it into a further tellable (Sacks 1992a: 776).

19. Goffman (1978: 795) suggests that bad news is in a class of "'all-too-human' crises" that "give us victims the passing right to be momentary centers of sympathetic attention, and provide a legitimate place for anything 'uncontrolled' we do during the occasion." The "uncontrolled" would include the production of "exclamatory imprecations" like swearing.

20. Sudnow (1967: 140) suggests that stoicism on the part of recipients may reflect the protectiveness of clients toward clinicians who, after all, as professionals are not their relational intimates. Psychologically, recipients may fear that if they let loose emotionally, it may cause the departure or social withdrawal of their informants.

21. I draw on both Heritage (1984a: 301–2, 306–7) and Drew (1984: 130–31) who have analyzed substantial parts of this excerpt.

22. Another arena in which we have seen this factual way of delivering and restrained manner for receiving bad news is when participants are monitoring the situation of a third party. Because of the close relationships such monitoring involves and displays, it is almost as if deliverers and recipients in those circumstances are themselves primary consequential figures. Through their monitoring and the modes of delivery and receipt performed as part of this monitoring, they embody how consequential the third party news also is for them.

23. In clinical settings, after the physician delivers a diagnosis, Heath (1992) observes a kind of passivity on the part of the patient that allows for movement to remedial discussion: "Withholding response, or producing a downward-intoned grunt or *yeh,* provides the doctor with the opportunity of progressing directly from diagnosis to management of the condition" (261). For further discussion of bad news in relation to proposals for remedy, and the preferencing of offers over requests, see chapters 6 and 8.

24. Pomerantz (1978a) writes, "While self-praise may not be publicly noticed on any given occasion, it is, nonetheless, a class of action which is noticeable and collectible with the possibility, on a subsequent occasion, of being turned into a complaint, a gossip item, an unfavorable character assessment, and so on." Self-pity also appears as a type of action that, having been exhibited on one occasion, may get turned into a subject of complaint or gossip on another occasion. Recall chapter 4, excerpt (11), in which Sally and Judy begin to gossip about

how a mutual friend, Vickie, had received the "official" news that her mother was terminal by becoming "very very upset." Sally and Judy figure that Vickie is inappropriately "upset" over the news recently received about her mother's advancing cancer, in a way that is somehow less about the impending death and more about Vickie's own unresolved "feelings."

25. For discussion of shocked and stoic responses to the diagnostic news of breast cancer see Fallowfield (1991: 38–42).

26. Included here should be the "repeat response," as in this instance of a man taking a treadmill test in the presence of his cardiologist, who then told him the result:

> "I'm sorry," he said, "but you failed the test."
> "Failed it," I said, amazed.
> "Yes, certain abnormalities have shown up" (Epstein 1999: 61).

27. See chapter 6 on good-news exits.

28. Besides reporting circumstances and citing evidence, there are other abstract ways of presenting a diagnosis. In an autobiographical account about breast cancer, Ehrenreich (2001: 44) reports that her physician told her the results of a biopsy immediately after the procedure was completed under general anesthesia: "I awake to find him standing perpendicular to me, at the far end of the gurney, down near my feet, stating gravely, 'Unfortunately, there is a cancer.' It takes me all the rest of that drug-addled day to decide that the most heinous thing about that sentence is not the presence of cancer but the absence of me — for I, Barbara, do not enter into it even as a location, a geographical reference point. Where I once was . . . 'there is a cancer.'"

Chapter Six

1. Editorial in the *Journal of Clinical Oncology* quoted in Holland (1989: 447).

2. See Abrahams (1963: 337), who culled this story from Hazlett's *New London Jest Book* (London, 1871), 43–44. Taylor (1987: 81) places the tale as type 2014.

3. Recall from chapter 1 that the "mum" effect (Rosen, Grandison, and Stewart 1974) is the experimentally demonstrated "reluctance" to communicate bad news, which, according to the review in Sussman and Sproull (1999: 151), happens by way of distortion, delay or delegation, and concealment. The mum effect has been documented in a wide variety of settings and across cultures; see, e.g., O'Neal, Levine, and Frank (1979). However, by their very design, experimental investigations do not enter the realm of actual behavior in real settings. They also neglect the interactional facets of news deliveries and, accordingly, recipients' contributions to the conveyance process.

4. Exceptions are Sudnow's (1967) chapter, "On Bad News," concerned with tidings about death, and McIntosh's (1977) study of communication processes in a hospital cancer ward. Each contains brief remarks about differences between good news and bad news in the hospital context. Several recent conversation analytic studies deal with bad and good news in clinical settings, and are discussed later in the chapter.

5. It is listed as number 2040 in folktale classifications. See Taylor (1987: 87) and Aarne (1961: 534). I am grateful to Steve Clayman for pointing me toward this example of the tale. Dick Bauman and Moira Smith got me further down the path, and Patrick Feaster supplied me with two recorded versions from 1908 and 1915 by the comedian Nat M. Wills. I have slightly edited Wills's versions.

6. None of the "House Is Burned Down" tales that I have seen feature women as protagonists and men as antagonists, and indeed many of them are characteristically misogynist.

7. My data suggest that "pretty good" may be equivocal–it can be precedent to either "troubles talk" and bad news or "prosperity talk" and good news, as we shall see. Hence, Schegloff's (1986: 130) characterization of such responses as being "qualified" is apt; they may be qualified to anticipate bad news or good news.

8. Lerner (1991: 441–44) observes ways in which utterances can *project* a [preliminary component + final component] compound turn format, for example through an if-then construction. No such construction is used here, which makes the projectability of what turns out to be a compound turn construction very weak and thereby may allow for Marvin to regard and align to Pete's utterance at lines 17–18 as complete in itself, even though that utterance turns out to be a preliminary component. Also see Ford and Thompson's (1996) analysis of how speaker change regularly occurs when the syntax, intonation, and pragmatics (action force) of an utterance converge to suggest that transition to next turn is relevant. Such convergence appears to have occurred here (in lines 17–18).

9. It is not only Andi who ignores Lucy's proposal about their moving; Bob's announcement succeeds in further deleting the sequential implicativeness of that proposal.

10. In other data (NBIV.10.R), Lottie, who has been trying unsuccessfully to reach Emma, engages in a my-side telling — "An' I called you earlier" — and this obtains an account from Emma as to her previous whereabouts. After Lottie acknowledges this account with "Oh," Emma says, "How was your trip?," thereby showing herself to be tracking Lottie's affairs, a readiness to hear news about those affairs, and possibly an interpretation that the attempts at calling had been to convey such news. This interchange also demonstrates that after a callee has accounted for her whereabouts and had the account receipted — after the search for an account is completed — is a slot in which the callee can ask about the (attempting) caller's (purported) reason for calling. In excerpt (4), the search for an account is unsuccessful, but closure of that search is reached at least by line 28, such that a slot for inquiry is available by then, if not earlier (line 26).

11. These patterns extend into and are reinforced by prosody. As noted earlier, bad news talk regularly features falling and/or low pitch, a narrower pitch range, breathy and creaky voice, quietness on key words, and slower pacing, whereas good news talk displays rising and/or high pitch, a wider pitch range, normal voice quality, loudness on key words, and faster pacing (Freese and Maynard 1998).

12. The asymmetries operate at remarkable levels of detail within sequences, if Schegloff's (1988b) "conjecture," concerning the signaling of guesses about bad news, is correct. The conjecture is that when someone has bad news to tell and a recipient is allowed or invited to guess at it, a rejection of an incorrect guess will be done as a *preferred* response (in an emphatic, quickened fashion) when the actual news is not as bad as the guess, and as a *dispreferred* response (in a delayed, less emphatic fashion) when the actual news is worse than the guess.

13. Ronnie's announcement response (arrow 2) is delayed relative to Edward's announcement completion, and it may be that Edward's turn-holding "uh::ah:::" is awaiting that response.

14. Bright-side sequences do not transform bad news into good news. Rather, as our analysis of the prosodic properties of this excerpt shows, participants preserve a negative stance toward the bad news and a positive stance toward the elaborating details that exhibits tempering but not replacing of the original stance (Freese and Maynard 1998: 211–12).

15. See, for example, the discussion in chapter 2 of historical and cultural variation in practices for disclosing cancer to its victims.

16. For example, see the discussion in Ehrenreich (2001) about how, in the "breast cancer culture"–in prescribed treatment paths, medical literature, autobiographies, journalist discourse, Web sites, fundraisers, organizations, and products for breast cancer–"cheerfulness is more or less mandatory, dissent a kind of treason." Breast cancer gets normalized, "prettied up," even presented "perversely, as a positive and enviable experience" in a kind of "relentless bright-siding." In clinics, this bright-siding occurs when, after a delivery of diagnosis, physicians and other clinicians admonish patients to "think positive." Although patients may appear to accept such admonishment at the clinic, a focus group study of women with breast cancer shows that, among themselves, women often are aware of the idiom's formulaic quality and may actively resist it (Kitzinger 2000). Research on actual episodes wherein oncologists make treatment recommendations to breast cancer patients (Roberts 1999: chap. 5) shows these doctors traversing a fine line between negative and positive aspects of treatment, but they do not relent in suggesting that adjuvant therapy should be pursued, even when patients raise strong reservations.

17. By referring to "normal societies," I want to note that there are also abnormal circumstances of terror, genocide, holocaust, and others that may render news in everyday life as anything but benign. An illustrative study is that of Fitzpatrick (1999), documenting the "fatalism" and "passivity" among Soviet Russians who, in the 1930s, suffered under the terror of the Stalinist regime. Recollecting their experiences, respondents in a Harvard post–World War II refugee interview project (cited by Fitzpatrick) reported that life was "abnormal" because of its unpredictability, the imposed dislocations and relocations for self and others, the state violence against citizens, and, above all, economic privation and hardship. Surely, there were myths, slogans, and propaganda with which citizens could affiliate–that conditions were a temporary sacrifice, that the Soviet Union was overcoming the "backwardness" of Tsarist Russia, that, as Stalin announced in 1935, "life has become better, comrades; life has become more cheerful" (90). However, except for the privileged few, these myths were very distant from the realities of everyday life. As well, secrecy, repression, quarreling, denouncing, informing, complaining, and other activities were endemic to the society. Evidently, although the Russian people were capable of and engaged in resistance to state impositions, in a variety of ways, opportunities were infrequent for shrouding the prevailing bad news and exposing good news. However, in the often-invoked academic phrase, this hypothesis is a matter for empirical inquiry–in this case, into the actualities of mundane interaction in such abnormal circumstances.

18. Leppänen's (1998) data are originally in Swedish and translated into English.

19. For discussion of deviant-case analysis in ethnomethodology and conversation analysis see Heritage (1984b: 248–51) and Clayman and Maynard (1995: 6–8).

20. Prosodically, the deliveries of bad and good HIV news were different, with good news being delivered with higher tones and volume than bad news.

21. The tests to which counselors refer in this and other excerpts are the ELISA (acronym for Enzyme Linked ImmunoSorbent Assay) and the Western blot. The ELISA, which is very sensitive but nonspecific, is used to screen blood for the HIV antibody, and when it is positive, the Western blot, which is more specific, is used to confirm the ELISA result.

22. It could be objected that the clients in both (13) and (14) are not being stoic and instead are silent because they were each expecting the bad news. However, even when clients are surprised or at least "kind of surprised," they still register the news in a minimal fashion:

CO: Well I'm- I'm not going to keep you guessing any longer uhm
        the test did come back po:sitive.

```
        (1.0)
CO:  Is that a surprise for you?
        (2.0)
CL:  (                    )
CO:  Mm hmm-
        (0.9)
CL:  Well it's kind of a surprise it's s- s- kind of a surprise.
```

This piece of data was supplied by David Silverman. For another example of HIV bad news and a stoic response see Silverman (1997: 91).

23. In a clinic for developmental disabilities, pediatricians might ask parents, "How do you see Ronald now, Mrs. C?," not initially proposing the existence of a "problem" (Maynard 1991b: 169).

24. The clinic had a number of preprinted informational brochures to give to clients who tested positive. These were usually kept in desk drawers. I assume that the counselor was looking for these, did not find any, and left the room to obtain a supply from the lobby.

25. The Department of Health in the state where this clinic resided had an official document entitled, "Post-test Counseling of Persons with Seropositive HIV Antibody Test Results," which operated as official policy for the clinic. The document stated:

A. Give the client the results of his or her HIV antibody test. Allow some time for the client to absorb the information.
B. Prompt the client who does not react after a time by asking them how they are feeling, or what they are thinking.
C. Address any client responses. Be prepared for a variety of reactions . . . anxiety and fear of death, guilt, depression, anger, denial, apathy.

Accordingly, the orientation in the clinic to eliciting emotional responsiveness from clients may have partially reflected official policy.

26. One counselor formulated the task to a client this way: "Okay so what I wanta do with you tonight is a couple of different things. Number one I wanna deal with the emotional side of this particular piece o' news. And then number two I wanna give you as many referrals and help–help you strategize what our next step is going to be as far as dealing with the situation as it stands" (B49A1: 4).

27. Recall that in excerpt (12), the counselor, who has good news, eventually announces, "so you're negative."

28. Having the client read his own test results may have features of bluntness, but there is some inbuilt caution as well, because it allows the clinician to confirm what the client himself pronounces from his reading.

29. Crying, of course, can be taken to exhibit happiness and is then forthrightly permissible. See excerpt (11).

30. For a study of how strong displays can impede the work of professionals in an organizational setting, see Whalen and Zimmerman (1998). They analyze the use of "hysteria" as a label that 9-1-1 call takers apply to callers whose behavior overwhelms the interactional demands of gathering information necessary to the dispatch of help.

31. Quotes are from my collection, case B57A1, page 6.

32. In the legal arena, McClenahen and Lofland (1976: 264) discuss "shoring" techniques, which seem to be versions of the bright-side sequence. Deputy marshals serving arrest

and other warrants employ such formulas as "it's not as bad as you think," "it could have been worse," "it may be blessing in disguise," and others.

33. For examples in educational settings see Rosenbaum, Miller, and Krei (1996), who address the topic of "gatekeeping" by counselors in high schools. Research in the 60s and 70s showed that counselors often counseled differentially trade colleges or lesser educational programs rather than regular colleges or universities for students from low socioeconomic, minority, or other disadvantaged communities. Partly as a result of this research, counselors are much more circumspect now than before, and properly so. On the other hand, counselors may avoid being realistic with students about their academic prospects because of two things–one is an increase in parental power, and the other is associated with having to give disappointing news to the students themselves: "Rather than confront a student with bad news and risk confronting an angry parent, open admission policy allows counselors the easy alternative of avoiding college advising almost entirely and urging college for every student" (Rosenbaum, Miller, and Krei 1996: 276).

34. The asymmetry that we have described between bad and good news can be appreciated ironically if we observe that no one ever seems to say that glad tidings should be withheld until they can be conveyed with some kind of sad counterpart.

35. See also Peräkylä's (1991) discussion of "hope work" and the differences between curative, palliative, and "dismantling" hope work.

36. See also our research concerning the communication between end-stage cancer patients and oncologists, who attempt to inform them that their cancers are no longer treatable and that palliative care is the present option (Lutfey and Maynard 1998). The conversational trajectories are highly contingent on the activities of the physicians, the patients, and the patients' family members–that is, on all participants in the informing episodes. As is mentioned in chapter 3, physicians are cautious in discussing death and dying with the patient and family members, and patients and family members strongly affect the course of the news delivery. That is, when a patient is dying, how far the physician's unpacking of that news can go is highly dependent on the responses to the physician's initiatives.

Chapter Seven

1. Ambassador Andrew Steigman, assistant dean, Georgetown School of Foreign Service, in an interview with Vicki O'Hara (1996) on National Public Radio.

2. See Heritage's (1984b) aptly titled chapter, "The Morality of Cognition."

3. See appendix 2 for discussion of preference structure.

4. A recorded phone message, in which an art gallery owner tells an artist, "Donald," whose work she has been promoting, that his paintings have been accepted into a juried exhibition, contains a more overt example of prospecting for compliments. The art gallery owner, "Martha Connor," was on the jury:

```
1   Hey Do:nald. It's Martha Connor. Can your voice be any lower?
2   Uhm- heh heh heh. I wanted to be the first ↑person to tell you
3   that >you made it into th-< Academy lineup for the year two
4   thousand one? You are (0.2) amazing? You had some stiff competition.
5   There was something like over sixty (.) applicants, and they only
6   selected eleven people? And, I um (.) was a major part of it heh
7   HEH HEH heh heh so you have me to thank. =No I'm only kidding.
```

```
8   Give me a call. I'll talk to you later. You'll be getting a letter
9   I guess from them (.) at some point. (0.2) Bye:::?
```

After greeting "Donald," identifying herself, and jokingly commenting on Donald's answering-machine voice (lines 1–2), Martha prefaces her good news announcement (lines 3–4) in a way that shows her to be competing to be in first-announcer position with the news (line 2). This is one way in which Martha inserts her agency as a feature of the news delivery. Then, after the announcement and several praising assessments directed to Donald (lines 3–6), Martha claims credit for the decision and asks for Donald's gratitude (lines 6–7), even if she laughs and declares herself to be "kidding."

5. The prosody of Jenny's announcements also conforms to what Freese and Maynard (1998) identify as the relatively subdued manner in which good news about self is delivered.

6. I use "unembellished" as a replacement for "unelaborated," which is Pomerantz's (1978b) term, because I refer to the third part of the news delivery sequence as an "elaboration" and do not want to confuse it with the phenomenon she describes.

7. See chap. 4, excerpt (16) and its analysis.

8. See chap. 5, excerpt (25) and its analysis.

9. See chap. 5, excerpt (29).

10. For a discussion of asymmetric attributions of responsibility in a journalistic setting see Clayman and Reisner (1998: 192–93). In newspaper conferences where participants decide which stories will go on the front page, editors act as advocates for their reporters, in part by giving explicit credit to them for strong stories and withholding blame for weaker ones.

11. See chap. 5, excerpt (4).

12. Following Austin (1970: 175–76), we can draw a distinction between "justifications" and "excuses." Justifications suggest that a given act was a "good," "right," or "sensible," while excuses admit that the act was "bad," but that the doer was, for some reason not fully responsible for the act. Drawing on Austin, Atkinson and Drew (1979: 140–41), go on to propose that an *interactional* distinction between justifications and excuses may reside in the different sequential positions in which these objects reside. Justifications occur in a position prior to an overt accusation, while excuses appear subsequent to such accusations. Consistent with this ordering, in the teacher–parent conversation here, Mrs. Stewart, having heard a covert type of blaming but no as yet bald accusation, deals with the blaming by justifying her teaching strategies (connecting them to those of the praiseworthy Mrs. Anderson and stating that she supplements them).

13. In the interests of space, I am glossing and simplifying approximately 15 minutes of discussion. Along the way, Mother grants that her child "has some weaknesses," and "maybe he just needs to get his rear end busy and start to study more," but that he "always had difficulty with pencil and writing." The two parties also go over the content of the tests. After Mrs. Stewart suggests that written work is the only way she can grade, Mother argues that John is "not a meticulous, detail-oriented person" which is necessary for writing. Mrs. Stewart responds to this as "a perfect example of what I mean by having him at least consider repeating the course."

Chapter Eight

1. Don DeLillo, *Underworld* (New York: Scribner, 1997), 542.

2. For wider-ranging discussions of these issues see Zimmerman and Boden (1991) and Drew and Heritage (1992).

3. Klein also suggests that inferences were made that the story was purposefully leaked by Clinton's legal adviser, Mickey Kantor (or someone else close to Clinton), sending a message to the president himself that he needed to "change" his story about the affair. However, another journalistic account also reports on the presidential pattern of preparing the public for bad news. Discussing Clinton's possible hiring of more counsel to deal with the Congressional inquiry into the Lewinsky allegations and even earlier questions about Whitewater real estate deals, Bennet (1998) writes, "Among the sorts of issues a new adviser might be expected to decide is what protected information the White House should release in advance of any hearings, to defuse revelations that might otherwise be bombshells. That is a technique the White House has used repeatedly during such Congressional investigations as the inquiry into donations during the 1996 campaigns."

4. In March 1991, shortly after the war had ended, a battalion of American combat engineers blew up an Iraqi ammunition depot containing nerve gas.

5. Whether the level of exposure was in fact too low to merit informing the troops and wearing protective gear has been subject to dispute. The Czech defense minister, General Miroslav Vacek, has argued, "There was a certain amount of underestimation of the problem by the Americans" (Shenon 1996), and the evidence of widespread illness tends to support this claim, despite longstanding denials on the part of the Pentagon, the CIA, and other U.S. organizations.

6. As Heimer (1988: 506) argues about poisonous hazards more generally, "If people learn about a complex of symptoms of acute poisoning from toxic substances, for instance, then when some group of people lacks those acute symptoms people may conclude that they cannot have been exposed to toxic wastes."

7. Rational choice and theories based upon it are, as Coleman (1990: 18) puts it, "constructed for a set of *abstract* rational actors" (emphasis added).

8. For example, Tversky and Kahneman (1974: 1130) write, "It is not surprising that useful heuristics such as representativeness and availability are retained, even though they occasionally lead to errors in prediction or estimation. What is perhaps surprising is the failure of people to infer from lifelong experience such fundamental statistical rules as regression toward the mean, or the effect of sample size on sampling variability. Although everyone is exposed, in the normal course of life, to numerous examples from which these rules could have been induced, very few people discover the principles of sampling and regression on their own."

9. When the primary figures are second parties, or recipients, a delivery of bad news, if it is also a warning, may be requesting or proposing that the second parties take remedial actions for themselves. However, second-party bad news can also operate differently. As chapter 5 showed, *after* the news has been received with a stoic and/or flooding-out response, *then* sequences of talk devoted to relieving the recipients' situation are enacted, and it may be the deliverer who is positioned to provide relief or remedy.

10. As Mandelbaum and Pomerantz (1991: 157) put it, "Although [Marcia] clearly was concerned with pursuing her own activities, she . . . turned down his inexplicit request in a way that claimed a willingness to have done the favor but for circumstances."

11. I draw on Sacks's ([1964–65] 1992a: 12–25). Lecture 2: "On Suicide Threats Getting Laughed Off." When responding to teller's report of feeling suicidal, a recipient who treats it seriously — as a suicide *threat* — may feel the obligation to help or intervene. However, a recipient who treats the report by laughing thereby suggests that it is a joke, and can avoid the obligation to help without being seen to refuse that obligation.

288 Notes to Pages 234–241

12. See Shilts's (1987) and Perrow and Guillén's (1990) early accounts of the national HIV crisis, two more recent books (Resnik 1999; Starr 1998), and a report from the National Academy of Sciences (Leveton, Sox, and Stoto 1995) more specifically concerned with HIV and contamination of the blood supply. Healy (1999) has written the most compelling socio-logical analysis of how different groups for distributing blood products, embedded in a situa-tion of uncertainty, responded to the crisis according to the character of their relations with sup-pliers and recipients of blood products.

13. For a discussion of "community" among hemophiliac sufferers see Resnik (1999).

14. This question can be raised in other contexts, because stories similar to the one sur-rounding the January 1983 CDC meeting in Atlanta pertain to international meetings and events in many countries. On what happened at a summer 1983 meeting at the World Hemo-philia Federation's annual meeting in Stockholm, and on the resistance to projected contami-nation of national blood supplies in France and Japan see Starr (1998). An article about more recent problems with the supply of safe blood products internationally summarized the situa-tion in the 1980s: "Over the last decade court cases have demonstrated to what extent early warnings about the virus that causes AIDS were ignored in the United States, France, Germany, Switzerland and other countries, with the result that thousands of hemophiliacs and others in need of blood may have been infected" (Crossette 2000).

15. In a different responsive fashion, a well-known physician at the meeting proposed that hemophiliacs should suspend their use of Factor VIII altogether and return to cryoprecipitate or treatment with frozen plasma (Starr 1998: 272), which was safer because it involved smaller pools of blood donation than Factor VIII. While the plasma companies were not happy with this proposal, which implied taking Factor VIII off the market, it indicates again that some rep-resentatives at the CDC meeting did take the presented information as bad news and did at-tempt remedial action: the physician continued using cryoprecipitate with his own patients (Resnik 1999: 66–67).

16. Both Elster (1989) and Sciulli (1992) argue that the key concept in rational choice is *optimality:* actors are rational if the actions they take are optimal relative to their desires and be-liefs, assuming that beliefs themselves are best related to available evidence. Or, as Coleman (1990: 14) puts it, "persons, when intending to act rationally, have systematic biases that lead their actions to be less than rational, according to some objective standard." Going by these statements, it seems that subsets of the participants in the 1983 CDC meeting, hearing the offi-cial presentation, acted in suboptimal, possibly even biased ways. Their beliefs, and consequent actions, were not suited to the evidence in hand, however sketchy and indeterminate it was.

17. Resnik (1999): 42–44, 52–53, 68–72, 78, 83. This was not true for the entire popu-lation of hemophiliac individuals. Access to the most sophisticated therapies for hemophilia was highly stratified along geographic, ethnic, and socioeconomic lines. See ibid., 90–92.

18. This belief of blood bank representatives was bolstered by a different argument from spokesmen for gay organizations also present at the CDC meeting in January 1983, who reflected a perspective articulated earlier in San Francisco in which donor screening was equated with racial discrimination and "scapegoating" (Shilts 1987: 220).

19. As a result, Healy (1999: 551) observes, "many more hemophiliacs contracted HIV than might otherwise have been the case." On this point, see also See Leveton, Sox, and Stoto (1995: 137, 164), and Starr (1998: 298).

20. See "Joint Statement on Directed Donations and AIDS" in appendix D of Leveton, Sox, and Stoto (1995: 297–98).

21. See also Resnik (1999: 127) and a similar account in Starr (1998: 273).

22. In particular, see Clarke's (1999) study concerning how governmental and other organizations may create "fantasy" documents as part of a "disqualification heuristic" that downplays potential bad news and stresses the good news of workable (in fiction) contingency plans for handling potential nuclear and other disasters.

23. For discussion of the linguistic problems in this case see Cushing (1994: 44–45).

Epilogue

1. Literatures in medicine and business have the most articles concerned with the how-to of bad news. In law, Smith (1998) observes a lack of attention to the problem of giving bad news as part of legal practice, and draws on medical "paradigms" to develop a protocol for the lawyer–client relationship.

2. Frankel and Stein (1999: 79) use the term *habit* "to denote an organized way of thinking and acting during the clinical encounter."

3. The list that follows adapts insights from several of my favorite clinical sources on the how-to of delivering bad news. The sources include Buckman (1992), Fallowfield (1991), Frankel (2000), Girgis and Sanson-Fisher (1995), Lo, Quill, and Tulsky (1999), Maguire and Faulkner (1988), Ptacek and Eberhardt (1996), Quill (1991), and Taylor (1988). To these insights, I add considerations from my own research.

4. The PDS was mentioned in chapters 2 and 3. See also Maynard (1991a, b).

5. On the distancing of emotional experience in various social settings see Scheff (1979).

6. For example, if a patient in a diagnostic medical interview, asks, "Is it cancer?," Maguire and Faulkner (1988) observe, "it is difficult to know what response is wanted by the patient. . . . Only the patient can suggest the direction he wishes to follow. You can usually discover this by saying, 'I would be happy to answer your question' and then reflecting his question back to him by asking, 'But what makes you ask that question?'"

7. Asking recipients about whether they want to talk first may beg a prior question about whether they want to know the news at all. In an extensive ethical consideration about whether patients should be told when they have cancer, and observing that patients have a "right" but not a "duty" to know, Freedman (1997: 336–37) argues for an approach of *offering* the truth. Physicians attempt to ascertain how much patients want to know about their condition, whether they prefer for family members to hear the news and make decisions on their behalf, or want themselves to be primarily involved. In short, "a patient will be offered the opportunity to learn the truth, at whatever level of detail that patient desires."

Appendix Two

1. Zimmerman, in turn, makes heavy use of Heritage's (1984b) chapter 8. See also, more recently, Clayman and Gill (forthcoming).

2. Not all assessments implicate agreement as the preferred next turn-type. When one party produces a self-deprecating utterance, for example, agreement from a recipient in next turn is dispreferred (Pomerantz, 1984a: 64).

REFERENCES

Aarne, Antti. 1961. *The Types of the Folktale*. Edited by S. Thompson. Helsinki: Suomalainen Tiedeakatemia.

Abbott, Andrew. 1988. *The System of Professions: An Essay on the Division of Expert Labor.* Chicago: University of Chicago Press.

Abrahams, Roger D. 1963. "'The House Burned Down' Again." *Journal of American Folklore* 76: 337–39.

Anderson, Elijah. 1976. *A Place on the Corner.* Chicago: University of Chicago Press.

Anderson, Robert J., John A. Hughes, and Wes W. Sharrock. 1985. "The Relationship between Phenomenology and Ethnomethodology." *Journal of British Sociology and Phenomenology* 16: 221–35.

Anspach, Renee R. 1993. *Deciding Who Lives: Fateful Choices in the Intensive-Care Nursery.* Berkeley: University of California Press.

Araton, Harvey. 1999. "Yogi and the Boss Complete Makeup Game." *New York Times,* 6 January.

Associated Press. 1989. "Ex-Student Indicted in Professor's Murder." *Capital Times* (Madison, WI), 26 September.

———. 1995. "Detective: Simpson Didn't Ask about Ex-Wife's Death." *Herald-Times* (Bloomington, IN), 17 February.

———. 1998. "Starr, Prosecutors Give In-depth Interview to ABC's Sawyer." *Herald-Times* (Bloomington, IN), 26 November.

Atkinson, J. Maxwell, and Paul Drew. 1979. *Order in Court: The Organisation of Verbal Interaction in Judicial Settings.* London: Macmillan.

Atkinson, Paul. 1990. *The Ethnographic Imagination: Textual Constructions of Reality.* London: Sage.

Austin, J. L. 1970. *Philosophical Papers.* London: Oxford University Press.

Aveline, David Timothy. 1998. "'My Son, My Son!' How Parents Adapt to Having a Gay Son." Ph.D. diss., Indiana University, Bloomington.

Bartlett, Kay. 1988. "Market Analyst Goes to Head of Class." *Wisconsin State Journal* (Madison, WI), 3 January.

Baugh, John. 1999. *Out of the Mouths of Slaves.* Austin: University of Texas Press.

Bauman, Richard. 1986. *Story Performance and Event: Contextual Studies of Oral Narrative.* Cambridge: Cambridge University Press.

Beach, Wayne A. 2001. "Stability and Ambiguity: Managing Uncertain Moments When Updating News about Mom's Cancer." *Text* 21: 221–50.

———. 2002. "Between Dad and Son: Initiating, Delivering, and Assimilating Bad Cancer News." *Health Communication* 14: 271–98.

Bearak, Barry. 1997. "Questions of Race Run Deep for Foe of Preferences." *New York Times,* 27 July.

Becker, Howard S. 1982. *Art Worlds.* Berkeley: University of California Press.

Belluck, Pam. 1998. "You Gotta Believe! 13's the Lucky Number." *New York Times,* 31 July.

Bennet, James. 1998. "White House Considers Adding to Defense Team." *New York Times,* 25 August.

Berger, Peter L., and Thomas Luckmann. 1967. *The Social Construction of Reality: A Treatise in the Sociology of Knowledge.* New York: Anchor Books.

Bergmann, Jörg R. 1992. "Veiled Morality: Notes on Discretion in Psychiatry." Pp. 137–62 in *Talk at Work: Interaction in Institutional Settings,* ed. P. Drew and J. Heritage. Cambridge: Cambridge University Press.

———. 1993. *Discreet Indiscretions: The Social Organization of Gossip.* Translated by J. John Bednarz. New York: Aldine De Gruyter.

———. 1998. "Introduction: Morality in Discourse." *Research on Language and Social Interaction* 31: 279–94.

Berkow, Ira. 1994. "Coach Still Battles as a Season Ends." *New York Times,* 10 June.

Best, Joel. 1995. *Images of Issues: Typifying Contemporary Social Problems.* New York: Aldine de Gruyter.

Beyene, Yewoubdar. 1992. "Medical Disclosure and Refugees: Telling Bad News to Ethiopian Patients." *Western Journal of Medicine* 157: 328–32.

Biesecker, Barbara Bowles. 1998. "Future Directions in Genetic Counseling: Practical and Ethical Considerations." *Kennedy Institute of Ethics Journal* 8: 145–60.

Billig, Michael. 1999. "Whose Terms? Whose Ordinariness? Rhetoric and Ideology in Conversation Analysis." *Discourse & Society* 10: 543–82.

Bloch, Maurice, Shelin Adam, Sandy Wiggins, Marlene Huggins, and Michael R. Hayden. 1992. "Predictive Testing for Huntington Disease in Canada: The Experience of Those Receiving an Increased Risk." *American Journal of Medical Genetics* 42: 499–507.

Blumer, Herbert. 1956. "Sociological Analysis and the 'Variable.'" *American Sociological Review* 21: 683–90.

Boden, Deirdre. 1994. *The Business of Talk.* Cambridge: Polity Press.

Boden, Deirdre and Harvey L. Molotch. 1994. "The Compulsion of Proximity." Pp. 257–86 in *NowHere: Space, Time, and Modernity,* ed. R. Friedland and D. Boden. Berkeley: University of California Press.

Bohannon, John Neil, III. 1988. "Flashbulb Memories for the Space Shuttle Disaster: A Tale of Two Theories." *Cognition* 5: 73–99.

Bor, Robert, and R. Miller. 1988. "Addressing 'Dreaded Issues': A Description of a Unique Counselling Intervention with Patients with AIDS/HIV." *Counselling Psychology Quarterly* 1: 397–405.

Bor, Robert, Riva Miller, Eleanor Goldman, and Isobel Scher. 1993. "The Meaning of Bad News in HIV Disease: Counseling about Dreaded Issues Revisited." *Counselling Psychology Quarterly* 6: 69–80.

Bourdieu, Pierre. 1977. *Outline of a Theory of Practice.* Cambridge: Cambridge University Press.

———. 1984. *Distinction: A Social Critique of the Judgement of Taste.* Cambridge, MA: Harvard University Press.

———. 1990. *The Logic of Practice.* Stanford: Stanford University Press.

———. 1991. *Language and Symbolic Power.* Cambridge, MA: Harvard University Press.

Boyd, Elizabeth. 1998. "Bureaucratic Authority in the 'Company of Equals': The Interactional Management of Medical Peer Review." *American Sociological Review* 63: 200–224.

Bragg, Rick. 1995. "For a Family of One Yet to Be Found, A Limbo of Suffering." *New York Times,* 2 May.

Brown, Roger, and James Kulik. 1977. "Flashbulb Memories." *Cognition* 5: 73–99.

Buchwald, Art. 1992. "Feminizing Bad News." *International Herald Tribune,* 31 March.

Buckman, Robert. 1992. *How to Break Bad News: A Guide for Health Care Professionals.* Baltimore, MD: Johns Hopkins University Press.

Burawoy, Michael. 1991. "The Extended Case Method." Pp. 271–87 in *Ethnography Unbound: Power and Resistance in the Modern Metropolis,* ed. M. Burawoy, A. Burton, A. A. Ferguson, K. J. Fox, J. Gamson, N. Gartrell, L. Hurst, C. Kurzman, L. Salzinger, J. Schiffman, and S. Ui. Berkeley: University of California Press.

Burgess, A., and A. Lazare. 1975. *Psychiatric Nursing in the Hospital and Community.* Englewood Cliffs, N.J.: Prentice-Hall.

Button, Graham. 1987. "Moving Out of Closings." Pp. 101–51 in *Talk and Social Organisation,* ed. G. Button and J. R. E. Lee. Clevedon: Multilingual Matters.

Button, G., and N. Casey. 1985. "Topic Nomination and Topic Pursuit." *Human Studies* 8: 3–55.

Button, Graham, and Wes Sharrock. 1993. "A Disagreement over Agreement and Consensus in Constructionist Sociology." *Journal for the Theory of Social Behavior* 23: 1–25.

Cahill, Larry, Bruce Prins, Michael Weber, and James L. McGaugh. 1994. "ß-Adrenergic Activation and Memory for Emotional Events." *Nature* 371: 702–4.

Canedy, Dana. 2001. "A Sentence of Life without Parole for Boy, 14, in Murder of Girl, 6." *New York Times,* 10 March.

Capital-Times. 1989. "Hackl Case: Man Heard 3 Gunshots." *Capital Times* (Madison, WI), 30 September.

Charmaz, Kathy. 1975. "The Coroner's Strategies for Announcing Death." *Urban Life* 4: 296–316.

———. 1991. *Good Days, Bad Days: The Self in Chronic Illness and Time.* New Brunswick, NJ: Rutgers University Press.

———. 1994. "Discoveries of Self in Illness." in *Doing Everyday Life: Ethnography as Human Lived Experience,* ed. R. Prus and W. Shaffer. Mississauga, Ontario: Copp Clark Longman.

Cherry, Keith. 1996. "Ain't No Grave Deep Enough." *Journal of Contemporary Ethnography* 25: 22–57.

Chisholm, Christian A., D. J. Pappas, and Michael C. Sharp. 1997. "Communicating Bad News." *Obstetrics and Gynecology* 90: 637–639.

Christakis, Nicholas A., and Elizabeth B. Lamont. 2000. "Extent and Determinants of Error in Doctors' Prognoses in Terminally Ill Patients: Prospective Cohort Study." *British Medical Journal* 320: 469–72.

Churchill, Larry R. 1997. "Bioethics in Social Context." Pp. 310–20 in *The Social*

Medicine Reader, ed. G. E. Henderson, N. M. P. King, R. P. Strauss, S. E. Estroff, and
L. R. Churchill. Durham, NC: Duke University Press.

Cicourel, Aaron V. 1963. *Method and Measurement in Sociology.* New York: Free Press.

———. 1974. *Cognitive Sociology: Language and Meaning in Social Interaction.* New York:
Free Press.

———. 1987. "The Interpenetration of Communicative Contexts: Examples from Medical Encounters." *Social Psychology Quarterly* 50: 217–26.

Clark, Robert E., and Emily E. LaBeff. 1982. "Death Telling: Managing the Delivery of
Bad News." *Journal of Health and Social Behavior* 23: 366–80.

———. 1986. "Ending Intimate Relationships: Strategies of Breaking Off." *Sociological
Spectrum* 6: 245–67.

Clarke, Lee. 1991. *Mission Improbable: Using Fantasy Documents to Tame Disaster.* Chicago: University of Chicago Press.

Clayman, Steven E. 1988. "Displaying Neutrality in Television News Interviews." *Social
Problems* 35: 474–92.

———. 1992. "Footing in the Achievement of Neutrality: The Case of News-Interview
Discourse." Pp. 163–98 in *Talk at Work: Interaction in Institutional Settings,* ed.
P. Drew and J. Heritage. Cambridge: Cambridge University Press.

Clayman, Steven E., and Virginia Teas Gill. Forthcoming. "Conversation Analysis." In
Handbook of Data Analysis, ed. A. Bryman and M. Hardy. Beverly Hills, CA: Sage
Publications.

Clayman, Steven E., and John Heritage. In press. "Questioning Presidents: Journalistic
Deference and Adversarialness in the Press Conferences of Eisenhower and Reagan."
Journal of Communication 52.

Clayman, Steven E., and Douglas W. Maynard. 1995. "Ethnomethodology and Conversation Analysis." Pp. 1–30 in *Situated Order: Studies in the Social Organization of Talk
and Embodied Activity,* ed. P. ten Have and G. Psathas. Lanham, MD: University Press
of America.

Clayman, Steven E., and Ann Reisner. 1998. "Gatekeeping in Action: Editorial Conferences and Assessments of Newsworthiness." *American Sociological Review* 63: 178–99.

Clough, Patricia T. 1992. *The End(s) of Ethnography.* Thousand Oaks, CA: Sage.

Coleman, James S. 1990. *Foundations of Social Theory.* Cambridge, MA: Belknap Press.

Corsaro, William A. 1981. "Communicative Processes in Studies of Social Organization:
Sociological Approaches to Discourse Analysis." *Text* 1: 5–63.

———. 1982. "Something Old and Something New: The Importance of Prior Ethnography in the Collection and Analysis of Audio-Visual Data." *Sociological Methods and
Research* 11: 145–66.

———. 1996. "Transitions in Early Childhood: The Promise of Comparative, Longitudinal Ethnography." Pp. 419–56 in *Ethnography and Human Development: Context
and Meaning in Social Inquiry,* ed. R. Jessor, A. Colby, and R. A. Shweder. Chicago:
University of Chicago Press.

Coulmas, Florian, ed. 1986. *Direct and Indirect Speech.* Berlin: Mouton de Gruyter.

Coulthard, Malcolm. 1977. *An Introduction to Discourse Analysis.* London: Longman.

Couper-Kuhlen, Elizabeth, and Margret Selting. 1996. "Towards an Interactional Perspective on Prosody and a Prosodic Perspective on Interaction." Pp. 11–56 in *Prosody*

in Conversation: Interactional Studies, ed. E. Couper-Kuhlen and M. Selting. Cambridge: Cambridge University Press.

Crossette, Barbara. 2000. "Most Nations Fail to Supply Safe Blood, W.H.O. Finds." *New York Times,* 7 April.

Cushing, Steven. 1994. *Fatal Words: Communication Clashes and Aircraft Crashes.* Chicago: University of Chicago Press.

Darling, Rosalyn Benjamin. 1979. *Families against Society: A Study of Reactions to Children with Birth Defects.* Beverly Hills, CA: Sage.

———. 1983. "Parent-Professional Interaction: The Roots of Misunderstanding." Pp. 95–121 in *The Family with a Handicapped Child,* ed. M. Seligman. New York: Grune & Stratton.

Davidson, Judy. 1984. "Subsequent Versions of Invitations, Offers, Requests, and Proposals Dealing with Potential or Actual Rejection." Pp. 102–28 in *Structures of Social Action,* ed. J. M. Atkinson and J. Heritage. Cambridge: Cambridge University Press.

Davies, Michele L. 1997. "Shattered Assumptions: Time and the Experience of Long-term HIV Positivity." *Social Science and Medicine* 44: 561–71.

Davis, Fred. 1963. *Passage through Crisis: Polio Victims and Their Families.* Indianapolis: Bobbs-Merrill.

De Bondt, Werner F. M., and Richard Thaler. 1985. "Does the Stock Market Overreact?" *The Journal of Finance* 40: 793–805.

DeBaggio, Thomas. 2000. "Loss of Memory, Loss of Hope." *New York Times,* 25 June.

Denzin, Norman K. 1991. *Images of Postmodern Society.* London: Sage.

Dingwall, Robert. 1997. "Accounts, Interviews and Observations." Pp. 51–65 in *Context and Method in Qualitative Research,* ed. G. Miller and R. Dingwall. London: Sage.

Douglas, Mary. 1986. *How Institutions Think.* Syracuse, NY: Syracuse University Press.

Dowd, Maureen. 1991a. "'Indispensability' of Sununu Is Creating Hard Questions." *New York Times,* 26 June.

———. 1991b. "The Senate and Sexism: Panel's Handling of Harassment Allegation Renews Questions About an All-Male Club." *New York Times,* 8 October.

Drennan, David. 1988. "How to Make the Bad News Less Bad and the Good News Great." *Personnel Management* 20: 40–43.

Drew, Paul. 1984. "Speakers' Reportings in Invitation Sequences." Pp. 152–64 in *Structures of Social Action,* ed. J. M. Atkinson and J. Heritage. Cambridge: Cambridge University Press.

———. 1992. "Contested Evidence in a Courtroom Cross-Examination: The Case of a Trial for Rape." Pp. 470–520 in *Talk at Work: Social Interaction in Institutional Settings,* ed. P. Drew and J. Heritage. Cambridge: Cambridge University Press.

———. 1998. "Complaints about Transgressions and Misconduct." *Research on Language and Social Interaction* 31: 295–325.

Drew, Paul, and John Heritage. 1992. "Analyzing Talk at Work: An Introduction." Pp. 3–65 in *Talk at Work,* ed. P. Drew and J. Heritage. Cambridge: Cambridge University Press.

Drew, Paul, and Elizabeth Holt. 1988. "Complainable Matters: The Use of Idiomatic Expressions in Making Complaints." *Social Problems* 35: 398–417.

———. 1998. "Figures of Speech: Figurative Expressions and the Management of Topic Transition in Conversation." *Language in Society* 27: 495–522.

Dreyfus, Hubert L. 1992. *What Computers Still Can't Do: A Critique of Artificial Reason.* Cambridge, MA: MIT Press.

Duneier, Mitchell. 1999. *Sidewalk.* New York: Farrar, Straus & Giroux.

Duneier, Mitchell, and Harvey Molotch. 1999. "Talking City Trouble: Interactional Vandalism, Social Inequality, and the 'Urban Interaction Problem.'" *American Journal of Sociology* 104: 1263–95.

Duranti, Alessandro. 1988. "The Ethnography of Speaking: Toward a Linguistics of the Praxis." Pp. 210–28 in *Linguistics: The Cambridge Survey,* vol. 4, ed. F. Newmeyer. Cambridge: Cambridge University Press.

———. 1997. *Linguistic Anthropology.* Cambridge: Cambridge University Press.

Eddington, Patrick G. 1997. *Gassed in the Gulf: The Inside Story of the Pentagon-CIA Cover-up of Gulf War Syndrome.* Washington, DC: Insignia.

Edgar, Timothy. 1994. "Self-Disclosure Strategies of the Stigmatized: Strategies and Outcomes for the Revelation of Sexual Orientation." Pp. 221–37 in *Queer Words, Queer Images: Communication and the Construction of Homosexuality,* ed. R. J. Ringer. New York: New York University Press.

Ehrenreich, Barbara. 2001. "Welcome to Cancerland: A Mammogram Leads to a Cult of Pink Kitsch." *Harper's,* November, pp. 43–53.

Ellis, Carolyn. 1993. "'There Are Survivors': Telling a Story of Sudden Death." *The Sociological Quarterly* 34: 711–30.

Elster, Jon. 1989. *Solomonic Judgements: Studies in the Limitations of Rationality.* Cambridge: Cambridge University Press.

Emerson, Robert M. 1998. "On Being Stalked." *Social Problems* 45: 289–314.

Emerson, Robert M., Rachel I. Fretz, and Linda L. Shaw. 1995. *Writing Ethnographic Fieldnotes.* Chicago: University of Chicago Press.

Epstein, Joseph 1999. "Taking the Bypass: A Healthy Man's Nightmare." *The New Yorker,* 12 April, pp. 58–63.

Erickson, Fred, and Jeffrey Schulz. 1982. *The Counselor as Gatekeeper: Social Interaction in Interviews.* New York: Academic Press.

Fairclough, Norman and Ruth Wodak. 1997. "Critical Discourse Analysis." Pp. 258–84 in *Discourse as Social Interaction,* ed. T. A. v. Dijk. London: Sage.

Fallowfield, Lesley. 1991. *Breast Cancer.* London, England: Tavistock/Routledge.

Fine, Gary Alan. 1987. *With the Boys: Little League Baseball and Preadolescent Culture.* Chicago: University of Chicago Press.

Firstman, Richard, and Jamie Talan. 1997. *The Death of Innocents.* New York: Bantam.

Fitzpatrick, Sheila. 1999. *Everyday Stalinism: Ordinary Life in Extraordinary Times: Soviet Russia in the 1930's.* New York: Oxford University Press.

Flaherty, Michael G. 1999. *A Watched Pot: How We Experience Time.* New York: New York University Press.

Ford, Cecilia E., and Sandra A. Thompson. 1996. "Interactional Units in Conversation." Pp. 134–84 in *Interaction and Grammar,* ed. E. Ochs, E. A. Schegloff, and S. A. Thompson. Cambridge: Cambridge University Press.

Frady, Marshall 1996. "An American Family." *The New Yorker,* 29 April, pp. 148–57.

Frank, Arthur W. 1991. *At the Will of the Body: Reflections on Illness.* Boston: Houghton Miflin.

Frankel, Richard M. 2000. "Challenges and Opportunities in Delivering Bad News." *Physician's Quarterly* 25: 1–6.

Frankel, Richard M., and Terry Stein. 1999. "Getting the Most out of the Clinical Encounter: The Four Habits Model." *The Permanente Journal* 3: 79–88.

Freedman, Benjamin. 1997. "Offering Truth: One Ethical Approach to the Uninformed Cancer Patient." Pp. 333–40 in *The Social Medicine Reader,* ed. G. E. Henderson, N. M. P. King, R. P. Strauss, S. E. Estroff, and L. R. Churchill. Durham, NC: Duke University Press.

Freese, Jeremy, and Douglas W. Maynard. 1998. "Prosodic Features of Bad News and Good News in Conversation." *Language in Society* 27: 195–219.

Fujimura, Joan H. 1996. *Crafting Science: A Sociohistory of the Quest for the Genetics of Cancer.* Cambridge, MA: Harvard University Press.

Gagné, Patricia, Richard Tewksbury, and Deanna McGaughey. 1997. "Coming Out and Crossing Over: Identity Formation and Proclamation in a Transgender Community." *Gender & Society* 11: 478–508.

Gans, Herbert. 1962. *The Urban Villagers: Group and Class in the Life of Italian-Americans.* New York: Free Press.

Garfinkel, Harold. 1963. "A Conception of, and Experiments with, 'Trust' as a Condition of Stable Concerted Actions." Pp. 187–238 in *Motivation and Social Interaction,* ed. O. J. Harvey. New York: Ronald Press.

———. 1967. *Studies in Ethnomethodology.* Englewood Cliffs, NJ: Prentice-Hall.

———. 1988. "Evidence for Locally Produced, Naturally Accountable Phenomena of Order, Logic, Reason, Meaning, Method, etc. in and as of the Essential Quiddity of Immortal Ordinary Society (I of IV): An Announcement of Studies." *Sociological Theory* 6: 103–9.

———. 1996. "Ethnomethodology's Program." *Social Psychology Quarterly* 59: 5–21.

Garfinkel, Harold, and D. Lawrence Wieder. 1992. "Two Incommensurable, Asymmetrically Alternate Technologies of Social Analysis." Pp. 175–206 in *Text in Context: Contributions to Ethnomethodology,* ed. G. Watson and R. M. Seiler. Newbury Park, CA: Sage.

Geertz, Clifford. 1973. *The Interpretation of Cultures.* New York: Basic Books.

Gieryn, Thomas F. 1983. "Boundary-Work and the Demarcation of Science from Non-Science: Strains and Interests in Professional Ideologies of Scientists." *American Sociological Review* 48: 781–95.

———. 1998. *Cultural Boundaries of Science: Credibility on the Line.* Chicago: University of Chicago Press.

Gill, Virginia Teas. 1998. "Doing Attributions in Medical Interaction: Patients' Explanations for Illness and Doctors' Responses." *Social Psychology Quarterly* 61: 342–60.

Gill, Virginia Teas, and Douglas W. Maynard. 1995. "On 'Labeling' in Actual Interaction: Delivering and Receiving Diagnoses of Developmental Disabilities." *Social Problems* 42: 11–37.

Girgis, Afaf, and Rob W. Sanson-Fisher. 1995. "Breaking Bad News: Consensus Guidelines for Medical Practitioners." *Journal of Clinical Oncology* 13: 2449–56.

Gladstone, Rick. 1998. "When the News Is Bad, Analysts Feel the Heat." *Wall Street Journal,* 12 July.

Glaser, Barney G. and Anselm L. Strauss. 1964. "Awareness Contexts and Social Interaction." *American Sociological Review* 29: 669–79.

———. 1965. *Awareness of Dying.* Chicago: Aldine.

———. 1967. *The Discovery of Grounded Theory: Strategies for Qualitative Research.* Chicago: Aldine.

Goffman, Erving. 1959. *The Presentation of Self in Everyday Life.* New York: Anchor Books.

———. 1961. "Fun in Games." Pp. 17–81 in *Encounters.* Indianapolis: Bobbs-Merrill.

———. 1971. *Relations in Public: Microstudies of the Public Order.* New York: Harper and Row.

———. 1974. *Frame Analysis: An Essay on the Organization of Experience.* New York: Harper and Row.

———. 1978. "Response Cries." *Language* 54: 787–815.

———. 1979. "Footing." *Semiotica*: 1–29.

———. 1983. "The Interaction Order." *American Sociological Review* 48: 1–17.

Good, Mary-Jo Delveccio, Byron J. Good, Cynthia Schaffer, and Stuart E. Lind. 1990. "American Oncology and the Discourse on Hope." *Culture, Medicine, and Psychiatry* 14: 59–79.

Goodwin, Charles. 1986a. "Audience Diversity, Participation, and Interpretation." *Text* 6: 283–316.

———. 1986b. "Between and Within: Alternative Sequential Treatments of Continuers and Assessments." *Human Studies* 9: 205–17.

———. 1996. "Transparent Vision." Pp. 370–404 in *Interaction and Grammar,* ed. E. Ochs, E. A. Schegloff, and S. A. Thompson. Cambridge: Cambridge University Press.

Goodwin, Charles, and Alessandro Duranti. 1992. "Rethinking Context: An Introduction." Pp. 1–42 in *Rethinking Context: Language as an Interactive Phenomenon,* ed. A. Duranti and C. Goodwin. Cambridge: Cambridge University Press.

Goodwin, Marjorie Harness. 1990. *He-Said-She-Said: Talk as Social Organization among Black Children.* Bloomington: Indiana University Press.

———. 1996. "Informings and Announcements in Their Environment." Pp. 436–61 in *Prosody in Conversation: Interactional Studies,* ed. E. Couper-Kuhlen and M. Selting. Cambridge: Cambridge University Press.

Gordon, Deborah R. 1990. "Embodying Illness, Embodying Cancer." *Culture, Medicine, and Psychiatry* 14: 275–97.

Gordon, Linda. 1988. *Heroes of Their Own Lives: The Politics and History of Family Violence.* New York: Penguin.

Gouldner, Alvin W. 1975. "The Dark Side of the Dialectic: Toward a New Objectivity." *Sociological Inquiry* 46: 3–15.

Greatbatch, David. 1992. "On the Managment of Disagreement between News Interviewees." Pp. 268–301 in *Talk at Work: Interaction in Institutional Settings,* ed. P. Drew and J. Heritage. Cambridge: Cambridge University Press.

Grimshaw, Allen D. 1982. "Sound-Image Data Records for Research on Social Interaction." *Sociological Methods and Research* 11: 121–44.

————. 1989. *Collegial Discourse: Professional Conversation Among Peers.* Norwood, New Jersey: Ablex.

Gubrium, Jaber F. 1975. *Living and Dying at Murray Manor.* New York: St. Martin's Press.

Gubrium, Jaber F., and James A. Holstein. 1997. *The New Language of Qualitative Method.* New York: Oxford University Press.

Gumperz, John. 1982a. *Language and Social Identity.* Cambridge: Cambridge University Press.

————. 1982b. *Discourse Strategies.* Cambridge: Cambridge University Press.

Gurwitsch, Aron. 1964. *The Field of Consciousness.* Pittsburgh: Duquesne University Press.

Hackett, T. P., and A.D. Weisman. 1962. "The Treatment of the Dying." *Current Psychiatric Therapies* 2: 121–216.

Hafferty, Fred. 1991. *Into the Valley: Death and the Socialization of Medical Students.* New Haven: Yale University Press.

Halkowski, Timothy. Forthcoming. "Realizing the Illness: Patients' Narratives of Symptom Discovery." in *Practicing Medicine: Structure and Process in Primary Care Encounters,* ed. J. Heritage and D. W. Maynard. Cambridge: Cambridge University Press.

Hanks, William F. 1996. *Language and Communicative Practices.* Boulder, Colorado: Westview Press.

Harre, Rom, ed. 1986. *The Social Construction of Emotion.* Oxford: Basil Blackwell.

Healy, Kieran. 1999. "The Emergence of HIV in the U.S. Blood Supply: Organizations, Oligations, and the Management of Uncertainty." *Theory and Society* 28: 529–58.

Heath, Christian. 1984. "Talk and Recipiency: Sequential Organization in Speech and Body Movement." Pp. 247–65 in *Structures of Social Action*, edited by J. M. Atkinson and J. Heritage. Cambridge: Cambridge University Press.

————. 1992. "Diagnosis and Assessment in the Medical Consultation." Pp. 235–67 in *Talk at Work: Interaction in Institutional Settings,* ed. P. Drew and J. Heritage. Cambridge: Cambridge University Press.

Heath, Christian, and Paul Luff. 2000. *Technology in Action.* Cambridge: Cambridge University Press.

Heath, Shirley Brice. 1983. *Ways with Words: Language, Life, and Work in Communities and Classrooms.* Cambridge: Cambridge University Press.

Heimer, Carol. 1985. "Allocating Information Costs in a Negotiated Information Order: Interorganizational Constraints on Decision Making in Norwegian Oil Insurance." *Administrative Science Quarterly* 30: 395–417.

————. 1988. "Social Structure, Psychology, and the Estimation of Risk." *Annual Review of Sociology* 14: 491–519.

Heise, David R. 1979. *Understanding Events: Affect and the Construction of Social Action.* Cambridge: Cambridge University Press.

————. 1999. "Controlling Affective Experience Interpersonally." *Social Psychology Quarterly* 62: 4–16.

Henriques, Diana B. 1998. "False Profits for 3 Years at Cendant." *New York Times,* 14 August.

Heritage, John. 1984a. "A Change-of-State Token and Aspects of its Sequential Placement." Pp. 299–345 in *Structures of Social Action: Studies in Conversation Analysis,* ed.
J. M. Atkinson and J. Heritage. Cambridge: Cambridge University Press.
———. 1984b. *Garfinkel and Ethnomethodology.* Cambridge: Polity Press.
Heritage, John, and David Greatbatch. 1991. "On the Institutional Character of Institutional Talk: The Case of News Interviews." Pp. 93–137 in *Talk and Social Structure,*
ed. D. Boden and D. H. Zimmerman. Cambridge: Polity Press.
Heritage, John and Anna Lindström. 1998. "Motherhood, Medicine, and Morality:
Scenes from a Medical Encounter." *Research on Language and Social Interaction* 31:
397–438.
Heritage, John, and Sue Sefi. 1992. "Dilemmas of Advice: Aspects of the Delivery and
Reception of Advice in Interactions Between Health Visitors and First Time Moth-
ers." Pp. 359–417 in *Talk at Work,* ed. P. Drew and J. Heritage. Cambridge: Cam-
bridge University Press.
Heritage, John, and Tanya Stivers. 1999. "Online Commentary in Acute Medical Visits:
A Method of Shaping Patient Expectations." *Social Science and Medicine* 49: 1501–17.
Hessler, Peter 2001. "Boomtown Girl: Finding a New Life in the Golden City." *The New
Yorker,* May 28, pp. 108–119.
Hester, Stephen, and David Francis. 2000. "Ethnomethodology, Conversation Analysis,
and 'Institutional Talk.'" *Text* 20: 391–413.
Hilbert, Richard A. 1984. "The Acultural Dimensions of Chronic Pain: Flawed Reality
Construction and the Problem of Meaning." *Social Problems* 31: 365–78.
———. 1992. *The Classical Roots of Ethnomethodology: Durkheim, Weber, and Garfinkel.*
Chapel Hill: University of North Carolina Press.
Hochschild, Arlie R. 1979. "Emotion Work, Feeling Rules, and Social Structure." *American Journal of Sociology* 87: 336–62.
Holland, Jimmie C. 1989. "'Now We Tell — But How Well?'" *Journal of Clinical Oncology*
7: 557–59.
Holland, Jimmie C., Natalie Geary, Anthony Machini, and Susan Tross. 1987. "An In-
ternational Survey of Physician Attitudes and Practice in Regard to Revealing the Di-
agnosis of Cancer." *Cancer Investigation* 5: 151–54.
Holstein, James A., and Gale Miller. 1993. *Reconsidering Social Constructionism: Debates
in Social Problems Theory.* New York: Aldine de Gruyter.
Holt, Elizabeth. 1993. "The Structure of Death Announcements: Looking on the Bright
Side of Death." *Text* 13: 189–212.
———. 1996. "Reporting on Talk: The Use of Direct Reported Speech in Conversation."
Research on Language and Social Interaction 29: 219–45.
Hopper, Robert. 1990/91. "Ethnography and Conversation Analysis after *Talking Cul-
ture.*" *Research on Language and Social Interaction* 24: 161–70.
Houtkoop-Steenstra, Hanneke. 2000. *Interaction and the Standardized Survey Interview:
The Living Questionnaire.* Cambridge, U.K.: Cambridge University Press.
Huggins, Marlene, Maurice Bloch, Sandi Wiggins, Shelin Adam, Oksana Suchowersky,
Michael Trew, MaryLou Klimek, Cheryl R. Greenberg, Michael Eleff, Louise P.
Thompson, Julie Knight, Patrick MacLeod, Kathleen Girard, Jane Theilmann, Amy

Hedrick, and Michael R. Hayden. 1992. "Predictive Testing for Huntington Disease in Canada." *American Journal of Medical Genetics* 42: 508–15.

Hughes, Everett. 1951. "Work and Self." in *Social Psychology at the Crossroads,* ed. J. H. Rohrer and M. Sherif. New York: Harper and Row.

Husserl, Edmund. 1970a. *Cartesian Mediations: An Introduction to Phenomenology.* Translated by D. Cairns. The Hague: Martinus Nijhoff.

———. 1970b. *The Crisis of European Sciences and Transcendental Phenomenology.* Evanston: Northwestern University Press.

Hutchby, Ian, and Robin Wooffitt. 1998. *Conversation Analysis.* Cambridge, England: Polity Press.

Hymes, Dell. 1974. *Foundations in Sociolinguistics: An Ethnographic Approach.* Philadelphia: University of Pennsylvania Press.

Izraeli, Dafna M., and Todd D. Jick. 1986. "The Art of Saying No: Linking Power to Culture." *Organization Studies* 7: 171–92.

Jacobs, Jerry. 1969. *The Search for Help: A Study of the Retarded Child in the Community.* Washington, DC: University Press of America.

Janofsky, Michael. 1998. "Family of Missing Girl, 13, Is Clinging to Hope." *New York Times,* 7 August.

Jefferson, Gail. 1980. "On 'Trouble-Premonitory' Response to Inquiry." *Sociological Inquiry* 50: 153–85.

———. 1981. "The Abominable 'Ne?': A Working Paper Exploring the Phenomenon of Post-Response Pursuit of Response." Department of Sociology, University of Manchester, Manchester, England.

———. 1984. "On the Organization of Laughter in Talk about Troubles." Pp. 346–69 in *Structures of Social Action,* ed. J. M. Atkinson and J. Heritage. Cambridge: Cambridge University Press.

———. 1985. "On the Interactional Unpackaging of a 'Gloss.'" *Language in Society* 14: 435–66.

———. 1988. "On the Sequential Organization of Troubles-Talk in Ordinary Conversation." *Social Problems* 35: 418–41.

———. 1990. "List Construction as a Task and Interactional Resource." Pp. 63–92 in *Interaction Competence,* ed. G. Psathas. Washington, DC: University Press of America.

Jefferson, Gail, and John R. E. Lee. 1981. "The Rejection of Advice: Managing the Problematic Convergence of a 'Troubles Telling' and a 'Service Encounter.'" *Journal of Pragmatics* 5: 399–422.

Jimerson, Jason B. 1998. "'Who Has Next?' The Symbolic, Rational, and Methodical Use of Norms in Pickup Basketball." *Social Psychology Quarterly* 2: 136–56.

Joas, Hans. 1985. *G. H. Mead: A Contemporary Re-Examination of His Thought.* Cambridge, MA: MIT Press.

Johnson, Dirk. 1996. "Gay Rights Movement Ventures beyond Urban America: Small Illinois City is Latest to Confront the Issues and Emotions Related to Homosexuality." *New York Times,* 21 January.

———. 1998. "Son Abducted 9 Years Ago, Mother Holds onto Hope." *New York Times,* 31 December.

Johnson, Jason B. 1990. "Avianca Transcript Indicates Communication Problem." *Los Angeles Times,* 28 March.

Jones, Charlotte. 1997. "'That's a Good Sign': Encouraging Assessments as a Form of Social Support in Medically Related Encounters." *Health Communication* 9: 119–53.

Katz, Jack. 1999. *How Emotions Work.* Chicago: University of Chicago Press.

Kaufmann, Felix. 1944. *Methodology of the Social Sciences.* New York: Oxford University Press.

Kemper, Theodore D. 1981. "Social Constructionist and Positivist Approaches to the Sociology of Emotions." *American Journal of Sociology* 87: 336–62.

Kennedy, Dana. 1998. "Neil LaBute's Good News." *New York Times,* 16 August.

Kifner, John. 1994. "Neighbors Anyone Would Want, And Most Wanted by F.B.I., Too." *New York Times,* 9 December.

Kinnell, Ann Marie K., and Douglas W. Maynard. 1996. "The Delivery and Receipt of Safer Sex Advice in Pretest Counseling Sessions for HIV and AIDS." *Journal of Contemporary Ethnography* 24: 405–37.

Kitzinger, Celia. 2000. "How to Resist an Idiom." *Research on Language and Social Interaction* 33: 121–54.

Klein, Joe. 1998. "Primary Cad." *The New Yorker,* 7 September, pp. 46–55.

Kleinfield, N. R. 1999. "Life, Death and Managed Care." *New York Times,* 14 November.

Kleinman, Arthur. 1988. *The Illness Narratives: Suffering, Healing, and the Human Condition.* New York: Basic Books.

Knorr-Cetina, Karin D., and Michael Mulkay. 1983. "Introduction: Emerging Principles in Social Studies of Science." Pp. 1–17 in *Science Observed: Perspectives on the Social Study of Science,* ed. K. D. Knorr-Cetina and M. Mulkay. London: Sage Publications.

Krull, John. 1998. "Branch Manager Known for Generosity Killed at Carmel." *Indianapolis Star/News,* 1 May.

Kutner, Jean S., John F. Steiner, Kitty K. Corbett, Dennis W. Jahnigen, and Phoebe L. Barton. 1999. "Information Needs in Terminal Illness." *Social Science and Medicine* 48: 1341–52.

Labov, William. 1972a. *Language in the Inner City: Studies in the Black English Vernacular.* Philadelphia: University of Pennsylvania Press.

———. 1972b. *Sociolinguistic Patterns.* Philadelphia: University of Pennsylvania Press.

Labov, William, and David Fanshel. 1977. *Therapeutic Discourse.* New York: Academic Press.

Lamont, Elizabeth B., and Nicholas A. Christakis. 2001. "Prognostic Disclosure to Patients with Cancer Near the End of Life." *Annals of Internal Medicine* 134: 1096–1105.

Landers, Ann. 2000. "It's Celebrants Job to Spread the Word." *Chicago Tribune,* 11 July.

Latour, Bruno and Steven Woolgar. 1979. *Laboratory Life: The [Social] Construction of Scientific Facts.* Princeton: Princeton University Press.

Lave, Jean, and Etienne Wenger. 1991. *Situated Learning: Legitimate Peripheral Participation.* Cambridge: Cambridge University Press.

Lavin, Cheryl. 1990. "Readers Tell How They Recognized Love." *Wisconsin State Journal* (Madison, WI), 4 February.

Lavin, Danielle. 2002. "Building a Case and Getting Out: Inmate Strategies for Obtaining Parole." Ph.D. diss., Bloomington, Indiana University.

Lavin, Danielle, and Douglas W. Maynard. 2001. "Standardization vs. Rapport: Respondent Laughter and Interviewer Reaction During Telephone Surveys." *American Sociological Review* 66: 453–79.

Leisner, Pat. 1989. "Father, Child Share Pain and Tears Trying to Cope with Baby Mix-Up." *South Bend Tribune* (South Bend, IN), 23 November.

Leppänen, Vesa. 1998. *Structures of District Nurse – Patient Interaction.* Lund, Sweden: Department of Sociology, Lund University.

Lerner, Gene H. 1991. "On the Syntax of Sentences-in-Progress." *Language in Society* 20: 441–58.

———. 1996. "Finding 'Face' in the Preference Structures of Talk-in-Interaction." *Social Psychology Quarterly* 59: 303–321.

Leveton, Lauren B., Harold C. Sox Jr., and Michael A. Stoto. 1995. "HIV and the Blood Supply." Washington D.C.: National Academy Press.

Levine, John M., Lauren B. Resnick, and E. Tory Higgens. 1993. "Social Foundations of Cognition." *Annual Review of Psychology* 44: 585–612.

Levinson, Stephen C. 1979. "Activity Types and Language." *Linguistics* 17: 356–99.

———. 1983. *Pragmatics.* Cambridge: Cambridge University Press.

Liebow, Elliot. 1967. *Tally's Corner.* Boston: Little, Brown.

Lind, Stuart E., Mary-Jo DelVecchio Good, Steven Seidel, Thomas Csordas, and Byron J. Good. 1989. "Telling the Diagnosis of Cancer." *Journal of Clinical Oncology* 7: 583–89.

Linell, Per, and Thomas Luckmann. 1991. "Asymmetries in Dialogue: Some Conceptual Preliminaries." Pp. 1–20 in *Asymmetries in Dialogue,* ed. I. Marková and K. Foppa. Hemel Hempstead, England: Harvester Wheatsheaf.

Linell, Per, and Ragnar Rommetveit. 1998. "The Many Forms and Facets of Morality in Dialogue: Epilogue for the Special Issue." *Research on Language and Social Interaction* 31: 465–73.

Lipton, Helene L. and Bonnie L. Svarstad. 1977. "Sources of Variation in Clinicians' Communication to Parents about Mental Retardation." *American Journal of Mental Deficiency* 82: 155–61.

Livingston, Robert B. 1967. "Brain Circuitry Relating to Complex Behavior." Pp. 499–514 in *The Neurosciences: A Study Program,* ed. G. C. Quarton, T. Melnechuck, and F. O. Schmitt. New York: Rockefeller University Press.

Lo, Bernard, Timothy Quill, and James Tulsky. 1999. "Discussing Palliative Care with Patients." *Annals of Internal Medicine* 130: 744–49.

Local, John. 1996. "Conversational Phonetics: Some Aspects of News Receipts in Everyday Talk." Pp. 177–230 in *Prosody in Conversation: Interactional Studies,* ed. E. Couper-Kuhlen and M. Selting. Cambridge: Cambridge University Press.

Lofland, John. 1981. "Collective Behavior: The Elementary Forms." Pp. 411–46 in *Social Psychology: Sociological Perspectives,* ed. M. Rosenberg and R. Turner. New York: Basic Books.

Long, Susan O., and Bruce D. Long. 1982. "Curable Cancers and Fatal Ulcers: Attitudes Toward Cancer in Japan." *Social Science and Medicine* 16: 2101–8.

Lucas, Mike. 1989. "Wins, Losses No Longer Big Deal for UNH Coach." *Capital Times* (Madison, WI), 9 January.

Luff, Paul, John Hindmarsh, and Christian Heath, eds. 2000. *Workplace Studies: Recovering Work Practice and Informing System Design.* Cambridge: Cambridge University Press.

Lutfey, Karen. 2000. "Social Dimensions of Noncompliance with Medical Treatment Regimens: The Case of Diabetes." Ph.D. diss., Bloomington, Indiana University.

Lutfey, Karen, and Douglas W. Maynard. 1998. "Bad News in Oncology: How Physician and Patient Talk about Death and Dying without Using Those Words." *Social Psychology Quarterly* 61: 321–41.

Lynch, Michael. 1993. *Scientific Practice and Ordinary Action: Ethnomethodology and Social Studies of Science.* Cambridge: Cambridge University Press.

Lyons, John. 1971. *Introduction to Theoretical Linguistics.* Cambridge: Cambridge University Press.

MacIntyre, Sally. 1976. "'Who Wants Babies' The Social Construction of 'Instincts.'" Pp. 150–73 in *Sexual Divisions and Society: Process and Change,* ed. D. L. Baker and S. Allen. London: Tavistock.

Macrae, Gillian. 1990. "The Patient's View: When the News is Not So Good." *Palliative Medicine* 4: 143–45.

Maguire, Peter, Susan Fairbairn, and Charles Fletcher. 1986. "Consultation Skills of Young Doctors." *British Medical Journal* 292: 1573–78.

Maguire, Peter, and Ann Faulkner. 1988. "Communicate with Cancer Patients: Handling Bad News and Difficult Questions." *British Medical Journal*: 907–9.

Mandelbaum, Jenny. 1993. "Assigning Responsibility in Conversational Storytelling: The Interactional Construction of Reality." *Text* 13: 247–66.

Mandelbaum, Jenny, and Anita Pomerantz. 1991. "What Drives Social Action." Pp. 151–166 in *Understanding Face-to-Face Interaction,* ed. K. Tracy. Hillsdale, NJ: Lawrence Erlbaum.

Manzo, John. 1996. "Taking Turns and Taking Sides: Opening Scenes from Two Jury Deliberations." *Social Psychology Quarterly* 59: 107–25.

Margolick, David. 1995. "Court Told Simpson Wasn't Curious about How Ex-Wife Died." *New York Times,* 17 February.

Marková, Ivana, and Klaus Foppa. 1991. *Asymmetries in Dialogue.* Hemel Hempstead, England: Harvester Wheatsheaf.

Marlaire, Courtney L., and Douglas W. Maynard. 1990. "Standardized Testing as an Interactional Phenomenon." *Sociology of Education* 63: 83–101.

Maynard, Douglas W. 1984. *Inside Plea Bargaining: The Language of Negotiation.* New York: Plenum Press.

———. 1989a. "Notes on the Delivery and Reception of Diagnostic News Regarding Mental Disabilities." Pp. 54–67 in *The Interactional Order: New Directions in the Study of Social Order,* ed. D. T. Helm, W. T. Anderson, A. J. Meehan, and A. W. Rawls. New York: Irvington.

———. 1989b. "On the Ethnography and Analysis of Discourse in Institutional Settings." in *New Perspectives on Social Problems,* ed. J. A. Holstein and G. Miller. Greenwich, CT: JAI Press.

———. 1991a. "Bearing Bad News in Clinical Settings." Pp. 143–72 in *Progress in Communication Sciences,* vol. 10, ed. B. Dervin. Norwood, NJ: Ablex.

———. 1991b. "Deliveries of Diagnosis and Problems of Meaning." Paper presented at conference on Current Work in Ethnomethodology and Conversation Analysis, University of Amsterdam, The Netherlands, July. Manuscript.

———. 1991c. "Interaction and Asymmetry in Clinical Discourse." *American Journal of Sociology* 97: 448–95.

———. 1991d. "The Perspective Display Series and the Delivery and Receipt of Diagnostic News." Pp. 164–92 in *Talk and Social Structure*, ed. D. Boden and D. H. Zimmerman. Cambridge: Polity Press.

———. 1992. "On Clinicians' Co-Implicating Recipients in the Delivery of Diagnostic News." Pp. 331–58 in *Talk at Work: Interaction in Institutional Settings*, ed. P. Drew and J. Heritage. Cambridge: Cambridge University Press.

———. 1997. "How to Tell Patients Bad News: The Strategy of 'Forecasting.'" *Cleveland Clinic Journal of Medicine* 64: 181–82.

———. 1998. "Praising versus Blaming the Messenger." *Research on Language and Social Interaction* 31: 359–95.

Maynard, Douglas W., and Steven E. Clayman. 1991. "The Diversity of Ethnomethodology." *Annual Review of Sociology* 17: 385–418.

Maynard, Douglas W., and Richard M. Frankel. Forthcoming. "On the Edge of Rationality in the Primary Care Encounter: Bad News, Good News, and Uncertainty." In *Practicing Medicine: Talk and Action in Primary Care Encounters,* ed. J. Heritage and D. W. Maynard. Cambridge: Cambridge University Press.

Maynard, Douglas W., Hanneke Houtkoop-Steenstra, Nora Cate Schaeffer, and Hans van der Zouwen. 2002. *Standardization and Tacit Knowledge: Interaction and Practice in the Survey Interview.* New York: John Wiley.

Maynard, Douglas W. and John Manzo. 1993. "On the Sociology of Justice: Theoretical Notes from an Actual Jury Deliberation." *Sociological Theory* 11: 171–193.

Maynard, Douglas W., and Courtney L. Marlaire. 1992. "Good Reasons for Bad Testing Performance: The Interactional Substrate of Educational Testing." *Qualitative Sociology* 15: 177–202.

Maynard, Douglas W., and Marilyn R. Whalen. 1995. "Language, Action, and Social Interaction." Pp. 149–75 in *Sociological Perspectives in Social Psychology,* ed. K. Cook, G. Fine, and J. House. Boston: Allyn & Bacon.

McClenahen, Lochlan, and John Lofland. 1976. "Bearing Bad News: Tactics of the Deputy U.S. Marshal." *Sociology of Work and Occupations* 3: 251–72.

McDonald, Steven, Patti Ann McDonald, and E. J. Kahn, III. 1989. *The Steven McDonald Story.* New York: Donald I. Fine, Inc.

McGovern, Raymond L. 1997. Foreword to P. G. Eddington, *Gassed in the Gulf: The Inside Story of the Pentagon-CIA Cover-up of Gulf War Syndome.* Washington, DC: Insignia.

McIntosh, Jim. 1977. *Communication and Awareness in a Cancer Ward.* New York: Prodist.

Mead, George Herbert. 1934. *Mind, Self, and Society.* Chicago: University of Chicago Press.

Meehan, Albert J. 1981. "Some Conversational Features of the Use of Medical Terms by Doctors and Patients." in *Medical Work: Realities and Routines,* ed. P. Atkinson and C. Heath. London: Gower Press.

Mehan, Hugh. 1991. "The School's Work of Sorting Students." Pp. 71–90 in *Talk and Social Structure,* ed. D. Boden and D. H. Zimmerman. Cambridge: Polity Press.

Mendoza, Martha. 1999. "Remains Are Those of Missing Girl, FBI Says." *San Francisco Gate News* and the Associated Press, 14 January.

Merleau-Ponty, M. 1962. *Phenomenology of Perception.* London: Routledge & Kegan Paul.

Miller, Gale. 1994. "Toward Ethnographies of Institutional Discourse: Proposal and Suggestions." *Journal of Contemporary Ethnography* 23: 280–306.

Miller, Gale, and David Silverman. 1995. "Troubles Talk and Counseling Discourse: A Comparative Study." *The Sociological Quarterly* 36: 725–47.

Moerman, Michael. 1988. *Talking Culture: Ethnography and Conversation Analysis.* Philadelphia: University of Pennsylvania Press.

Monk, Ray. 1991. *Wittgenstein: The Duty of Genius.* New York: Penguin Books.

Moore, Robert, and Douglas W. Maynard. 2002. "Achieving Understanding in the Standardized Survey Interview: Repair Sequences." Pp. 281–311 in *Standardization and Tacit Knowledge: Interaction and Practice in the Survey Interview,* ed. D. W. Maynard, H. Houtkoop-Steenstra, N. C. Schaeffer, and H. van der Zouwen. New York: Wiley Press.

Nelson, Christian Kjaer. 1994. "Ethnomethodological Positions on the Use of Ethnographic Data in Conversation Analytic Research." *Journal of Contemporary Ethnography* 23: 307–29.

Novack, Dennis, Robin Plume, Raymond L. Smith, Herbert Ochitil, Gary R. Morrow, and John M. Bennett. 1979. "Changes in Physicians' Attitudes toward Telling the Cancer Patient." *Journal of the American Medical Association* 241: 897–900.

O'Hara, Vicki. 1996. "Diplomatic Immunity." In National Public Radio Morning Edition Transcripts, 7 January. Landover MD: Federal Document Clearing House.

O'Neal, Edgar C., Douglas W. Levine, and James F. Frank. 1979. "Reluctance to Transmit Bad News When the Recipient Is Unknown: Experiments in Five Nations." *Social Behavior and Personality* 7: 39–48.

Ochs, Elinor. 1979. "Introduction: What Child Language Can Contribute to Pragmatics." Pp. 1–17 in *Developmental Pragmatics,* ed. E. Ochs and B. B. Schieffelin. New York: Academic Press.

Oken, D. 1961. "What to Tell Cancer Patients: A Study of Medical Attitudes." *Journal of the American Medical Association* 175: 1120–28.

Olshansky, Simon. 1962. "Chronic Sorrow: A Response to Having a Mentally Defective Child." *Social Casework* 43: 191–94.

Parker, Ian. 2001. "Dept. of Memory: Where Were You, Really?" *The New Yorker,* 8 October, p. 32.

Parkes, Colin M. 1974. "Comment: Communication and Cancer—A Social Psychiatrist's View." *Social Science and Medicine* 8: 189–90.

Parsons, Talcott. 1951. *The Social System.* New York: Free Press.

Peräkylä, Anssi. 1991. "Hope Work in the Care of Seriously Ill Patients." *Qualitative Health Research* 1: 407–33.

———. 1997. "Reliability and Validity in Research Based on Tapes and Transcripts."

Pp. 201–20 in *Qualitative Research: Theory, Method and Practice,* ed. D. Silverman. London: Sage.

———. 1995. *AIDS Counselling: Institutional Interaction and Clinical Practice.* Cambridge: Cambridge University Press.

———. 1998. "Authority and Accountability: The Delivery of Diagnosis in Primary Health Care." *Social Psychology Quarterly* 61: 301–20.

Perrow, Charles, and Mauro F. Guillén. 1990. *The AIDS Disaster.* New Haven: Yale University Press.

Pilkington, Neil W., and Anthony R. D'Augelli. 1995. "Victimization of Lesbian, Gay, and Bisexual Youth in Community Settings." *Journal of Community Psychology* 23: 34–56.

Pillemer, D. B. 1984. "Flashbulb Memories of the Assassination Attempt on President Reagan." *Cognition* 16: 63–80.

Plashke, Bill. 1997. "The Fall Guy: Robinson Came Away with a Moral Victory." *Los Angeles Times,* 18 December.

Polanyi, Michael. 1958. *Personal Knowledge: Towards a Post-Critical Philosophy.* Chicago: University of Chicago Press.

Pollner, Melvin. 1987. *Mundane Reason: Reality in Everyday and Sociological Discourse.* Cambridge: Cambridge University Press.

Pollner, Melvin, and Robert M. Emerson. 1999. "Ethnomethodology and Ethnography." Department of Sociology, the University of California, Los Angeles. Manuscript.

Pomerantz, Anita. 1978a. "Compliment Responses: Notes on the Co-Operation of Multiple Constraints." Pp. 79–112 in *Studies in the Organization of Conversational Interaction,* ed. J. Schenkein. New York: Academic Press.

———. 1978b. "Attributions of Responsibility: Blamings." *Sociology* 12: 115–21.

———. 1980. "Telling My Side: 'Limited Access' as a 'Fishing' Device." *Sociological Inquiry* 50: 186–98.

———. 1984a. "Agreeing and Disagreeing with Assessments: Some Features of Preferred/Dispreferred Turn Shapes." Pp. 57–101 in *Structures of Social Action: Studies in Conversation Analysis,* ed. J. M. Atkinson and J. Heritage. Cambridge: Cambridge University Press.

———. 1984b. "Pursuing a Response." Pp. 152–63 in *Structures of Social Action: Studies in Conversation Analysis,* ed. J. M. Atkinson and J. Heritage. Cambridge: Cambridge University Press.

———. 1986. "Extreme Case Formulations: A Way of Legitimizing Claims." *Human Studies* 9: 219–29.

———. 1990/91. "Mental Concepts in the Analysis of Social Action." *Research on Language and Social Interaction* 24: 299–310.

Potter, Jonathan. 1997. "Discourse Analysis as a Way of Analysing Naturally Occurring Talk." Pp. 144–60 in *Qualitative Research: Theory, Method and Practice,* ed. D. Silverman. London: Sage.

———. 1998. "Cognition as Context (Whose Cognition?)." *Research on Language and Social Interaction* 31: 29–44.

Psathas, George. 1995. *Conversation Analysis: The Study of Talk-in-Interaction.* Thousand Oaks, CA: Sage Publications.

Ptacek, J. T., and Tara L. Eberhardt. 1996. "Breaking Bad News: A Review of the Literature." *Journal of the American Medical Association* 276: 496–502.

Purdum, Todd. 1996. "Ickes to Leave His White House Post." *New York Times,* 12 November.

Purdy, Matthew. 1996. "Farewell to a Slain Officer and His Father-in-law." *New York Times,* 28 December.

Quill, Timothy E. 1991. "Bad News: Delivery, Dialogue, and Dilemmas." *Archives of Internal Medicine* 151: 463–68.

Quint, Jeanne C. 1965. "Institutionalized Practices of Information Control." *Psychiatry* 2: 119–32.

Rawls, Anne W. 1996. "Durkheim's Epistemology: The Neglected Argument." *American Journal of Sociology* 102: 430–82.

———. 2001. "Durkheim's Treatment of Practice: Concrete Practice vs. Representations as the Foundation of Reason." *Journal of Classical Sociology* 1: 33–68.

Raymond, Geoff. 2000. "The Structure of Responding: Type-conforming and Nonconforming Responses to Yes/No Type Interrogatives." Ph.D. diss., University of California, Los Angeles.

Resnik, Susan. 1999. *Blood Saga: Hemophilia, AIDS, and the Survival of a Community.* Berkeley: University of California Press.

Richardson, Laurel. 1991. "Postmodern Social Theory: Representational Practices." *Sociological Theory* 9: 173–79.

Rinken, Sebastian. 1997. "After Diagnosis: HIV, the Prospect of Finitude, and Biographical Self-Construction." Working Paper SPS no. 97/10. European University Institute, Florence, Italy.

Roberts, Felicia D. 1999. *Talking about Treatment: Recommendations for Breast Cancer Adjuvant Therapy.* New York: Oxford University Press.

Roberts, Karlene H., and Charles A. O'Reilly, III. 1974. "Failures in Upward Communication in Organizations." *Academy of Management Journal* 17: 205–15.

Rorty, Richard. 1979. *Philosophy and the Mirror of Nature.* Princeton: Princeton University Press.

Rosen, Sidney, Richard J. Grandison, and John E. Stewart, III. 1974. "Discriminatory Buckpassing: Delegating Transmission of Bad News." *Organizational Behavior and Human Performance* 12: 249–63.

Rosenbaum, David E. 2001. "Washington Memo: For Bush, a Chronicle of Bad News Foretold." *New York Times,* 19 March.

Rosenbaum, James E., Shazia Rafiullah Miller, and Melinda Scott Krei. 1996. "Gatekeeping in an Era of More Open Gates: High School Counselors' Views of Their Influence on Students' College Plans." *American Journal of Education* 104: 257–79.

Rotheram-Borus, Mary J. and Joyce Hunter. 1994. "Suicidal Behavior and Gay-Related Stress among Gay and Bisexual Male Adolescents." *Journal of Adolescent Research* 9: 498–508.

Rubin, David C. and Marc Kozin. 1984. "Vivid Memories." *Cognition* 16: 81–95.

Ryle, Gilbert. 1949. *The Concept of Mind*. New York: Barnes & Noble.

Sack, Kevin, and Frank Bruni. 2000. "How Gore Stopped Short on His Way to Concede." *New York Times,* 9 November.

Sacks, Harvey. 1972. "An Initial Investigation of the Usability of Conversational Data for Doing Sociology." Pp. 31–74 in *Studies in Social Interaction,* ed. D. Sudnow. New York: Free Press.

———. 1975. "Everyone Has to Lie." Pp. 57–80 in *Sociocultural Dimensions of Language Use,* ed. M. Sanches and B. G. Blount. New York: Academic Press.

———. 1984a. "Notes on Methodology." Pp. 21–27 in *Structures of Social Action,* ed. J. M. Atkinson and J. Heritage. Cambridge: Cambridge University Press.

———. 1984b. "On Doing 'Being Ordinary.'" Pp. 413–29 in *Structures of Social Action,* ed. J. M. Atkinson and J. Heritage. Cambridge: Cambridge University Press.

———. 1987. "On the Preferences for Agreement and Contiguity in Sequences in Conversation." Pp. 54–69 in *Talk and Social Organisation,* ed. G. Button and J. R. E. Lee. Clevedon, England: Multilingual Matters.

———. 1992a. *Lectures on Conversation,* vol. 1, ed. G. Jefferson. Oxford, England: Basil Blackwell.

———. 1992b. *Lectures on Conversation,* vol. 2, ed. G. Jefferson. Oxford: Blackwell.

Sacks, Harvey, and Emanuel A. Schegloff. 1979. "Two Preferences in the Organization of Reference to Persons in Conversation and Their Interaction." Pp. 15–21 in *Everyday Language: Studies in Ethnomethodology,* ed. G. Psathas. New York: Irvington.

Sacks, Harvey, Emanuel A. Schegloff, and Gail Jefferson. 1974. "A Simplest Systematics for the Organization of Turn-Taking for Conversation." *Language* 50: 696–735.

Schaeffer, Nora Cate. 1991. "Conversation with a Purpose — Or Conversation? Interaction in the Standardized Survey." Pp. 367–91 in *Measurement Errors in Surveys,* edited by P. P. Biemer, R. M. Groves, L. E. Lyberg, N. A. Mathiowetz, and S. Sudman. New York: John Wiley & Sons.

Schaeffer, Nora Cate, and Douglas W. Maynard. 1996. "From Paradigm to Prototype and Back Again: Interactive Aspects of 'Cognitive Processing' in Standardized Survey Interviews." Pp. 75–88 in *Answering Questions: Methodology for Determining Cognitive and Communicating Processes in Survey Research,* ed. N. Schwarz and S. Sudman. San Francisco: Jossey-Bass.

Scheff, T. J. 1979. *Catharsis in Healing, Ritual, and Drama*. Berkeley: University of California Press.

Schegloff, Emanuel A. 1979. "Identification and Recognition in Telephone Openings." Pp. 23–78 in *Everyday Language,* ed. G. Psathas. New York: Irvington.

———. 1986. "The Routine as Achievement." *Human Studies* 9: 111–51.

———. 1987a. "Between Macro and Micro: Contexts and Other Connections." Pp. 207–34 in *The Micro-Macro Link,* ed. J. Alexander, R. M. B. Giesen, and N. Smelser. Berkeley: University of California Press.

———. 1987b. "Some Sources of Misunderstanding in Talk-in-Interaction." *Linguistics* 25: 201–18.

———. 1987c. "Some Sources of Misunderstanding in Talk-in-Interaction." *Linguistics* 25: 201–18.

———. 1988a. "Goffman and the Analysis of Conversation." Pp. 89–135 in *Erving Goffman: Exploring the Interaction Order,* ed. P. Drew and A. Wootton. Cambridge: Polity Press.

———. 1988b. "On an Actual Virtual Servo-Mechanism for Guessing Bad News: A Single Case Conjecture." *Social Problems* 35: 442–57.

———. 1991a. "Conversation Analysis and Socially Shared Cognition." Pp. 150–171 in *Perspectives on Socially Shared Cognition,* ed. L. B. Resnick, J. M. Levine, and S. D. Teasley. Washington, DC: American Psychological Association.

———. 1991b. "Reflections on Talk and Social Structure." Pp. 44–70 in *Talk and Social Structure,* ed. D. Boden and D. H. Zimmerman. Berkeley: University of California Press.

———. 1992a. Introduction. Pp. ix–lxii in Harvey Sacks, *Lectures on Conversation,* vol. 1, ed. G. Jefferson. Oxford: Basil Blackwell.

———. 1992b. Introduction. Pp. ix–lii in Harvey Sacks, *Lectures on Conversation,* vol. 2, ed. G. Jefferson. Oxford: Basil Blackwell.

———. 1996. "Issues of Relevance for Discourse Analysis: Contingency in Action, Interaction and Co-Participant Context." Pp. 3–35 in *Computational and Conversational Discourse: Burning Issues—An Interdisciplinary Account,* ed. E. H. Hovy and D. R. Scott. Berlin: Springer-Verlag.

———. 1997. "Discourse, Pragmatics, Conversation Analysis." *Discourse Studies* 1: 405–35.

———. 1998. "Reply to Wetherell." *Discourse & Society* 9: 413–16.

———. 1999. "'Schegloff's Texts' as 'Billig's Data': A Critical Reply." *Discourse & Society* 10: 558–72.

Schegloff, Emanuel A., Gail Jefferson, and Harvey Sacks. 1977. "The Preference for Self-Correction in the Organization of Repair in Conversation." *Language* 53: 361–82.

Schegloff, Emanuel A., and Harvey Sacks. 1973. "Opening Up Closings." *Semiotica* 8: 289–327.

Schellhardt, Timothy D. 1996. "Employees Dislike Reviews; Bosses Look for Alternatives." *Wall Street Journal,* 19 November.

Schemo, Diana Jean. 1999. "The Soldier: Fighting Heartache, A Family Endures G.I. Son's Capture." *New York Times,* 24 April.

Schmalz, Jeffery. 1992. "Holidays and the Bad Tidings of H.I.V." *New York Times,* 31 December.

Schmitt, Eric. 1999. "Two Victims in U.S. Raid Reportedly Were Spies." *New York Times,* 25 June.

Schoene-Seifert, Bettina, and James F. Childress. 1986. "How Much Should the Cancer Patient Know and Decide." *CA—A Cancer Journal for Clinicians* 36: 85–94.

Schragg, Bruce. 1987. "About Men: A Degree of Detachment." *New York Times Magazine,* 26 July, 48.

Schutz, Alfred. 1962. *Collected Papers I: The Problem of Social Reality.* The Hague: Martinus Nijhoff.

———. 1964. *Collected Papers II: Studies in Social Theory.* The Hague: Martinus Nijhoff.

Sciulli, David. 1992. "Weaknesses in Rational Choice Theory's Contribution to Comparative Research." Pp. 161–80 in *Rational Choice Theory: Advocacy and Critique*, ed. J. S. Coleman and T. J. Fararo. Newbury Park, CA: Sage.

Scott, Derek, and Vicente Ponsoda. 1996. "The Role of Positive and Negative Affect in Flashbulb Memory." *Psychological Reports* 79: 467–73.

Seale, Clive. 1991. "Communication and Awareness about Death: A Study of a Random Sample of Dying Patients." *Social Science and Medicine* 32: 943–52.

Sharrock, Wes, and Jeff Coulter. 1998. "On What We Can See." *Theory & Psychology* 8: 147–64.

Sheckler, Jackie. 1998. "Rare Disorder Doesn't Slow Down Bloomington Teen." *Herald-Times* (Bloomington, IN), 7 August.

Shenon, Philip. 1996. "Czechs Say They Warned U.S. of Chemical Weapons in Gulf." *New York Times*, 19 October.

Shibutani, Tamotsu. 1961. *Society and Personality: An Interactionist Approach to Social Psychology*. Englewood Cliffs, NJ: Prentice-Hall, Inc.

Shilts, Randy. 1987. *And the Band Played On*. New York: St. Martin's Press.

Siebert, Charles 1995. "The DNA We've Been Dealt." *New York Times Magazine*, 17 September, pp. 50–104.

Silverman, David. 1993. *Interpreting Qualitative Data: Methods for Analysing Talk, Text, and Interaction*. London: Sage.

———. 1997. *Discourses of Counselling: HIV Counselling as Social Interaction*. London: Sage.

———. 1998. *Harvey Sacks: Social Science and Conversation Analysis*. New York: Oxford University Press.

Simers, T. J. 1994. "Business as Usual for Rams." *Los Angeles Times*, 7 August.

Simmel, Georg. 1950. "The Secret Society." Pp. 345–76 in *The Sociology of Georg Simmel*, ed. K. H. Wolff. New York: Free Press.

Singer, Stacey. 1988. "Death in an Instant: Teen Said Gun Wasn't Loaded." *Capital Times* (Madison, WI), 7 September.

Smith, Linda F. 1998. "Medical Paradigms for Counseling: Giving Clients Bad News." *Clinical Law Review* 4: 391.

Souhami, R. L. 1978. "Teaching What to Say about Cancer." *The Lancet*: 935–36.

Spector, Malcolm, and John Kitsuse. 1977. *Constructing Social Problems*. Menlo Park, CA: Cummings.

Spencer, J. William. 1994. "Mutual Relevance of Ethnography and Discourse." *Journal of Contemporary Ethnography* 23: 267–79.

Sproull, Lee, and Sara Kiesler. 1986. "Reducing Social Context Cues: Electronic Mail in Organizational Communication." *Management Science*: 1492–1512.

Starr, Douglas. 1998. *Blood: An Epic History of Medicine and Commerce*. New York: Alfred A. Knopf.

Stivers, Tanya. 1998. "Pre-diagnostic Commentary in Veterinarian-Client Interaction." *Research on Language and Social Interaction* 31: 241–77.

Stubbs, Michael. 1983. *Discourse Analysis: The Sociolinguistic Analysis of Natural Language*. Oxford: Blackwell.

Suchman, Anthony L., Kathryn Markakis, Howard B. Beckman, and Richard Frankel.

1997. "A Model of Empathic Communication in the Medical Interview." *Journal of the American Medical Association* 277: 678–82.

Sudnow, David. 1967. *Passing On: The Social Organization of Dying.* Englewood Cliffs, NJ: Prentice-Hall.

Sullivan, Andrew. 1996. "When Plague Ends: Notes on the Twilight of an Epidemic." *New York Times Magazine,* 10 November, pp. 52–84.

Surbone, Antonella. 1997. "Truth Telling to the Patient." Pp. 326–30 in *The Social Medicine Reader,* ed. G. E. Henderson, N. M. P. King, R. P. Strauss, S. E. Estroff, and L. R. Churchill. Durham, NC: Duke University Press.

Sussman, Stephanie W., and Lee Sproull. 1999. "Straight Talk: Delivering Bad News through Electronic Communication." *Information Systems Research* 10: 150–66.

Svarstad, Bonnie L., and Helene L. Lipton. 1977. "Informing Parents about Mental Retardation: A Study of Professional Communication and Parent Acceptance." *Social Science and Medicine* 11: 645–51.

Taylor, Archer. 1987. "A Classification of Formula Tales." *Journal of American Folklore* XLVI: 77–92.

Taylor, Kathryn M. 1988. "'Telling Bad News': Physicians and the Disclosure of Undesirable Information." *Sociology of Health & Illness* 10: 103–32.

ten Have, Paul. 1999. *Doing Conversation Analysis.* London: Sage Publications.

Terasaki, Alene. 1976. "Pre-Announcement Sequences in Conversation." Social Science Working Paper 99. School of Social Sciences, University of California: June.

Tesser, Abraham and Sidney Rosen. 1975. "The Reluctance to Transmit Bad News." Pp. 192–232 in *Advances in Experimental Social Psychology,* vol. 8, ed. L. Berkowitz. New York: Academic Press.

Tracy, Karen. 1998. "Analyzing Context: Framing the Discussion." *Research on Language and Social Interaction* 31: 1–28.

Turner, Victor. 1969. *The Ritual Process: Structure and Anti-Structure.* Chicago: Aldine.

Tversky, Amos, and Daniel Kahneman. 1974. "Judgment under Uncertainty: Heuristics and Biases." *Science* 185: 1124–31.

———. 1981. "The Framing of Decisions and the Psychology of Choice." *Science* 211: 453–58.

Uchitelle, Louis, and N. R. Kleinfield. 1996. "On the Battlefields of Business, Millions of Casualties." *New York Times,* 3 March.

Ulmer, Jeffery T. 1997. *Social Worlds of Sentencing: Court Communities under Sentencing Guidelines.* Albany: State University of New York Press.

van Dijk, Teun. 1985. *Handbook of Discourse Analysis.* 4 vols. London: Academic Press.

———. 1999. "Critical Discourse Analysis and Conversation Analysis." *Discourse & Society* 10: 459–60.

van Gennep, Arnold. 1909. *The Rites of Passage.* London: Routledge and Kegan Paul.

van Maanen, John. 1995. *Representation in Ethnography.* Thousand Oaks, CA: Sage.

van Oss, Alex. 1998. "Reincarnation: Tibetan Buddhism." National Public Radio, Weekend Edition, Saturday, January 10. Transcript.

Volosinov, V. N. 1973. *Marxism and the Philosophy of Language.* Cambridge, MA: Harvard University Press.

Vygotsky, Lev. 1986. *Thought and Language.* Cambridge, MA: MIT Press.

Wambaugh, Joseph. 1989. *The Blooding.* New York: Bantam.

Watson, D. R. 1978. "Categorization, Authorization and Blame Negotiation in Conversation." *Sociology* 12: 105–13.

Watson, Rod. 1997. "Some General Reflections on 'Categorization' and 'Sequence' in the Analysis of Conversation." Pp. 49–75 in *Culture in Action: Studies in Membership Categorization Analysis,* ed. S. Hester and P. Eglin. Lanham, MD: University Press of America.

———. 2000. "The Character of 'Institutional Talk': A Response to Hester and Francis." *Text* 20: 377–89.

West, Candace. 1996. "Ethnography and Orthography: A (Modest) Methodological Proposal." *Journal of Contemporary Ethnography* 25: 327–52.

West, Candace, and Richard M. Frankel. 1991. "Miscommunication in Medicine." Pp. 166–94 in *'Miscommunication' and Problematic Talk,* ed. N. Coupland, H. Giles, and J. M. Wiemann. Newbury Park, CA: Sage.

West, Morris. 1994. "Time is Not the Enemy." *Parade Magazine,* 15 April, pp. 24–25.

Wetherell, Margaret. 1998. "Positioning and Interpretative Repertoires: Conversation Analysis and Post-Structuralism in Dialogue." *Discourse & Society* 9: 387–412.

Whalen, Jack, and Don H. Zimmerman. 1998. "Observations on the Display and Management of Emotion in Naturally Occurring Activities: The Case of 'Hysteria' in Calls to 9-1-1." *Social Psychology Quarterly* 61: 141–59.

Whalen, Jack, Don H. Zimmerman, and Marilyn R. Whalen. 1988. "When Words Fail: A Single Case Analysis." *Social Problems* 35: 335–62.

Whalen, Marilyn, and Don H. Zimmerman. 1990. "Describing Trouble: Practical Epistemology in Citizen Calls to the Police." *Language in Society* 19: 465–92.

Whyte, William F. 1943. *Street Corner Society.* Chicago: University of Chicago Press.

Wikler, Lyn, Mona Wasow, and Elaine Hatfield. 1981. "Chronic Sorrow Revisited: Parent vs. Professional Depiction of the Adjustment of Parents of Mentally Retarded Children." *American Journal of Orthopsychiatry* 51: 63–70.

Wilkinson, Alec 1992. "Annals of Crime: A Violent Act—I." *The New Yorker,* 8 June, pp. 40–78.

Wilson, Thomas P. 1991. "Social Structures and the Sequential Organization of Interaction." Pp. 22–43 in *Talk and Social Structure,* ed. D. Boden and D. Zimmerman. Cambridge: Polity Press.

Wittgenstein, Ludwig. 1953. *Philosophical Investigations.* New York: Macmillan.

Wooffitt, Robin. 1992. *Telling Tales of the Unexpected: The Organization of Factual Discourse.* London: Harvester Wheatsheaf.

Woolgar, Steve. 1988. *Science, the Very Idea.* London: Ellis Horwood and Tavistock Publications.

Wright, D. B. 1993. "Recall of the Hillsborough Disaster Over Time: Systematic Biases of 'Flashbulb' Memories." *Applied Cognitive Psychology* 7: 129–38.

Wright, Daniel B. and George D. Gaskell. 1995. "Flashbulb Memories: Conceptual and Methodological Issues." *Memory* 3: 67–80.

Zimmerman, Don H. 1988. "On Conversation: The Conversation Analytic Perspective." Pp. 406–432 in *Communication Yearbook 11.* Newbury Park, CA: Sage.

———. 1992. "The Interactional Organization of Calls for Emergency Assistance."

Pp. 418–469 in *Talk at Work: Social Interaction in Institutional Settings,* ed. P. Drew and J. Heritage. Cambridge: Cambridge University Press.

Zimmerman, Don H., and Deirdre Boden. 1991. "Structure-in-Action: An Introduction." Pp. 3–21 in *Talk and Social Structure,* ed. D. Boden and D. H. Zimmerman. Cambridge: Polity Press.

Zimmerman, Don H., and Melvin Pollner. 1970. "The Everyday World as a Phenomenon." Pp. 80–103 in *Understanding Everyday Life: Toward the Reconstruction of Sociological Knowledge,* ed. J. D. Douglas. Chicago: Aldine.

AUTHOR INDEX

SUBJECT INDEX

accent of reality, 5
adjacency pairs, 261, 271n.11
ADL. *See* attitude of daily life
affinity, 65; HIV counseling and, 192–93; interactional detail and, 76–77; limited, 65, 73–77, 192–93; mutual, 67–68; settings and, 73–74
agency: bad news and, 207–12; causal texture and, 32; good news and, 201–7
agreement, 262–63; good news agency and, 207; positive assessment and, 172; prior, 89; rational choice and, 238; token, 223
AIDS. *See* HIV virus
American Red Cross, 236, 239, 241
analytic control, 70–71
announcement: agency and, 32, 201–12; asymmetry and, 30–32; blaming messenger and, 52–54; clinicians and, 79–80 (*see also* clinicians); death and, 42–43, 132; disorientation and, 12–15; first-party news and, 138–48; HIV and, 66–67; in-course modification and, 105–7; joking, 52; local contingencies and, 57–60; longitudinal analysis and, 78; noetic resolution and, 15–17; occasioning, 89–93; relationship and, 30; remedy, 177–79; response, 98–107; second-party news and, 148–53; shrouding and, 162 (*see also* shrouding); standardized assessment and, 103–5; third-party news and, 126–28; turn, 94–98. *See also* preannouncement
anticipatory leakage, 166–70
apologies, 39–40
assessment, 14, 279n.15; announcement response and, 98–107; cognitive risk, 229–31; detail and, 83–85; first-party news and, 138–48; foregoing components and, 112–16; lexical, 93; news delivery sequence and, 110–16; problematic presumptiveness and, 113; second-party news and, 148–53; sequelae and, 174–82; standardized, 103–5;

sympathy and, 209–10; third-party news and, 126–37; turns of, 110–16
asymmetry, 30–32, 159; moral issues in, 212; shrouding/exposing news and, 170–74
attitude of daily life (ADL), 4–5, 200, 230
autonomous structures, 69

bad/good news, 1–3; ADL and, 4–5; agency and, 32, 201–12; analytic precepts for, 259–62; asymmetries in, 30–32; bluntness and, 34, 49–55, 58, 64, 87, 188–90; causal texture and, 32; conversation analysis and, 64–87; delivery strategies and, 45–60, 247–52 (*see also* delivery strategies); disorientation and, 12–15, 238; everyday frame and, 21–24; first-party, 138–48; forecasting and, 34–60, 64, 161–62, 178, 193, 268n.2; HIV and, 187–99, 233–43; initial elicitors and, 122–26; misattribution and, 221–25 (*see also* misattribution); moral issues in, 54, 62–63, 201–25; mum effect and, 31, 160, 281n.3; news delivery sequence and, 88–119; noetic crisis and, 11–20 (*see also* noetic crisis); participant's subjectivity and, 26–28; phenomenological approach to, 7–11, 20–21, 32–33; premonitoring of, 170; public manipulations of, 227–33; realization and, 24–26, 34–45; real-time interaction and, 26; relational implications and, 28–30; relationships and, 120 (*see also* relationships); retrospective interpretations and, 17–19; second-party, 148–53; sequelae to, 174–82; shrouding and, 162–75, 185–99 (*see also* shrouding); social interaction and, 19–20; stalling and, 45–49; stoicism and, 120–22, 152–53, 186–87, 190–92, 277n.2, 284n.22; subject-predicating format and, 126; third-party, 126–37; timing and, 37–38; topic initial elicitor, 122–23; topic shifting and, 174–75; typification and, 6–7

sociopolitical environment and, 236–37; stoicism and, 187
Hollingshead Index of Social Position, 81
hopefulness, 54
Hospice, 76

illusion, 8–9, 69
indexical expressions, 64–65
initial elicitors, 122–26
intentionality, 9
intersubjectivity, 73
Iraqi War, 228–31, 287n.4
isolation, 57

joking, 51–52, 88, 115, 121

limited affinity, 65, 73–77, 192–93
linguistics, 69–70, 272n.19, 278n.6
literature, 160–62
local determination, 260–61
longitudinal conversation analysis, 78–79

MEDLINE database, 267n.15
memory, 2–3, 265nn. 2–4
misattribution, 200, 244–45; asymmetry in, 212; blame negotiations and, 210–12, 219–25; blaming messenger and, 28–32, 49–52; clinical environment and, 213–25; contaminated blood supply and, 236–42; credit and, 201–12; Iraqi War and, 228–31; moral issues and, 200–225; praising predecessor and, 221–25
moral issues, 54, 270n.18; agency and, 201–12; asymmetry in, 212; blame and, 201–12, 219–25; clinical environment and, 62–63; contaminated blood supply and, 236–42; credit and, 201–12; information conveyance and, 231–33; Iraqi War and, 228–31; praising predecessor, 221–25
Müller-Lyer figure, 8–9
mum effect, 31, 160, 281n.3
mutual affinity, 65, 67–68

National Academy of Sciences (NAS), 235, 238
National Gay Task Force, 236
National Hemophilia Foundation (NHF), 234, 236
National Institutes of Health (NIH), 65, 236
naturalism, 68, 86
news, bad/good. See bad/good news
news delivery sequence, 153; announcement

response and, 98–107; announcement turn, 94–98; assessment and, 110–16; clinical environment and, 117–19; elaboration and, 100–103, 107–10; in-course modification and, 105–7; occasioning and, 89–93; pre-announcement and, 88–91; problematic presumptiveness and, 113; standardized response and, 103–5; steps of, 91, 94; See also delivery strategies
news inquiries, 90; accusatory tones and, 123; anticipatory leakage and, 166–70; asymmetry and, 170–74; initial elicitors and, 122–26; preannouncements and, 92–93; recognitionals and, 127; relationships and, 122–26; sequelae to, 174–82; subject-predicating format and, 126; topic initial elicitor, 122–23; topic shifting and, 174–76
newsmarks, 102–3, 107–10
news receipts, 99–102
noetic crisis: blaming messenger and, 52–53; bluntness and, 49–52; clinical environment and, 86–87; confirmation and, 41–44; conversation analysis and, 65 (see also conversation analysis); courses of action and, 17–19; data collection and, 65–67; disorientation and, 12–15; orderliness and, 53–54; preknowledge and, 44–45; resolution of, 15–17; retrospective interpretation and, 17–19; social interaction and, 19–20; stalling and, 46–49
normalization, 46–48, 53–54

objectivist knowledge, 71
objects, 4–5
occasionalist illusion, 69, 244
occasioning, 89–93
optimality, 288n.16
optimism, 179–82, 282n.14, 284n.32

perception, 2–5; assessment and, 5–6; asymmetry and, 170–74; bracketing and, 10; collective behavior and, 6–7; constancy hypothesis and, 9–10; contingency and, 9–10; ethnomethodology and, 4–6; ideal typical, 6–7; illusion and, 8–9, 69; intentionality and, 9; noetic crisis and, 11–20; phenomenological approach and, 7–11; retrospective interpretations and, 17–19; slowed time and, 13–15; transmission theory and, 8–9; typification and, 6–7